I0187581

# LORD CORNWALLIS IS DEAD

# LORD CORNWALLIS IS DEAD

∞

*The Struggle for Democracy in the United States and India*

· NICO SLATE ·

Harvard University Press

Cambridge, Massachusetts
London, England
2019

Copyright © 2019 by the President and Fellows of Harvard College
All rights reserved

Second printing

*Library of Congress Cataloging-in-Publication Data*
Names: Slate, Nico, author.
Title: Lord Cornwallis is dead : the struggle for democracy in the
United States and India / Nico Slate.
Description: Cambridge, Massachusetts : Harvard University Press, 2019.
Identifiers: LCCN 2018007627 | ISBN 9780674983441 (alk. paper)
Subjects: LCSH: Democracy—United States. | Democracy—India. |
India—Civilization—American influences. |
United States—Civilization—Indian influences.
Classification: LCC JC423 .G638 2019 | DDC 320.954—dc23
LC record available at https://lccn.loc.gov/2018007627

*In memory of*
Kamaladevi Chattopadhyay
*and*
Pauli Murray

We have frequently printed the word Democracy,
yet I cannot too often repeat that it is a word the real gift
of which still sleeps, quite unawakened, notwithstanding
the resonance and the many angry tempests out of which
its syllables have come, from pen or tongue. It is a great
word, whose history, I suppose, remains unwritten,
because that history has yet to be enacted.

—WALT WHITMAN

# CONTENTS

# LORD CORNWALLIS IS DEAD

# Introduction

## *A Grave on the Ganges*

∞

OUTSIDE THE CITY of Ghazipur, an hour east of Varanasi, the tomb of Lord Charles Cornwallis overlooks the Ganges. A marble dome, seventy-five feet high and sixty feet in diameter, the Cornwallis mausoleum embodies the ambitions of the British Raj. While the Ganges swells and shrinks, the stone crypt holds firm. Cornwallis would be proud. As governor-general of British India from 1786 to 1793, Cornwallis oversaw the growth of one of history's greatest empires. In 1757, the Battle of Plassey had given the British a foothold on the subcontinent. Cornwallis transformed that foothold into an empire that was built to last. His most famous innovation, a new revenue system, was known as the "permanent settlement." Cornwallis knew, however, that what seems permanent today may crumble tomorrow. He had, after all, come to India in defeat.[1]

Five years before he arrived in India, Cornwallis lost one of the most momentous battles of the modern era. On October 19, 1781, over six thousand miles west of Ghazipur, a joint force of French and American troops, led by the rebel George Washington, defeated Cornwallis and his soldiers in the bustling port of Yorktown, Virginia. Cornwallis lost much more that day than Yorktown. By surrendering his troops, he guaranteed victory for the rebels. Thirteen British colonies would become the United States of America, and Cornwallis would be shipped home in disgrace. As if his defeat was not sufficiently humiliating, Cornwallis was captured by a French ship while on his way home.[2]

The emergence of the United States, a nation dedicated to democracy, threatened the very idea of empire. The battle of Yorktown did not, however, mark the end of empire or even of the British Empire. The defeat of Cornwallis is better understood as a transition point between empires. Defeated in the New World, the British turned to conquer the Indian subcontinent. As one British Empire died, another was born. Lord Cornwallis embodied the death and resurrection of the British Empire. His journey from Yorktown to Ghazipur reveals that American freedom was, from its inception, bound up with Indian freedom—or what might be called India's enslavement.[3]

The rise of the British Raj was not a simple tale of freedom overcome by tyranny. In India, the British did not encounter egalitarian democracies. They displaced older empires. Cornwallis extended British rule by defeating the great Tipu Sultan. Tipu declared he would rather live a day like a lion than a hundred years like a jackal, and he died on the ramparts of his city. His courage inspired later freedom fighters. But Tipu was no democrat. Like the Mughal emperors that ruled much of India, Tipu Sultan occupied the apex of a divided and unequal society.[4]

As in India so in America, British imperialism was not the only impediment to freedom. What did American independence mean to the hundreds of thousands of enslaved Africans living in the rebellious colonies? The Revolution did nothing to break their shackles. At the inception of American independence, it was the British who offered freedom to the enslaved. At the battle of Yorktown, many slaves fled across British lines. Some were turned away by Cornwallis. Others were re-enslaved in the British Caribbean. But many found their freedom with the help of the redcoats.[5]

The story of India and America is a story of many freedoms and many slaveries. In 1920, the African American scholar W. E. B. Du Bois declared, "Most men today cannot conceive of a freedom that does not involve somebody's slavery." Du Bois imagined an expansive freedom and then strove to achieve it on a global scale. He was not alone. Thousands of patriots in India and the Unites States struggled to make real the democracy of their dreams. They fought for a freedom that would stretch not only across the borders that divide India from America but also across the borders that divide Indians from Indians, and Americans from Americans.[6]

Today, India and the United States are often celebrated as the world's two largest democracies. They are also among the most diverse. One of the central arguments of this book is that diversity can enrich democracy by connecting local, national, and transnational social movements. The "fragments" of the nation can inspire freedom struggles that defy the borders of the nation. Yet neither Indians nor Americans have fully achieved their democratic ideals, and their diversity remains fraught with intolerance and inequality. Other large, diverse democracies bear equally bold aspirations and equally tragic flaws. Think of Brazil or South Africa. But the story of democracy in India and the United States is uniquely significant. While the United States remains the world's most powerful democracy, India—the world's most populous democracy—is growing in wealth and influence. Together, the United States and India will play a predominant role in shaping the future of democracy.[7]

This book traces the many bridges—political, economic, cultural, and intellectual—that have linked India and the United States. But this is not a simple tale of the triumph of connection over difference. Indeed, many of the "connections" at the heart of this book were misconnections defined by mistakes, misunderstanding, or self-centered efforts to appropriate the foreign for intellectual or material profit.[8]

The relationship between India and America began with a mistake. Believing he had reached that fabled land of spices, Christopher Columbus named his new discovery India. Since 1492, India and America have been intertwined. Trade networks carried ice from Walden Pond to Calcutta and an elephant from Calcutta to New York. Transcendentalists corresponded with Indian thinkers. American missionaries flocked to India. Hindu gurus attracted crowds across America. Two hundred thousand American soldiers served in India during the Second World War. While Gandhian civil disobedience inspired the American civil rights movement, the Indian American community fought its own battle for civil rights. Often estranged during the Cold War, India and the United States became allies in its aftermath. From yoga to nuclear politics, and Hollywood to Bollywood, Indo-American relations have become increasingly important to both countries—and increasingly misunderstood.

Columbus launched one of many misunderstandings that would link India and America. The very word *India* was invented by an earlier band of hapless explorers who labeled everyone to the east of the Indus River "Indians," lumping together a variety of peoples and languages. The word *America* emerged from an equally reckless generalization. A Florentine merchant, Amerigo Vespucci, gave his name to two continents, and "America" was born. New worlds yielded new words—new, that is, for those outsiders who declared themselves to have discovered lands long known, long loved, by other names.[9]

Named by ignorant foreigners, neither India nor the United States can claim purity of origin. Nor should they. Their mixed histories helped make both countries bastions of diversity. It is tempting to celebrate that diversity, to praise the border crossing that bound together distant lands. Yet as Columbus himself made clear, border crossing is often a bloody business in which some gain vast fortunes while others lose everything, even the right to name their loss.

The history of India and America resounds with powerful words charged with legacies of loss and forgetting. This book contains three short chapters that explore the history of particular keywords—*Indian, caste,* and *thug*—that traveled between India and the United States. These chapters frame the three sections of the book, demonstrating the significance of language as a source of transnational connection and disconnection. While there are many vital words at the heart of Indo-American histories, *Indian, caste,* and *thug* are all uniquely connected to Indo-American relations—and to the struggle for democracy in both countries. All three words speak to the exclusion and oppression at the heart of this story—as well as the transnational resistance to that oppression. All are controversial terms that have been interpreted in many different ways and toward many different ends. Such hermeneutic conflict also marks the most important keywords in the long history of Indo-American relations: *freedom* and *democracy*.

As freedom struggles reflected back and forth between India and America, the definition of *freedom* was itself called into question. In India, words like *swaraj* (self-rule) and *swadeshi* (of one's own country), burdened with their own contested histories, influenced how people understood the word *freedom*. In both the United States and India, terms like *liberty, independence,* and *democracy* shifted in relation to each other, and as a result of larger historical developments. It took the American Civil War, for example, to force Americans to acknowledge that a country could not claim to be free if it contained millions of enslaved people.

And it took the civil rights movement to grant the descendants of those slaves the rights of citizens—or, at least, some of those rights. The modern history of India can similarly be understood as a long struggle to expand the meaning of *freedom*. Indian independence led to full adult suffrage, a remarkable achievement for a country as poor and diverse as India. Yet, as in the United States, the story of freedom remains incomplete in India, a country with a rapidly growing economy and hundreds of millions of people trapped in poverty.[10]

Neither Indians nor Americans can claim to have achieved the full potential of the words *freedom* and *democracy*. In defense of "free markets," the word *freedom* has been refashioned to mean only freedom from government interference—not from hunger, illiteracy, discrimination, or oppression. Just as a mirror image reverses the original, so the United States and India have achieved a freedom that perpetuates its opposite. Rather than carry forward the struggle to achieve real democracy, our leaders spout hollow paeans to freedom. The ongoing struggle against oppression and inequality is hidden behind reassuring narratives of national triumph. The bitter victories of the past are stripped of their unresolved complexities. We celebrate the achievements of our ancestors and forget their dreams.[11]

It would be a mistake to ignore the progress that has been achieved in both India and the United States, countries that despite their many problems can claim with good reason to be bulwarks of democracy. Yet the very achievements of democracy, from regular elections to an independent judiciary to a vibrant press, can breed complacency by obscuring the persistence of inequality and oppression. Such complacency finds transnational support when the history of shared struggle that links the United States and India is repackaged as empty praise for the "world's two largest democracies." The myth of the two democracies is more powerful because it is not entirely false. Indians and Americans have good reason to celebrate the history that has connected our democracies. But when our achievements are framed as a culmination rather than a new beginning, we dishonor the struggles that brought us where we are today—close enough to our democratic aspirations to forget them.

When Cornwallis died, his compatriots carved a short inscription on his tomb: "This monument, erected by the British inhabitants of Calcutta, attests their sense of those virtues which will live in the remembrance of grateful millions, long after it shall have mouldered into dust." They got it wrong. The Cornwallis monument maintains its watch over the Ganges. It is the virtues of empire that have moldered into dust. But what has taken their place? As I write, the specter of populist authoritarianism stalks the globe. Even the basic trappings of democracy are under threat, not just in places like Russia and China, but in the United States and India too. In this time of democratic crisis, it is not enough to safeguard the basic liberties gifted to us by generations of struggle. We must reawaken the courage and creativity with which our forebears expanded the limits of democracy. We must ask again what it means to be free.[12]

# PART I

# INDIAN

Brothers, on the other side of the Great Water, far
beyond the nations of white people, there are many
nations of Indians who have dark skins, black hair &
black eyes, like you.
—Timothy Pickering, addressing the Grand Council of the
Six Nations of the Iroquois Confederacy, 1791

IT WAS A LONG July day, and the frontier hamlet of Newtown, New
York, buzzed with activity. Timothy Pickering, official agent of President George Washington and of the newly formed United States of America, had come to tell the Indians about India. Before him sat leaders of
the Mohawk, Oneida, Onondaga, Cayuga, Seneca, and Tuscarora people,
all gathered under the banner of the Haudenosaunee or Iroquois Confederacy. Pickering preferred an even more capacious label: Indians. By
applying that label to his listeners, Pickering prepared for a daring linguistic leap. Thousands of miles away, he told his audience, "on the other
side of the Great Water," lived "many nations of Indians who have dark
skins, black hair & black eyes, like you." Unlike the Iroquois, the Indians of India were "farmers, carpenters, smiths, spinners and weavers,
like the white people." Pickering aimed to convince *these* Indians to be
more like *those* Indians, and ultimately to be more like "the whites."
Holding up the subcontinent as a model of civilization, he used India to
turn the Indians into good Americans. He continued a long tradition in
which the words *India* and *Indian* were bent and stretched in order to
advance particular forms of knowledge and power.[1]

It began with the river. The Indus River sweeps across what is today China, India, and Pakistan. When Alexander the Great arrived at that great ribbon of water in 326 BC, the Indus was less a barrier between distinct lands than a crossroads of trade long traversed by a variety of peoples. The names *Indus, Indos,* and *Sindhu* had come to refer both to the river and to the people who lived beyond its eastern shore. These labels were neither indigenous nor widely accepted. As diverse as the many "Indian" nations that Pickering lumped together in New York, the peoples of India would live for thousands of years before they came to see themselves as "Indians." Many still prefer other labels. But Alexander returned to Europe with tales of the Indos and the Indikoi, Greek words that obscured the diversity of India as they moved through Latin into modern European languages. The first recorded use of the English word *Indian* may have been by King Alfred the Great in 893, although it remains unclear if he used the word *India* and, if so, what exactly he had in mind. As to Columbus, his first letter home from "the new world" makes several references to the "Indians" he had discovered. Perhaps most telling is his casual confession that he had enslaved some of the generous people who had welcomed him: "I took by force some Indians."[2]

Columbus gave birth to what we might call "the problem of the two Indians." Timothy Pickering turned that problem into an opportunity. Once it was known that there was a difference between the Indians of America and those of India, that difference could be employed to rhetorical and political ends. In Pickering's eyes, Asian Indians were role models for the "uncivilized" Indians he lectured in New York. It is remarkable that Pickering held up the inhabitants of India as models of civilization. It would not be long before many Americans came to associate India with barbaric heathens. That shift in the American understanding of India—from beacon of civilization to the epitome of savagery—hinged on how Americans viewed the other word that came from the Indus river: *Hindu.*

Over the course of the nineteenth century, the word *Hindoo* replaced *Indian* as the American term of choice for the people of India. *Hindoo* gained popularity as a way to sidestep the problem of the two Indians. *Here they are Indians; there they are Hindoos.* The shift from *Indian* to *Hindoo* also marked the increasing impact of religion on how Americans viewed India. For some, the Hindu faith was a source of inspiration. In New

England, in particular, a variety of well-known figures, from Unitarian theologians to Transcendental philosophers, came to see Hindu thinkers as partners in a shared quest to know God. For many Americans, by contrast, Hinduism embodied the foreign and the uncivilized. Consider the strange fate of Daniel Ullmann, a promising politician whose career was hampered in the 1850s by rumors that he had been born in Calcutta. Ullmann was a leading figure in the anti-immigrant American Party, known by its critics as the Know-Nothings. As a leader of a rabidly nativist organization, he must have found it galling to be tarnished by a foreign birth. To be from an "uncivilized" country like India was especially damning. Opponents quickly dubbed the American Party the "Hindoos."[3]

For many Americans, all Indians—whether Sioux, Apache, or "Hindoo"—were heathen savages whose souls called out to be saved. This created a dilemma for American missionaries attracted to the subcontinent. Why should they travel to India when there were "Indians" whose souls needed saving closer to home? One of the longest-serving American missionaries in India, John Christian Frederick Heyer, grappled with the problem of the two Indians when choosing where to direct his energies. While working in Pittsburgh, he decided to dedicate his life to saving the souls of poor Indians. But which Indians? Convenience seemed to suggest American Indians. But Heyer was not convinced. "If we undertake to establish a mission among our Indians," he wrote, "we should, probably, have to go across the Rocky Mountains to a place perhaps as difficult of access as the peninsula of Hindustan." Compared to the residents of India, he stated, "Our Indians are of a roving disposition, and hence it is very difficult to get hold of them." Convinced that his calling was among those Indians rather than among "our Indians," Heyer left for India in October 1841.[4]

Even as the word *Hindoo* gained in popularity, many Americans continued to use *Indian* to refer to residents of the subcontinent as well as to those who would later be deemed "Native Americans." In 1854, the ambiguity of the Indian proved crucial to a landmark decision of the California Supreme Court. Strangely, the decision concerned neither the Indians of India nor those of America. Rather, the issue in question was whether a Chinese witness could testify against a "white" defendant. California had passed a law that prohibited "Blacks, Mulattos and Indians" from providing testimony against "whites." The question before the court was whether that law should be understood to also exclude the testimony of someone of Chinese descent. In an act of geographic daring, the court declared, "The name of Indian, from the time of Columbus to the present day, has been used to designate, not alone the North American Indian, but the whole of the Mongolian race." Thus, the court used the word *Indian* as a linguistic bridge between the "Mongolian race" and the "Indians" Columbus had encountered in 1492. Such reasoning was flimsy at best. Should American law be guided by the erroneous geography of a fifteenth-century Genoese sailor? To be safe, the court offered a different justification that lumped both kinds of Indians with other nonwhite peoples. "Even admitting the Indian of this continent is not of the Mongolian type," the court declared, "the words 'black person,' in the 14th section, must be taken as contradistinguished from white, and necessarily excludes all races other than the Caucasian." The court suggested that the Chinese were "black" if they were not "Indian." Thus, the testimony of the Chinese witness was ruled inadmissible, and the ambiguity of the Indian was used to reinforce white supremacy.[5]

The idea of the "Indian" was also useful as a prop for patriarchy. In 1790, the citizens of Philadelphia gathered to watch *The Widow of Malabar*, an English-language adaptation of a play written in French twenty years earlier. The new version included a prologue that juxtaposed the plight of women in India with the struggles of women in other "barbarous" societies: "Doom'd the mean vassals of unfeeling lords, / By Western Savages, and Tartar hords! / Through Asian climes, see custom reason braves, / And marks the fairest of their sex for slaves." The reference to "Western Savages" lumped *these* Indians with *those* Indians, both uncivilized societies that "enslaved" their women. *The Widow of Malabar* hinged on the ritual immolation of a Brahmin woman, an act known as sati. As a colonial trope, sati allowed Western imperialists to claim superiority over the barbaric East. Sati would remain a popular controversy throughout the nineteenth century, one of several colonial clichés that affected how Americans thought of India and Indians.[6]

The gendered lens through which Americans saw India was shaped by the esteemed Sanskrit scholar and social reformer Pandita Ramabai. Ramabai arrived in America in 1886 to attend the graduation of her cousin from the women's medical college in Philadelphia. She quickly became one of the most well-known Indians in America. The American Ramabai Association, formed in 1887, boasted members up and down the East Coast, with large concentrations in Boston and New York. Ramabai's fame dovetailed with prevailing stereotypes of India, many of which revolved around the "plight" of Indian women. A Christian convert who became famous for advocating on behalf of child widows, Ramabai was a useful figure for imperialists, missionaries, and all those who wished to "save" India from itself. As *The Widow of Malabar* made clear, the suffering of Indian women had long served as justification for foreign intervention, political and spiritual. In Ramabai, Americans found a living witness to the tragedy of Indian womanhood. But they also found a dynamic speaker who contradicted in her person some of the stereotypes she was used to support.[7]

Ramabai attacked the treatment of India's "thousands of child widows" as a form of "slavery" and contrasted that injustice with what she saw as the idyllic treatment of American girls. She told one Philadelphia audience to "compare the condition of your own sweet darlings at your happy firesides with that of millions of little girls of a corresponding age in India, who have already been sacrificed on the unholy altar of an inhuman social custom." Ramabai's maudlin appeal assumed that America's "sweet darlings" never faced discrimination. While denouncing the oppression of Indian women, Ramabai largely overlooked American sexism. Her impressions of America were not, however, entirely positive. Upon returning to India, Ramabai published a wide-ranging book on the "Peoples of the United States." Her use of the plural is significant. Ramabai recognized that there was more than one "people" within the United States, and devoted considerable attention to the struggles of American minorities.[8]

In January 1888, Ramabai met with the renowned freedom fighter and former slave Harriet Tubman. In a letter to her daughter, Ramabai praised Tubman as a role model. "You know, my dear child," she wrote, "there are thousands of little children like you and women like me in our dear India who are as badly treated as the slaves in olden times. I hope my child will remember the story of Harriet and try to be as helpful to her own dear countrywomen as Harriet was and is to her own people." Ramabai realized that, in her words, "The belief in the inferiority of the non White races, such as the Negro race, has been deeply ingrained." She used American racism as a foil to highlight the injustices of Indian society—not just sexism but also caste oppression. Despite the depths of American racism, Ramabai wrote, "There is no fear whatsoever that racial discrimination and prejudice here would reach the level of caste discrimination and prejudice in India."[9]

In addition to criticizing the oppression of African Americans, Ramabai decried the racism faced by the people she called "the Red Indians." In the process, she demonstrated that the problem of the two Indians could be wielded against white supremacy. Ramabai lamented the "strong hatred" many Americans felt "for the Red Indians, the original inhabitants of America." She linked that racism to decades of illegal dispossession. In her words, "After making treaties with different Indian tribes pertaining to their lands, the United States Government violated the clauses of those treaties and wrested the lands from them; it then turned very respectable and branded the Indians as rogues." Ramabai denounced the mistreatment of American Indians as a failure of American democracy. "The Indian people have no rights as American citizens," she concluded.[10]

Even as she condemned the oppression of "the Red Indians," Ramabai reproduced stereotypes used to justify that oppression. "The Indians are a very long-suffering people, either because of ignorance or by nature," she wrote. She praised the Cherokee for giving up "savage customs." By contrast, Ramabai believed, most Indian tribes had been "scattered all over America like fragments of a broken glass bowl." Overlooking the ways in which American Indians continued to fight for their land and their culture, Ramabai concluded that most Indians in America had been "broken." In her words, "Their only aim in life now is to eat and drink whatever is provided by their White enemies and rulers, to be utterly dependent on them, to live out the lives they are born to, and to die like wild animals or birds hunted by the White people." Thus, Ramabai vividly portrayed the oppression of American Indians, even while failing to recognize how Indians struggled against that oppression.[11]

Ramabai drew on her knowledge of American Indians to advance arguments about India. First, she argued that a lack of Indian unity—both in America and in India—had facilitated conquest by outsiders: "Our countrymen's feuds allowed foreigners to gain entry into our internal matters, and we lost our independence, as everyone familiar with the history of India knows. Our Red Brethren ended up the same way." Ramabai used the problem of the two Indians to urge her countrymen to unite and thus reclaim their independence. For a model of self-reliance, she turned to the American Revolution: "The American said that drinking

*Figure 1.* Pandita Ramabai, who visited the United States in 1886 and denounced the "racial discrimination and prejudice" she found there as well as the "caste discrimination and prejudice in India." From Pandita Ramabai, *The High-Caste Hindu Woman* (Philadelphia: J. B. Rodgers, 1888). F. Gutekunst Phototype, Philadelphia. Courtesy of the University of California Libraries.

the tea and wearing the clothes imported from England harms the industries of his country; therefore he would never drink such tea or wear English clothes." Such economic self-reliance led to independence and prosperity. In India, by contrast, dependence on foreign goods had led to poverty. "Like the Indians of North America," Ramabai wrote, "we have sold our precious gem-studded land to foreigners in return for glass beads and glass bottles filled with wine." Fooled by shiny trinkets, Ramabai's "Red Brethren" emerge yet again as caricatures of the naïve native.[12]

Ramabai was not the first visitor from India to traffic in stereotypes of the American Indian. In 1883, Harriet Beecher Stowe, author of *Uncle Tom's Cabin,* attended an unusual sermon in the Hartford Congregational Church. The speaker was Protap Chunder Mozoomdar, a prominent Bengali religious figure. After the lecture ended, Stowe invited Mozoomdar to her home. Mozoomdar later complained that Stowe did not have "very accurate notions" of India. She thought Indians were, in Mozoomdar's words, like "Dacotas and Cherokees, savage, heathenish and illiterate." Thus, Mozoomdar repeated one Indian stereotype in order to reject another. It is unclear whether he thought that the Dakotas and the Cherokee were in fact "savage, heathenish and illiterate." That was, for him, beside the point. The issue was that Stowe had failed to recognize the advanced culture—and especially the advanced Western education—of many Indians. "When I told her how the young men of India at one time read and wept over Uncle Tom's Cabin," Mozoomdar lamented, "she asked me whether they read it in English." Mozoomdar had good reason to be sensitive to American impressions of India. In a letter to his colleagues in India, he noted, "It was doubted whether any of the respectable hotels would receive me as a customer, because my complexion was that of the liberated slave." His opposition to racial discrimination might have fostered warm bonds between Mozoomdar and Stowe. But Mozoomdar focused more on American impressions of India than the racial discrimination faced by African Americans—or, for that matter, the Dakota and the Cherokee. Ignoring white supremacy, he told one American audience that theirs was "a free nation" and "a nation of brothers."[13]

Unlike Mozoomdar, Ramabai used the plight of American Indians to upend the dichotomy between the civilized and the uncivilized. Her emphasis on the color of "our Red Brethren" allowed her to distinguish these Indians from those Indians, but also facilitated a sharp criticism of white Americans and of the color line they sustained. She told her Indian readers that "our Red Brethren" were often accused of cannibalism. She dismissed such claims, and instead accused the West of its own form of cannibalism. In her words, "Usually civilized people do not in reality eat the flesh of fellow human beings; but they have mastered the art of 'eating' others of their kind without actually eating their flesh." By flipping the narrative of cannibalism, Ramabai urged her Indian readers to challenge the superiority of the white world and the voracious appetite of Western imperialism. Lest her Indian readers forget their own forms of injustice, Ramabai concluded by turning her cannibalism analogy inward: "Take care that you yourselves do not eat one another!"[14]

Cannibalism—a powerful analogy for the tragedy of the modern world. The strong consumed the weak, as the great coming together of peoples and ideas that marks modernity was corrupted by greed, oppression, and the rise of modern racism. The more the world became interconnected, the more ways were devised to separate nation from nation and people from people. Beginning with Columbus, the word *Indian* embodied the paradoxical relationship between border crossing, racism, and inequality. From *The Widow of Malabar* to the California Supreme Court, many of the "connections" between the Indians of India and of America were in fact disconnections when viewed from the perspective of human unity. Indians were compared and contrasted in order to defend conceptions of liberty and democracy from which Indians were consistently excluded. The global history of "the Indian" is an indictment of democracy. The key point is not just that Indians, slaves, and other "barbarians" were excluded from democracy, but that their labor, their land, and their exclusion were all vital to democracy itself. From colonial Athens to revolutionary America, the people Paulin Ismard has called "democracy's slaves" were not outsiders but oppressed insiders, trapped by the chains of democracy.[15]

The history of the word *Indian* reminds us to be cautious about celebrating the transnational spread of democracy and freedom. Rather than breaking down barriers, transnational "democratic" forces have often reinforced boundaries of race, gender, class, caste, and nation. As the scholar Lisa Lowe has written, "Liberal forms of political economy, culture, government, and history propose a narrative of freedom overcoming enslavement that at once denies colonial slavery, erases the seizure of lands from native peoples, displaces migrations and connections across continents, and internalizes these processes in a national struggle of history and consciousness." Consider Andrew Jackson, icon of American democracy and of Indian removal. Or consider how a globe-trotting social reformer like Ramabai was used to justify imperial rule. But even while Ramabai reproduced stereotypes of the Indians of America, she offered a radical approach to transnational solidarity, an approach that suggested new anti-imperial alliances and that offered a revolutionary vision for how to bring real democracy to both India and America.[16]

## Red, White, and Colored

Ramabai gestured toward solidarity with American Indians and other racial minorities, but it would fall to later generations to build a transnational struggle against white supremacy. The relationship between the two Indians would become a pillar of what W. E. B. Du Bois called the "colored world." The idea of being "colored"—whether red, yellow, brown, or black—inspired new solidarities and acts of resistance. Those solidarities were neither natural nor limitless. The power of colored unity was constrained by the demands of nation, language, and religion. Few saw being "colored" as more important than being Muslim or Nigerian or

Bengali. Rather than weakening its significance, however, the humility of colored unity allowed it to bestow new meanings on a range of identities—including the Janus-faced *Indian.*

The problem of the two Indians became revolutionary when infused with colored unity. The radical potential of the colored world is evident in the life of the most famous "Indian" of the twentieth century: Mohandas Karamchand Gandhi. Unlike Ramabai, Gandhi never visited the United States. His understanding of American Indians is nevertheless revealing. In 1903, Gandhi demonstrated the "coloring" of the American Indian in an article on the African American educator Booker T. Washington. Gandhi quoted the French writer and Nobel Prize winner Romain Rolland, who had described one of Washington's mentors as "a sort of apostle who devoted his life to the coloured races, whose needs he thoroughly understood, and who founded in 1868 in Virginia the Hampton Normal and Agricultural Institute to train young men and women of the negro and (Red) Indian races to become teachers among their own people." By inserting the word *Red* in parentheses, Gandhi aimed to help his Asian Indian readers make sense of Rolland's reference to the "Indian races." Gandhi's choice of the word *Red* is telling. Later in the article, he wrote of Washington, "Being himself a negro, he had some difficulty with the American Indians, but by his gentleness and prudence he soon succeeded in disarming all opposition to himself." Whether "Red" or "American," those Indians needed to be distinguished from these Indians. But unlike the adjective *American,* Gandhi's use of the word *Red* signaled his growing awareness of the color-coded division of humanity that underpinned the racist hierarchy at the heart of the imperial project.[17]

Over time, Gandhi developed a robust critique of the racist imperialism that oppressed Indians, whether "Red" or otherwise. During his time in South Africa, Gandhi made a series of derogatory statements about black South Africans. But his experiences in South Africa—and his reading of racial oppression in America—would steer him toward a more critical colored cosmopolitanism. Fifty years later, in the midst of the Second World War, Gandhi made clear that he fought for the freedom of all "colored" peoples. In October 1944, Gandhi was asked, "Are we right in thinking that your stand against world imperialism is intended to benefit as much the African, Chinese, Red Indians and other non-white masses as the 400 millions of India?" Gandhi replied, "My correspondence with the Government while under detention shows that most clearly."[18]

Gandhi was not the first Indian anticolonial figure to oppose the imperial racism that oppressed both sorts of Indians. The firebrand nationalist Lala Lajpat Rai spent five years in the United States during and after the First World War. Like Pandita Ramabai, Lajpat Rai turned his American travels into a book for Indian readers. Also like Ramabai, he used the struggles of American Indians to educate his fellow Indians about the injustice of American white supremacy. In order to explain the injustice suffered by American Indians, Lajpat Rai turned to the story of Columbus. Echoing stereotypes of the uncivilized savage, he wrote that the "natives" that Columbus encountered "were savages of a reddish skin and long, straight, black hair, living the tribal life of hunters." Thus, Lajpat Rai naturalized the racial classification of the "red Indians," as if the language of racial difference directly mirrored natural distinctions of skin color. He failed to see that racial distinctions were historical developments that deserved to be challenged along with the racial inequalities they facilitated. But although he largely embraced the idea of racial difference, Lajpat Rai rejected white supremacy and traced the injustice of European imperialism back to the conquest of the Americas. Beginning with Columbus, the European powers "never dreamt of the possible right of the native Indian to the land of his birth. Wherever the white men had first come into contact with the red man, he had been received with great friendliness, but the treachery and cruel treatment with which he treated the red man, soon turned the latter into his bitter enemy." Lajpat Rai's contrast between "white" and "red" better matched the divided world in which he lived than the complexities of ethnic identity in the early years of European imperialism. But by lumping all American Indians under the heading "red" and bracketing their oppressors with the word "white," Lajpat Rai attacked the displacement and genocide of American Indians while connecting that savagery to the brutality of twentieth-century imperialism.[19]

Even in the twentieth century, whiteness and redness continued to be constructed and contested in a dynamic process that shaped the lives of "Indians" in America and India. That process had a unique impact on Indian Americans, racially suspect not just because of the racial ambiguities of the word *Indian,* but also because Americans were unable to decide where Indians fit in a society divided between black and white.

In 1906, Bhicaji Balsara applied for American citizenship. Because naturalization was limited to "whites" and those of African descent, Balsara's case depended on whether the government would accept his claim to whiteness. In its decision, the court distinguished the "white race" from the "black, red, yellow, or brown races." Although the court found "no difficulty in saying that the Chinese, Japanese, and Malays and the American Indians do not belong to the white race," it proved more difficult to define which groups did belong to the "white race." In the absence of conclusive evidence to the contrary, the court accepted Balsara's arguments, found that he belonged to the white race, and affirmed his citizenship. American Indians were red, but Indian Americans were white. Or at least some Indian Americans were white. The court made a point of distinguishing Balsara as a member of the Parsi community, "a settlement by themselves of intelligent and well-to-do persons, principally engaged in commerce" who were "as distinct from the Hindus as are the English who dwell in India." Thus, Balsara gained citizenship by distinguishing himself from American Indians and Hindu Indians.[20]

Some Indian Americans chose to use the word *Hindu* for all Indians. In 1918, the anticolonial newspaper *Young India*, founded by Lala Lajpat Rai in New York, offered a revealing note on terminology: "In the United States the word Hindu stands for all East Indians regardless of their religion." "The word 'Indian' is used for American Indians," the editors explained. "So in this magazine we shall frequently use the word 'Hindu' instead of 'Indian' for all the peoples of India." For an Indian American newspaper to embrace the term *Hindu* as a moniker for the entire population of India risked obscuring the subcontinent's religious minorities. Lajpat Rai was a leading figure within the Arya Samaj, an organization that defended pan-Hindu unity by fighting against caste discrimination but also by opposing conversions to Christianity and Islam. To emphasize the importance of unity, Lajpat Rai turned to the history of American Indians. The European conquerors "whipped up rivalry and hatred between the different tribes for the sole purpose of having them fight and exterminate each other to make the work of advance easier for the white man." Such divide-and-rule tactics had been employed by the British in India as well—most prominently along religious lines. Imperial apologists had long maintained that British rule was necessary to prevent religious conflict. To combat imperialism, Lajpat Rai encouraged his readers to forge unity within India and between Indians and other oppressed peoples throughout the world. But whether such unity could be respectful of difference remained an important question for Lajpat Rai and all those struggling against racism and imperialism in India and America.[21]

In addition to religious divides, class, gender, and sexual identities were also called into question by links between the Indians of India and of America. Unlike Lajpat Rai or Pandita Ramabai, the majority of Indian Americans were working-class laborers based on the West Coast. In the fields, mills, and cities of the American West, Indian Americans encountered American Indians not as one side of a rhetorical comparison, but as colleagues, competitors, friends, and lovers. In the first decades of the twentieth century, the vast majority of Indian Americans were men. Some of these men forged romantic and sexual relationships with American Indians. These relationships crossed divides of race, language, and culture. When both partners were men, they also defied the law. The historian Nayan Shah has uncovered several relationships between "Indian" men that were deemed illicit at the time. Take, for example, the encounter between a Punjabi migrant named Tara Singh and an eighteen-year-old American Indian named Hector McInnes. Singh befriended McInnes in downtown Sacramento, and offered the younger man money for food and lodging. When the two men checked into adjoining rooms, they aroused suspicions. The police were called and both men were arrested. Many same-sex relationships between "Indian" men are remembered only in legal records that testify to the constraints placed on men whose lives and identities were policed in more ways than one.[22]

While working-class Indian Americans forged their own connections with American Indians, activists from India continued to envision a larger unity in the struggle against white supremacy in India and America. Persistent stereotypes marred these imagined solidarities. In 1921, a letter to the *Bombay Chronicle* complained that "the name Indian suggests to Americans semi-savages." Rather than attack the myth of the Indian savage, the author of the letter blamed the British for leading Americans to believe that "the Indians are a people deserving of no more consideration than the Negroes and Red Indians." Instead of denouncing the equation of the Indian and the savage, the letter elevated these Indians over those Indians, echoing the hierarchy suggested by Timothy Pickering 130 years earlier.[23]

The "savage" nature of the Indian found partial redemption in the writings of Sarojini Naidu, the first female president of the Indian National Congress and a renowned poet. During a tour of the United States in 1928, Naidu visited American Indian communities in the Southwest and envisioned her own link between Indians. In a letter she sent Gandhi, Naidu wrote movingly of American Indians: "The Arizona Desert is the home of many Red Indian tribes, who live their own picturesque and primitive lives, so strangely aloof and alone in the land that was once their ancestral heritage. They are more akin to us than to the foreign Western peoples who have taken away that heritage." By describing the lives of American Indians as "picturesque and primitive," Naidu reproduced tired stereotypes of the noble savage. She complicated those stereotypes, however, by stating that the "Red Indian tribes" were "akin" to the people of India because both groups had been dispossessed of their land and their rightful heritage. In addition to a history of oppression, cultural similarities linked both groups of Indians. Naidu celebrated a "folk spirit" that "whether in India, Romania, Zululand or the Arizona Desert expresses itself very much in the same symbols and reveals very much the same primal virtues through the folk music, folklore and folk dance." With her emphasis on the "primal," Naidu again advanced limiting tropes. White supremacists would be happy to grant Indians "primal virtues," while reserving more refined achievements for the so-called civilized races. But Naidu did not understand "primal" as the opposite of "civilized." As an example of a "primal virtue" Naidu offered "valor." "One of the primal key virtues," valor linked all Indians, Naidu wrote, "and nowhere does it find more stirring expression than in the dances I saw of the Hopi tribe on the edge of the Grand Canyon, the Eagle Dance, the Dance of the Buffalo Hunt and the Victory Dance."[24]

Naidu's emphasis on folk culture risked oversimplifying complex traditions and overlooking the many differences between cultures. Consider, for example, a conversation Naidu shared with "a proud young representative of an Indian tribe" who attended a speech Naidu gave about India. Afterward, the young Indian man thanked her for her speech, and then turned to America: "This country once belonged to me and my people. We are dying out, but they may kill us, they can never conquer us." After quoting this defiant declaration, Naidu added, "Yes, these desert children are children of the Eagle and the Wind and Thunder. Who can conquer their spirit?" Her repeated reference to Indians as children continued a long tradition of infantilizing American Indians, the "children of the Great White Father." But while Naidu's language was patronizing, her message was one of Indian resilience in the face of oppression. Gandhi published Naidu's letter in his newspaper, sharing her message of pan-Indian solidarity with his many readers.[25]

Like Naidu, Cedric Dover turned the problem of the two Indians into an opportunity for solidarity between oppressed peoples. A scholar born in Calcutta of mixed racial heritage, Dover developed strong ties with a variety of African American intellectuals. A visit to several Indian reservations broadened his sense of connection to America's racial minorities. "I have lived in Negro ghettoes with an overpowering feeling of intimacy," Dover wrote in 1952. "I have felt the same kinship on American Indian reservations, and even the dour Apaches have welcomed me inside their *tipis*." In his characterization of the Apaches as "dour" and his reference to tipis, Dover evoked hackneyed stereotypes not unlike those that proved irresistible to Naidu, Lajpat Rai, and Pandita Ramabai. Dover aimed to celebrate the "kinship" he felt with American Indians as evidence of a broader solidarity in the struggle against white supremacy. But his recourse to stereotypes called into question the depth of such a kinship.[26]

Unlike many of her compatriots, the feminist and anticolonial nationalist Kamaladevi Chattopadhyay rejected many of the stereotypes of the American Indian. In the midst of the Second World War, Kamaladevi spent eighteen months traveling across the United States. Her itinerary included a journey "across the long desert country in the South-West to wander over the Indian Reservations, and see those ancient people in their own setting, hear their brave sagas, listen to their songs, see their arts and crafts and trace the pattern of their social life." Her description of American Indians as "ancient people" did not prevent her from recognizing their dynamism and diversity. In her words, "The Amer-Indians, as the American Indians are called, are no longer the 'Vanishing Tribe,' as symbolized by the famous painting 'The End of the Trail,' nor the fanciful bogeyman, 'The Wild Men with the Feathers' who do war-dances for the delectation of the tourists, the last pathetic remnants of a great people." This rejection of Indian stereotypes came in 1946 in *America: The Land of Superlatives*, a book Kamaladevi published about her American journey. The book included a chapter on American Indians titled "The Disinherited," which conveyed the diversity of

American Indian cultures while portraying the poverty that plagued most Indian peoples. Kamaladevi praised American Indians for fighting against those inequalities and, like Ramabai and Lajpat Rai, upended the equation of civilization with whiteness. Sarcastically, she wrote, "The Indians were not 'civilized' enough to pin up 'Keep off' sign boards" when Europeans first began to arrive. "Of course," she added, "the enlightened arrivals took whatever land they could in their 'civilising' stride." She lauded American Indians for giving "long and stiff resistance to the white invader," and told her Indian readers that the Indians of America "had been through the same kind of traumatic experience as ours, of being dispossessed, isolated." Kamaladevi praised American Indians for creating democratic traditions, what she called "a real League of Nations, an actual meeting point for all problems to be amicably settled." Thus, she celebrated pan-Indian solidarity twice over—first among American Indians themselves and then between American Indians and the citizens of what she hoped would soon be a free and united India.[27]

By praising American Indian communities as "a real League of Nations," Kamaladevi revealed the most important lesson that South Asian anticolonial activists took from their engagement with American Indian struggles: a layered conception of sovereignty, a vision of democracy in which no one was left out. Although often marred by stereotypes of the American Indian, the colored cosmopolitanism that thrived in the first half of the twentieth century helped inspire a generation of Indian freedom fighters to forge solidarities with American Indians and other oppressed peoples throughout the world. Such solidarities influenced how Indians understood the United States by rendering hollow American claims to champion liberty and democracy. Even more important, solidarities with American Indians impacted how South Asian activists connected their own fight to the global struggle for freedom and democracy. Many came to feel that they were fighting not just for the freedom of India but for all oppressed peoples, all "Indians" everywhere.


## The Real Indians

What have American Indians made of India? From Pandita Ramabai to Kamaladevi Chattopadhyay, several generations of South Asian activists and thinkers studied the history of American Indians. But what about the reverse? American Indian reflections on India are hard to find in the historical record—a fact that points to the different impact of colonialism in the subcontinent as versus the United States. While the British remained a minority in India, European Americans and their diseases decimated the American Indian population. In addition to vast differences in population, economic divides also help to explain the unequal history of intra-Indian reflection. Despite the British drain on India's economy, India retained much greater wealth and thus educational opportunities than did American Indian communities. The lopsided nature of intra-Indian commentary also reflects the relatively large numbers of Asian Indians who traveled to America. Working-class connections in the American West offered American Indians the opportunity to meet migrants from India. Such connections undoubtedly generated some curiosity about India on the part of American Indians. But unlike prominent Indian visitors to America, most American Indians who worked and lived alongside Indian Americans did not have the opportunity or the resources to publish reflections on their experiences. Thus, the inequality that divided Indians from each other shaped how that difference has been remembered—and forgotten.

There is at least one other explanation for why we find more Asian Indians commenting on American Indians than vice versa: namely, the fact that people from India being called "Indian" demands less explanation. That final possibility—the relative naturalness of Indians from India—is at the heart of a revealing exception to the general trend, an exception that occurs in the prefatory note to Joseph Marshall's classic history, *The Day the World Ended at Little Bighorn: A Lakota History.* "We prefer to be identified by our specific tribes or nations," Marshall wrote, "of which there are nearly five hundred ethnically identifiable in the United States." Despite such a preference, Marshall explained, the word *Indian* remained indispensable. "I have chosen to use the word Indian," he wrote, "mostly in those instances when there is a necessary reference to more than a specific tribe or native nation." He then turned to the problem of the two Indians and offered an apology: "There are no references herein to the people of India, who are, of course, the real Indians. I extend my apologies to them for being dragged into this confusion over labels. But then, neither they nor anyone from North, South, or Central America started this confusion. We are simply forced to live with it, and sometimes answer for it." Marshall's willingness to name "the real Indians," a generous act of etymological humility, overlooks the essential foreignness of that word even in the subcontinent. Some residents of contemporary India prefer *Bharat,* a Sanskrit word that is often identified as "the original" term for the Indian subcontinent. But as the history of the word *Indian* makes clear, names are defined less by their origins than by their utility. As Marshall himself noted, the word *Indian* remains useful precisely because it can unite peoples often known by other names.[28]

Beginning in the 1960s, American Indians began to be widely known as Native Americans. Unlike *Indian*—long saddled with racist stereotypes—*Native American* offered more dignity and recognized the indigeneity of those peoples who first made the Americas home. But even as *Native American* became popular, a political and cultural struggle known as the American Indian Movement led to a resurgence of pride in the label *Indian.* In 1977, a delegation from the International Indian Treaty Council voted to embrace the label *American Indian* at the United Nations Conference on Indians in the Americas. Some activists continue to prefer *American Indian* to *Native American.* The word *native* carries pejorative connotations. And *Native American* sounds too banal and generic, as if it were the real name for what are in fact hundreds of distinct peoples. The word *Indian,* by contrast, speaks to the history of violence that aimed to erase the specific identities of the many nations that lived in the Americas before the arrival of Europeans.[29]

While *Native American* began to rival *American Indian,* the term *Indian* was also losing ground in the United States as a referent to migrants from India. Especially on college campuses and in policy circles, *Indian* became replaced by the bland but more inclusive geographic phrase *South Asian.* The idea of South Asia as a geographic unity gained traction as a result of the growth of area studies. In 1948, the University of Pennsylvania created a Department of South Asia Regional Studies. In 1955, the University of Chicago launched the Committee on South Asian Studies. In 1960, the University of Wisconsin created a South Asia Area Center. The rise of the term *South Asia* was aided by the problem of the two Indians, as well as by the fact that the phrase allows for transnational discussions of India and its neighbors, especially Pakistan. *South Asian* also recognizes the ways in which migrants from the subcontinent to the United States have been lumped together and racially profiled as a group.[30]

For generations, the word *Indian* helped foster antiracist solidarities. If the "Indians" that Columbus encountered fell victim to violence, slavery, and disease, the Indians subjected by the British were impoverished by hundreds of years of foreign rule. But the rhetorical power of such connections has dwindled since the 1950s. In part, the decline in comparisons between the two communities of Indians is a result of India's independence. No longer do comparisons between Indians seem revealing. Until the 1940s, both groups of Indians were oppressed and dispossessed and struggling against white racism and imperialism. Now, the Indians of India have their own country.

In the wake of Indian independence, a more apt comparison might be between American Indians and the indigenous peoples of India, often known as *Adivasis,* a word that means "original inhabitants." Still commonly known as "tribals," the Adivasis number slightly under 10 percent of the population of India, or approximately one hundred million people. Many live in the forested hills that snake up the center of India, a landscape of stunning beauty and rich resources that has been under assault by mining and timber companies and that has seen terrible violence between Maoist rebels, armed mercenaries, and government soldiers. Like American Indians, Adivasi communities face widespread attacks on their land and culture.[31]

Regardless of the analogy—whether *American Indian* versus *Adivasi, American Indian* versus *Indian American*, or simply *Indian* versus *Indian*—such comparisons risk overlooking difference and erasing diversity. The homogenizing potential of any transnational analogy is especially severe when that analogy is being used to attack a distant wrong rather than confront injustice closer to home. In their rush to denounce American racism, visitors from India like Pandita Ramabai or Cedric Dover overlooked the complexities of American Indian struggles. Even the most well-meaning historical actors oversimplified in order to render useful the problem of the two Indians. Like the other keywords that linked India and America, the term *Indian* was used to attack some stereotypes even while buttressing others. What allowed such selective stereotyping was a particular kind of ignorance: that of the explorer who knows what he will discover long before he has found it.

From the days of Columbus onward, the problem of the two Indians reproduced myths that masqueraded as knowledge. Early European explorers knew little of India, and even less of the indigenous peoples they branded "Indians." In the words of Vine Deloria Jr., "The absence of elephants apparently did not tip off the explorers that they weren't in India." That telling comment appeared in 1969 in *Custer Died for Your Sins: An Indian Manifesto,* a best seller that emerged alongside the American Indian Movement. In returning to the confusion that inspired the original naming of the Indian, Deloria made a vital point about the arrogance of imperial systems of knowledge. "By the time they realized their mistake," Deloria wrote of the explorers who believed they had found India, "instant knowledge of Indians was a cherished tradition."[32]

The problem of the two Indians was ultimately a problem of knowledge, of who was known and who did the knowing. It should not be a surprise, then, that the problem of the two Indians remains alive in the realm of scholarship. Cherokee scholar Jace Weaver has described "postcolonial writing" as "oddly detached when discussing indigenous peoples and their lives." Focusing on the work of the Bengali writer and activist Mahasweta Devi—and, in particular, on Devi's writings "on behalf of the tribal peoples of India"—Weaver found "the same sense of patronizing care reflected by those in the dominant, Western culture." One thinks of the stereotypes of the American Indian employed by Cedric Dover, Sarojini Naidu, Lala Lajpat Rai, and Pandita Ramabai—except what is at issue here is not how the Indians of India saw the Indians of America, but rather how the Indians of India continue to see indigenous people within India itself. This is not the place to assess whether Devi's writings are in fact patronizing, although it should be noted that Devi is known as an outspoken defender of India's indigenous peoples. What deserves attention is what is at stake when American Indian scholars challenge scholars of Indian descent to reconsider the indigenous peoples of India—what is at stake when scholar Jodi Byrd, a member of the Chickasaw Nation, writes, "South Asians have become the signposts of the condition of postcoloniality within the academic centers of the global North. Within an increasingly canonized discipline that is still innovating the language to account for deep settler colonialism within (post)colonized localities, the slippages inherent in 'Indian' bear the complications of indigenous peoples in the Americas." Put differently, even within contemporary India there are layers of inequality built into what Byrd calls "Indianness."[33]

Perhaps every country has its Indians. But let us not fall into the trap of false equivalence—the same path that leads from the problem of the two Indians into the realm of stereotypes. The Indians of America have their own histories, even if those histories have long been bound up with global processes. In the words of Paul Chaat Smith, "the Indian experience, imagined to be largely in the past and in any case at the margins, is in fact central to world history." Recognizing that centrality must entail seeing "the Indian experience" as simultaneously unique and interconnected. We must be wary of yet again comparing these Indians to those Indians—unless such analogies lead to critical self-reflection within both India and the United States. Even the Indians of America were not free of what the historian Pekka Hämäläinen calls "reversed colonialism" or "indigenous imperialism." But while recognizing that every society must confront its own legacy of discrimination and injustice, it would be foolish to conclude by equating all wrongs—as if genocide and slavery are nothing but useful rhetorical gestures, as if the meaning of the word *Indian* did not vary radically over time and space.[34]

Timothy Pickering lumped together distant "Indian" peoples marked by "dark skins, black hair and black eyes." Such physical commonalities were not, for Pickering, as important as the cultural and economic differences between the Indians of America and the Indians of India. Later generations of Americans would have been shocked to hear Pickering praise India as a model of modern civilization. But Pickering lived at a time when American ships regularly returned from India laden with expensive paintings, fine furniture, and intricate fabrics. When Pickering needed proof of India's advanced civilization, he offered the clothes on his back. As he told his audience, "The vessels of the United States sail to those Indian countries, and bring back silks, callicoes and other cotton cloths of the best kind." Lest his audience forget that they too could create such products of modernity, Pickering added, "These muslin cloths of mine, and this silk handkerchief, were also made in those distant countries by people of your colour."[35]

It is unclear what his Indian audience made of Pickering's pronouncements. One chief, Red Jacket, later declared, "It won't do to talk much more—for perhaps we have been deceived in the whole!" But three years later, Pickering would sign a treaty with the Iroquois at Canandaigua, New York. That treaty included a regular payment of the calico cloth that Pickering had extolled, a cloth that takes its name from the South Indian city of Calicut, where it first became famous. As the word *calico* makes clear, *Indian* was but the first of many words to travel from India to America. Historian Wendy Doniger provides a telling list of English words of Indian origin: "bungalow, calico, candy, cash, catamaran, cheroot, curry, gymkhana, jodhpur, juggernaut, loot, madras, mango, mogul, moola (British slang for 'money,' ultimately from the Sanskrit *mula*, 'root,' as in 'root of all evil'), mosquito, mulligatawny, pajama, Pariah, posh, pukka, punch, pundit, thug, tourmaline, veranda." Many of these words traveled across borders of language and nation because they referenced things that were similarly mobile, things like the calico cloth that Pickering saw as an emblem of civilization. To this day, the United States government gives a yearly allotment of cloth to the descendants of the Iroquois nations, in keeping with a treaty sometimes called the Pickering Treaty but also known as the Calico Treaty. Woven cloth dyed in colorful patterns, calico became increasingly popular throughout the United States over the course of the eighteenth century—one example of a flourishing trade that connected India and America.[36]

While enriching merchants in both America and India, the "India trade" influenced what people wore, drank, ate, and thought. Not everyone benefited equally from this commerce of goods and ideas. Free trade did not guarantee other freedoms. Just as the word *Indian* was used to buttress racism and patriarchy, so the ships that connected India and America strengthened prevailing inequalities. But those ships also created channels of resistance, as much more than cloth traveled the bustling sea routes between India and America.

# CHAPTER 1

# Elephants and Ice

∞

The pure Walden water is mingled with the sacred
water of the Ganges.

—Henry David Thoreau, *Walden*

T HE FIRST ELEPHANT to set foot in America left Calcutta on December
3, 1795. Her ship, appropriately called *America,* also carried a New
Englander named Nathaniel Hathorne. Nathaniel's son would add a "w"
to his father's name, penning *The Scarlet Letter* as Nathaniel Hawthorne.
Nathaniel senior was more a sailor than a writer. Fortunately for pos-
terity, however, he did like to keep a journal. He noted when the crew
"took on board several pumpkins and cabbages, some fresh fish for
ship's use, and greens for the elephant." Lest that final detail go unno-
ticed, he added in large letters, "ELEPHANT ON BOARD."[1]

The captain of the *America,* Jacob Crowninshield, had four brothers.
All five Crowninshield boys plied the busy shipping lanes between India
and New England. The Crowninshields were one of several prominent
families to make fortunes in the India trade. Their ships ferried a range
of goods—from raw sugar to fine calico cloth. No one had yet tried to
bring an elephant, however. Even in a family of adventurous sailors,
Jacob Crowninshield was a maverick. Writing home from India in November 1795, he reported, "We take home a fine young elephant two

years old." He bragged that the elephant was "almost as large as a very large ox." Every day, the young elephant grew bigger still, as did the captain's ambition. "It will be a great thing," young Crowninshield proclaimed, "to carry the first elephant to America."[2]

It would also prove quite lucrative. Crowninshield paid $450 for the elephant in Calcutta. He boasted to his brothers that he would get $5,000 for the animal in America. In 1795, such a profit on a single journey would be remarkable. But Crowninshield had actually underestimated the value of his magnificent cargo. The elephant sold for $10,000, a substantial fortune in eighteenth-century America. Crowninshield's success inspired other merchants to import animals from India. Elephants, monkeys, and at least one large Bengal tiger crossed the Atlantic to the delight of American audiences, and the profit of savvy sailors.[3]

Adventurous merchants like Crowninshield learned how to profit from the distance—both figurative and literal—between India and America. Novelty sold, and nothing was more exotic than the mysterious East. Even as they benefited from the divide between India and America, merchants built bridges across that divide. With every shipload of goods, Americans became more familiar with the products of India and thus, to some degree, with India itself. Of course, wearing calico cloth or gazing at Crowninshield's elephant did not require Americans to learn anything about the intricacies of Indian culture. Indeed, the India trade reinforced a peculiar dualism that would define Indo-American relations for generations. Even as connections between India and the United States multiplied, many Americans remained remarkably ignorant of India and Indians.

The interplay of the foreign and the familiar, so central to the India trade, also defined the intellectual networks that linked India and the United States in the first half of the nineteenth century. While the Crowninshields ferried goods from India to New England, a variety of American thinkers—from Unitarian theologians to Transcendental philosophers—consumed the intellectual fruits of Indian culture. Just as Americans enjoyed Indian material goods without learning much about India, so thinkers mined Hindu texts without respecting their context. From material culture to ancient philosophy, American Indophiles often engaged in a hollow form of cultural, intellectual, and material appropriation. But despite a certain shallowness, their interest in Indian culture stands in sharp relief to the views of those Americans who rejected Indian philosophy and religion as backward and barbaric. The largest number of Americans to travel to India during the nineteenth century were missionaries bent on converting the subcontinent to Christianity. While some expressed admiration for Indian art and literature, many denounced Indian culture as uncivilized.

American missionaries worked alongside British missionaries—and shared their prejudices. National divisions proved less salient than notions of race and culture, a consequence of the fact that British imperialism varied dramatically between India and the thirteen colonies that would become the United States. In America, British colonists had come to dominate the land. The "Indians" they encountered had been killed in large numbers, victims of disease and war. In India, by contrast, the British remained a tiny minority in a land they would continue to see as inextricably foreign. Many explained that foreignness in terms of race. The color line divided the British from India while connecting them to the new rulers of the United States. The modern idea of race, shaped by the European encounter with the Americas, solidified in the plantations of the American South and the colonial cities of India. A sharp distinction between white and nonwhite came to dominate the world.[4]

That distinction fueled two massive conflicts that rocked India and the United States in the middle of the nineteenth century. In India, the rebellion of 1857 shook the foundations of British rule. Four years later, the American Civil War erupted. The rebellion of 1857 led to the consolidation of British rule. It was a victory for empire. By contrast, the emancipation of America's slaves framed the American Civil War as a victory for freedom. It seemed as if the United States was marching toward democracy even while India slid further into despotism. But the resurgence of white supremacy in the United States defies such a contrast. Consider the production of cotton. In the last decades of the nineteenth century, in both India and the United States, cotton was produced by an impoverished labor force controlled with violence and set apart from the ruling elite by a steep racial hierarchy. Despite the myth of American freedom that still clings to narratives of the Civil War, the late nineteenth century saw both India and the United States become more deeply wedded to a global system of imperial white supremacy.[5]

India and the United States were not equal in their relationship to the imperial power structure. While the United States emerged as an industrial powerhouse, India became a source of raw goods for imperial

Britain. In 1700, India had been the greatest manufacturer of cotton textiles in the world. By the mid 1800s, India's manufacturing prowess had been gutted, its economy reduced to producing raw cotton for export. Much had changed since Timothy Pickering praised India's advanced economy and the Crowninshields sailed toward India's riches.[6]

The earliest commerce between India and America involved the transport of raw goods—not *from* India, however, but *to* India. In the sixteenth and seventeenth centuries, at a time when the Mughal Empire was among the wealthiest in the world, India was a consumer of raw materials from America. Then, the most important commodity was not the white gold of the cotton fields, but gold itself, along with silver, emeralds, and other precious jewels. Mined by "Indians" whose lands were conquered by Europeans, the riches of the Americas were hoarded by the rulers of India. From the beginning, inequalities of power dictated who gained and who lost as the economies of India and America began their long journey toward interconnectedness but not equality.

## The Rich Indies

The earliest trade between India and America occurred on Spanish and Portuguese ships. Wooden carracks, about the size of modern yachts, carried Columbus on his fateful journey. Carracks continued to cross the Atlantic for centuries after 1492, joined by larger galleons that were used for both trade and battle. Armed force was necessary to protect the prized cargo of these Iberian adventurers. Among their loot were precious jewels bound for the royal courts of the subcontinent. Emeralds from Columbia adorned Mughal emperors, a tribute to global interconnectedness but also to the vast inequality that marked the European plunder of the Americas as well as Mughal rule in India. As the "Indians" of America saw their lands looted, India was itself divided and unequal.[7]

Here is the great tragedy of the modern world: increasing interconnectedness did not mean increasing equality. There were winners and losers in the grand Columbian exchange—the movement of plants, animals, ideas, and maladies between the New World and the old. New encounters led to intermixture and connection, but also to new forms of oppression and division. The European encounter with the Americas and with India—a great coming together of peoples, ideas, and traditions—culminated in a global system of empire and white supremacy.[8]

By the time Lord Cornwallis surrendered at Yorktown, India and America had long been connected by Europeans bent on controlling lands they labeled foreign but simultaneously claimed as their own. First it was the Spanish and the Portuguese. Only six years after Columbus "discovered" America, believing he had found India, the Portuguese explorer Vasco da Gama became the first European to reach the real "Indies" by sea. The Portuguese established colonies in India, as did the French. But it would be the British who would conquer the vast majority of the subcontinent.

Long before Britain took control of the subcontinent, however, India's wealth inspired the British to found colonies in the Americas. As early as 1612, one advocate of colonization encouraged his fellow Englishmen "to consider, to conceave, and apprehend Virginia, which might be, or breed us a second India." By the late seventeenth century, British ships dominated the shipping routes that connected India to North America. As London became the hub of a growing empire, British trade created new connections between India and America. Not everyone benefited equally from these trade linkages. South Asian sailors, often known as lascars, were employed on British ships in conditions that approximated slavery. By contrast, certain merchants, ship captains, and government officials earned fortunes from the burgeoning trade between India and America.[9]

Elihu Yale embodied the centrality of money to the earliest phases of Indo-American relations—and the unequal and often illicit manner in which that money was earned. Born in Boston but raised in England, Yale made a fortune as the governor of the East India Company settlement in Madras, now Chennai, the largest city in South India. Much of Yale's money came via illegal ventures, but his dubious dealings did not prevent Cotton Mather, the famous New England Puritan, from asking Yale to supply funds for the Collegiate School of Connecticut. Yale agreed, and the school was eventually renamed in his honor. Yale University testifies to the importance of trade to the early links between India and New England. Yale's gift: "nine bales of goods, 417 books, and a portrait of King George I."[10]

Elihu Yale's philanthropy is but one way in which the American colonies benefited economically from the early trade with India. But the imperial authorities in London strove to ensure that the bulk of the profit remained in England. They tried to force all trade between America and India through London. American colonists responded by colluding with French and Dutch merchants and smuggling Indian goods into the colonies without paying import duties. In 1700, an admiralty judge in Pennsylvania denounced the illegal traffic of cargo from India into the colonies. In one summer, the judge estimated, goods worth some £20,000 were smuggled through a single port—Cape May, New Jersey—while untold amounts of Indian contraband entered at other points up and down the Atlantic Coast. While imperial authorities struggled to protect the monopoly of the British East India Company, many colonists came to see that monopoly as the epitome of despotism. It was in opposition to such despotism that a band of rebellious Bostonians dressed up as "Indians" and dumped crates of East India Company tea into Boston Harbor. The Boston Tea Party made evident not only American opposition to "taxation without representation," but also the centrality of trade with Asia to the economy of the American colonies and the growing hatred of the East India Company for having monopolized that trade.[11]

American opposition to the East India Company was further enflamed by the scandal of Company rule in India. In 1770, news spread of a terrible famine in Company-controlled Bengal, a famine that would lead to the deaths of some ten million people. The brutality of the Company in India became a cautionary tale for American colonists outraged by what they saw as imperial tyranny and fearful that America would soon meet the same fate as India. In 1778, Thomas Paine declared that the East India Company had "filled India with carnage and famine." The British plunder of India "was not so properly a conquest as an extermination of mankind." Other revolutionary leaders joined Paine in denouncing the fate of India. But how much was American sympathy with India driven by a self-interested desire to attack the East India Company? Consider how readily Americans collaborated with the Company in the wake of the American Revolution.[12]

In the decades after the revolution, New England merchants took advantage of the opportunity to trade directly with India. On the day after Christmas, in 1784, the ship *United States* arrived in Pondicherry, a French port on the East Coast of India. It is not surprising that an American ship would aim for one of the few French outposts in India. The American Revolution had ended only a few years earlier, and the ship's captain, Thomas Bell, had reason to believe that the French would prove more welcoming than the British. Unfortunately for Captain Bell, the British had conquered Pondicherry, and had yet to restore it to France as required by the Treaty of 1783. It was the Union Jack that greeted the crew of the *United States* as it edged its way into Pondicherry's harbor, loaded with tobacco, ginseng, copper, and a "considerable sum in dollars."[13]

The *United States* was allowed to carry on its trade. But unbeknownst to Captain Bell and his crew, British officials were actively debating how much to allow Americans to trade in India. Two years earlier, in 1782, an anonymous letter to the East India Company had warned that "certain leading Members of the American Congress have had in agitation some time a scheme to open a Trade from America to the East Indies." As if the Americans had not caused enough trouble in the new world, now they wanted to meddle in other parts of His Majesty's empire. Any foreigners posed some risk to the stability of a colony. But the rebellious Americans were especially troublesome. To allow the Americans to mix with "the quiet Gentoo Natives of Indostan" would be like "the Devil sowing the Tares amongst the Wheat." The "Tares" or weeds were, in this case, ideas of liberty and self-rule. By bringing such rebellious ideas into India, Americans might contaminate the "quiet Gentoo Natives." The British consul in Egypt, George Baldwin, shared similar concerns about the spread of American ideals. He worried about Americans arriving in India "free, exulting, broke loose from all restraints."[14]

Even more troubling than the contagion of American liberty was the threat of American competition. The British coveted their dominance of the trade between India and Europe. Nevertheless, some British leaders argued that Americans should be given greater access to trade in India. In September 1807, Sir Francis Baring noted that the United States had yet to industrialize and thus still purchased finished goods from its old imperial supplier. "If an American is successful and thereby increases his consumption of luxuries," Baring argued, "those luxuries are again Indian or British manufactures." Whatever money American merchants might accrue by trading in India would ultimately wend its way back to London. American profit was British profit. "Reduce them to their original poverty," Baring wrote of the Americans, "and like their red neighbors, their only consumption would be blankets, and for those, we should get ill paid." Thus, Baring used the poverty of "red" Indians to defend

American access to India. Baring's arguments resonated, especially with those influenced by the writings of Adam Smith and other advocates of free trade. Even Lord Cornwallis welcomed the Americans as "most favored foreigners." Any lingering resentment he felt did not prevent him from seeing the benefits of American trade.[15]

Whatever impact American trade with India may have had on British fortunes, it certainly brought wealth to some Americans. The value of the India trade was substantial. One historian has estimated that American trade with India in 1806–1807 was worth over $4 million, a magnificent sum in those years and more than twice the American trade with China. Yankee ships carried everything from tea and spices to cloth, furniture, and the occasional elephant. It was not uncommon for a particular journey to earn a profit of over 10 or even 15 percent. One journey involved carrying 1,500 Spanish-milled dollars from Salem to Calcutta. There, the dollars were exchanged for "2 bales containing 200 pieces of Alliabad cossas [muslin], 2 bales containing 200 pieces Tanda cossas, 2 bales containing 300 pieces Mahurazgunzu [another type of cloth], and 1 box containing 130 pieces Bandanna handkerchiefs." Those goods were sold for $2,866 in New York. After subtracting the costs of the journey, the total profit was more than 17 percent. Although the rate of return was not always so high, trade with India remained important to the American economy well into the nineteenth century. As late as 1856, Freeman Hunt, the eminent founder of *Hunt's Merchants Magazine,* praised commerce with India. "India has been," he wrote, "through all stages of history the leading star of mercantile enterprise."[16]

Trade between the United States and India enriched American merchants and ship captains, British officials, and some wealthy Indian landowners and merchants. Little trickled down to the Indian peasants who farmed jute or cotton or sugar, the Indian laborers who transported products to the coast and loaded them on ships, or the American seamen who worked those ships. The British need not have feared that Americans would disrupt the social order with rebellious ideas of liberty. On the contrary, American trade benefited those already in power. National distinctions proved less significant than the class rifts and racial divisions that united Americans and the British in opposition to the Indian other.

The line between being British and being American remained blurry long after the American Revolution. Take the case of William Duer, the first assistant secretary of the United States Treasury. Duer was born in

Devon, England, in 1743. As a young man, he accompanied Robert Clive, the governor-general of British India, on a tour of duty in the subcontinent. After returning to England, he traveled to the United States, where he became a prominent member of the Continental Congress. He was British at birth, and British when he served the empire in India. He died a proud American. But if he had returned to India at the end of his life, it would have been his skin color, his wealth, and his English heritage that would have decided how he was received.[17]

The racial segregation of colonial India lumped together the Americans and the British along with others deemed "white" or "European." Across the subcontinent, French and British cities were divided into "white" and "black" sections—the "black" reserved for "natives" regardless of the color of their skin. The crew of the *United States* noticed the racial segregation of Pondicherry. One ship official recorded his concern for the treatment of the local "Blacks," who were kept "in the most abject state of slavery & Bondage to the Europeans." So long as the division was between "Black" and "European," the American crew might position themselves as objective outsiders. But they were well aware that *European* was used interchangeably with *white,* a category that included white Americans. "The white Town," the ship's log noted, was "separate from the black." Such segregation was not peculiar to the French. In 1800, the Salem, Massachusetts, sailor Dudley Leavitt Pickman found the same division in British Madras. Pickman wrote, "No Black is permitted to go into the Fort in a Palanquin—they must walk in from the gates." The equation of Indians with black people, common to both European colonists and American visitors, reveals the early stages of a white supremacy bound up with slavery and empire. Like the word *Indian,* the term *black* was used to lump together distant peoples at the bottom of a global racial hierarchy.[18]

Some American sailors were critical of European rule in India. Commander Richard S. Rogers sailed the ship *Tartar* to India in 1817. He denounced the British for "satisfying their thirst for conquest" by disregarding "justice and humanity," fomenting war, and dethroning "rightful sovereigns." William Rogers, the log keeper on the *Tartar,* offered his own criticism of British "rapacity." Neither sailor made his criticisms public. By contrast, William Duane, a reporter born to Irish immigrants in Lake Champlain, New York, published his views of British rule and paid a price for his candor. In 1794, he was deported for publishing what Company officials saw as anti-British propaganda. Duane was the first in a long line of Irish American critics of British rule in India. Upon returning to America, he entered local politics. His opponents hoped to use the Alien and Sedition Acts against him, and so questioned whether Duane had been born in America. Having been deported from Calcutta as an American, he faced being deported from America as an Irishman.[19]

In the aftermath of the revolution, Americans routinely contrasted their freedom with the bondage imposed by the British. They claimed to be, in the words of Thomas Jefferson, an "Empire of Liberty." Duane's life does not support such a claim, and neither does the history of emancipation. In 1833, London ended slavery throughout the empire some thirty years before Abraham Lincoln's emancipation proclamation. American freedom remained undermined by American slavery. And slavery was not the only obstacle to America becoming the "land of the free." The persecution of indigenous peoples, the oppression of women, and the swelling ranks of the poor combined with the slavery of Africans to yield an American society dominated by wealthy white men. The inequalities of the United States help to explain why American merchants did not hesitate to profit from Indian societies that were similarly divided by race, class, and gender.[20]

Although British officials had worried that Americans would spread dangerous ideas of self-rule in India, most Americans either supported British rule or were indifferent so long as they earned profit. In 1791, John Gibaut, a New England sea captain, wrote home about the war between the British and Tipu Sultan. An American patriot might have been expected to side with Tipu against the redcoats who had only a decade before been the enemy of American freedom. Tipu's adversary was none other than Lord Cornwallis. But Captain Gibaut showed little interest in the legitimacy of British rule in the subcontinent. His concern was with his bottom line. "The seat of the war is so near the Coast of Malabar," he explained, that "it makes business more than commonly brisk."[21]

The briskness of business inspired the United States government to protect American commercial interests in India. In 1792, George Washington appointed Benjamin Joy the first American consul to India. Joy arrived in Calcutta in April 1794. The East India Company refused to recognize his official capacity, but did allow him to stay in Calcutta as a "Commercial Agent." That was his primary purpose—to help American merchants. Joy wrote Thomas Jefferson, asking him to increase the money that could be used to support sick seamen in Calcutta. "There is an excellent hospital at Calcutta supported at great expense by the East India Company," Joy reported, "to which all white men that are sick are admitted on their paying after the rate of ten sicca rupees per month." Joy's letter reveals the privileges that white American sailors experienced on account of their ethnic status. Neither Joy nor Jefferson seemed interested in whether America's "Empire of Liberty" might inspire freedom struggles in the subcontinent.[22]

American trade with India grew as the British expanded and consolidated their power. In the eighteenth century, the decline of the Mughal Empire led regional powers to jockey for power. The British encouraged such conflicts as a way to solidify their own standing. Americans also profited from the divisions within India. In 1789, John Parker Boyd helped equip the army of the Nizam of Hyderabad. Six years later, Boyd fought as a mercenary for the Nizam in a battle against the Maratha Confederacy. It was a disastrous defeat for the Nizam. For Boyd, however, it was merely a career setback. He escaped alive and took his military experiences back to America, where he became a brigadier general in the United States Army.[23]

Rather than representing conflicting ideals, American trade and British rule grew together, fueled by a shared Anglo-American desire to extract profit from India and Indians. At the turn of the nineteenth century, Indian ports swelled with American vessels. So many Yankee ships plied Indian waters that American sailors complained of competition from their compatriots. "I hear India is full and full of Americans in particular," John Crowninshield wrote his father from Mauritius, then known as the Isle of France. That was in 1796. Ten years later, an agent of the East India Company reported that American sailors remained omnipresent. "The vessels of these enterprising Merchants are to be seen traversing the seas in every part of India," he wrote. At the height of the India trade, thirty to fifty American ships sailed for India every year.[24]

Conducting business in India had its challenges, even for the most seasoned Americans. After leaving Madras, Benjamin Crowninshield reported that he "paid some enormous bills and endeavored to get away from so vile a place as fast as possible." Crowninshield's negative assessment of Madras may have been influenced by those "enormous bills." Later in life, he would retain warm memories of India. Living in

Washington as the secretary of the Navy, Crowninshield wrote his wife, "I dream about home, about India, & indeed about any thing but Washington." In another personal letter, he declared that he had "spent considerable time in Hindustan, & had become acquainted with the amicable manners of that mild & much misrepresented people."[25]

Trade increased the familiarity between Indian and American businessmen. Like Benjamin Crowninshield, many American sailors developed close relationships with Indian merchants. Indian brokers charged smaller fees than European merchants. They were also good sources of information. One astute businessman, Ramdoolal Dey, shared valuable tips with the New England merchant Francis Cabot Lowell. "There is now about to sail for America three ships," Dey wrote Lowell on April 29, 1800, "the *Recovery*—Captain Philips—the *Ulysses,* Captain Menkford and the *Winthrop & Marcy,* Captain Colling." In addition to such knowledge, Indian traders offered invaluable local connections. Some made fortunes by working with American sailors. Ramdoolal Dey was reported to be worth £400,000.[26]

It remains unclear what Indian merchants thought of their American partners, or how poor and working-class Indians viewed Yankee sailors. We know that the residents of Calcutta became accustomed to Americans. It took at least three weeks to load a big ship, ample time for sailors to make themselves known about town. But were Americans seen as different from the British? To a dockworker or a rickshaw driver, the differences might have been slight. But we need more historical sources to know for sure. Also unclear are the impressions of most of the American sailors who traveled to India in those years. The historical record contains far more concerning captains and merchants than of the sailors who did the bulk of the work. But despite the many holes in our knowledge, one thing is clear: the India trade had its greatest impact far from Madras and Calcutta. It was in the bustling shipping towns of New England that the trade left its greatest legacy.

## The Most Respectable Animal in the World

Salem is famous for witches. The witch trials that rocked the Massachusetts town in 1692 left an image of a closed community, backward looking and intent on punishing difference. But by the 1790s Salem had become one of the most cosmopolitan cities in the United States. A busy port, Salem connected New England to the riches of the world, and to India in particular. The Crowninshield brothers were based in Salem, as were several other enterprising families with strong ties to India. The town's motto speaks to the importance of India and its wealth to the people of Salem: *Divitis Indiae usque ad ultimum sinum,* or "To the farthest port of the rich Indies."[27]

Well before the American Revolution, trade with India brought wealth to New England merchants and sailors. With that wealth came a fear of decadence and other forms of corruption. As historian Jonathan Eacott has demonstrated, Americans worried about the social and moral impact of Indian luxury goods. In Boston in 1721, the Reverend Thomas Paine lamented that "the most distant Indies" were "searched with the greatest cost and peril, for the finest Sattins, Silks or at least Chences and Callicoes to fit up thousands of Women, who really are not worthy to be advanced one Ace above the Dunghill." In addition to moral corruption, critics worried about the economic drain of consuming so many foreign goods. But even while some decried the moral and economic impact of the India trade, Americans continued to buy the newest fashions from India.[28]

The influence of the India trade stretched far beyond New England. The goods themselves brought touches of India into American homes and American English. The word *bandanna,* for example, comes from the Sanskrit *bandhana,* meaning "to tie." In 1792, the wealthy Salem merchant William Gray sent a letter to the captain of his ship encouraging him to seek "sugar, saltpeters, Bandanno silk Handerchiefs, or such other goods as you suppose will answer best in this market." Americans also began to smoke "cheroots," a type of cigar whose name came from the Tamil for "roll." In August 1804, Gray recorded, a ship brought "sugar, indigo, and cheroots" from Calcutta. The pages of the *Boston Daily Advertiser* were filled with goods from India: "sawns, bafts, sannas, gilla, the madras pattern, sooty ruman handkerchiefs, custers, fine Gourypore checks, gurrahs, Calcutta goatskins, chintz, mahmuddis, Bengal ginghams, mogadore skins, sea-horse teeth and leopard hides. Physicians recommend India rubber shoes. Citizens are encouraged to buy Bengal or Jessore indigo, India muslins, choppas, bandannas, and Calcutta twines." Although Boston and other New England towns were deeply involved in the India trade, New York and Philadelphia received even more goods from India. And those goods traveled throughout British America. By the early seventeenth century, probate lists from across the colonies were filled with Indian merchandise, usually clothes and drapery made of silk or cotton. Did this avalanche of Indian commodities pique American curiosity about India itself? Americans wore calico bandannas, built bungalows, and smoked cheroots. But what did they know of India?[29]

Let us return to Jacob Crowninshield's elephant. Transported up and down the East Coast, the animal drew crowds of curious onlookers. Thousands turned out to pay a quarter per person to witness the magnificent creature. One advertisement, printed in Boston in 1797, called the elephant "the most respectable Animal in the world," not just for its size but also because of its intelligence, which "makes as near an approach to man, as matter can approach spirit." Simultaneously humanizing the elephant and exaggerating its difference, the ad declared that the animal drank "all kinds of spirituous liquors; some days he drank 30 bottles of porter, drawing the corks with his trunk." Here was something new. But the elephant's novelty did not depend on its Indian origin. Indeed, advertisements often ignored its nativity. The word *India* had yet to gain the mystique it would hold for later generations of Americans.[30]

Travelogues published by sea captains introduced some Americans to India. But such books were biased by the perspectives of their authors, colorful characters who often prized a fanciful yarn above objective reporting. Take, for example, *A Narrative of Voyages and Travels in the Northern and Southern Hemispheres,* a sweeping memoir written by Amasa Delano, a sailor from Duxbury, Massachusetts. Delano found Bombay "an old, dirty, weather beaten place," but his account brims with curiosity about everything from the "extraordinary octagon building" used for pressing cotton, to the different kinds of cobras one must avoid, to the burial rituals and culinary delicacies of different Indian communities. Delano expressed admiration for the British and their achievements. He was more critical of Indians and especially Brahmins. "Notwithstanding the ancient purity and benevolence of the Bramins," Delano wrote, "they are now often immoral, ignorant, and cruel." Americans often decried caste and Brahmins in particular as examples of Indian barbarism. But Delano used the Brahmin to make a larger point about the dangers of privilege. "Many of them do honour to their cast," Delano wrote of Brahmins, "but like all other classes of privileged men, there are many also extremely corrupt."[31]

While sailors like Delano reported on India, the India trade brought some Indians to America. On December 29, 1790, Reverend William Bentley encountered an unusual visitor walking the streets of Salem. In his diary that day, the reverend wrote, "Had the pleasure of seeing for the first time a native of the Indies." Bentley noted that the man was from Madras and was "of very dark complection, long black hair, soft countenance, tall, & well proportioned." It was the man's skin color that most attracted Bentley's attention. "He is said to be darker than Indians in general of his own cast," Bentley explained, "being much darker than any native Indians of America." Simultaneously locating the Madrasi sailor within his caste and in relation to American Indians, Bentley placed both groups of "Indians" on the edge of civilization, linked not just by the name *Indian* but by all the strangeness that name evoked. It is unclear whether Bentley spoke to the Indian sailor. "I had no opportunity to judge of his abilities," he wrote, "but his countenance was not expressive."[32]

Bentley's comparison between Indians came just one year before Timothy Pickering told the Iroquois at Newtown about the "nations of Indians" across the water from America. Pickering was himself from Salem. The India trade inspired his comparison between those Indians and these Indians. There is some evidence that an Indian sailor had already bridged that divide—and not just, like Bentley and Pickering, through an act of analogy. As early as 1787, it appears that "an East Indian, a native of Bombay" had married a Mashpee Indian woman and had settled on Cape Cod. That "native of Bombay" might be the first Indian American—the first person of Indian descent to settle in the United States. It would be strangely fitting if the first Indian American had married an American Indian.[33]

In Salem, Indian sailors continued to arrive as trade with the "rich Indies" boomed. In the words of historian Joan Jensen, "One captain brought back a tall, black-bearded Sikh who could be seen walking down Derby Street in his blue turban, long white tunic, loose trousers, and red sash." By 1851, six Indians marched in Salem's Fourth of July parade. "They were said by New England chroniclers," Jensen wrote, "to have married Negro women and become part of the black population of Salem."[34]

Intermarriage with African Americans and American Indians might be celebrated as a defiant rejection of racial boundaries. But these marriage patterns also make clear that Indians arriving in the United States were slotted into the lower ranks of a highly racialized society. Whereas white American merchants positioned themselves on par with the British, Indian sailors were seen as racially different. Trade networks may have crossed geographic boundaries, but they did little to challenge racial or class borders. The boldness of the India trade and its social limitations were both on display in perhaps the most daring commercial initiative ever to link the United States and India.

In 1806, Frederick Tudor, a Boston businessman, developed a revolutionary idea: to export ice. In some ways, ice was the ideal commodity: free and plentiful in some places, scarce and expensive in others. But how to move it? Most cargo was not at risk of melting away. Fortunately, ice would remain frozen if packed tight in sawdust and hay. Tudor first transported ice from New England to the West Indies. In 1833, he expanded to Calcutta. The first shipment, around a hundred tons of ice, sold well at three pence per pound. Within a few years, several merchants were shipping ice to India—not only to Calcutta but also to Madras and Bombay. A large structure was constructed in Calcutta to house the ice. One resident wrote, "The arrival of our English mail is not more anxiously expected than that of an American Ice-ship." The American Tudor Ice Company quickly monopolized the trade, and Tudor made more than $200,000 in profit.[35]

The ice trade provided Henry David Thoreau with a metaphor for the power of ideas to cross time and space. "In the morning," Thoreau wrote in one of the most famous passages in *Walden*, "I bathe my intellect in the stupendous and cosmogonal philosophy of the Bhagavat-Geeta, since whose composition years of the gods have elapsed, and in comparison with which our modern world and its literature seem puny and trivial." Thoreau's liquid metaphor—"bath[ing]" his intellect in the Gita's philosophy—was chosen purposefully. He continued, "I lay down the book and go to my well for water and lo! There I meet the Brahmin, priest of Brahma and Vishnu and Indra, who still sits in his temple on the Ganges reading the Vedas." Ice from Walden pond refreshed "the sweltering inhabitants . . . of Madras and Bombay and Calcutta." Thoreau drew inspiration from that transit of waters. In his writing, as well as in the world, "The pure Walden water is mingled with the sacred water of the Ganges."[36]

Even as he celebrated such transnational connections, Thoreau demonstrated their superficiality. His references to Hinduism appear gratuitous, almost random. Indra is a Vedic god, for example, not usually seen in the company of Brahma and Vishnu. Many references to Hinduism were added after Thoreau had already written a full draft of *Walden*. Thoreau's use of Hindu iconography reveals that, like the trade in goods, the exchange of ideas between India and America thrived on difference. Even more than the physical economy, the intellectual circuits that bound together India and America were built on myth, fantasy, and ignorance.

## The Spirit of the East

In 1844, Ralph Waldo Emerson told Thomas Carlyle, "I only worship Eternal Buddh in the retirements and intermissions of Brahma." What did it mean for a Yankee philosopher to "worship Eternal Buddh" or ponder "the retirements and intermissions of Brahma"? The Hindu god of creation, Brahma eludes description for the same reason that many Jews refuse to write the name of God. The presumption of knowledge is sacrilege. It was the elusiveness of Brahma, and of Hinduism and Buddhism more generally, that fascinated Emerson. In his essay "Poetry and Imagination," Emerson wrote, "I think Hindoo books the best gymnastics for the mind." Their esoteric foreignness worked the brain and stretched the soul. But was Emerson's fascination anything more than mental aerobics?[37]

Despite his respect for the esoteric traditions of the East, Emerson did not hesitate to claim those traditions as his own. In his poem "Brahma," he used the vastness of the Hindu god to lead his audience beyond the apparent divisions of the world. In the first stanza of the poem, Emerson lets the god speak directly to the reader: "If the red slayer think he slays, / Or if the slain think he is slain, / They know not well the subtle ways / I keep, and pass, and turn again." Like the Book of Job, Emerson's poem reminds us that God transcends our understanding. Yet Emerson presumed to write in the voice of Brahma. It was the sage of New England that allowed the Hindu god to speak.[38]

Emerson's poem reveals a tension at the heart of American perceptions of Indian religion. Even while Americans proclaimed the vast sublimity of Indian spirituality, they did not hesitate to offer confident readings of that spirituality. When readers expressed difficulty with Emerson's *Brahma,* he suggested that they put the text in a Christian context. "Tell them," he wrote, "to say 'Jehovah' instead of 'Brahma' and they will not feel any perplexity." In that bold translation, Emerson typified the hubris, the flattening universalism, that marked many early American accounts of Indian religion. It was the intellectual version of the India trade. Like the Crowninshields, American scholars aimed to profit by domesticating the exotic.[39]

But while merchants focused on the material world, intellectuals were drawn to India precisely because of its nonmaterial or "spiritual" heritage. Their understanding of that heritage was shaped by intermediaries, none more important than Raja Rammohan Roy. A Bengali scholar and social reformer, Roy gained fame in the West for his opposition to sati and for his efforts to reconcile Christianity and Hinduism. Often credited with introducing the word *Hinduism* into English, Roy worked to unify and demystify the many strands of Hindu faith in service of a rational, socially progressive monotheism. Although he refused to fully embrace Christianity, Roy was an appealing figure for many American Christians. In 1824, his correspondence with the Harvard professor Dr. Henry Ware Sr. was quoted in the *Quarterly Christian Spectator.* Ware asked "whether it is desirable that the inhabitants of India should be converted to Christianity." Roy responded, "I am led to believe from reason, which is set forth in scripture, that 'in every nation, he that feareth God and worketh righteousness, is accepted with him.'" Thus, Roy used Christian scripture to defend his religious pluralism.[40]

Roy introduced many Americans to classic Hindu texts, but even more influential were the European scholars who came to be known as "orientalists." The term *orientalist* has become an epithet as a result of Edward Said's scathing critique of the "orientalism" that homogenized the East. But many orientalists were careful readers who approached their work with humility and admiration for Indian philosophy. Perhaps the most influential, Sir William Jones, inspired many Americans to read Indian classics. In 1817, John Adams cited Jones in a letter to Thomas Jefferson. "In the eleventh discourse of Sir William Jones," Adams wrote, "We find that Materialists and Immaterialists existed in India and that they accused each other of athiesm, before Berkly or Pristley, or Dupuis, or Plato, or Pythagoras were born. Indeed, Newton himself, appears to have discovered nothing that was not known to the Ancient Indians."[41]

The two faces of orientalism—humble scholarship and colonial fascination with the exotic—were intertwined in the way that many Americans approached India in the first half of the nineteenth century. Nothing better embodies the ambivalence of orientalism than Benjamin Silliman's remarkable *Letters of Shahcoolen*. Originally published serially in the *New York Commercial Advertiser,* Silliman's letters were republished as a book in 1802. Readers encountered the correspondence of, in the words of Silliman's subtitle, "A Hindu Philosopher Residing in Philadelphia to His Friend El Hassan an Inhabitant of Delhi." An American's view of what an Indian would have made of America, *Letters of Shahcoolen* reveals what Silliman thought both of America and of India. Like many orientalists, Silliman associated particular virtues with particular nations or peoples. "How happy would that poet be," he wrote, "who should combine the imagination and copiousness of the Hindu, with the sublimity and correctness of the American!" Such stereotypes were explained as the result of differences in climate. A note from the editors of Silliman's volume linked the Indian weather to the imaginations of Indian poets. "Enjoying a milder atmosphere," the editors wrote, "their feelings and imaginations are more warm and vivid, their language and mode of expression will of course be more brilliant, and be ornamented with a greater variety of metaphorical allusion." Such "positive" stereotypes were pernicious. They slid easily into dismissive prejudice. A people with such "warm and vivid" feelings could not be trusted to handle the sober affairs of state.

Despite his recourse to stereotypes that divided Indian from American, Silliman rejected the supposed superiority of Western culture. He compared favorably the *Gitagovinda* with the *Song of Solomon* and praised the love of Krishna and Radha as embodying "the reciprocal attraction between the divine goodness and the human soul." His letters present Hinduism as a rich faith tradition with strong moral principles. By contrast, Christians emerge as exemplars of hypocrisy. In London, Shahcoolen was shocked to find that many Christians "every day insulted and blasphemed" even "their holy Veda and Shahstah, denominated the Bible." Silliman used an idealized version of ancient Indian tradition to critique the modern corruption of the West.[42]

In the 1840s and 1850s, American literary discourse was filled with references to Indian philosophy and religion. The philosopher James Elliot Cabot published "The Philosophy of the Ancient Hindoos." Bronson Alcott, the educational reformer and father of Louisa May Alcott, peppered a public address with quotes from the Bhagavad Gita. The eminent literary journal *The Dial* published a series of excerpts from Hindu texts introduced by Emerson. His first selection of Hindu wisdom for *The Dial* included a passage that could serve as a motto for Emerson's relationship to Indian philosophy: "*Is this one of us, or is he a stranger?* is the enumeration of the ungenerous; but to those by whom liberality is practiced, the whole world is but as one family."[43]

In sacred Hindu texts—the Bhagavad Gita and the Upanishads, in particular—Emerson found a philosophy that resonated with his own belief in transcending divisions. The idea of Vedanta, the unity of the individual and of God, helped Emerson move toward what would come to be known as Transcendentalism. Emerson's first engagement with what he called "the wonderful riches of Indian theological literature" came in the form of a poem that he wrote as a student at Harvard. Entitled "Indian Superstition," Emerson's poem praised ancient India, "once illustrious in the elder time," but lamented that now "dishonored India clanks her sullen chain." Emerson did not doom the subcontinent to perpetual ruin. He imagined a future India undergoing a "godlike birth." But he remained focused on days long gone. Like most Indophiles, Emerson praised the Indian past at the expense of the Indian present. He celebrated the texts of a distant age rather than the beliefs of living Hindus.[44]

Even the most ardent Indophiles indulged crude dichotomies between East and West, or in the words of Thoreau, "the Oriental and the Occidental." "The former has nothing to do in this world," Thoreau wrote, "the latter is full of activity." Emerson offered a similar distinction. In 1857, he wrote, "We read the orientals, but remain occidental." "Orientalism is Fatalism, resignation," he explained, "Occidentalism is Freedom and Will." Emerson explained the difference in terms of race, and then linked that racial difference to a justification of empire. In his words, "It is race, is it not, that puts the hundred millions of India under the dominion of a remote island in the north of Europe." Such a racist apology for imperialism contradicted the best intentions of Thoreau and Emerson, both of whom often ignored distinctions between East and West in pursuit of a transcendent truth.[45]

Thoreau and Emerson both kept notebooks filled with quotes from Hindu scripture, and translated key passages into their own vernacular. In his poem "Hamatreya," Emerson expanded upon a famous passage in the Vishnu Purana: "Foolishness has been the character of every king who has boasted, 'All this earth is mine—everything is mine—it will be in my house forever'; for he is dead." Emerson condensed this antimaterialist wisdom: "Mine and yours; Mine, not yours. Earth endures." Thoreau similarly drew upon Indian philosophy. *Walden* abounds with references to Indian literature. From the Vedas, Thoreau offers this dictum: "All Intelligences awake with the morning." From the Vishnu Purana, he takes the following: "The house-holder is to remain at eventide in his courtyard as long as it takes to milk a cow, or longer, if he pleases to await the arrival of a guest." Many of *Walden*'s references to Hindu theology were grafted onto the second and third additions. This timing suggests that the Indian texts had only a marginal influence on *Walden*. Nevertheless, Thoreau's analysis of Hindu classics shows real understanding. He grasped one of the key arguments of the Gita, for example, when he wrote in *A Week on the Concord and Merrimack Rivers*: "But they, who are unconcerned about the consequences of their actions, are not therefore, unconcerned about their actions." If Indian sources were not formative for Thoreau, neither were they inconsequential.[46]

Thoreau repeatedly elevated Hindu texts above their Western counterparts. In his journal, he wrote, "The religion and philosophy of the Hebrews are those of a wilder and ruder tribe, wanting the civility and intellectual refinements and subtlety of the Hindoos." One sentence from the Vedas was "worth the state of Massachusetts many times over." In *A Week on the Concord and Merrimack Rivers*, Thoreau compared Hindu texts to the most beloved writer in the English language. "Beside the vast and cosmogonal philosophy of the Bhagvat-Geeta," he declared, "even our Shakespeare seems sometimes youthfully green and practical merely."[47]

While some scholars have written volumes on the impact of Indian traditions on American Transcendentalists, others have dismissed that impact as inconsequential. Three things are clear. First, both Emerson and Thoreau, like many of their contemporaries, found meaning in making reference to Indic philosophy and religion. Second, those references operated not solely as examples of a distinct and foreign culture, but also as opportunities to reflect on a larger, more universal truth. Third, for many American thinkers, Hindu scripture was less inspirational than confirming. As the biographer of Thoreau, Walter Harding, wrote about the author of *Walden*, "He accepted from Oriental literature only that which appealed to him and ignored the rest." We might argue that the "universal" was deployed to support truths found closer to home— if not for the fact that the American engagement with India had always connected the local and the universal.[48]

It was in the space between the local and the foreign, the particular and the universal, that these efforts at intercultural understanding were most successful. The halfway, in-between nature of such encounters is embodied in the story of King Trishanku. The story, told to Lord Rama in the Hindu epic the *Ramayana*, begins when King Vishvamitra attempts to steal a magic cow from the Brahmin Vasistha. Vasistha is too clever and uses the cow to destroy the king's armies. Humbled, King Vishvamitra vows to become a Brahmin himself. Meanwhile, a different ambitious king, Trishanku, makes it known that he wishes to go to heaven in his own body. Vasistha rejects such an ambition as impossible and his sons curse Trishanku, turning him into a Pariah, an untouchable. Vishvamitra learns of Trishanku's fate and decides to intervene to send Trishanku directly to heaven. On the way, however, the king of the gods, Indra, learns of the attempt and hurls poor Trishanku back toward the ground. Vishvamitra has become quite powerful, however, and is able to halt Trishanku's fall in midair. In the end, poor Trishanku is stuck in the sky, halfway between earth and heaven. The American poet Henry Wadsworth Longfellow turned the story into a poem titled "King Trisanku":

> Viswamitra the Magician
> By his spells and incantations,
> Up to Indra's realms elysian
> Raised Trisanku, king of nations.
>
> Indra and the gods offended
> Hurled him downward, and descending
> In the air he hung suspended,
> With these equal powers contending.

Thus by aspirations lifted,
By misgivings downward driven,
Human hearts are tossed and drifted
Midway between earth and heaven.

Longfellow used the story of King Trishanku to offer a sweeping pro-nouncement on the human condition. We are, all of us, torn between our highest aspirations and our earthbound "misgivings." Like Thoreau and Emerson, Longfellow failed to engage the larger context of his In-dian referent. We learn nothing from the poem about the role of caste conflict, for example, in creating King Trishanku's predicament. But like Thoreau and Emerson, Longfellow found positive lessons in a seemingly foreign world, and strove to uncover a truth that could speak across the divides of his time.[49]

Many Indian thinkers admired Thoreau and Emerson and appreci-ated their engagement with Indian texts. After his wife died in labor in 1890, the great Bengali anticolonial leader Bipin Chandra Pal "found solace in the writings of Emerson." He later remembered, "It was Em-erson who first initiated me into that transcendental Monism which I found more fully expounded in the Upanishads, the Bhagavad-Geeta and the Vedantra Sutras." Another Bengali thinker, Protap Chunder Mo-zoomdar, declared that Emerson was "a geographical mistake." "He ought to have been born in India," Mozoomdar explained. In 1909, Mahatma Gandhi praised Emerson from South Africa's Pretoria Prison. Emerson's essays were, the Mahatma wrote, "Indian wisdom in a western garb." "It is refreshing," Gandhi added, "to see our own sometimes thus dif-ferently fashioned."[50]

Gandhi also admired Thoreau. In 1907, Gandhi published an article praising Thoreau's use of civil disobedience to protest slavery. With a con-viction notable for its transnational sympathy if not for its historical ac-curacy, Gandhi concluded, "Historians say that the chief cause of the abolition of slavery in America was Thoreau's imprisonment and the pub-lication by him of the above mentioned book after his release." A week later, Gandhi translated an antislavery passage from Thoreau into Guja-rati and published it as an inspiration for his readers. In 1918, Gandhi told those living at his ashram, "Thoreau has said that, where injustice prevails, an upright man simply cannot prosper and that, where justice prevails, such a one would experience no want."[51]

Indian admiration for Emerson and Thoreau surged long after both men had died. That timing matters. Without significant connections to Indian thinkers and writers, Emerson, Thoreau, and their contemporaries interacted with Indian sources predominantly through European interpreters. As more Indian thinkers began to travel to the United States in the late nineteenth century, the intellectual ties between India and America would become more of a dialogue. But in the years before the Civil War, only two groups of Americans established direct connections to India: first, the merchants and sailors who, as we have seen, were less interested in philosophical wisdom than material bounty and, second, the missionaries who traveled to India to win souls. Missionaries spent more time in India than any other group of Americans in the nineteenth century. Many saw the peoples of the subcontinent as akin to the Indians of the American West—barbaric heathens who needed to be saved. But like Emerson, Thoreau, and other American philosophers, some missionaries came to respect Indian history, society, and culture—and to learn from those they had hoped to save.

## Missions

In March 1837, six New England couples, all Christian missionaries, sailed toward India's Coromandel Coast on a ship, the *Saracen*, packed with over one hundred tons of ice. Thoreau had been inspired by the ice trade to imagine meeting "the Brahmin, priest of Brahma and Vishnu and Indra, who still sits in his temple on the Ganges reading the Vedas." Unlike Thoreau, most missionaries were not inclined to celebrate Indian philosophy. As early as 1721, Cotton Mather had published *India Christiana* in order "to show the best ways of converting India to Christianity." Conversion meant breaking the hold of false religions, a category in which Protestant missionaries placed not just Hinduism, Islam, and other non-Western faiths, but also the Roman Catholicism brought to India by the Portuguese. Timothy Dwight, the president of Yale and a key figure in the American Board of Commissioners for Foreign Missions, envisioned a time "when the Romish cathedral, the mosque, and the pagoda, shall not have one stone left upon another, which shall not be thrown down." The young missionaries who arrived in India on the *Saracen* were equally zealous, although their enthusiasm was dampened by the shock of racial difference. Upon seeing dark-skinned laborers board the ship, several of the missionaries were overcome with fear and had to retreat to their cabins to pray. One exclaimed to his wife, *"These* are the Hindus, *these* the people among whom we came to dwell!"[52]

While Transcendentalists found metaphysical inspiration in the journeys of New England sailors, the India trade was even more intimately connected to the work of American missionaries. The same ships that took ice to India ferried eager missionaries. Most captains were happy to have the paying travelers, but not all appreciated the religious zeal of their passengers. Captain Nathaniel Ames thought missionaries were "obnoxious" cargo. He remained uninterested in the "battle between Calvin and Vishnoo," and declared sarcastically, "It is sincerely to be hoped that the time is not far distant when these 'poor ignorant heathen' will be compelled to eat pork and lace tight, when intemperance, fraud, adultery, murder and all other 'evidence of christianity' will be introduced among them." Benjamin Crowninshield knew many Indians who "had examined our religion & were familiar with its doctrines, & who could teach our missionaries the history of their church." The Indians he knew "were perfectly satisfied with their own religion, & wanted no change." Many American sailors avoided religious questions lest they complicate relationships with Indian rulers and merchants.[53]

The gap between the gospel and the bottom line was nowhere more evident than in the family of Nathaniel Higginson, Elihu Yale's replacement as the leader of Madras. Higginson was born and raised in Guilford, Connecticut. His grandfather and father were both prominent ministers. His father had hoped young Nathaniel would follow in the family tradition. But after graduating from Harvard in 1670, Nathaniel moved to England, where he spent several years working for the British government. In 1683, he found employment with the British East India Company, and was dispatched to India. An ambitious striver, Higginson worked his way up to become the first mayor of the Corporation of Madras. Like Yale, Higginson would make a fortune. Unlike Yale, he sent little of that fortune back to New England—despite multiple appeals from his cash-strapped family. News of Higginson's fortune prompted a remarkable letter from his seventy-seven-year-old father. After soliciting funds, the reverend asked three questions: "1) how ye breach betwene ye English & Indians is made Up & whethr be like to hold, 2) whethr their be any track or footsteps of Christianity in those parts som authrs have writtin of ye Christians of Saint Thomas, 3) What Reallity & progress of Christianity by ye dutch in ye Ile of Ceylon not far from you some years ago we heard their had been 300000 Baptized."

The reverend's first question pointed toward the still tenuous nature of British rule in India. What would come of the "breach" between the English and the Indians? His second and third questions reveal curiosity about the progress of Christianity in South Asia. Well into the nineteenth century, American missionaries would sail toward the subcontinent without much knowledge of what to expect.[54]

Adoniram Judson, Samuel Nott, Samuel Newell, Gordon Hall, and Luther Rice had all studied at Andover Theological Seminary before volunteering to serve in India. Before leaving, they were given explicit instructions by the American Board of Commissioners for Foreign Missions: "Withhold yourselves most scrupulously from all interference with the powers that be" and, in the words of scripture, "render unto Caesar the things that are Caesar's." At first, their efforts to prevent conflict with the East India Company seemed doomed to fail. The five young men arrived in India in 1812—an inauspicious year to travel from the United States to the British Empire. War had erupted. Washington would be sacked, the White House burned to the ground. What kind of reception could American missionaries expect at a time of war? As soon as they arrived in Calcutta, the governor ordered them to sail back to America. But a group of British missionaries pleaded the cause of their American colleagues, and the governor granted permission for the Americans to travel to another part of India.[55]

American missionaries continued to arrive on the subcontinent. As one explained in 1823, "India is the most important field in the world for the Propagation of the Gospel." India was "immensely populous, highly civilized, easily assessable," and "most important . . . united in one vast empire under a regular, stable and Christian government." What at first appeared an obstacle—the rule of the East India Company—had become a boon. Yet again Americans found British rule expedient. By 1912, there were some 1,890 Americans striving to save souls in India.[56]

Along with rendering unto Caesar what was Caesar's, the first cohort of American missionaries was instructed to respect those they wished to convert. "You go, dear Brethren," their official instructions explained, "as the messengers of love, of peace, of salvation, to people whose opinions and customs, habits and manners, are widely different from those, to which you have been used." They were to make themselves "easy and agreeable" to those they hoped to convert. While some missionaries followed such advice, others chose to excoriate Indian faiths. Samuel Nott, one of the first missionaries to arrive in India, declared that the Hindu gods were prone to "adultery, uncleanliness, lasciviousness, hatred, wrath, strife, envying, and murders." Another missionary wrote home that the Hindu gods embodied "wretchedness & moral death!"[57]

Like the puritans who came to America, many missionaries tried to establish "cities on a hill" that would model what they saw as an upright, moral life. At the heart of that life was the family. Of the first five missionaries to India, four traveled with their wives. Some missionary wives taught Indian girls or served as nurses in medical clinics. Most were treated as appendages of their husbands regardless of their own achievements. Charlotte White was the first female missionary to travel to India without a husband. From Lancaster, Pennsylvania, White applied to serve in India after her husband and first child died within a year of each other. The Baptist Board of Foreign Missions was not sure how to handle her request. Eventually, a compromise was struck. White was allowed to travel to India "as a helper and companion" for the wife of another missionary. Unlike male missionaries, White was required to pay her own expenses. Her rebellion against gender norms was significant, if short-lived. Soon after arriving in Calcutta in 1816, she married a widower, and the two moved near Patna, where they directed a series of missionary schools. White later wrote a Hindustani spelling book for children.[58]

American missionaries sent millions of dollars to India, a vast sum in the nineteenth century. Some of that money went to support the lavish lifestyles expected of upper-class "European" residents in India. Horace B. Putnam, a merchant sailor from Danvers, was startled by the "luxury" lifestyle of the missionaries he encountered in Bombay in 1850. Driven about in "costly carriages" or "carried in 'Pallanquins' upon the shoulders of four natives," many missionaries lived in "beautiful country seats which would be quite palaces at home." Not all lived so extravagantly. George Bowen, originally of Middlebury, Vermont, earned renown for living a simple life in a small rented room in Bombay. The editor of the *Bombay Guardian*, Bowen wrote passionately in defense of his Christian faith. But his deeds spoke louder than his words. Known as the

"Christian Fakir," the "Christian Rishi," or "the White Saint of India," Bowen lived in Bombay for forty years, until his death in 1888. The *Dinbandhu,* an Anglo-Marathi weekly, remembered his "philanthropy, large heartedness, charity and humility" as "in every way typical of the old sages of India." Bowen's humble lifestyle stood in sharp relief to the excesses of other missionaries. After memorializing Bowen, one paper wrote that "missionaries inspired with deep, ardent, comprehensive, Christian sympathy" had once been common in India, but with Bowen's death, "their race is extinct."[59]

Missionaries like George Bowen were rare, but many strove to serve India and to learn about Indian culture. Because of the need to translate the Bible, many missionaries became expert linguists. Nathan Brown was born in 1807 in the heartland of the India trade: New Ipswich, New Hampshire. Brown traveled to Burma and then Assam, a hilly region in the Northeast of India. While the British imposed the Bengali language, Brown worked to learn the local tongue, Assamese. In 1848, he published an Assamese grammar, followed two years later by an Assamese version of the New Testament. At the same time, another Baptist missionary, Lyman Jewett, was patiently translating the Bible into the South Indian language, Telugu. Samuel Henry Kellogg, a Presbyterian missionary, helped draft a Hindi Bible and a popular textbook of the Hindi language.

While linguists like Brown, Jewett, and Kellogg brought attention to the diversity of Indian languages, many American missionaries aimed to serve India in a less academic fashion—as doctors. John Christian Frederick Heyer, one of the first Lutheran missionaries to be sent abroad from the United States, trained in both Sanskrit and medicine before sailing for India in 1841. Heyer's life reveals the mix of luxury and difficulty that marked many missionary experiences. When he arrived in Tamil Nadu in 1842, Heyer hired a palanquin and bearers to travel inland. Being carried did not trouble his Christian humility, in part because racial stereotypes alleviated any concern he might have felt for the men tasked with bearing his weight. "Compared with the Aryans of North India," Heyer wrote, "the Dravidians have a darker complexion, longer heads, flatter noses, more irregular features, and are shorter in stature. In lieu of physical strength and vigor they possess, to a marked degree, the power of patient endurance." The power of patient endurance: what could be more fitting for men charged with lugging missionaries across great distances? Heyer's name was often confused for Aiyar, a common surname for Brahmins. It was ironic that, in Heyer's words, "the first Lutheran missionary to the Telugus should be a priest, a Brahmin, by name and by office." But Heyer's privileged status as a white man and honorary Brahmin did not protect him from all hardships. During his second trip to India, he moved inland to an area with a high risk of malaria. A practical man, he had his own coffin built and a grave dug near his home. His preparations proved unnecessary. He lived a long and healthy life. But his efforts did not go to waste. When the roof of his home began to leak, he slept in the coffin.[60]

It was Heyer who had decided that converting the residents of "the peninsula of Hindustan" was easier than saving American Indians, who were "of a roving disposition" and thus "very difficult to get hold of." While other American missionaries made a similar calculation, their numbers in India were further increased through reproduction. Like New England sea captains who passed their trade down the generations, missionaries were often born to other missionaries. Three generations of McGavrans contributed some 279 years of service in India. The Scudder family may hold the record for combined service. The Reverend Doctor John Scudder Senior was born in New Jersey in 1793. After graduating from Princeton and the New York College of Physicians and Surgeons, he left for South Asia in 1819. John, his wife Harriet, and their six sons and two daughters all served as missionaries. The family focused on medicine. John's granddaughter, Ira Scudder, founded the renowned Christian Medical College and Hospital in Vellore.[61]

Many missionaries came to see India as home. Mary Reed, born in Ohio in the 1850s, served in Cawnpore (now Kanpur) for eight years before returning to the United States. She might have settled in Ohio if she had not developed a strange tingling in her finger and noticed a peculiar spot on her face. She had leprosy. Reed decided to return to India to work among other victims of leprosy. She founded a hospital in the Himalayas, where she lived and worked for the next fifty-three years. Her letters reveal a woman at peace with God's will. In November 1894, she wrote a friend:

> I began this letter before sunrise, and while sitting at my eastern window writing to you, the sun rose in splendour over the majestic mountains, lighting them up with a halo of glory. The magnificent views I have of

the eternal snows and of the beautiful forest-clad heights are a never-ceasing delight to me. Pray for me, please, that my soul's life may be strengthened by the lessons and thoughts suggested by these glorious works of God which lie about me.

Many American missionaries—even those who struggled to respect Indians—found in the subcontinent "glorious works of God."[62]

Some Americans became prominent members of India's missionary world. Born in Ohio in 1836, James Thoburn went to India in 1859, eventually rising to the rank of bishop of the Methodist Episcopal church. Thoburn founded a renowned boys' school in Calcutta, built one of the largest congregations in India, and edited one of the leading missionary journals in the subcontinent, *Indian Witness.* Thoburn demonstrated the success of American missionaries as judged by their status in colonial society. But as Thoburn himself recognized, their success at converting Indians was far less significant.

Although missionaries failed to achieve a Christian India, they left a lasting mark on Indian society and Indo-American relations. Some of the earliest Indians to come to the United States were young men trained for missionary service at the Foreign Mission School, also known as the Heathen School, a remarkable seminary in rural Connecticut dedicated to educating "heathens" from throughout the world. The goal was for these young men to return to India to spread the good news, but their numbers paled in comparison to the hordes of American missionaries who traveled to India. Until the Second World War, missionaries constituted the largest contingent of Americans in India. From the handful that journeyed there in 1812 to over one thousand in 1900 and over three thousand in 1920, missionaries accounted for more than 90 percent of the Americans who traveled to India. They represented not just Christianity, but also the United States.[63]

But which United States? Nearly all missionaries were white Protestants. Very few were unmarried women. Such homogeneity renders more remarkable the journey of Amanda Smith. In November 1879, Smith arrived in Bombay to preach the gospel. What distinguished Smith from other American missionaries was twofold. First, she was a woman unaccompanied by a husband. Second, she was black. Born a slave, Smith was one of the first African Americans to visit India. She traveled across the subcontinent for over two years. Everywhere she went, she drew huge crowds. "During the seventeen years that I have lived in Calcutta," Bishop Thoburn wrote, "I have never known anyone who could draw and hold so large an audience as Mrs. Smith." What did her Indian audiences make of her racial identity? The vast majority of American missionaries were middle-class whites. Most of their Indian converts were low-caste and poor. Amanda Smith might have bridged that divide by speaking against oppressions of race, caste, and class. But there is no evidence that she did. Her interactions with Indians were limited by her missionary zeal. Smith noted the peculiarities of caste, and lamented the poverty of many Indians, but dwelled more on her own spiritual journey than on India or Indians.[64]

Many Indians already admired African American struggles. Missionaries taught the history of emancipation, and helped popularize antislavery books like *Uncle Tom's Cabin*. But it was Indians themselves who found in black struggles a source of inspiration. Some joined the fight against slavery by enlisting as soldiers or sailors in the American Civil War. Their stories reveal the patriotism of Indian Americans, as well as the persistence of racism among those who claimed to fight for freedom.

## Bloody Cotton

In the spring of 1862, Antonio Frank Gomez sailed toward New Orleans on the *USS Iroquois*. His mission was to retake the mouth of the Mississippi River from Confederate forces. Born Conjee Rustumjee Cohoujee Bey, the son of a wealthy Parsi family, Gomez had been raised in India and educated in London before arriving in New York in 1860 at the age of twenty-four. Inspired by the renowned preacher and abolitionist Henry Ward Beecher, Gomez converted to Christianity, changed his name, and enlisted in the Union Navy. He served on the *USS North Carolina* before transferring to the *Iroquois* and participating in the capture of New Orleans. In 1867, Gomez moved to San Francisco, where he worked as an administrator for the Navy for forty-four years. He died in February 1911 and was buried with full military honors in the National Cemetery in San Francisco. His career might serve as evidence of the social mobility afforded Indian migrants in post–Civil War America. But although Gomez contributed to destroying the Confederacy and thus slavery, his success depended on his ability to pass as white.[65]

Most Indian Americans who fought for the North were identified as black. Even as they fought for their new country, they were treated as second-class citizens. Most were merchant seamen recruited as sailors for the Union Navy. John Joseph, from Bombay; Joseph Sortee, from Madras; and James Bradshaw, from Calcutta—all became American sailors, and all were labeled black. Even when they were not described as black, most South Asian recruits were not seen as white. One Indian sailor named Joseph Raimen was listed as "Creole." Others were deemed "Mulatto."[66]

Indian American soldiers were the most direct link between India and the United States during the American Civil War. But their numbers were small, and their service largely unrecognized in the United States and India. A more significant connection came in the form of cotton. The Bombay Chamber of Commerce saw the "emancipation of American slaves" as "a matter of paramount importance," but primarily because emancipation might rob Southern planters of cheap labor, providing Indian cotton with a strategic advantage. As Union forces choked Confederate shores, cutting off supplies of cotton to Europe, Indian merchants and cotton farmers benefited dramatically. So did the Indian stock market. The flood of profits created a boom, but only for a few years. The end of the war returned American cotton to the world stage. Indian markets crashed, revealing the dangers of being connected to the increasingly global economy.[67]

The middle of the nineteenth century was a time of great turmoil in both the United States and India. Only a few years before the American Civil War began, a massive rebellion swept North India, fueled by a range of grievances against the British East India Company. Many Americans sided with the British in what was seen as a racial conflict between civilized whites and barbaric natives. A newspaper in Louisville predicted "the certainty and decisiveness of the triumph of the English" given that "one European is equal to at least ten natives." The *New York Times* similarly played up the racial dimensions of the conflict. "The mutineers," the *Times* reported, "under the inspiration of their Mohammedan leaders, made this outbreak from the first a contest of race with race." Many Americans cheered as the British gained the upper hand. Their victory depended on help from local Indian partners and a relatively new invention: the telegraph. But many Americans saw it as a victory for the white race. According to the *Times*, the British had "restored the threatened supremacy of their race."[68]

Even antislavery Indophiles could not resist the romance of British soldiers standing firm against the uncivilized hordes. The Quaker poet and abolitionist John Greenleaf Whittier had written hymns in praise of the Brahmo Samaj, and lauded Indian intellectuals like Keshub Chunder Sen and Protap Chunder Mozoomdar. In his poem "The Pipes of Lucknow," however, Whittier celebrated the bagpipe tune "Auld Lang Syne," and the empire with which it was associated:

> Round the silver domes of Lucknow,
> Moslem mosque and Pagan shrine,
> Breathed the air to Britons dearest,
> The air of Auld Lang Syne.

But even while welcoming British victory, many Americans did not hesitate to criticize what was widely perceived as imperial overreach. A newspaper in Louisville suggested that "the entire question of the British rule in India will come up for investigation and reform."[69]

Americans gained a sympathetic view of India's rebels from an unlikely source: Karl Marx. In his column for the *New York Daily Tribune*, Marx explained the rebellion as a direct result "of England's own conduct in India." He described Company rule as a form of "torture" and the rebellion as "historical retribution." While many American journalists focused on the violence of the Indian rebels, Marx chronicled British atrocities. He used the words of a British officer to reveal the racial prejudice at the heart of the empire. "We hold court-martials on horseback," the officer declared, "and every nigger we meet with we either string up or shoot."[70]

America has its own tradition of lynching "niggers." The racial dynamics of British India were familiar to Frederick Douglass, who compared the subjugation of Indian soldiers by their white officers to the racism faced by black abolitionists. Douglass made that comparison in August 1857, a few months after the rebellion erupted in India and three years before the outbreak of the American Civil War. We might contrast the outcome of the Civil War with the triumph of British colonialism; America's slaves were free, while Indians had been shackled by a resurgent empire. But the slaveholders of the American South proved resilient, and white supremacy returned in the form of Jim Crow. In both India and America, cotton production was guaranteed with a new system of forced labor driven by debt peonage and violence. In both nations, war led to the consolidation of state power and of white supremacy.[71]

Well into the twentieth century, white supremacy linked imperialists in the United States, Britain, and British India. In the aftermath of the Spanish-American War, Rudyard Kipling published an influential poem calling for Americans to take up "the white man's burden." Kipling's appeal resonated with many Americans, including Teddy Roosevelt. In December 1908, Roosevelt told John Morley, the British secretary of state for India, "I realize the immensity of the burden which England has to bear in India." Roosevelt asked Morley for information for a major speech on India. Roosevelt gave that speech to members of the Methodist Episcopal Church in January 1909. He praised British rule and predicted violence if India were given freedom. "The successful administration of the Indian Empire by the English," Roosevelt declared, "has been one of the most notable and most admirable achievements of the white race during the past two centuries."[72]

Roosevelt's defense of the Raj was prompted by his disgust at what he called a "silly speech and hysterical pronunciamento" given by the renowned Democratic politician William Jennings Bryan. According to Roosevelt, Bryan had dared to suggest that "there should be a kind of Indian republic established out of hand." One of America's most renowned political figures, Bryan visited India soon after the turn of the century. He concluded, "British rule in India is far worse, far more burdensome to the people, and far more unjust—if I understand the meaning of the word—than I had supposed." In the Raj, there was "money for an army, none for irrigation." Bryan rejected the old excuse that India was too divided for independence, and concluded, "Let no one cite India as an argument in defense of colonialism."[73]

Many Americans who visited India sought a middle ground between Bryan's anticolonialism and Roosevelt's imperialism. A series of American writers toured India over the second half of the nineteenth century. Many offered qualified praise for the British administration. Bayard Taylor, a poet and literary critic, criticized the East India Company for depressing "the prosperity of India and the civilization of its people." He compared British residents of India to American advocates of slavery. Still, Taylor concluded that the Raj was a "well-regulated despotism" that was better than the "capricious tyranny" of previous Indian rulers. Similar praise marks the travel writing of perhaps the highest-profile American to visit India in the Victorian era, former president Ulysses S. Grant. Grant toured India in 1878. His visit was widely discussed in India and the United States. In a private letter, Grant reported that he was "very much pleased with English rule and English hospitality in India." In British India, he declared, "two hundred and fifty millions of uncivilized people are living at peace with each other and are not only drawing their subsistence from the soil but are exporting a large excess over imports from it." Grant drew upon racial distinctions between the civilized and the uncivilized, while failing to recognize that India's economy enriched the British by impoverishing the majority of Indians.[74]

No figure better expressed the ambivalence many Americans felt toward the British Raj than Mark Twain. In January 1896, Twain arrived in Bombay. He would later call India "the only foreign land I ever daydream about or deeply long to see again." Twain could not resist the breathless stereotypes used by many foreigners: "A bewitching place, a bewildering place, an enchanting place—the Arabian Nights come again!" But Twain's sarcasm prevented him from fully embracing such orientalist cant. Even before he visited India, Twain ridiculed the tropes of the Raj. "You must be ready," Twain told Rudyard Kipling in 1895. "I shall come riding my ayah with his tusks adorned with silver bells and ribbons and escorted by a troop of native howdahs richly clad and mounted upon a herd of wild bungalows; and you must be on hand with a few bottles of ghee, for I shall be thirsty." Purposefully misusing words like *ayah* (housemaid), *howdah* (elephant carriage), and *ghee* (clarified butter), Twain laughed at himself, but also at the pretenses of the civilization that Kipling celebrated.[75]

Twain's religious pluralism helped him avoid the racial superiority Kipling shared with Roosevelt. After attending the Kumbh Mela, the great pilgrimage that brings millions to the Ganges, Twain penned a moving portrait of Hindu faith in action:

> It is wonderful, the power of a faith like that, that can make multitudes upon multitudes of the old and weak and the young and frail enter without hesitation or complaint upon such incredible journeys and endure the resultant miseries without repining. It is done in love, or it is done in fear; I do not know which it is. No matter what the impulse is,

the act born of it is beyond imagination marvelous to our kind of people,
the cold whites.

Twain's contrast between the Hindu pilgrims and "the cold whites"
maintained common racial stereotypes, but inverted their standard
hierarchy. Twain's interaction with Hindus strengthened his religious
pluralism. After meeting with Swami Bhaskarananda Saraswati at
Banaras, Twain offered a defense of pluralism. "The reverence which
is difficult," he wrote, "and which has personal merit in it, is the respect
which you pay, without compulsion, to the political or religious attitude
of a man whose beliefs are not yours."[76]

Twain described India as "a sorrowful land—a land of unimaginable
poverty and hardship." After watching a hotel worker struck by his "European" employer, Twain wrote in his journal, "I had not seen the like
of this for fifty years. It carried me instantly back to my boyhood and
flashed upon me the forgotten fact that this was the usual way of explaining one's desires to a slave." Witnessing the assault upon the hotel
worker made Twain recall seeing, at the age of ten, a slave killed "for
merely doing something awkwardly—as if that were a crime." After juxtaposing these memories, Twain wrote, "It is curious—the space-
annihilating power of thought. For just one second, all that goes to make
the *me* in me was in a Missourian village, on the other side of the globe,
vividly seeing again these forgotten pictures of fifty years ago, and wholly
unconscious of all things but just those; and in the next second I was
back in Bombay, and that kneeling native's smitten cheek was not done
tingling yet!" The "space-annihilating power of thought" allowed Twain
to connect American slavery to the European colonization of India.

But despite his religious pluralism and his shock at the racially-based
inequality he found in India, Twain remained guardedly sympathetic
toward British rule. His anticolonialism and his respect for the Hindu
faith did not save Twain from the blinkered view most Americans held
of the British Raj. Like Ulysses Grant, Twain portrayed British rule as
preferable to the alternative. "When one considers what India was under
her Hindu and Mohammedan rulers, and what she is now," Twain wrote,
"he must concede that the most fortunate thing that has ever befallen
that empire was the establishment of British supremacy."[77]

Twain's ambivalence toward the British Raj mirrors a larger paradox
that emerges from the early history of connections between the United

States and India. Many of those "connections" reinforced divides of race, nation, and class. New England sailors, Transcendental philosophers, and Christian missionaries all sought in India some form of profit, whether material, intellectual, or spiritual. Many approached the cultures and traditions of India with respect and humility. Like Twain, they used the "space-annihilating power of thought" to learn new truths and to oppose injustice. But the imbalance of power between Americans and Indians—an imbalance that grew over the course of the nineteenth century—allowed Americans to take from India what they wanted while leaving in place hierarchies of privilege and power. Like the word *Indian*, relationships between the United States and India linked disparate forms of inequality in ways that could be used to fight for freedom, but that could also perpetuate its opposite.

The imbalance of wealth and power between the United States and India helps to explain why most of the figures in this chapter were Americans engaging India—rather than Indians exploring America. But even while Americans like Twain toured India, more and more Indians began to arrive in the United States. Most came not as visitors but as workers. Their goal was to make money to support their families back home. The fact that they were willing to leave their families and travel across the globe speaks to the lack of opportunity in colonial India. India's loss would prove to be America's gain. The Indian American community would eventually become an overwhelming success story. But the early pioneers who journeyed from India to the United States struggled in the face of harsh labor conditions and fierce racism. When they organized to demand their rights, they encountered a government as repressive as the colonial state back home. And unlike in India, their very identity was called into question. In the United States, a society divided by the color line, it remained unclear whether Indians were white, black, or something altogether different.

# CHAPTER 2

# The Color of Freedom

∞

The Hindu resembles us except that he is black—and
we are shocked to see a black white man.
—A professor of chemistry, Los Angeles, 1924

I N 1922, Annette Thackwell Johnson, a reporter based in New York,
traveled to California to look for Punjabis. Johnson had lived in India
and had learned Hindi. She used her language skills with the Indian men
she found working the fields of the Golden State. Indian women were
harder to find. After several days, Johnson came upon a young woman,
the wife of one of the Indian men she had met. The encounter evoked
long-distant memories of India. "As my hand closed over the slim brown
one extended to me," Johnson remembered, "I should not have been surprised if a wild elephant had trumpeted from the shadowy fig trees in the
far corner of the vineyard." She continued, "The white *chadder* that draped
the calm oval face did not deviate by a hair's breadth from the time-
immemorial North India woman's costume; and the pig-tailed little girl
who ran up to stare at me might, with her loose-above, tight-at-the-
ankle trousers, have stepped from the heart of a Punjab village." Only
after speaking to the young woman in Hindustani and receiving a stony
silence did Johnson realize that her "pig-tailed" Punjabi, the essence of
"time-immemorial" India, was in fact Mexican American.[1]

Thousands of Punjabi-Mexican marriages were celebrated in California in the first decades of the twentieth century. They faced many challenges. While many Indian migrants spoke some English, most were more comfortable in Punjabi or Hindi—neither of which were useful when communicating with someone whose native tongue was Spanish. Language was only one of the divides that separated Punjabis from Mexican Americans. Whereas most Punjabi migrants were Sikh, the Latino community in California was overwhelmingly Roman Catholic. Every couple approached differences of faith in their own way, but most chose to raise their children Catholic. These transnational, interreligious families embodied the power of love to transcend the borders of nations, languages, and religions. But they also revealed the racism that labeled Indian migrants undesirable "asiatics" and made it difficult for them to marry white women.[2]

In the first decades of the twentieth century, most Indian migrants to America were men, many of them veterans of the British military. Their years in military service exposed them to living abroad, and provided the seed money necessary to begin their travels. Neither extremely poor nor especially wealthy, they were attracted by the prospect of making enough money to return to India to buy land and support their families. Significant communities of South Asian merchants, sailors, and street peddlers dotted American cities from New York and Chicago to Atlanta and New Orleans. But the largest contingent of Indian Americans was on the West Coast. Many worked in lumberyards in the Pacific Northwest or as farmers in California. The majority did not plan to stay long. But thousands did stay, despite the many obstacles they found in a land that became increasingly hostile to their very existence.[3]

The Indians who came to America were only a small percentage of the millions of Indians who traveled abroad in the nineteenth century and the first few decades of the twentieth century. Many went to South Africa and the Caribbean as "indentured" laborers, bound to serve a set number of years in conditions that often resembled slavery. Indentured Indians came to the United States too, but in small numbers. The life of James Dunn, indentured in Calcutta and brought to Georgia, illustrates the dangers these migrants faced in the racialized climate of the United States. Dunn's master died before the end of his indenture. The executors of the will forced Dunn to burn the evidence of his indenture, and then proceeded to treat him as a slave. Dunn sought his freedom in court.

But his dark skin spoke louder than the few documents he had to prove his right to freedom.[4]

Not all Indian migrants faced such dire circumstances. In 1889, Rudyard Kipling stumbled upon three Parsi traders in Philadelphia. By 1900, there were some five hundred Indian merchants and petty salesmen in the United States. Their experiences of America varied. Those who were affluent and light in complexion were welcomed into elite white society. Those with fewer resources and darker skin found the path to the American dream more challenging. But even for the many working-class Indians who arrived on the West Coast, racism did not always define their experience of America. On April 6, 1899, the *San Francisco Chronicle* announced the arrival of "four Sikhs" on a Japanese ship, the *Nippon Maru*. "The quartet formed the most picturesque group that has been seen on the Pacific Mall dock for many a day," the *Chronicle* announced. While they were all "fine-looking men," one was "a marvel of physical beauty." Such praise speaks to the curiosity with which many Americans greeted such "exotic" visitors. Even while romanticizing the Sikh travelers, the *Chronicle* simultaneously normalized them by noting that one of the four spoke English fluently, and all had served as soldiers and policemen in Hong Kong. Readers were offered no reason to worry about such men, courageous explorers who had journeyed thousands of miles "to make their fortunes here and return to their homes in the Lahore district, which they left some twenty years ago."[5]

Such a warm welcome would not last. By 1910, the West Coast had become a bastion of anti-immigrant hysteria. Indians were routinely forced to live in ethnically segregated ghettos, restricted to the lowest-paying occupations, and denied access to hotels and movie theaters. They encountered racism throughout America, but its character varied geographically. In the East and the South, Indians were often mistaken for African American—and suffered discrimination accordingly. On the West Coast, by contrast, they were discriminated against not as blacks but as Asians. Anti-Asian racism that had long targeted the Chinese was broadened to include the "Hindoo menace." Fearful that cheap Asian labor would drive down wages, white labor unions joined with xenophobic groups to lobby for an end to migration from India.[6]

In the face of such hostility, migrants formed mutual-benefit organizations and houses of worship, and turned to each other for financial and emotional support. Their relationships defied the heteronormative expectations of the Raj and of early-twentieth-century America. As the historian Nayan Shah has revealed, some South Asian men forged erotic ties with each other and with men from other ethnic communities. Like Punjabi-Mexican marriages, these intimate relationships flouted the constraints of a divided world, but were also shaped by those constraints, especially the racism that strained relations between Indian migrants and white American workers.[7]

It matters that anti-Indian racism was at its worst in the American West, where the land had been, not long before, American Indian. The discrimination faced by migrants from India was part of a larger racial system that simultaneously attacked nonwhite bodies and coveted their labor. Alongside workers from China and Mexico, freed slaves and their children, and those American Indians who survived the massacres of the nineteenth century, migrants from India built railroads, cleared forests, planted and harvested food, and in myriad other ways created an economy and a society that refused to accept them as equals. In 1893, the American historian Frederick Jackson Turner famously argued that American democracy was born on the frontier, "the meeting point between savagery and civilization." Connecting the genocide of American Indians to the oppression of Indian Americans both echoes and subverts Turner's argument. The experience of the frontier was constitutive of American democracy—but it was a democracy built on racial inequality. Who was the savage and who the civilized?[8]

Even as the United States became increasingly inhospitable, Indians continued to arrive. They were encouraged by reports from friends and family members who had managed to make money despite the challenges. They were attracted by American companies, which plastered India with advertisements for workers. And they were pushed by the dire economic situation in colonial India. While the majority of Indian migrants were working class, a steady stream of professionals also made the journey to America. They encountered anti-Asian discrimination like their working-class counterparts, but they had more options to cope with that discrimination. One of those options entailed distinguishing themselves racially.

Confronted with a sharp color line between white and black, some Indian Americans made use of contemporary racial science to claim the privileges of being "Aryan" and "Caucasian" and thus white. Between 1908 and 1922, some sixty-nine Indians gained citizenship by identifying as white. Most were middle class, and their class status helped them avoid the worst of American racism. Some found a warm welcome in the elite circles that had patronized figures like Pandita Ramabai. Many of the first Indians to come to America were religious figures hailed as prophets by adoring audiences, especially on the East Coast, where interest in India had been stoked by the India trade and the writings of the Transcendentalists, and being "Hindoo" remained suffused with alluring mystery. But even that allure revealed imbalances of power and knowledge, as well as the danger of a society divided by racial lines that were never as clear as they seemed.

## The Voice of God

At sunrise on July 4, 1898, on a houseboat floating on a tranquil lake in the valley of Kashmir, Swami Vivekananda recited a poem he had written in honor of the American Declaration of Independence. While a home-made American flag billowed from the mast of the boat, Vivekananda praised the United States for spreading "the light of Freedom." But Vivekananda's long relationship with the United States complicates an attempt to read his poem as an uncritical hymn to all things American. He had personally experienced the limitations of American democracy.[9]

Vivekananda came to the United States in 1893 to attend the World's Parliament of Religions in Chicago. A Hindu scholar and social reformer, Vivekananda was lauded for his blend of ancient wisdom and modern sensibility. In the words of a professor at Harvard, "Here is a man who is more learned than all of our learned professors put together." Many of Vivekananda's most devoted disciples were women. Christina Greenstidel first heard Vivekananda speak in Detroit in February 1894. "Never have I heard such a voice, so flexible, so sonorous," she recalled. "It was the voice of God to me!" In 1902, Greenstidel traveled to India, where she was embraced by Vivekananda's followers as "Sister Christine"; she spent a dozen years teaching in Calcutta. Josephine MacLeod met Vivekananda in January 1895 in New York, and also made her way to India. Vivekananda's most famous American devotee, Mrs. Sara Bull, left half a million dollars to the Vedanta Society, an organization Vivekananda founded in New York in 1894. Bull's daughter contested the gift in court, claiming that her mother had been "inoculated with the bacteria of faith taught by Indian swamis." The trial led to a surge of anti-Hindu news-paper stories with titles like "American Women Going after Heathen Gods."[10]

But despite waves of anti-Hindu hysteria, Vivekananda remained widely respected and his influence continued to grow. In 1897, he dis-patched Swami Abhadamanda to lead the Vedanta Society in New York. According to the American consul in Calcutta, Abhadamanda was "one of the first to put across the idea that in return for the religions which America has been receiving from India she should and doubtless will impart to India that technical and industrial skill which she made fa-mous throughout the world." That idea of a reciprocal relationship be-tween India and America would prove appealing for generations. John Haynes Holmes, a prominent Unitarian minister, put it this way: "Amer-ica can contribute her energy, inventive capacity and her century and a half experience of self-government while in return America may receive from India her great capacity for self-control, and patient philosophy." Such dichotomies flattened the complexities of both countries and ob-scured their similarities. Both India and America struggled to achieve real "self-government." Both nations were full of people struggling for "self-control." Moreover, praise for India's "patient philosophy" could easily slide into a condescending stereotype of Indian docility—spiritual "self-control" at the expense of "energy" and "inventive capacity."[11]

The dichotomy between the spiritual East and the material West fails to explain the success of the Vedanta Society and many of its leaders. Consider the career, for example, of Swami Trigunatita. In 1903, Trigu-natita arrived to helm the Vedanta Society in San Francisco and to oversee the construction of a new temple, often heralded as "the first Hindu Temple in the western world." Trigunatita personally designed the building, an impressive structure adorned with domes and towers that, in his words, "may be considered as a combination of a Hindu temple, a Christian church, a Mohammedan mosque, a Hindu math or monas-tery, and an American residence." Trigunatita founded a monastery and a convent and published a monthly journal called the *Voice of Freedom*. He authored articles on immigration policy and American participation in the Great War, and gave lectures on "The Future of the American Woman" and "Vedanta and Socialism." Trigunatita openly identified as a socialist. To a gathering of the Socialist Party, he gave a speech enti-tled "Every Man and Woman is a Born Socialist." His socialism was not just philosophical. Under his direction, the Vedanta Society purchased two hundred acres just outside San Francisco with the intention of founding a utopian society. Trigunatita defied the stereotype of the reclusive guru, as had Vivekananda.[12]

There was profit to be made in such stereotypes. Henry Ballentine, the American consul in Bombay beginning in 1889, made a small fortune by sending Indian jugglers and other circus performers to America. He convinced more than one Indian swami to travel to the United States to be displayed at circuses and county fairs. Ballentine ran into trouble when he was accused of pocketing precious jewels that he had promised to return to India after they had been displayed in America. He resigned his position and promptly left India.[13]

Ballentine was far from alone in turning India and Indians into a circus act. Buffalo Bill Cody's "far east show" featured a "Hindu fakir" and a team of Sinhalese dancers. It is telling that someone who made his fortune selling the conquest of American Indians as a carnival show would do the same with the cultures of Asia. The romance of the Indian knew no bounds. In 1904, Coney Island housed a replica of Delhi with seventy elephants and forty camels, as well as three hundred Indian men, women, and children—all paraded as curiosities before eager American eyes. The appeal of the exotic Indian inspired several Americans to reinvent themselves as Indian gurus. A few of the most successful were African American. Paschal Beverly Randolph, a free black man, claimed to have learned esoteric mysteries from an Indian maharajah. In 1855, he encouraged an African American audience to emigrate to India. Joe Downing, described by a contemporary as having a "coal-black visage," went on the vaudeville circuit with the name Joveddah de Raja. He landed a position on the radio dispensing "Oriental" wisdom. African Americans had a unique ability to reinvent themselves as Indian, given that many Americans equated "Hindoos" with dark-skinned foreigners. Black Americans also had a strong incentive to embody Hindu personas and thus to escape the fierce antiblack racism that dominated American life.[14]

White Americans also saw profit in embodying the mystical East. Some tried to do so respectfully. Ruth St. Denis, a prominent figure in the history of contemporary American dance, gained popularity for "oriental" dance routines that drew upon stories that Americans associated with the mystical East. Among her most famous works was *Radha*, a piece that evoked the famous lover of Krishna. St. Denis had been inspired by Coney Island's infamous Indian village. But she went well beyond such limiting caricatures. Her dance troupe toured India, earning the praise of Rabindranath Tagore, who invited St. Denis to teach dance at his school. Her husband, Ted Shawn, helped introduce Americans to the South Indian classical dance form, Bharatanatyam, by promoting an Indian dancer named Balaraswati, one of the first masters of the art to visit America.[15]

Many Americans were less interested in Indian culture than in how to profit from stereotypes of that culture. Perhaps the most renowned American guru was Oom the Omnipotent, formerly known as Peter Bernard, a professional baseball player who reinvented himself as an expert on the Hindu tradition known as Tantra. Now associated with sex, Tantra was originally a less titillating form of Hindu philosophy. Oom the Omnipotent deserves some of the credit for sexualizing Tantra. In 1904 and 1905, Oom established himself in San Francisco, where he launched an organization that would eventually become known as the Tantric Order in America. In a journal associated with his movement, Oom declared sex to be "the cause of our individual existence" and "the wellspring of human life and happiness." Such an argument was dangerous, at least from the vantage point of the authorities. In 1906, the San Francisco police charged Oom with morals violations, and the press attacked him for seducing "young women interested in learning hypnotism and soul charming." The charges were eventually dropped, but Oom decided to move to New York. There he was again charged by the police after neighbors reported hearing "wild Oriental music and women's cries, but not of distress." Despite a wave of negative publicity, Oom was never convicted, largely because his female "victims" refused to testify. One told the press, "He is the most wonderful man in the world. No women seem able to resist him."[16]

While Oom the Omnipotent reimagined Tantra, many of the most popular American gurus embraced yoga—but not the kind of yoga popular today. Yoga arrived in America as an idea and thrived as a spiritual movement long before it became a trendy form of exercise. As early as 1849, Thoreau wrote a friend, "I would fain practice yoga faithfully. To some extent and at rare intervals I am a yogi." What did Thoreau mean by *yoga*? "Free in this world as the buds in the air," he wrote, "disengaged from every kind of chains, those who have practiced the yoga

gather in Brahma the certain fruit of their works." Yoga was a form
of gathering. The word *yoga* literally means connection or unity, and
the word has long been used to reference the unity of the physical and the
spiritual. In 1884, the prominent Hindu scholar Protap Chunder Mozoomdar praised Emerson for embodying yoga. Mozoomdar wrote of
Emerson that "the tranquil landscape and the distant line of the horizon
gave him that perception of occult relationship between man and all
things which is the key to the sublime culture known as Yoga."[17]

Emerson and Thoreau were drawn to the philosophical implications
of yoga. Many Americans were more interested in its popular appeal.
In 1905, William Walker Atkinson published several tracts on yoga with
the penname Yogi Ramacharaka. His titles included "The Hindu-Yogi Science of Breath: A Complete Manual of the Oriental Breathing Philosophy of Physical, Mental, Psychic, and Spiritual Development" and
"Hatha Yoga; or, The Yogi of Physical Well Being, with Numerous Exercises." Atkinson's emphasis on breathing and "physical well being" reveals that yoga had already begun to shift from a philosophical tradition to a mixture of philosophy, spirituality, and physical exercise.[18]

It was such a hybrid form of yoga that exploded in popularity in the
first few decades of the twentieth century. Although American gurus
remained active, the most prominent advocates of yoga came to the
United States from India. Manibhai Haribhai Desai came in 1919 and
stayed for three years. Desai blended mental, spiritual, and physical forms
of training and gave yoga an institutional structure by founding the Yoga
Institute in New York. What might be called the first "yoga studio" in
America, the Yoga Institute more resembled an office and library than an
exercise space. In 1920, another prominent yogi, Swami Paramahansa
Yogananda, came to the United States to attend an ecumenical religious conference in Boston. He stayed for more than thirty years,
traveling across the country and popularizing his brand of yoga. The
all-encompassing nature of Yogananda's approach is evident in a promotional blurb for his "system for Harmonious and Full Development
Of Body, Mind and Soul . . . A Practical, Scientific Technique of Con-
centration And Meditation Leading to Conscious Contact With Inner
Divine Forces." Disseminated by the Yogada Sat-Sanga Society of Los
Angeles, the blurb helps to explain the allure of yoga for those Americans
drawn to an exotic "system" that unified the physical and spiritual.[19]

That allure took a strange turn in the hybrid spiritual movement known as Theosophy. Although Theosophy positioned the East as the original source of all wisdom, it was founded by two Westerners, Helena Blavatsky and Henry Steel Olcott. Born in Russia in 1831, Blavatsky traveled extensively before settling in New York. There, she met Olcott, a veteran of the Civil War who had developed an interest in spiritualism, a diverse movement that attracted those intrigued by the occult. In 1875, Blavatsky and Olcott founded the Theosophical Society, a religious community that blended "Mesmerism, Spiritualism, and Other Secret Sciences" with a hodgepodge of Eastern religious traditions. Blavatsky and Olcott moved to Bombay, where they published a journal, *The Theosophist*. The first edition defended "the necessity for an organ through which the native scholars of the East could communicate their learning to the Western world."[20]

Theosophy offered Americans a reason to once again see India as a source of positive spiritual, ethical, and philosophical traditions. But the Theosophical reading of those traditions, shot through with Western occultism, remained more popular outside India than within. By contrast, several of the Hindu reformers who traveled to the United States in the 1880s and 1890s brought with them considerable respect and institutional support within India. They might be seen as reverse missionaries, except their goal was not to convert Christians to Hinduism, but to suggest ways in which all faiths might find common ground.

Such ecumenical inclusivity defined the career of Protap Chunder Mozoomdar, one of the most renowned Indian religious figures to visit the United States in the nineteenth century. Mozoomdar arrived in Boston in August 1883. He understood his journey as a mission of religious unification. As he told one audience, "The spirit invites all men, all races, all churches, to exchange with each other their inner experiences, that all experiences may be assimilated, all ideals summed up, and one great ideal formed." Soon after arriving in America, Mozoomdar traveled to Concord to visit Emerson's home and speak to the local Unitarian church. The *Boston Globe* declared that "a preacher from Hindostan" had lectured about "his conversion to Unitarianism & the Progress of That Church on the Banks of the Ganges." The *Globe* was mistaken. Mozoomdar was careful to distinguish himself from the Unitarians as well as other Christian communities. A leader of the Brahmo Samaj, Mozoomdar saw himself as advocating "a new dispensation" that took the best from all world religions. In the United States, he found a ready audience for that kind of syncretism. From Boston, Mozoomdar traveled to Saratoga, in his words "a fashionable watering place" where "the wealth, the intellect, and the aristocracy of America gather." His reception is best summed up by the *New York Observer*: "We have had statesmen and generals, ministers of the Church and of the State, distinguished foreigners not a few, but no one of them has made such a sensation, or so profound an impression, as this traveller from the East, a Hindoo philosopher, teacher, and reformer."[21]

Over the course of several months, Mozoomdar gave dozens of speeches in churches, spoke to five hundred young women at Wellesley College, chatted with Harriet Beecher Stowe (and accused her, as we have seen, of conflating Indians with "Dacotas and Cherokees, savage, heathenish and illiterate"), and met the president of the United States, Chester Alan Arthur. He also published a book, *The Oriental Christ*, that challenged Christians to think about what Jesus might mean outside of a Western context. Mozoomdar inspired many liberal Christians to question the conceits of Christian dogma. In Boston, the *Christian Register* asked, "Would it not be a good idea for the home missionary societies to import a score of missionaries from the Brahmo Somaj [*sic*], to teach us loftier conceptions of God and humanity than commonly prevail?" Not all of Mozoomdar's Christian hosts were so humble. In Boston, Mozoomdar's talk titled "The Sympathy of Religions" was delayed by what one audience member remembered as a "long and tedious introduction" by one Reverend Joseph Cook. Cook had gone to Calcutta in 1882, met with Keshub Chunder Sen, Ramakrishna, and other leading Bengali intellectuals, and lectured in the Calcutta Town Hall. But rather than gain respect for Indian faiths, Cook returned even more committed to converting all Indians to Christianity. Rather than cede the floor to the stated speaker, Cook "could not refrain from sandwiching a missionary effort to convert the distinguished heathen guest." He failed. Mozoomdar would remain proud of his Hindu roots, and would return ten years later to represent the Brahmo Samaj at the World's Parliament of Religions in Chicago. But then he would be overshadowed by another Hindu reformer with universalist ambitions, Swami Vivekananda.[22]

Vivekananda came, like Mozoomdar, with a message of unity but not uniformity. The East and West should come together not because they were fundamentally the same, but precisely because their differences were complementary. "By uniting the materialism of the West with the spiritualism of the East," Vivekananda explained, "I believe much can be accomplished." Like Mozoomdar, Vivekananda encountered many sympathetic Americans, but also had to speak to less receptive audiences, including at the Parliament of Religions. Although often described as a cosmopolitan gathering aimed at fostering tolerance and pluralism, the Parliament of Religions was, Vivekananda complained, "organized with the intention of proving the superiority of the Christian religion over other forms of faith."[23]

Vivekananda struggled against more than Christian supremacy. American racism also proved challenging for the dark-skinned visitor from the East. Like many Indians in the United States, Swami Vivekananda was repeatedly mistaken for an African American. One woman described Vivekananda as "dark, about the colour of a light quadroon, and his full lips, which in a man of Caucasian race would have been brilliant scarlet, had a tint of bluish purple." In 1895, he wrote one of his supporters in India, "At Baltimore, the small hotels, being ignorant, would not take in a black man, thinking him a negro. So my host, Dr. Vrooman, had to take me to a larger one, because they knew the difference between a negro and a foreigner." A biography written by his disciples portrays Vivekananda reaching out to African Americans, such as the "Negro porter" who shook Vivekananda's hand and explained that he saw in the Swami "one of his own people [who] had become a great man." According to the biography, "the Swami warmly clasped his hand and exclaimed, 'Thank you! Thank you, brother!'"[24]

The color line in the United States descended from the history of two Souths: the American South and the global South. American white supremacists looked with interest and admiration upon the racial hierarchies established by European imperialists in Africa and Asia. But as Swami Vivekananda's travels make clear, the link between the American color line and the global color line cannot be explained solely in terms of intellectual circuits within transnational white supremacy. Vivekananda's fame challenged American conceptions of the East, and his embrace of African Americans presaged the rise of a global struggle against white supremacy. The migratory streams created by empire would prove vital to that struggle. While renowned figures like Vivekananda defied racist binaries, thousands of Indian workers confronted racial apartheid on America's West Coast.

### Far from Home

In 1907, a mob of five hundred people violently expelled a community of Indian mill workers from Bellingham, Washington. The violence began as white workers paraded through town to celebrate Labor Day. Some broke ranks to attack Indians who were watching the parade. The next day, a mob gathered and swept through the Indian part of town, attacking anyone they could find, stealing anything of value. Two hundred Indian workers took refuge in city hall, before being forced out of town. Crowds cheered as the homeless, jobless Indians fled for their lives.[25]

The Bellingham riot had been brewing for months, fostered by a toxic mix of economic insecurity and racist xenophobia. The economic underpinnings of the conflict help to explain why it was on Labor Day that the trouble began. White workers felt threatened by the growing numbers of Indians working in the mills, and complained that the Indians undercut pay by working for lower wages. The fact that Indians had asked for better pay did nothing to mollify the antipathy of the white workers. But competition for jobs only partly explains the violence in Bellingham.

A few days after the riot, the *Bellingham Herald* offered another justification for the riot: "The Hindu is not a good citizen. It would require centuries to assimilate him, and this country need not take the trouble. Our racial burdens are already heavy enough to bear." By referencing "racial burdens," the *Herald* made clear that anti-Indian bias derived as much from racial prejudice as from economic angst. Politicians stoked such anti-Asian bigotry. Senator Frank Flint from California was quoted in the *Bellingham Herald* supporting the riot. "We don't want these Hindus," he declared. Flint promised to "protect the Pacific coast from the brown horde."[26]

Anti-immigrant activists portrayed the Indians as outsiders despite the fact that the United States had only just wrested much of the West from Mexico. Originally, the land had been Indian—American Indian. It might be tempting to contrast the mythic rootedness of the American Indian with the mobility of migrants from India. Yet the borders of American Indian communities were neither timeless nor rigid. Indeed, geographic mobility became central to how many American Indians resisted the confines of the reservation and defied the arbitrary boundaries of settler states. Such radical mobility remains a political tool and a way of life for some indigenous communities. In *Mohawk Interruptus,* Audra Simpson writes, "It is through their actions and, in particular, their mobility that Indigenous border crossers enact their understandings of history and law." While recognizing the emancipatory potential of movement, it is important to also acknowledge the ways in which mobility was historically used to brand American Indians as wild nomads, not unlike the unwanted arrivals from Asia. Indeed, as Jodi Byrd has noted, "The constructed imaginary arrival of peoples in the Americas thousands of years ago across a land bridge from Asia performs nineteenth- and twentieth-century concerns over Asian immigrants and the perceived 'threat' they posed to the United States." American Indians became "the first wave of a 'yellow peril' invasion that infested the lands already (or destined to be) inhabited by Europeans."[27]

The violence directed against Indians in Bellingham was a continuation of a long history of brutal expropriation—a history embodied in the word *Indian.* As early as the seventeenth century, the conquest of the American West had been linked to India. From colonial Virginia, expeditions headed west "to find out the East India Sea," as Governor William Berkeley wrote in 1669. The journey of Lewis and Clark reinvigorated dreams of a new passage to India, despite the fact that Meriwether Lewis himself told Thomas Jefferson that there was little prospect that an overland route would serve as an effective way to transport the "productions of the East Indias to the United States and thence to Europe." Even as Americans learned more about the vast territory that stretched between the Atlantic and Pacific oceans, and the many nations of "Indians" who lived there, the prospect of reaching India itself continued to inspire advocates of "manifest destiny." Senator Thomas Hart Benton called the Central Pacific Railroad "an American road to India," and supported the occupation of Oregon by declaring, "There is the East; there lies the road to India." Benton got it wrong. The West would prove less "the road to India" than "the road from India." Migration from India and other parts of Asia would, alongside the persistence of American Indians and Mexican Americans, challenge visions of the American West as a paradise for Anglo-Saxon Americans. The racial conflict that ensued was part of a global struggle for land and power shaped by the collision of white supremacy and migration.[28]

In January 1908, a group of Indian laborers was attacked by a mob in the Central Valley of California. The Indians were robbed of $2,000 and driven from town. In March 1910, a suburb of Portland erupted in another anti-Indian riot. South Asian men were beaten, their turbans ripped from their heads. Local newspapers blamed the violence on the sexual misconduct of South Asian men. The racist magazine *The White Man* wrote that Indian men loitered in the "entrances of stores and would stare at and frighten the women and children." Demonizing South Asians as threats to white women continued a timeworn tradition of using sexual anxiety to prop up white supremacy, a strategy that had for generations justified violence against African American men.[29]

Anti-Asian racism dovetailed with antiblack discrimination. In early 1913, real estate agents in Port Angeles, Washington, pledged to never sell property to "Hindoos and Negroes." They lumped together South Asians and African Americans as "undesirable" groups who had "materially depreciated the value of adjacent property and injured the reputation of the neighborhood." Thus, the real estate agents of Port Angeles opposed two forms of migration—one transnational and the other internal—and conflated racial hierarchy with financial gain.[30]

On the West Coast, Indian migrants had limited contact with African Americans. But in places like New Orleans, New York, and Detroit, some South Asian migrants passed as black in order to evade immigration controls. They made their homes in African American communities and married African American women. Historian Vivek Bald has chronicled these Black-Indian families. Even in relatively cosmopolitan cities like New York and Boston, Indians who passed as black risked incurring antiblack racism. On the West Coast, by contrast, Indian migrants suffered discrimination because they were Asians. The anticolonial activist Lala Lajpat Rai catalogued the variety of racist dangers that confronted the Indian migrant: "In the South he is confounded with the Negro and the only way to escape the indignities, that are heaped on the Negro there, is to put on a turban. In the West, a turban has to be scrupulously tabooed, because with a turban you stand the chance of being excluded from hotels, restaurants and theaters and of being looked down upon." Lajpat Rai identified what might be called the "turban paradox": the fact that turbans could help Indians avoid racism in the South and East, but often aggravated racism in the West, where Indians were often pejoratively called "rag-heads."[31]

California congressman John Raker highlighted the turban when he told a congressional committee that migrants from India were stealing work from Americans. "We saw them build the Western Pacific," Raker declared, "working for hundreds of miles with their red turbans around their heads when that work should have been done by American citizens." Like other Asian migrants, Indians were seen as a threat to the livelihood of white workers. Labor leaders argued that Asians drove down wages because they were willing to accept unconscionably low standards of living. But even while attacking Indians for stealing jobs, anti-immigrant groups simultaneously demonized Indians as lazy. Immediately after the riot in Bellingham, the local paper denounced the Indian immigrant as "not even a good workman." In January 1910, the *San Francisco Call* declared Indians "indifferent workers." A cartoon in one San Francisco paper depicted Uncle Sam dangling a turbaned figure over the Atlantic. The figure was labeled with three equally misleading words: "incompetence," "indolence," and "Hindu." Incompetence and indolence were not why hard-working Indian migrants were competing for jobs.[32]

The "Hindu" label was, of course, also misleading. With its erasure of Sikh and Muslim immigrants, *Hindu* was almost as confusing a term as *Indian*. Treating all Indian migrants as a homogenous block of "incompetent" workers, immigration officials used the specter of Indians becoming a "public charge" to deny them entry to the United States. As historian Seema Sohi has documented, the overwhelming majority of Indians were gainfully employed. Nevertheless, officials used the fear of the "public charge" to exclude about half of all Indians trying to enter the United States.[33]

Economic anxiety served as cover for other fears and forms of exclusion, both racial and sexual. In January 1909, Harnam Singh applied for a visa to move from Vancouver to Bellingham, Washington. It had been less than two years since the South Asian workers in Bellingham had been driven from the city. But Singh had reason to believe he would find employment there, and was able to convince the immigration authorities that he could support himself. Twenty-eight years old and married, Singh impressed officials as a trustworthy figure. His visa application was approved. But two days later, Singh was arrested and accused, in the words of the Vancouver police department, of "the charge of sodomy, his companion in the offence being a Chinaman." Informed of the charges, the U.S. immigration service quickly withdrew the visa and branded Singh as "likely to be a public charge."[34]

As immigration officials tightened access to the continental United States, hundreds of Indian migrants tried to enter through the Philippines or Hawaii. Once admitted to part of the American empire, it was easier to gain access to the mainland. Thus, American empire worked against racial exclusion. But not for long. American authorities quickly acted to close that loophole.[35]

Women faced special hurdles while traveling from India to America. Historian Nayan Shah has uncovered the revealing case of Raj Kaur, who arrived in San Francisco in November 1923. A twenty-year-old widow, Kaur was accompanied by her brother, Bagh Singh Chotia. Chotia had lived in the United States for more than ten years and had married a white woman. But immigration authorities received a letter accusing him of trying to smuggle a woman of "bad character" into the country. Chotia explained that Kaur was not a woman of "bad character," but his sister and a widow. Women migrants traveling without husbands or fathers were routinely demonized as welfare cases who would drain public funds or turn to immoral methods to make ends meet. Pressed regarding her finances, Kaur outlined her share of the family land and declared that she had sufficient amounts of silver to pay for her time in the country. The immigration commissioner rejected her claims. But the U.S. Secretary of Labor overruled that decision and granted her a six-month tourist visa. Kaur entered a public high school, and applied to extend her visa. The Secretary of Labor rejected her request, as did the Attorney General. But Kaur was able to gain an extension through a personal bill passed by the House Committee on Immigration and Naturalization. She tried again six months later, and this time bolstered her application with recommendations from the principal of her high school and from a YWCA board member. But Kaur's string of successes came to an end, and she was deported. Her story reveals the determination with which Indian women struggled against the gendered obstacles created by American immigration officials and their British counterparts.[36]

British and American officials worked together to constrain the movement of Indian migrants. Anthony W. Caminetti, the American Commissioner of Immigration, cooperated closely with William C. Hopkinson, a British spy sent to keep tabs on Indians in North America. Fluent in Hindi, Hopkinson was known to wear a turban and fake beard in order to pass as an Indian laborer. In addition to such antics, Hopkinson relied on paid informants. He built a surveillance network composed, in his words, of "secret agents connected with the Consulates in centres of Hindu population in the United States." Hopkinson and Caminetti shared intelligence information and a fierce suspicion of Indian migrants.[37]

Such antimigrant cooperation extended to India itself. Colonel William Michaels, the American Consul-General in Calcutta from 1905 to 1912, did everything he could to prevent Indians from moving to America. He explained his procedure with brazen openness:

> When Indians apply to this office whether they are going to the United States to become permanent citizens or to make money and come back to India, I give them a thorough examination. I find out their moral character, question them regarding their sentiment with regard to government, determine whether they are in favor of sedition in India, qualifications as farmers, artisans, etc., and lastly their educational and financial condition. After these examinations I turn down practically all of them.

Colonel Michaels justified such discrimination in terms of racist hierarchies. According to him, the Asian man lacked the "standard of modesty that lifts him above the beast." He praised Britain for working on "the problem of civilizing India," and declared that "the want of real unity among the Indian people, as a whole, must forever deny them self-government." More than just a racist American in British India, Colonel Michaels embodied the growing connection between British and American authorities committed to defending white supremacy throughout the world. Ironically, the very definition of "whiteness" would create a loophole through which some Indians would turn American racism to their own advantage.[38]

## Almost White

At the dawn of the twentieth century, the United States was divided by race. But the color line was not as clear as white supremacists would have liked. Despite the "one drop rule," some light-skinned African Americans managed to "pass" as white. Immigrants from Southern and Eastern Europe, long despised by the "Anglo-Saxon" old guard, were growing in number and political strength. And a variety of smaller ethnic groups—from the Syrians to the Japanese—refused to slot neatly into the prevailing racial boxes. Indians were especially hard to categorize. "A number of the Hindoo immigrants have kinky hair like a negro's wool," one Indian reporter, Saint Nihal Singh, wrote in 1909. Others had hair as straight as straw. Skin color also varied dramatically. As Singh explained, "The hide of the Hindoo varies from the dull, pale, sallow-brown of a Mexican to the extreme black of an African."[39]

In 1924, a professor of chemistry in Los Angeles offered a remarkable description of Indian racial ambiguity. He wrote, "The Hindu resembles us except that he is black—and we are shocked to see a black white man." Being a "black white man" had its advantages, at least to the degree that Indians could claim the privileges that came with whiteness. In Savannah, Georgia, in 1910, Abba Dolla, a native of Calcutta, asked a doctor to certify his "pure Caucasian blood." The doctor's testimony was not enough to convince a judge who described Dolla as follows: "The applicant's complexion is dark, eyes dark, features regular and rather delicate, hair very black, wavy and very fine and soft." Uncertain how to categorize Dolla's racial identity, the judge asked him to pull up his shirt sleeves to expose "the skin of his arm where it had been protected from the sun." Fortunately for Dolla, the judge found the skin "to be several shades lighter than that of his face and hands, and was sufficiently transparent for the blue color of the veins to show very clearly." Convinced of Dolla's whiteness, the judge granted citizenship.[40]

Indians less pale than Abba Dolla found a different path to whiteness: the idea of the Caucasian. In 1775 Johann Friedrich Blumenbach popularized the idea of a "Caucasian race." He took the name *Caucasian* from the Caucasus Mountains, which he believed had produced "the most beautiful race of men." Despite such arbitrary foundations, the idea of a "Caucasian race" gained currency over time. Many experts on race classified Indians as Caucasian, but not all Indians were so blessed. Geography and caste both helped decide who was Caucasian. By the mid-nineteenth century, scholars had distinguished two large and distinct language families in the Indian subcontinent. This discovery helped inspire "the two-race theory of Indian civilization," in which certain Indians were associated with Europeans while others were linked with "Negroes." The key distinction was between those deemed "Aryan" and those labeled "Dravidian." Often associated with the Nazis, the word *Aryan* originated in the Vedas, a collection of ancient Indian religious texts. The idea that racial differences defined the Aryans finds little support in the Vedas themselves. Nevertheless, the Aryan idea became a prop for racial hierarchy.[41]

Confronted with a system in which whiteness conferred citizenship, many Indians strove to prove their whiteness by claiming Caucasian and Aryan identities. In 1922, the Pacific Coast Khalsa Diwan Society published a booklet by Dr. Pardaman Singh that aimed to prove that the "Hindustanees at present residing in California and other Pacific Coast states belong to the Aryan race." Not surprisingly, given the predominance of Punjabis among early Indian migrants, Singh singled out Punjabis as "handsome white men and hence eligible to be citizens of the United States." His emphasis on Punjabis aligned with the common belief that migrants from the north of India were Aryan and thus white. Caste also played an important role in these divisions. According to another Indian American author, Godha Ram, "high caste Hindus" from the north of India were "light white or dark white," while the "lower castes" were darker and of Dravidian ancestry. Ram explained such distinctions as the result of universal taboos concerning sex across racial lines. It was only natural for "Aryans" from North India to marry amongst themselves while shunning the darker castes. "Do not the Christians do about the same thing when it becomes a question between the Anglo-Saxon and the Negro or even the Red Indian?" Ram used American racism and aversion to "miscegenation" to defend the racial purity of high-caste Indians.[42]

Unlike Pardaman Singh and Godha Ram, some Indian Americans argued that all Indian migrants deserved to be classified as white. Although he admitted that some Indians had skin that matched "the extreme black of an African," Saint Nihal Singh still asserted, "All the Hindoos who come to the land of the Stars and Stripes are descended from the same branch of the human family as the Anglo-Saxons." Even fierce critics of white supremacy claimed the privileges of whiteness. In the fall of 1917, Lala Lajpat Rai stood next to W. E. B. Du Bois at the Intercollegiate Socialist Society and proclaimed, "The problem of the Hindu and of the negro and cognate problems are not local, but world problems." A year earlier, Lajpat Rai had written extensively and sympathetically of African American struggles in his book *The United States of America: A Hindu's Impressions and a Study*. In the same book, however, Lajpat Rai complained that "most Americans know that the Hindus come from the same stock as the Europeans; yet they exclude them from America even more rigorously than the black of Africa." Lajpat Rai's opposition to racism did not prevent him from arguing that Indians deserved the benefits of whiteness. In June 1916, he told several United States senators that it had "been acknowledged by the highest scholastic authority in the world, that the Hindus are from the Aryan Stock."[43]

The United States government was not convinced. Indian Americans may have seen themselves as white, but that did not make them so. In August 1907, Charles Bonaparte, the United States Attorney General, wrote a private note on Indian racial identity. "It seems to me clear," Bonaparte declared, "that under no construction of the law can natives of British India be regarded as white persons." In 1908, the head of the Bureau of Naturalization directed all U.S. attorneys to oppose the naturalization of "Hindus or East Indians," regardless of what racial identity they might claim. Ultimately, however, the racial status of Indian migrants was not for U.S. attorneys to decide. It was a matter for the courts. Despite the opposition of the government's attorneys, federal judges repeatedly decided in favor of Indian American claims to whiteness. Caste played a crucial role in these decisions.[44]

Akhay Kumar Mozumdar, the first Indian to gain naturalization on the West Coast, argued that the racial purity of his caste lineage made him "more white" than other Indians in the United States. Mozumdar told the court, "I am a high-caste Hindu of pure blood, belonging to what is known as the warrior caste, or ruling caste." By contrast, he stated, "The great bulk of the Hindus in this country are not high-caste Hindus, but are what are called sihks, [*sic*] and are of mixed blood." Blending class, caste, and religion, Mozumdar elevated himself above the "mixed blood" Sikhs. "The laboring class," he explained, "those who do the rough manual labor, are not high-caste Hindus at all, but are in an entirely separate class, having quite a different religion and a different ancestry." The court accepted Mozumdar's claim to racial and caste purity, and granted him citizenship.[45]

Anti-Indian racism applied to nearly everyone from the subcontinent. The mob that attacked Indians in Bellingham did not make distinctions based on caste. Nor did most advocates of "Hindu exclusion" distinguish between dark-skinned Dravidians and fair Aryans. The all-inclusive nature of anti-Indian racism encouraged many Indian Americans to see beyond divisions of caste and faith. Ironically, such inclusivity was complicated by the racially structured nature of American naturalization laws. By encouraging some Indians to claim whiteness, American law reinforced caste divides.

The ability of Indians to gain citizenship by claiming whiteness ended in 1923. That year, the Supreme Court denied citizenship to a veteran of the United States Army, Bhagat Singh Thind. Born in 1892, Thind had come to the United States in 1913 to advance his education. He enrolled at the University of California, Berkeley, found part-time work in a lumber mill, and joined the army. Wearing his military uniform, Thind proudly received the certificate of U.S. citizenship on December 9, 1918. Only four days later, however, the Immigration and Naturalization Service revoked his citizenship on the grounds that he was not a "free white person" as required by American law. Six months later, Thind applied again. The Immigration and Naturalization Service again opposed his claim to citizenship. In addition to arguing that Thind was not white, the government raised concerns about his political activities on behalf of Indian independence. The presiding judge ruled in his favor nonetheless, and Thind gained citizenship for the second time on November 18, 1920.[46]

The government appealed the decision, and the case made its way to the U.S. Supreme Court. A few months earlier, the Court had denied citizenship to a Japanese man because he was not "Caucasian." It seemed that Thind needed only to prove that Indians were "Caucasian," a position that contemporary racial "science" had validated and that several courts had accepted. To be safe, Thind employed notions of caste hierarchy to claim a privileged Caucasian lineage. He proudly told the Court, "The high class Hindu regards the aboriginal Indian Mongoloid in the same manner as the American regards the Negro speaking from the matrimonial standpoint." The Court was unconvinced. Writing for the majority, Chief Justice Sutherland concluded "that the words 'free white persons' are words of common speech, to be interpreted in accordance with the understanding of the common man." Treating "scientific" arguments as irrelevant, Justice Sutherland declared, "It is a matter of familiar observation and knowledge that the physical group characteristics of the

*Figure 2.* Bhagat Singh Thind in his United States Army uniform. In 1923, the United States Supreme Court decided that Thind was not legally white, denying his application for United States citizenship and casting into doubt the legal status of all Indian Americans. Bhagat Singh Thind Materials, South Asian American Digital Archive, Philadelphia. Courtesy of David Thind.

Hindus render them readily distinguishable from the various groups of persons in this country commonly recognized as white." Establishing "the common man" as the supreme judge of whiteness, Sutherland rejected Thind's claim to racial and caste purity.[47]

The *Thind* decision devastated the Indian American community. Authorities moved to retroactively cancel naturalizations. Because alien land laws prohibited anyone ineligible for citizenship from owning land, suddenly all Indians were denied the right to own land. Those who had already purchased land scrambled to put the legal title in the name of white partners. Others were forced to sell at below-market rates. Thus, the *Thind* decision undercut both the political and economic rights of Indian Americans.[48]

News of Thind's defeat traveled quickly to India. An editorial in the prominent Indian journal *Modern Review* found "a sort of international irony" in the fact that Indian law placed "Americans in a privileged position" while "in America the natives of India are discriminated against and placed in a humiliating condition." That discrepancy inspired Indians to pass their own alien land laws and to try to bar Americans from entering India. The small hamlet of Lalitpur, Punjab, refused to allow a group of American missionaries to buy land. Explaining the refusal, the local municipal board resolved "that in view of the fact that in America the Indians do not enjoy full rights of citizenship, the board as a protest against said fact is not prepared to grant any plots in lease or otherwise to any American within the limits of this municipality." Indians also targeted American immigration policies. The lawyer and anticolonial activist Govind Ballabh Pant sponsored a "reciprocity bill" that would have denied Americans the right to enter India.[49]

Most Americans never learned of such gestures. Even those Americans that traveled to India had little reason to worry about Indian public opinion. They could count on the British to prevent any meaningful inconvenience. But one group of Americans did worry about Indian opinion. A group of American missionaries published an article in *Indian Social Reformer* and the *Nation* declaring that the *Thind* case had "caused deep resentment in the mind of India." They worried that the decision "may help to widen the gulf between the East and West and will give added impetus to the rising tide of resentment and bitterness against white exclusion."[50]

Indians in the United States had been attacked by racist mobs, relegated to poorly paid manual labor, and denied the right to become American citizens. But despite the fierce bigotry they encountered, many found ways to thrive. Among the most resourceful were the hundreds of students who came to America to pursue higher education. Despite American racism and the indifference of colonial officials, many students left the United States with advanced degrees and new skills. Even the hardships they faced could be educational. Indeed, many students learned as much from their struggles as they did in the classroom.

## Learning America

In April 1908, the British Ambassador to the United States, James Bryce, warned officials in London that Indian students should not be allowed to study in America lest their experience "encourage their political delusion." Bryce was wise to be worried. Hundreds of Indian students would come to the United States in the first half of the twentieth century. Many would return to India determined to throw off the British yoke. "We came here to imbibe free thoughts from free people," one student wrote in 1907, "and teach the same when we go back to our country and to get rid of the tyranny of the rule of the universal oppressor." It would be an exaggeration to claim that studying in America transformed loyal subjects into seditious rebels. Many Indian students harbored anticolonial commitments long before they arrived in America. Some were inspired by living in a country that had rejected British rule, a country that prided itself on its democratic traditions. Just as transformative, however, were the ways in which those traditions failed Indian students, many of whom confronted racism, political repression, and stark inequality—all while living and studying in a land that claimed to be free.[51]

Students occupied an intermediate position among Indian migrants. Unlike such dignitaries as Ramabai or Vivekananda, many Indian students struggled to pay their bills. But unlike the majority of Indian workers, most students spoke fluent English and had more opportunities for upward mobility. These distinctions should not be overdrawn. Indian students often hosted famous visitors and socialized in the same cosmopolitan, India-loving communities that embraced yoga and Vedanta. Many also worked in the fields and the mills to cover the costs of their education. Bhagat Singh Thind, for example, worked at an Oregon mill in the summer in order to pay his way through UC Berkeley. The economic struggles of Indian students inspired a tribute from Lala Lajpat Rai. "The Indian student in America is a prodigy of enterprise and industry and resourcefulness," he wrote in 1916. "Picture to yourself an Aggarwal young man of U.P. coming from a respectable family, working on a railroad track under construction, either cutting stones or doing other hard work, sleeping on the ground at night and cooking his food in tin cans thrown on the road by wayfarers." Such resourcefulness was especially noteworthy, in Lajpat Rai's opinion, when demanded of a high-caste man from a "respectable" background. But it was the poorest Indians who struggled the most to gain an education in America.[52]

In December 1911, Sarangadhar Das, an alumnus of the University of California, published an article in Calcutta's *Modern Review* entitled "Information for Indian Students Intending to Come to the Pacific Coast of the United States." Das offered practical advice on everything from transportation routes to clothing to finances. Total expenses for a student at UC Berkeley averaged $350 per year, or some one hundred rupees per month. Some students were able to rely on family support to cover such charges. But even those who could not afford such payments could make ends meet by working part-time during the year and full-time in the summer. They could also expect help from benevolent Americans.[53]

In Seattle, Mrs. Evelyn Burlingame Covington was something of a one-woman welcoming committee. Covington would greet Indian students on their ship and take them to her home. In his article for *Modern Review,* Sarangadhar Das quoted Covington: "I love and cherish every Hindu, whether laborer, student, priest or prince; and my heart and home, wherever I may be, will always be open to each and every one of you." Covington helped lead the Association for the Promotion of Education of the People of India, an organization drawn largely from faculty at the University of Washington. The organization was created "to help the people of India at home and abroad by all possible means especially in the acquirement of scientific, industrial and technical education and to establish free primary schools in India to spread secular education among the masses." While raising funds to build schools in India, Covington used her own money to help Indian students in the United States. She appealed to Indian students to come to Seattle, where, she asserted, they would not encounter too much "color-prejudice." "Of course, at times there have been some disagreeable incidents," she added, "but no more (and not as much I think) as in other sections of the United States." It is unclear whether Covington included the Bellingham riot in the category of "disagreeable incidents," or simply ignored it given that it had not occurred in Seattle proper.[54]

Indian students faced racism throughout America. In Boston, an MIT student failed to find housing in "districts where there exists a prejudice against negroes." In Chicago, a dental student applied to over a dozen potential landlords, all of whom refused to rent to the dark-skinned foreigner. The Indian press often reported on the racism that Indian students faced in the United States. In 1922, *Modern Review* noted that for "the bronze and colored students" in the United States, "life is made miserable by the exhibition of color prejudice."[55]

Despite American racism, Indian students carved space for themselves on campuses nationwide and built networks across those campuses. The most important Indian student organization was called the Hindustan Association of America. The association's name indicated a desire to serve all Indians in America, but its primary purpose was advancing "the educational interests of the Hindusthanee students, present or prospective." The organizers also strove to "stimulate healthy American interest in India" and to "propagate Indian ideas from the Indian standpoint." Those ideas included a critique of British rule framed as a celebration of American freedom: "America is about the only country where we Indians have perfect freedom of expression." These grateful words, published in August 1913, would not be borne out by future events. Indian students would come under increasing surveillance and repression from both British and American authorities. They would learn to connect oppression in the United States and India—and to fight both simultaneously. No figure embodied that interconnected struggle more than the most famous Indian American intellectual in the first half of the twentieth century, Har Dayal.[56]

Born in Delhi in 1884, Dayal studied at Oxford and lived in Paris, Algeria, Martinique, and Puerto Rico before moving to Berkeley in 1911 and taking a job as a lecturer at Stanford. In an article for the Hindustan Association of America, Dayal framed education as inherently anticolonial. "If a young man does not return to India with a love of liberty and a sense of social justice in all its forms," he declared, "he has learned nothing abroad." Dayal encouraged Indian students to cultivate friendships with American "lovers of freedom" and to "take part in American movements of all kinds." "Go to meetings, join societies, join any fight that is on," he wrote. "All students should be ardent partisans and combatants in American politics."[57]

Dayal's vision for a socially engaged education explicitly included women. Like the flow of laborers, the Indian student population in the United States was dominated by men. But a small cohort of female students did make the journey to America. Indeed, some of the first Indian students in America were young women like Dr. Anandibai Joshee, who completed her medical degree in 1886 at the Women's Medical College of Pennsylvania. As the overall population of Indian students swelled, some called for greater numbers of women to make the journey. In the bulletin of the Hindustan Association of America, one student leader, Sayad Muhammad Khuda, encouraged "the women of India to fight their battles for freedom" by first traveling to America to get an education. "This is an age when women are claiming and wresting their natural rights from men all over the world," Khuda wrote. He believed that women had the power to attack injustice throughout society. "Like swords of flame they must cut asunder all social tyranny and burn all the hypocrisy of man and thus purge the social body of its ills."[58]

The effort to "purge the social body of its ills" brought together many Indian students, men and women, who became actively involved in political struggles that bridged India and America. College campuses became important sites of Indian American protest as students packed events like the Nation Day celebration held at UC Berkeley on October 12, 1912. It was a young and passionate crowd that heard Har Dayal and several American professors speak in support of Indian nationalism. Student protest was not confined to campus. When missionaries attacked the Hindu faith at a YWCA meeting in San Francisco, sixteen Indian students stood up, one after the next, to defend their heritage. In the midst of the first major Gandhian civil disobedience campaign, the Indian students of Pittsburgh, Pennsylvania, passed a resolution in support of noncooperation. They cabled the resolution to the Indian National Congress. The Congress recognized the power of Indian students to shape American opinion in favor of Indian independence. In the early 1920s, N. S. Hardikar, an anticolonial activist, recommended that "some of our first class students" should be trained to spread India's message overseas. Students had long served as ambassadors—not just between India and America, but also between different factions within the Indian American community.[59]

The prominence of such factions was revealed in a remarkable letter sent to Swami Trigunatita, the leader of the San Francisco Vedanta society, by Sarangadhar Das, the UC Berkeley alumnus who had advised prospective students in the pages of *Modern Review*. On July 16, 1911, Das wrote Trigunatita a blunt note in which he denounced the swami as "a rude man of very rough manners and a slick priest to boot." According to Das, Trigunatita had sabotaged plans to create a home for Indian students in Berkeley. The funds for the home were to be provided by a Mrs. Pettie, who also happened to be an important supporter of the Vedanta Center. Das accused Trigunatita of convincing Mrs. Pettie to drop the idea of a student house and to dedicate her funds to the Vedanta Center instead. He also charged the Swami with abandoning the cause of Indian freedom. "I belong to a slave nation," Das wrote. "I want you to understand that we, the slaves stand not only against the present governing class, but also against all the privileged classes, whether foreign or Swadeshi." What Trigunatita made of these charges remains unclear. On December 28, 1914, Trigunatita was directing a Sunday service when a former student burst toward the front of the room and hurled a bomb at the eminent monk. Both the student and the swami were killed.[60]

Differences of personality and of vision would continue to divide the Indian American community. In the face of those divisions, many Indian Americans struggled to forge unity. Workers fought to build communities that transcended caste and religion. Students reached out to the laborers they joined in the fields and the mills. And religious figures like Swami Vivekananda—and Swami Trigunatita—inspired Americans to support India and Indians. Sarangadhar Das may have had good reason to denounce Trigunatita's politics, but American support for India's independence would flourish in part as a result of the popularity of Indian religious figures. Indeed, even secular Indians were often seen by Americans through the lens of "Eastern" spirituality.

Take, for example, the most famous Indian to visit the United States in the first half of the twentieth century, Rabindranath Tagore. A renowned poet and playwright, Tagore was welcomed in America as something more: a spiritual authority. Tagore visited the United States five times over eighteen years. He praised those strands of American culture that were indebted to India. "I love your Emerson," he declared. "In his work one finds much that is of India." He also praised Whitman, whose poems were "deeply imbued with Eastern ideas and feelings." But despite appreciating Whitman and Emerson, Tagore was critical of Western materialism and echoed the complaints of many Indian visitors, including Vivekananda. "These Western people have made their money but killed their poetry of life," the poet lamented. "They do not have the time to realize that they are not happy."[61]

In April 1924, Tagore told an audience at the Anglo-American Association of Peking that during his travels in the United States he had
seen the "deliberate cultivation of contempt for other races." He added,
"This was neither Christian in a people who were supposed to be Christians, nor was it prudent. It must some day end in universal disaster to
humanity." Tagore's stature as a famous writer usually protected him
from the "contempt for other races" that many Indians had experienced
in America—but not always. Tagore's fourth visit to America, in
April 1929, ended just hours after it began. He left in protest after American officials in Vancouver harassed him at the border.[62]

Tagore recognized that India had its own struggle with "contempt"
for those deemed inferior. In the summer of 1910, he wrote Myron Phelps,
an American lawyer who was a strong supporter of India and Indian
Americans. Phelps had met Swami Vivekananda and become active in
the Society for the Advancement of India, a group of prominent liberal
intellectuals and philanthropists dedicated to the uplift of India. Tagore
told Phelps, "It has never been India's lot to accept alien races as factors
in her civilization. You know very well how the caste that proceeds from
colour takes elsewhere a most virulent form." He added, "I need not cite
modern instances of the animosity which divides white men from negroes in your country, and excludes Asiatics from European colonies."
Tagore contrasted Western racism with an Indian inclusiveness that
he traced to caste by returning to the two-race theory of Indian civilization: "When, however, the white-skinned Aryans on encountering
the dark aboriginal races of India found themselves face to face with the
same problem, the solution of which was either extermination, as has
happened in America and Australia, or a modification without the possibility of either friction or fusion, they chose the latter." Without directly
referencing the problem of the two Indians, Tagore used the "extermination" of American Indians to mitigate the injustice of caste in India.
Caste was a "frictionless" alternative to genocide. Tagore stated that he
"need not dwell at length on the evils of the resulting caste system." Instead, he defended caste by arguing that "it served a very useful purpose
in its day and has been even up to a late age of immense protective
benefit to India."[63]

In the decades after the American Civil War, anticaste activists
offered a different comparison between racism in America and caste
inequality in India. Some turned to the emancipation of American

slaves for hope and guidance in the struggle against caste. Others argued that casteism was worse than American racism. In both India and the United States, scholars and activists debated the race / caste analogy. Many claimed that their country's problems were not as bad as the problems of those other people—whether the other was "racist Americans" or "casteist Indians." Meanwhile, millions of people—oppressed because of their racial or caste-based identities—struggled to survive in the face of crushing poverty and oppressive violence. What did it mean to them whether race was a form of caste or vice versa? Could a new name help right such an old wrong?

# PART II

# CASTE

The millions of untouchables in India might as well
regard the negroes [sic]struggle for equality and human
dignity as their own struggle. . . . It may be that the
American negro is fighting not only for himself and for
his brethren in America but for all the submerged
castes, for all the blacks of the world whether they be
in America or in India.
                    —"The Freedom March," *United Asia,* 1963

ABRAHAM LINCOLN STOOD on the banks of the Ganges surrounded
by Brahmins. The crowd chanted, "He is a Brahmin, he is one of
us!" A horde of Kshatriya warriors fought their way into the circle,
clanging their swords and yelling, "He is a warrior; he is one of us!" The
merchants, the Vaisyas, also tried to claim Lincoln as their own, as did
the Sudras, "the mechanics and laborers." But when Lincoln spoke, it
was to the humblest that he turned: "the scavengers, the Pariahs, the
outcasts, the men from the dust of the dust." So imagined the American poet Nicholas Vachel Lindsay in 1929 in a short story entitled, "A
Vision, Called: 'Lincoln in India.'" Lindsay's vision is one of many colorful
episodes in the history of America's obsession with caste in India, an
obsession that was ultimately about caste in America.[1]

In Lindsay's story, next to India's Brahmins stood "the rich from all the
world who consider themselves Brahmans." Thus, Lindsay suggested that
class was a form of caste and America was itself caste-ridden. Like Lindsay,

many Americans used the word *caste* to decry the gap between the rich and the poor. Indians did likewise. Lala Lajpat Rai found something akin to caste in the American "industrial system," which he compared to feudalism and branded "cruel and crushing and demoralizing." "America is doubly caste-ridden," Lajpat Rai concluded in 1917. In addition to class, Lajpat Rai found caste in another pillar of American inequality: race. Like the comparison between caste and class, analogies between caste and race worked to expose America's own forms of caste. But the race / caste analogy could also be flipped to oppose caste in India.[2]

Less than a decade after Abraham Lincoln was gunned down in Ford's Theater, the anticaste activist Jotirao Phule deployed his knowledge of American racism to attack caste in India. Phule had been moved by reading *Uncle Tom's Cabin*. "Anyone who reads this book," he declared, "will have to cry with shame in public like the Marwadi women drawing the pallu of their saree over their heads and will have to sigh and sob." In 1873, Phule published his own book about slavery. At least, that was its title: *Slavery*. The subject of Phule's book was better known by another name: caste. Phule dedicated the book "to the good people of the United States" who had struggled against slavery. He hoped "their noble example" would help spark "the emancipation" of India's oppressed castes "from the trammels of Brahmin thraldom." In his dedication, as well as in the title of his book, Phule equated slavery and caste. But his knowledge of slavery was limited. His gratitude to the "good people of the United States" presented emancipation as the end of a happy story. He said nothing about the continued plight of African Americans. In the boldness of his vision as well as its limitations, Phule epitomized the long tradition of race / caste comparison.[3]

Most historical figures who juxtaposed race and caste were more interested in one than the other, and tended to oversimplify race or caste or both. Concerned with the political impact of race / caste analogies, they ignored what was lost in translating messy identities into the words *race* and *caste* and then again translating between these words. The danger of such a double translation is epitomized by the limitations of the word *caste*. From the Portuguese *casta*, the word *caste* conflates two separate forms of identity: *varna* and *jati*. *Varna* is the division of Hindu society into Brahmins, Kshatriyas, Vaishyas, and Sudras, a hierarchical system that excludes those once known as "untouchables" and now more commonly called Dalits (from the Marathi for "broken" or "crushed") as well as the indigenous peoples known as "Tribals." *Jati* refers to the hundreds of endogamous groups, sometimes associated with a specific occupation, that have come to be the primary social identifier for many Indians. While distinctions of *varna* and *jati* exist throughout the subcontinent, their meanings vary between regions and in relation to other social divisions such as class and gender.[4]

The complexity of caste complicates transnational comparisons. The same could be said of race. Both are powerful words that are applied to widely divergent social categories. At their best, comparisons between race and caste empowered those fighting to create more democratic and inclusive societies. But the complexities of these identities did not prevent one-sided critics from denouncing the wrongs of others while ignoring injustice closer to home. Unlike Jotirao Phule, who criticized racism and casteism, or Vachel Lindsay, who denounced "Brahmans" throughout the world, many Americans attacked caste without acknowledging the hierarchies of status and power that divided the United States as well.[5]

## Boston Brahmins

In his poem "Indian Superstition," Ralph Waldo Emerson attacked caste and the violence with which he believed Brahmins maintained caste. "In the mid path to Honour's glittering shrine," Emerson wrote, "Stands the stern Bramin armed with plagues divine." Lest his readers fail to understand the link between caste, violence, and the Brahmin, Emerson provided a note: "The following paragraph alludes to the degradation of the lowest caste in India and the punishment which attends an attempt to alter their condition." Emerson's critique might have resonated with an anticaste activist like Jotirao Phule. But Emerson's poem was less a sharp attack on caste inequality than a blunt assault on Hinduism in general. Rather than recognize that the United States had its own forms of caste, Emerson distinguished between the "degradation" of India and the egalitarianism of the West.[6]

Emerson's attack on caste would prove rare among Transcendentalists, most of whom romanticized caste. Even Emerson himself later referenced the Brahmin positively in his poem "Brahma." But it was Thoreau, the staunch critic of social hierarchies, who embraced caste with the most surprising ardor. In January 1843, *The Dial* published Thoreau's translation of passages from the *Laws of Manu*, a canonical text for many Hindus that is often credited with formalizing the idea of caste. The association between the *Laws of Manu* and caste is so strong that anticaste activists have publicly burned copies. But according to Thoreau *The Laws of Manu* expressed "what is deepest and most abiding in man." "It belongs to the noontide of the day," he wrote, "the midsummer of the year and after the snows have melted, and the waters evaporated in the spring, still its truth speaks freshly to our experience." It is telling that Thoreau chose natural metaphors to express his esteem for the *Laws of Manu*. Praising the work as a force of nature allowed him to separate the text from its social and political significance and thus to ignore its embrace of caste hierarchy.[7]

Walt Whitman cut out and kept several of Thoreau's passages on the *Laws of Manu*. Like Thoreau, Whitman approached caste not as a contemporary social reality, but as a myth that might be deployed for literary ends. In the poem "Chanting the Square Deific," Whitman envisioned a four-dimensional god, one of whose sides he described as a Sudra: "Aloof, dissatisfied, plotting revolt, / Comrade of criminals, brother of slaves, / Crafty, despised, a drudge, ignorant, / With sudra face and worn brow, black." It is unclear how much Whitman knew about the category "Sudra," or how much Thoreau or Emerson cared about what it meant to be a Brahmin in nineteenth-century India. The Brahmin and the Sudra were archetypal figures of the distant past, useful as a foil for an America that was categorically different.[8]

But even while many Americans understood caste as distinctly ancient and foreign, the vocabulary of caste became useful for describing contemporary America. In the late nineteenth century, the term "Boston Brahmin" gained currency as a label for the upper crust of Boston society. Oliver Wendell Holmes coined the term in 1860 in an article for the *Atlantic Monthly* entitled "The Brahmin Caste of New England." Holmes made clear that his use of the term *Brahmin* was not a critique of Boston's status hierarchy. On the contrary, Holmes used the word *caste* "not in any odious sense," but as a neutral term for "the repetition of the same influences, generation after generation" that yielded "a distinct organization and physiognomy."[9]

Unlike Thoreau, Whitman, and Holmes, many Americans despised caste, at least as they imagined it operating within India. In 1849, the business periodical *Hunt's Merchant's Magazine* declared that the caste system rendered Hindus "the most enslaved portion of the human race." It took a remarkable degree of hypocrisy for a magazine which advertised goods produced by American slave labor to decide that a distant population was "the most enslaved." Jotirao Phule had come to the same conclusion—that India's lowest castes were equivalent to slaves—but he did so to combat caste oppression. By contrast, *Hunt's Merchant's Magazine* aimed to praise the accomplishments of the British Empire. If the caste system was a form of slavery, then the British Raj could be framed as an emancipatory initiative. But what of the slaves still toiling the fields of the American South? The hypocrisy of labeling India's lower classes "the most enslaved portion of the human race" is especially jarring given the fact that the word *caste* was often used by abolitionists to denounce American slavery.[10]

On the first page of the first edition of William Lloyd Garrison's newspaper *Liberator,* a petition to Congress called for educating former slaves so that they could be saved "from continuing, even as free men, an unenlightened and degraded caste." A variety of prominent antislavery activists, from Horace Greeley to Theodore Parker to William E. Channing, labeled slavery a form of caste. Such an analogy allowed antislavery activists to demean slavery as fundamentally un-American, and to link slavery to the racism that plagued free blacks throughout the United States. Caste was especially useful for attacking racial inequality in free states. The *Liberator* declared that "blacks are a degraded caste in all the states." Introducing the autobiographies of Frederick Douglass, James M'Cune Smith wrote, "From the depths of chattel slavery in Maryland, our author escaped into the caste-slavery of the north." Douglass himself described segregation in New England as "fostering the spirit of caste."[11]

After abolition, caste became a powerful rhetorical tool for those fighting to grant African Americans full citizenship rights. In October 1869, the renowned abolitionist and statesman Charles Sumner gave a speech titled "The Question of Caste." Sumner envisioned a "transcendent Future, where man shall be conqueror, not only over nations, but over himself, subduing pride of birth, prejudice of class, pretension of Caste." Whereas most abolitionists used the idea of caste without directly referencing India, Sumner lectured his audience on the history of caste in the subcontinent. "Let me carry you to that ancient India," he declared, "with its population of more than a hundred and eighty millions, where this artificial discrimination, born of impossible fable, was for ages the dominating institution of society, being in fact, what Slavery was in our Rebellion, the corner-stone of the whole structure." Sumner's portrayal of ancient India as hopelessly caste-ridden ignored the diversity of social structures across time and space, as well as the role of British colonialism in rigidifying the institutions of caste.[12]

Sumner was more attuned to the transnational circuits of the language of caste. Consider his analysis of the "pariah," originally a Tamil word for those deemed untouchable. "In the well-known language of our country, once applied to another people," Sumner explained, the pariah "has no rights which a Brahmin is bound to respect." By using both *pariah* and *Brahmin*, Sumner demonstrated how the idea of caste had influenced the English language. Along with the word *caste*, a vocabulary of hierarchy and difference traveled across the English-speaking world. Sumner used the vocabulary of caste to attack anti-Asian as well as anti-black racism. He told his American audience, "Here the Caste claiming hereditary rank and privilege is white; the Caste doomed to hereditary degradation and disability is black or yellow." Thirteen years before the Chinese Exclusion Act, Sumner's inclusion of the word *yellow* demonstrates his opposition to racism—to caste—in all its forms. "Let Caste prevail," Sumner declared, "and Civilization is thwarted."[13]

While Sumner used the idea of caste to defend Asian Americans, anti-Asian nativists employed the specter of caste to oppose migration from India. In 1910, the *San Francisco Call* complained that Indian migrants brought "caste prejudices" to America. In 1914, William B. Wilson, the Secretary of Labor and a fierce opponent of Asian migration to the United States, criticized Indian "clannishness, caste ideas, superstitions, and habits of life." It is ironic that anti-immigrant forces used caste to disparage migrants from India, given that many Indian Americans believed that caste was weakened by the process of migrating to America. As Sarangadhar Das explained in his advice to Indian students coming to America, "We never know or care to know to what caste anyone belongs."[14]

Das exaggerated the casteless nature of the Indian American community. But it was not without good reason that Saint Nihal Singh declared in 1909 that migration to America had "broken the back-bone of caste." Singh explained the process in two steps. First, there was the force of necessity. "Despite their origins and hereditary caste-prejudices," Singh wrote, Indian migrants were "willing to make common cause with each other and do any kind of work they may be able to secure." In addition to the challenge of surviving in a new land, Singh credited the American commitment to equality with undermining caste sentiment. As he put it, "The East-Indian immigrant, when he leaves America, takes home with him a dynamic love of liberty and sentiments of democracy. America sandpapers his caste-exclusiveness and instills within his heart a sense of brotherhood and co-operation." By praising American democracy, Singh overlooked the degree to which American racism, which treated all Indians as unwanted, had also helped erode caste distinctions.[15]

Many Indian Americans denounced caste in India and racial caste in America. Shridhar Venkatesh Ketkar, while completing a PhD in sociology at Cornell, decided to focus his dissertation on caste in India. But Ketkar's years in the United States had convinced him that the United States also had a "caste system," which he outlined as follows: "1. The blue bloods; 2. The New Englanders; 3. The born gentile Americans; 4. The English and Scottish immigrants; 5. The Irish; 6. Gentile immigrants from other countries of Western Europe; 7. Dagoes (Italians); 8. The Jews; 9. The Mongolians; 10. Negroes." Ketkar used what he called "the caste system in the United States" to critique the practice of caste in India. He lamented the fact that "very many of the low castes believe, or are made to believe, that they justly suffer in this condition as a retribution for the sins which they did in the past life." He sarcastically concluded, "How much better it would have been for the whites in the United States, had they taught the negroes the doctrines of Transmigration of Soul and Karma instead of Christianity!"[16]

Despite his disdain for caste, Ketkar stopped short of calling for its complete abolition. A Chitpavan Brahmin, Ketkar approached caste as did many high-caste reformers, lamenting the divisiveness of caste while arguing that caste was too embedded in Indian culture and religion to allow dramatic reforms. A more radical critique emerged from the Indian American community on the West Coast. The *Independent Hindustan,* an anticolonial newspaper, repeatedly attacked caste as a source of India's internal divisions and thus of British rule. "Independent Hindustan is against any practices that hinder the unification of India," the paper declared in 1921. If India was to gain its freedom, all its people would have to come together "to keep religion out of politics, to do away with the spirit of caste and creed and class, and to bring all the people together, for the common good of all." Caste was anathema to Indian American activists who struggled to gain American support for Indian independence. The scandal of caste repelled Americans who might otherwise champion Indian independence. In the United States, the *Independent Hindustan* noted, "Everyone has heard of the caste system of India."[17]

Americans came to expect Indians to define themselves in terms of caste—and many did, regardless of their personal feelings about caste. In 1923, Dhan Gopal Mukerji published a memoir that would become the first commercially successful book to provide Americans with an Indian perspective on India. Given its impressive sales and glowing reviews, it is telling that Mukerji chose to title his memoir *Caste and Outcaste.* The first thing Mukerji told readers—"I am a Hindu of Brahmin parentage"— situated the narrative in terms of caste. On the final page, Mukerji compared the inequity of caste and race. He wrote, "America lynches Negroes. India illtreats her untouchables."[18]

As Mukerji knew, it was challenging to write in America about untouchability without reinforcing stereotypes that supported British rule. American interest in caste—and comparisons between race and caste— surged after the publication in 1927 of Katherine Mayo's *Mother India,* a damning account of Indian society in which caste justified British imperialism. Over 250,000 copies of *Mother India* were sold over the course of twenty-seven editions. Not all Americans believed Mayo's account. A group of American missionaries in India publicly denounced "the unfairness of Miss Mayo's book." But many Americans took the book as an authoritative portrait of a dissolute India in need of imperial salvation. "With the facts in Mother India available," an editorial in the *Chicago Evening Post* declared, "there will henceforth be no excuse for criticism of the administration of the British or even of their presence in India at all." While Mayo attacked many facets of Indian society, caste oppression was one of her primary targets. She did not explicitly compare race and caste in *Mother India.* A few years later, however, she wrote that, in India, "every fourth person is a slave held in a type of bondage compared to which our worst Negro slavery was freedom."[19]

Many Indian authors responded to *Mother India* by attacking American racism. Their purpose was not to achieve racial equality in the United States but to defend India against the scorn of outsiders like Mayo. In *Father India: A Reply to Mother India,* C. S. Ranga Iyer declared that the

"Aryan" invaders of India were "better than the white Brahmins of the twentieth century." In *Uncle Sham: Being the Strange Tale of a Civilisation Run Amok,* Kanhaya Lal Gauba proclaimed that the initials "K. K. K." were "well known throughout the world as symbols of terrorism, barbarity and murder." In *A Son of Mother India Answers,* Dhan Gopal Mukerji argued that Mayo's worst inaccuracies were "as fantastic as saying that Miss Jane Addams believes in Negro lynching." In *My Mother India,* Dalip Singh Saund chastised Americans for believing "that there is no caste in the United States" while black Americans had "absolutely no opportunity" to vote or run for office. Saund himself would later become the first U.S. congressman of Indian descent.[20]

In 1929, an American woman asked Mahatma Gandhi, "Is the plight of the untouchable as hard as that of the Negro in America?" Gandhi responded that caste was problematic, but he offered four reasons why the "plight of the untouchable" was not as dire as the oppression of "the Negro in America." First, he claimed that Dalits did not face legal discrimination. Second, he suggested that the "tradition of non-violence" protected Dalits from lynching. Third, he noted that a few Dalits had become "saints." Lastly, he stated that prejudice against Dalits was "fast wearing out." All of Gandhi's comparisons between race and caste understated the brutality of caste oppression in India. Like other critics of Katherine Mayo, Gandhi whitewashed untouchability in defense of India's reputation.[21]

The most sweeping response to *Mother India* came from Lala Lajpat Rai. Published in 1928, Lajpat Rai's *Unhappy India* attacked caste as "an absolutely indefensible, inhuman and barbarous institution, unworthy of Hinduism and the Hindus." Nevertheless, Lajpat Rai recycled the argument made by Gandhi: that American racism was worse than caste prejudice. In 1916, Lajpat Rai had proclaimed, "The Negro is the PARIAH of America." In *Unhappy India,* he argued, "The Negro in the United States is worse than a pariah." Shifting from equating wrongs to ranking them, Lajpat Rai transformed a transnational analogy he had used to attack injustice in the United States and India into a reactionary shield, defending domestic inequality in the face of foreign criticism.[22]

The most renowned Dalit leader of the twentieth century, Bhimrao Ramji Ambedkar, praised Lajpat Rai as "a friend of the untouchables" but criticized him for suggesting "that untouchability as an evil was nothing as compared with slavery." By contrast, Ambedkar declared, "Untouchables have been worse off than slaves." Whereas Lajpat Rai understated the brutality of untouchability, Ambedkar diminished the horrors of slavery. The contrast between Lajpat Rai and Ambedkar fades, however, when their respective audiences are considered. Like Jotirao Phule, Ambedkar spoke to an Indian audience and attacked caste. Lajpat Rai, by contrast, spoke to an American audience and denounced American racism. Both Lajpat Rai and Ambedkar used the race / caste analogy to advance equality and to oppose injustice.[23]

Lajpat Rai and Ambedkar oversimplified race and caste, but their goal was to eradicate injustice, not to understand its complexities. By contrast, the race / caste analogy gained leverage in the United States among scholars who understood their efforts as part of a scientific quest for the truth. In 1936, the American sociologist Lloyd Warner published an article in the *American Journal of Sociology* arguing that the Jim Crow South could best be understood in terms of caste. The following year, John Dollard, another leading sociologist, published *Caste and Class in a Southern Town*. Warner and Dollard helped found what became known as the "caste school" of American race relations. The term was something of a misnomer for what was a large and diverse assortment of arguments linking Jim Crow to caste. Between 1936 and 1950, at least a dozen books made overt reference to caste as a way to understand race in America. At times, scholars advanced older arguments that racism in America was worse than caste in India. In 1939, for example, Lloyd Warner and Allison Davis published an article that presented caste as relatively weak and flexible compared with Jim Crow segregation. But unlike Lala Lajpat Rai or Dalip Singh Saund, proponents of the caste school weren't interested in defending India from American criticism. Their goal was to provide a new way to understand race.[24]

Not all scholars of race were convinced that caste was a useful analytical category. Two of the most renowned African American sociologists of the twentieth century, E. Franklin Frazier and Charles S. Johnson, both used the term *caste* early in their careers but eventually came to reject the idea that American racism was a kind of caste. In Frazier's words, the "concept of caste" was "essentially static" and thus "failed to provide an orientation for the dynamic aspects of race relations." The most vociferous critic of the caste school was the African American sociologist Oliver Cromwell Cox. Cox criticized "the false outlook derived from the caste belief." Unlike caste, Cox argued, race was "not an abstract, natural, immemorial feeling of mutual antipathy between groups, but rather a practical exploitative relationship."[25]

The anthropologist Gerald D. Berreman rejected Cox's belief that caste was more static than race. Berreman argued that Dalits and African Americans were similar in having directly confronted the injustices of their respective societies. In his response to Berreman, Cox went so far as to state, "There has been no progressive social movement for betterment among outcaste castes in Brahmanic India." Cox ignored one of the largest social movements in twentieth century India: the Dalit struggle for freedom from caste oppression. In 1964, the American political scientist Harold Isaacs published a book titled *India's Ex-Untouchables*. Isaacs agreed with Berreman that both race and caste were deeply rooted injustices that were being actively challenged.[26]

Academic interest in the race / caste analogy dissipated over the course of the 1960s. In 1971, a team of sociologists led by Sidney Verba concluded that the race / caste analogy was helpful "only if one does not look too closely." But even as academic interest in race / caste comparison waxed, the Cold War invested new meaning in such comparisons. While the Soviet Union and its supporters in India portrayed the United States as a hopelessly racist country, Americans fought back by arguing that racism in America was no worse than caste in India.[27]


## Race, Caste, and the Cold War

In 1956, the *New Yorker* published a cartoon that used the race / caste parallel to dismiss Indian critiques of American racism. Two Indian men sit on a bench. One looks up from a newspaper to remark, "More controversy in Alabama! You'd think those people were being asked to send their children to school with Untouchables!" It was hypocritical, the cartoon suggested, to denounce racism and not casteism. During the Cold War, many Americans tried to deflect Indian concerns about American racism by referencing caste. In 1948, the American consul in Madras wrote the secretary of state that "an oft-repeated answer by the recent Consul General at this post to questions about the 'color problem' in the United States was 'Yes, it's almost as bad as it is in India.' This often caused such embarrassed confusion that the subject was immediately dropped." As in the days of Katherine Mayo, the race/caste analogy stifled dialogue, prevented constructive self-criticism, and buttressed blind nationalism.[28]

African Americans who strove to defend the United States without defending American racism found caste especially useful. Caste offered a way to respond to Indian critiques without directly condoning American racism. Such reasoning helps to explain why the African American diplomat Edith Sampson declared in Delhi, "I would rather be the lowliest, most downtrodden Negro in the United States than one of your Untouchables." Sampson's purpose was to defend the United States in the context of the Cold War. But by asserting that American racial oppression was less severe than caste oppression, Sampson earned criticism from civil rights activists back home. Other African Americans employed by the American government strove to walk a finer line when Indians asked about American racism. Carl Rowan, an African American journalist and diplomat, denied using caste "as an excuse for, or mitigating factor in regard to, American racial discrimination." As an example, he wrote, "I admitted to Indians that, as reported in my book, I *had* grown up in a town where, as a Negro, I couldn't get a drink of water in a drug store unless the fountain clerk could find a paper cup. I also told them how I had visited Manimangalam, an Indian village where untouchables could not draw water from the well." Although Rowan claimed that he did not use caste as a "mitigating factor," his many references to caste in his travelogue, *The Pitiful and the Proud,* operated primarily to parry Indian questions regarding race in America.[29]

Like Edith Sampson and Carl Rowan, the African American columnist George Schuyler used caste to shield American racism from foreign criticism. In an article in which he argued that "each nation has its own prejudices and discriminations," and thus that American racism did not deserve the world's condemnation, Schuyler offered as evidence that "India's castes are notorious." Schuyler defended Edith Sampson by asserting that when African Americans were chosen to go abroad, they should "speak as an American," not as a black American. As an example of a minority leader who pursued justice within the nation rather than appeal to international opinion, Schuyler offered Dr. Ambedkar, whom Schuyler called "the brilliant leader of India's outcasts and untouchables." Schuyler asserted that if Ambedkar was chosen as an ambassador from India to the United Nations, "it is highly unlikely that he will so far forget his position as to wash his country's dirty linen (the treatment of his people) before the world audience."[30]

It is difficult to imagine Ambedkar, who dedicated much of his life to the cause of his fellow Dalits, remaining silent on issues of caste before the United Nations. Ambedkar repeatedly used African American history to better understand the struggles of Dalits in India. In 1943, he denounced the denial of equal rights "to Negroes in America, to the Jews in Germany, and to the Untouchables in India." In 1946, he wrote to W. E. B. Du Bois, "There is so much similarity between the position of the Untouchables and the position of the Negroes of America that the study of the latter is not only natural but necessary." With Ambedkar as the chair of its drafting committee, the Indian constitution would outlaw untouchability as well as any discrimination based on caste. Ambedkar and other Indian legal authorities studied American attempts to use the law to achieve racial equality. The Indian constitution went further than American law by reserving seats in the legislatures for the lowest castes, and declaring that the state "shall promote with special care the education and economic interests" of those "castes and tribes" that occupied the lowest positions in Indian society.[31]

When confronted with comparisons between American racism and Indian caste oppression, many high-caste Indians defended Indian progress toward equality, even while recognizing that caste remained a significant problem. In a book entitled *Ambedkar Refuted,* the veteran anticolonial activist Chakravarti Rajagopalachari wrote that improvements in the treatment of Dalits did not "compare ill with what has been done in America for Negroes." Rajagopalachari chose his words carefully in order to avoid apologizing for caste injustice. Not all Indians were so careful. "Untouchability Banished in India: Worshipped in America," declared an article in the left-leaning Bombay journal *Blitz.* The idea that untouchability had been banished ignored the gap between Indian law and the injustice that continued to confront Dalits throughout India.[32]

Some Indians attacked casteism and racism with equal passion. In the spring of 1943, Bharatan Kumarappa was imprisoned in Nagpur as an outspoken opponent of British rule. In jail, he gave a series of lectures about his time as a student in the United States. In 1945, Kumarappa published these talks as a book in which he directly compared American racism with caste oppression. "America has a long way to go before it can come anywhere near the tyranny we have practised in regard to the Harijans," he wrote. Indians discriminated against the lowest castes, Kumarappa declared. "Shall we now complain if other nations treat us as untouchables, brahmins of the purest blood though we may be?" Thus, Kumarappa compared African Americans to Dalits and then to all colonized Indians. By using the race / caste analogy to encourage his readers to combat caste oppression, imperialism, and racism, Kumarappa demonstrated that transnational solidarities could oppose multiple injustices.[33]

Like Kumarappa, the Bombay journal *United Asia* connected race and caste. In September 1963, *United Asia* reported on the March on Washington for Jobs and Freedom, during which Martin Luther King Jr. famously shared his "dream" for America. Only a few months earlier, police dogs and fire hoses had been unleashed on nonviolent protesters in Birmingham. Denouncing such brutality, *United Asia* declared, "The atrocities on negro demonstrators reminded people in India of their experience of the British methods of suppression during Gandhiji's great movements of 1920, 1930 and 1942." "These memories of the past rose up to our minds," the editorial added, "and we could almost feel physically the pain, the anguish, the suffering of the negroes." Their "we" spoke for all Indians, but the editorial acknowledged that Dalits had a special connection to the struggles of African Americans:

> The millions of untouchables in India might as well regard the negroes [*sic*] struggle for equality and human dignity as their own struggle. . . . Their struggle against the high caste tyranny is almost identical in content with the great battle the negroes of America are fighting. It may be that the American negro is fighting not only for himself and for his brethren in America but for all the submerged castes, for all the blacks of the world whether they be in America or in India.

King's legacy—and the "I Have a Dream" speech in particular—have become neatly contained in a national story in which the goals King fought for are presented as having already been accomplished. By connecting race and caste, the editors of *United Asia* offered a more expansive understanding of the African American struggle, a struggle that continues to have relevance for "all the blacks of the world."[34]

King developed his own understanding of the links between race and caste. In an article for *Ebony,* he wrote that independent India confronted "the problem of segregation." "We call it race in America; they call it caste in India," he explained. Although King recognized the ongoing brutality of caste in India, he concluded that "India appears to be integrating its untouchables faster than the United States is integrating its Negro minority." Both nations had laws against discrimination. "But in India," he wrote, "the leaders of Government, of religious, educational and other institutions have publicly endorsed the integration laws." Furthermore, the Indian government had "set forth a constitutional provision making untouchability illegal" and had spent "millions of dollars a year in scholarships, housing, and community development to lift the standards of the untouchables."[35]

By using the race / caste comparison, civil rights leaders like King reframed American racism as an international problem. Their efforts inspired American power brokers to worry that racism was hurting American foreign policy by damaging the nation's reputation abroad. On June 11, 1963, President John F. Kennedy addressed the nation on live television after the National Guard had forcibly integrated the University of Alabama. Kennedy used the idea of caste to explain his commitment to civil rights: "We preach freedom around the world, and we mean it, and we cherish our freedom here at home, but are we to say to the world, and much more importantly, to each other that this is the land of the free except for the Negroes; that we have no second-class citizens except Negroes; that we have no class or caste system, no ghettoes, no master race except with respect to Negroes?" By juxtaposing caste with two other imported terms, *ghettoes* and *master race,* Kennedy placed caste on par with Nazi fascism, and then equated both to racism in the United States. If racism was caste, it must be un-American.[36]

Reversing the analogy also had power. In July 1959, delegates to the First Southwide Institute on Nonviolent Resistance to Segregation passed a resolution that declared, "We make common cause with the oppressed and submerged peoples of the world—particularly the unfreed peoples of Africa and the former 'untouchables' of India. We call upon them to adhere to the principles of nonviolence in our common world struggle." By invoking a "common struggle," the resolution suggested that the fight against racial caste in America could inspire struggles against caste in India.[37]

On August 15, 1973, the twenty-sixth anniversary of Indian independence, two hundred people marched through the streets of Bombay in a celebration of what they called "Black Independence Day" (Kala Swatantrya Din). The march was organized by the Dalit Panthers, an organization inspired by the Black Panthers. A Dalit Panther manifesto, written in 1973, declared, "Due to the hideous plot of American imperialism, the Third Dalit World, that is, oppressed nations, and Dalit people are suffering. Even in America, a handful of reactionary whites are exploiting blacks. To meet the force of reaction and remove this exploitation, the Black Panther movement grew. From the Black Panthers, Black Power emerged. . . . We claim a close relationship with this struggle." Like the Black Panthers, the Dalit Panthers positioned their struggle within a global community of the oppressed. One of their publications stated, "The Dalit Panthers aspire to join hands with the Dalits (oppressed) of the world which includes the oppressed and the exploited [*sic*] people in Cambodia, Vietnam, Africa, Latin America, Japan and even in USA (especially with the Blacks)."[38]

Much like their American namesake, the Dalit Panthers found their political and economic goals stymied by official repression and undermined by internal disagreement. Nevertheless, they inspired a variety of ongoing struggles. A new Dalit Panther political party arose in the South Indian state of Tamil Nadu. Like its predecessor, the new party drew on analogies with African American struggles. The most lasting impact of the Dalit Panthers occurred at the intersection of politics and culture. Just as the Black Panthers contributed to a resurgence of pride in the word *black,* the Dalit Panthers encouraged Dalits to embrace aspects of their identity that had been used to denigrate them. Several Dalit authors compared African American and Dalit struggles in order to emphasize the power that stems from embracing adversity. In 1974, Janardan Waghmare wrote, "The Negro should not change the colour of his hide, nor the Untouchable his caste. There is no difference between the place of the Negro in America and the step or level of the Untouchable in India." That same year, another Dalit author, Gangadhar Pantawane, opened a seminal article on Dalit literature by quoting James Baldwin: "Our humanity is our burden, our life, we need not battle for it; we need only to do what is infinitely difficult—that is accept it."[39]

In the choice of their name, the Dalit Panthers gestured toward a global struggle against caste in all its forms. That struggle continues. Although a middle class has emerged among both African Americans and Dalits, both communities remain disproportionately poor. In India, the public murder of Dalits, often reported as "lynchings," remains all too common. In the United States, antiracist activists continue to frame American racism as a form of caste. In 2010, the legal scholar Michelle Alexander, writing about the mass incarceration of people of color, declared, "We have not ended racial caste in America; we have merely redesigned it."[40]

Alexander demonstrated the power of the word *caste* to highlight structural and institutional inequalities. As many antiracist, anticasteist activists have argued, the problem is not just the psychological prejudices that cling to the divides of race and caste, but also the ways in which those divides are written into the political, economic, and legal structures that reproduce inequality across generations. Race and caste are not just thought and felt but lived. From our neighborhoods to our schools to our offices and places of worship, what are the lines that decide where certain people can live or work or study or play? In addition to buttressing such structural inequalities, caste, race, and other forms of difference serve as useful tools for power brokers eager to divide and rule. As Ambedkar declared in *The Annihilation of Caste*, "Caste in the hands of the orthodox has been a powerful weapon for persecuting the reformers and for killing all reform." The same could be said of race in America. As Anupama Rao has written, caste is central to "the manner by which the production, recognition, and distribution of social difference serve as the explicit predicate for the state's authority to govern legitimately." The act of keeping people apart has long been central to the state's claim to legitimacy, a fact that helps to explain why many anticaste activists turn to apartheid as an analogy for caste.[41]

Faced with caste-based or racial apartheid, many antiracist and anticaste activists have simultaneously embraced and transcended the language of identity and difference. In the words of the mixed-race antiracist intellectual Cedric Dover, "We must be both 'racial' and anti-racial at the same time, which really means that nationalism and internationalism must be combined in the same philosophy." Writing of Chamar activists, the scholar Ramnarayan Rawat has written, "Moving beyond the confines of identity or ethnicity politics, Dalit struggles have offered a resounding critique of social and cultural practices that have defined the shared frameworks of colonialism and nationalism."[42]

At their most powerful, race / caste analogies have been used to oppose the intersectionality of multiple injustices. In 1946, in a book called

*America: The Land of Superlatives,* Kamaladevi Chattopadhyay encouraged her Indian readers to learn from African Americans, even while suggesting that African Americans would benefit from the liberation struggles of Asians and Africans. She wrote, "Soon Africa too, will come back, and come into her own, and the dark ones will cease to be the 'untouchables' of the world. The international colour line has been challenged and stormed by Asia. No more the colonials will allow themselves to be jim-crowed the world over." Kamaladevi placed the struggles of African Americans in a global framework in which "colonization" was akin to "Jim Crow." Her concern with the interconnection of racism and imperialism did not blind her to India's own legacy of "Jim Crow." Her reference to "untouchables" reminded her readers that the Indian struggle for freedom was about more than political independence from Britain. By comparing African American struggles simultaneously to the efforts of Dalits and of all Indians, Kamaladevi used analogies of struggle between Indians and African Americans like a prism, refracting Indian nationalism into a broader opposition to the intersection of imperialism, racism, and oppressions based on gender, class, and caste.[43]

Kamaladevi's opposition to multiple oppressions was rooted in a global struggle against white supremacy that emerged during the First World War. In 1900, when W. E. B. Du Bois declared, "The problem of the twentieth century is the problem of the color line," he globalized the color line, referring not only to the "millions of black men in Africa, America and the Islands of the Sea" but also to "the brown and yellow myriads elsewhere." His vision was prophetic. Soon, the Great War would reveal the weaknesses of the white imperial order, and inspire anticolonial revolutionaries to imagine a new world. As African American activists like Du Bois envisioned India's independence movement within a global fight against white supremacy, Indians and Indian Americans reconceptualized their own battles in global terms. Struggles against racism, imperialism, and casteism became intertwined, as both India and the United States grappled with the meaning of a war fought in the name of freedom.[44]

CHAPTER 3

# Rebellions

∞

We aim at nothing less than the establishment in India
of a republic, a government of the people, by the
people, for the people in India.
—Ram Chandra, *New York Times*, 1916

IN AUGUST 1914, soon after the outbreak of the First World War, Jawala
Singh, a wealthy California farmer known as the Potato King, donated his property to a revolutionary political party and sailed to his
native India to fight against British imperialism. Singh was not alone. The
organization that inherited his land, the Ghadar Party, attracted thousands of supporters in North America and throughout much of the
world. *Ghadar* means "rebellion" in Urdu. Its members rebelled against
imperialism in India and racism in America.[1]

Most Indians who traveled to America came to build a better life for
themselves and their families. They strove to get ahead in the world, not
to transform it. But arrogant border agents, violent white mobs, and the
everyday struggle to survive in a profoundly unequal society forced Indian migrants to confront the root causes of injustice and inequality.
Many recognized that their future in America hinged on the freedom
of India. When Japanese Americans faced discrimination, the Japanese
government intervened on their behalf. The British Raj, by contrast, did

little to protect the rights of Indians abroad. In the wake of the Bellingham riot, for example, Indians demanded that the British "take effective measures for the protection of British Hindus both in the United States and Canada." But nothing changed. In the words of Har Dayal, "as long as the Indians remained in subjection to the British they would not be treated as equals by Americans or any other nation." Dayal urged his fellow Indians to attack white supremacy from the fields of California to the streets of Calcutta.[2]

In the United States, Ghadar was nonviolent and invisible to most Americans. While some Indian Americans challenged American racism in the courts and in the press, the Ghadar movement failed to produce a sustained public protest within the United States. Rather, the United States became a launching pad for rebellion in India. But although Ghadar members focused on the freedom of India, their efforts had deep roots in the struggle for survival and civil rights in the United States.

Of the roughly ten thousand Indians in the United States at the time of the First World War, some two thousand sailed back to India to foment violent rebellion. Many traveled in small groups, or *jathas*, of four or five young men. Each *jatha* raised its own funds, often barely enough to make the journey. Many would sail for India without arms or training. Their faith might seem naïve, their plans reckless. But the First World War gave them hope that the world was changing, and they did not feel alone in risking their lives in the fight against British rule. Once the struggle had begun, they believed, millions of their countrymen in India would join them. Plus, they had the support of a powerful ally: Germany.[3]

The German government provided funds and training to Indian radicals in the United States. The relationship seemed natural to many Indian revolutionaries. In July 1914, the Ghadar newspaper declared, "All intelligent people know that Germany is an enemy of England. We also are mortal enemies of England. So the enemy of our enemy is our friend." But the "friendship" between Germany and Indian radicals risked alienating Americans—especially once the United States entered the war on the side of Great Britain.[4]

The transnational radicalism of Ghadar fed an equally transnational surveillance regime—British, British Canadian, and American. The more radical the Indian American community became, the more British officials were able to gain the support of their American counterparts. But as historian Seema Sohi has demonstrated, Indian American radicalism was itself driven by the oppressive overreach of American and British officials. As the First World War destroyed the old world order, the fate of Ghadar would hinge on an intricate dance between rebellious migrants, anxious officials, and government spies.[5]

## The United States of India

As early as 1907, British officials found "seditious pamphlets" in the Punjab that had come from "some Natives of India now in the United States." The pamphlets aimed to convince Indian soldiers "how easy it would be to throw off British rule." In 1908, the director of intelligence for the British Raj, C. J. Stevenson Moore, warned that the struggle for Indian rights in America was becoming "an integral part of the whole political movement directed against our supremacy in India." British intelligence officials worked to enlist their American counterparts in an ambitious transnational surveillance scheme. In the summer of 1914, C. R. Cleveland, director of the Department of Criminal Intelligence, wrote to the American consulate in Bombay that "a group of seditious Indians" in San Francisco had "become intoxicated by the freedom of restraint which they are allowed to enjoy in the United States."[6]

British officials worried about Indians like Taraknath Das. A Bengali scholar and revolutionary, Das fled India in 1905 to avoid imprisonment. After arriving in Seattle in the summer of 1906, he became the first Indian migrant to claim political asylum in the United States. He was twenty-two years old. To earn a living, Das picked celery and worked in a chemistry lab at Berkeley before landing a job as an interpreter for the American immigration service in Vancouver. In 1908, he began publishing a bimonthly journal called *Free Hindusthan*. After the British government complained, American authorities offered Das a choice: stop publishing the paper or quit his job. He quit, and began traveling up and down the West Coast, urging his countrymen to rebel against British rule. Das alarmed British authorities by enrolling at a military academy in Vermont and encouraging other Indians to seek military training. After pressure from British officials and American military intelligence, the academy expelled the Bengali radical, ostensibly for making speeches against British rule. But despite British opposition, Das managed to gain American citizenship in June 1914.[7]

Like Taraknath Das, Har Dayal embodied the connection between migration and radicalism. Also like Das, Dayal believed in the power of ideas and of the written word. As he told the American writer Van Wyck Brooks, "Your pen can do much for the renovation of American life." But Dayal was not content to revolutionize the world of ideas. He traveled the Pacific Coast, meeting with Indian workers and encouraging them to support the cause of India's freedom. With funds raised from his tours, Dayal bought a building in San Francisco, renamed it the Yugantar Ashram, and began publishing a newspaper that would give a name to a movement: *Ghadar*.[8]

Taraknath Das and Har Dayal both helped guide the Ghadar movement. But Ghadar was a popular struggle with deep roots in the national pride and daily struggles of thousands of Indian workers in North America. Indian Americans had formed political organizations before Ghadar. In the spring of 1912, a group of Indian lumber mill workers organized to demand their rights. Their initiative would empower leaders like Dayal and Das, as well as lesser-known figures like the lumber worker Sohan Singh Bhakna. When workers gathered to create the Pacific Coast Hindustan Association, an important predecessor of Ghadar, it was Bhakna who was elected president.[9]

The Ghadar movement demonstrated the unity of the Indian American community across divides of class, religion, and caste. But that unity was not perfect. Differences of strategy and long-term vision threatened to tear apart fragile coalitions. Personality clashes intensified in the context of a life-and-death struggle. These divisions were strained by the machinations of an increasingly repressive American government.

Aware that they risked alienating Americans, Ghadar activists turned to history to portray their movement as fundamentally American. Taraknath Das echoed Lincoln when he declared, "the government of India must be a government of the people of India, by the people of India, and for the people of India." Another prominent Ghadar leader, Ram Chandra, declared in the *New York Times*, "We aim at nothing less than the establishment in India of a republic, a government of the people, by the people, for the people in India." In 1914, Ram Chandra assumed leadership of the Pacific Coast Hindustan Association and editorship of the Ghadar newspaper. He also created an Indian News Service that provided stories sympathetic to India's cause to American newspapers. He told readers of the *Times* that living in the United States had created a new kind of Indian who saw beyond differences of caste and creed to embrace "a United States of India."[10]

Despite the patriotic gestures of Ram Chandra and Taraknath Das, American authorities became increasingly suspicious of Indian radicals. They worked with British spies to track the movement of Indians suspected of radicalism. In January 1913, William Hopkinson, the turban-sporting British spy, began a secret mission to California. With the help of paid informants, he identified Har Dayal as his chief target. In March 1914, Dayal was arrested at the Bohemian Hall in San Francisco. He was accused of being "an anarchist or advocating the overthrow of the United States government by force." Dayal's arrest was a victory for Hopkinson, and a significant setback for the Ghadar movement. But although he was no longer able to help lead the movement in America, Dayal would continue to be a thorn in the side of the empire. Rather than face deportation back to India, he skipped bail and fled to Switzerland before eventually traveling to Germany.[11]

The growing ties between Ghadar and Germany fed American paranoia about Indian American radicalism. In 1915, Ghadar party members and German officials together orchestrated a plot to ship $200,000 of guns and ammunition from the United States to India. The weapons were to be transported on a ship, the *Annie Larsen*, to a second vessel, the SS *Maverick*. But the boats failed to rendezvous as planned, and the arms-laden *Annie Larsen* returned to the United States, where its cargo was promptly confiscated.[12]

The American government had long tracked ties between Indian American radicals and Germany. But once the United States entered the war, such ties became treason. The day after the United States entered the war, thirty-four Indian Americans were arrested on suspicion of conspiracy. Their trial, known as the Hindu Conspiracy Trial, began in November 1917. It helped the government's case that Wilhelm von Brincken, the military attaché of the German consulate in San Francisco, had written home, "I am the head and organizer of the Hindu Nationalists on the Pacific." Von Brincken's claim was patently false, but it fit prevailing racial beliefs that such an elaborate revolutionary effort must have been planned by a white man.[13]

The defendants strove to present their efforts as the patriotic struggles of an oppressed people. On their side, they had the tradition of American rebellion against British colonialism, as well as the more recent pronouncements of Woodrow Wilson in support of self-determination. Wilson framed the war as a struggle for freedom and independence—precisely the goals of Ghadar activists. Ram Chandra wrote Wilson that Indians were "entitled to independence, especially as the Government we propose to set up, will be a democracy." Later, it would become clear, in the words of the *Indian Social Reformer,* that "Woodrow Wilson never meant to have his pet doctrine of self-determination applied to Asiatic nations." But in the midst of the Great War, many hoped that Wilson would champion democracy across the planet.[14]

Despite the democratic aims of the Ghadar movement, Wilson's government zealously prosecuted the Hindu Conspiracy Trial. Indians lost hope in the president and turned to other prominent anti-imperial Americans. The defense subpoenaed William Jennings Bryan in the hope that he would testify in support of India's need for independence. A copy of Bryan's article, "British Rule in India," had been donated to the Yugantar Ashram by Har Dayal. But at a time of war and widespread white supremacy, few Americans dared support Indian Americans accused of associating with the enemy. Those who did rally to the cause of Ghadar tended to be radical themselves—William and Marian Wotherspoon, for example, a pacifist couple who opened their San Francisco home to Indian activists. The absence of high-profile American supporters was a major problem for the Ghadar movement. Even more troubling were the divisions within the movement itself.[15]

The courtroom was packed when Ram Singh pulled out his pistol and shot dead Ram Chandra, only to be immediately killed by a U.S. marshal. Thus, the Hindu Conspiracy Trial ended with a dramatic revelation of the divisions within Ghadar, divisions stoked by British spies. The British were deeply involved in the trial. While the American government spent $450,000 on the trial, the British contributed some $2.5 million. Among other things, that money paid for the over two hundred spies, double agents, and "experts" that were called as witnesses. Ram Singh believed Ram Chandra was one of those double agents. He had reason to be paranoid about British spies. Ten of the Indian defendants and six of the Germans testified for the prosecution in exchange for leniency.[16]

In addition to the specter of double-dealing, the Ghadar movement also suffered differences of vision and method. While all Ghadarites envisioned the ultimate freedom of India, some also focused on the civil rights of Indians within the United States. Some pursued armed rebellion, but others argued that peaceful methods were better suited to undoing injustice in India and America. In South Africa, the Indian community was similarly divided along multiple lines, and yet a majority rallied around a young lawyer named Mohandas Gandhi. Why did America not produce a Gandhi? Demographics provide one answer. Unlike in South Africa, the vast majority of Indian migrants in the United States hailed from the Punjab, a region with a strong connection to the military. Many Indian Americans had served in the British military, a fact that helps to explain their preference for armed rebellion. Timing also provides a clue. Gandhi's nonviolent rebellion in South Africa began a decade before the First World War. Ghadar arose at a different historical moment. At a time of widespread armed conflict, many Indian radicals became convinced that only violence could bring them their freedom. In the short term, they were wrong. India remained under British rule, and Indian Americans continued to suffer discrimination. But in both America and India, the Ghadar movement had profound effects.[17]

The willingness of Indian rebels to take up arms, and to foment rebellion among soldiers in the British Indian Army, pushed the imperial government toward increasingly severe repression. That repression backfired, inspiring greater rebellion and ultimately contributing to the fall of the British Raj. As one former Ghadar activist remembered, the worst British repression was not inspired by "the daring deeds of the National Congress, but the activities of the Gadar Party and its members."[18]

In addition to hastening the day of India's freedom, Ghadar members left an enduring vision of that freedom. In March 1920, one Ghadar volunteer, Santok Singh, sent a revealing note to the nationalist congressman N. S. Hardikar. Singh declared, "India needs a revolution, political, social, industrial. An Independent India with social and economic problems unsolved does not appeal to my reason." From the beginning of the movement, Ghadar activists had debated how to solve India's "social and economic problems." In a speech at UC Berkeley in October 1912, Har Dayal made clear that he did not believe in a "narrow view of nationalism." He encouraged his fellow Indians to seek freedom from

Britain but also "a revolution in social ideals so that humanity and liberty would be valued above property, special privilege would not overshadow equal opportunity, and women would not be kept under subjection."[19]

Like the Indian American community from which it arose, Ghadar was overwhelmingly male. Nevertheless, a variety of Ghadar figures called for an end to patriarchy. The newspaper founded by former Ghadar activists, the *Independent Hindustan,* regularly championed women's empowerment. In March 1921, the paper reported that "the women of India are quite alive to their needs, without waiting for the men to decide." A few months later, the paper declared that a future India must "give full rights of every kind to women."[20]

In addition to women's empowerment, Ghadar activists also championed religious tolerance, building on the inclusivity of earlier Indian American organizations. The Pacific Coast Hindustan Association included Hindus, Sikhs, and Muslims. The masthead of its publication bore the names "Ram, Allah, and Nanak." When a group of speakers was sent to travel the Pacific Coast recruiting volunteers, the team included one Hindu, one Sikh, and one Muslim. In the words of a poem published by the Ghadar press, "Muslims, Pathans, Dogras and Sikh heroes should join together. The power of the oppressors is nothing if we unitedly attack him."[21]

The inclusivity of Ghadar extended to caste. In 1909, a Dalit laborer named Mangu Ram found work picking fruit in California. He was twenty-three years old. After spending four years in the fields, Ram became a full-time employee of the Ghadar party in San Francisco. He participated in a mission to smuggle weapons into India, and was forced to flee to the Philippines. After years in exile, Ram returned to India, inspired by his experiences in the Ghadar movement to struggle against caste inequality.[22]

Ghadar also defied the borders of class. A British spy, codenamed "C," recalled that Ghadar leaders would "go out to the ranches, where poor labourers are working." The leaders would "preach revolution to them until these poor and illiterate people think they must drive the English out of India or kill them." Such a paternalistic reading of Ghadar overlooked the fact that many of its leaders, like Mangu Ram, began as laborers. Ghadar activists connected their struggles against British colonialism to the global labor movement. Both Sohan Singh Bhakna and

Har Dayal joined the Industrial Workers of the World. Dayal encouraged his fellow Indians to join "the strenuous struggle which is going in *all countries*, between the oppressors and the oppressed, the rich and the poor, the powerful and the weak." Ghadar activists like Dayal fostered an interclass culture of resistance. In April 1914, Ghadar press published *Ghadar-di-Gunj*, or *Echoes of Revolt*, a collection of poetry. Many of the poems frame the Indian American struggle in terms of class. One declares, "The world calls us coolie. / Why doesn't our flag fly anywhere?"[23]

Ghadar activists developed an inclusive vision that opposed multiple oppressions. One California newspaper attacked Har Dayal as the leader of "an international anarchist society" that was "in cooperation with the Industrial Workers of the World for the promotion of industrial organization and the General Strike, the abolition of patriotism and race feeling, the economic, intellectual and sexual freedom of women, and the 'movements of progress and revolt' in Asia and Africa." This list was meant to be scandalous, but it was a catalog of struggles that Dayal heartily embraced. Like Dayal, many Ghadar activists recognized the intersectionality of oppressions, and fought on many fronts to build a more just world. Even after the Ghadar Party was crushed, its members killed or imprisoned, a legacy of inclusive struggle survived to inspire other activists seeking true democracy in the United States and India.[24]

## Partnerships for Freedom

In the fall of 1920, a group of Indian workers was arrested at the Bethlehem Steel factory seventy miles north of Philadelphia. They were taken to Ellis Island to be deported. Rather than send the workers back to India, however, corrupt immigration officials arranged for them to be forced into labor on a British ship. When the workers learned of these plans, they refused to leave the detention center. One was a naturalized American citizen. Still, all the workers might have languished in jail if word of their plight had not made its way to the Friends of Freedom for India (FFI), a new organization that brought together Ghadar veterans with sympathetic Americans. The FFI had more resources and political connections than earlier Indian American groups. FFI lawyers secured freedom for the workers, and unearthed what the *Independent Hindustan* called "a gigantic conspiracy between powerful British shipping interests and certain American immigration authorities to shanghai Indian workers out of this country." Between eighty and one hundred Indian immigrants had been forced into labor on British ships. But legal action and political pressure from the FFI put an end to this illegal system of forced labor, demonstrating the power of new collaborations between Indian radicals and American supporters.[25]

The FFI was founded in late 1918 by Taraknath Das, Agnes Smedley, and Sailendranath Ghose. Like Das, Ghose had come to the United States already a committed anticolonial activist. He arrived in Philadelphia in January 1917, and was in San Francisco as the Hindu Conspiracy Trial began. Aware of the need for American partners, Ghose penned an open letter to "American Radicals" that was published in the journal *Young Democracy* and republished as a pamphlet by the FFI. He asked, "You liberals and radicals of America, what are you doing about the Indian revolution? Where is your voice? Where, indeed, has been your voice while Hindu revolutionaries in your country have been sentenced to prison because they have tried to free their country from a foreign and autocratic rule?" He appealed for the support of "idealistic Americans," and concluded, "We shall learn whether your idealism transcends racial and national boundaries."[26]

Of the growing number of Americans who supported India's freedom, none was more influential than the third founder of the FFI, Agnes Smedley. Born in Missouri in 1892, Smedley grew up in a small Colorado mining town. In early 1917, she moved to New York and found herself socializing with Indian radicals, including Sailendranath Ghose. As she became more committed to India's cause, Smedley drew the attention of Lala Lajpat Rai, who tried to convince her to avoid advocates of violence lest she attract the attention of the authorities. She refused such caution, and was soon rerouting correspondence between Indian revolutionaries in the United States, Mexico, Germany, and elsewhere. She moved homes multiple times a year to evade surveillance. Despite such precautions, Smedley was twice imprisoned for her efforts.[27]

If the FFI had only reached a few radicals like Smedley, its influence would have remained small. But the organization attracted a variety of influential Americans. The executive board included ACLU leader Roger Baldwin, birth-control advocate Margaret Sanger, and renowned socialist Norman Thomas. Robert Morss Lovett, an English professor at the University of Chicago, served as president. Many of these figures were committed to a world free of colonial oppression and to an America welcoming of immigrants. The FFI called upon the government "to protect the traditional right of asylum for political refugees on American soil and to sever all connection with the British agents seeking to prosecute those representatives of the Indian people who are lawfully presenting their cause to the people of the United States."[28]

The British had long worried that the American public would turn against the Raj. In 1908, the Secretary of State for British India, John Morley, wrote the viceroy that "Hindu anti-British propaganda has not produced any sensitive effect so far on United States opinion." Morley's "so far" is telling. He knew that American opinion might shift against the British empire. White supremacy and anti-immigrant hysteria predisposed many Americans to support the British. After the Hindu Conspiracy Trial portrayed Indian radicals as traitorous pawns of the Germans, it seemed as if the Anglo-American alliance was safe. Yet over the course of the 1920s and 1930s, the British steadily lost the propaganda battle, as organizations like the FFI successfully turned American opinion against British rule in India.[29]

That victory was the result of decades of collaborative work, much of it based in New York. Ghadar arose on the West Coast among laborers and students struggling against racial discrimination. On the East Coast, by contrast, Indian organizations were driven by a relatively small group of activists who gained influence by building alliances with American reformers. Those alliances would prove crucial in shifting American opinion toward Indian independence.

In 1906, seven years before Ghadar erupted in California and twelve years before the FFI emerged, the first Indian American political organization, the Pan-Aryan Association, was founded in New York. Whereas Ghadar was overwhelmingly Sikh and Hindu, the Pan-Aryan Association was founded by a Christian and a Muslim, neither of whom was especially devout. Samuel Lucas Joshi, the son of a Christian pastor, came to the United States to teach languages to aspiring missionaries. After earning a master's degree from Columbia, Joshi gravitated away from religion and toward radical politics. He was inspired by the other founder of the Pan-Aryan Association, Mohamed Barakatullah. Barakatullah would later travel the Pacific Coast recruiting volunteers for Ghadar, flee the United States for Germany, and eventually establish himself as the head of a "provisional government of India" just outside Afghanistan.

The fact that Barakatullah and Joshi found each other in New York in 1906 speaks to the small size of the Indian American community. But although the community was small, it lacked cohesion when Barakatullah and Joshi created the Pan-Aryan Association.[30]

In 1906, the word *Aryan* had yet to be tarnished by the Nazis. Barakatullah and Joshi used the word, like the German Indologist Friedrich Max Müller, as a bridge between white Europeans and high-caste Indians from the North of India. Their goal was to forge solidarity amongst Indian Americans, and between Indians and those white Americans who could also be seen as Aryan. Ironically, their greatest success was with a group that was, in 1906, still seen as neither fully white nor fully American: the Irish. The Pan-Aryan Association was in many ways an Indo-Irish creation. Its first president was Irish American. The organization's founding was announced in the *Gaelic American*. And Barakatullah and Joshi both frequented Irish American events. At a gathering of the United Irish League, for example, Barakatullah discussed imperial politics with the Irish journalist and politician T. P. O'Connor.[31]

The most prominent pro-India Irish American was Myron Phelps, the wealthy New York lawyer to whom Rabindranath Tagore wrote concerning caste. In 1907, Phelps founded the Indo-American National Association and the Society for the Advancement of India. The following year, he funded the creation of New York's India House, a student hostel and center for community organizing that was modeled on London's India House. Phelps wrote a series of public "Letters to the Indian People" that were published in the *Gaelic American* and reprinted in *The Hindu*, a prominent newspaper in Madras (now Chennai). His letters used American history to encourage Indians to fight for their independence. Phelps met Gandhi in London, and corresponded with several prominent Indian figures. He also spent a year in India seeing British tyranny for himself. Phelps was not without his critics. Several Indian American activists, including Barakatullah and Joshi, were put off by what they saw as Phelps's domineering approach to the Indian cause. India House failed to attract significant support and was forced to close only a year after it had opened. But Phelps was successful enough to be closely watched by British intelligence officers who worried about his impact on American opinion.[32]

The British also worried about Jabez T. Sunderland, a Unitarian minister who became one of the most outspoken American supporters of

Indian freedom. Sunderland traveled to India in 1896. He met with prominent Indian political figures, including the social reformer Mahadev Govind Ranade. After returning to America, Sunderland authored a series of articles and books denouncing British rule as a form of slavery. In the first chapter of his revealingly entitled *India in Bondage: Her Right to Freedom,* Sunderland wrote, "The impression is widespread in America that British rule in India has been good." Similarly, Sunderland argued, "During the days of chattel-slavery in the Southern States of the American Union, so long as the world knew of slavery only through the representations of it given by slave-holders, the impression was common that slavery was a beneficent institution." To fight against the slavery of colonial rule, Sunderland served as the president of the most effective pro-India coalition organization in the United States before the FFI, the India Home Rule League of America.[33]

The Home Rule League was founded in 1917 in New York by Lala Lajpat Rai. By 1918, it boasted nine hundred dues-paying members, and branches in at least ten cities. At the height of anti-Ghadar sentiment, the league attracted government suspicion. On behalf of federal intelligence operatives, the New York police secretly read Lajpat Rai's mail, followed visitors to his apartment, and tapped his phone. Other members of the Home Rule League were similarly monitored. But unlike Ghadar, Lajpat Rai's organization expressly rejected violence. The newspaper of the Home Rule League, *Young India,* declared that the organization's work was "purely educational." While educating the American public, the league also cultivated powerful American supporters, from the prominent liberal activist Oswald Garrison Villard to Republican senators George Norris and A. J. Gronna.[34]

When it came to garnering American supporters for India's independence, no organization was as successful as the FFI. On December 5, 1920, over four hundred people packed New York's Hotel McAlpin to attend the National Convention of the FFI. Many of the delegates came from labor organizations, Socialist party branches, or Irish American organizations. Mary White Ovington, one of the founders of the NAACP, also attended, as did Roger Baldwin and W. E. B. Du Bois. Surendranath Karr, a Ghadar veteran who had been indicted in the Hindu Conspiracy Trial, challenged the audience "to destroy British imperialism and raise the banner of freedom—political, economic, social and intellectual, all over the world." "India is being sandwiched between British Imperialism on the one hand," he told delegates, "and Capitalism on the other." Karr's critique of capitalism must have resonated with the labor activists who made up a substantial proportion of the audience.[35]

The support of labor was vital to the FFI's ability to broaden its coalition beyond elite reformers. In the winter of 1920, Taraknath Das spoke at the annual convention of the Illinois State Federation of Labor. He portrayed the Indian independence movement as part of the global class struggle and appealed for solidarity between the world's working people. The delegates responded warmly. They passed a resolution extending their "moral support to the cause of the independence of India." In Fresno, the California State Federation of Labor expressed "deep sympathy with the people of India in their struggle for freedom." Reporting on such successes, the *Independent Hindustan* declared that "the interests of the proletariat are identical everywhere."[36]

In the wake of the Hindu Conspiracy Trial and the Russian Revolution, many Indian American activists embraced socialism. In 1921, the *Independent Hindustan* described Ghadar as a rebellion for "the peasants and the workers who have led a most horrible life for decades and centuries in India." It deemed the Communist International the "League of the Oppressed Peoples," and lauded Soviet efforts to bring together the world's working classes. When military intelligence agents raided Taraknath Das's home, they found a letter to the "Workingmen's and Soldiers' Council of Russia." Addressed to Leon Trotsky, the letter offered support for the Russian Revolution and declared that Russia was "the leader of the movement for true freedom in the world." In November 1922, two Ghadar representatives attended the fourth congress of the Comintern. Lala Lajpat Rai praised the Soviet Union for giving birth "to a new order of society aglow with the spirit of a new and elevated kind of internationalism."[37]

The impact of the left on Indian Americans was exemplified by the career of the great socialist firebrand Jayaprakash Narayan. Narayan arrived in San Francisco in October 1922. He was twenty years old. Over the next seven years, Narayan worked his way through college, first at the University of California at Berkley and eventually at the University of Wisconsin at Madison. To earn his tuition and living costs, he picked grapes, waited tables, and washed dishes. In the fields of California, he developed an awareness of class inequality that was nurtured on campus as well. "Strangely enough," Narayan later remembered, "it was in the land of resilient and successful capitalism, in the United States of America . . . that I became a convert to Marxism."[38]

Narayan credited "the pungent writings of M. N. Roy" with completing his "conversion to Marxism." Born near Calcutta in 1887, Manabendra Nath Roy embraced the revolutionary ferment that roiled his native Bengal. During the Great War, he traveled in secret from India to Japan, where he posed as a seminary student in order to gain an American visa and purchase a ticket for San Francisco. In Palo Alto, he fell in love with a Stanford graduate student. The two married and traveled to New York. American authorities identified Roy as a key suspect in the Hindu-German conspiracy. According to the U.S. Attorney for the Northern California District, Roy was "steeped in crime" and "one of the most violent revolutionaries India has produced." But before he could be arrested and deported to India, Roy fled to Mexico, where he embraced communism and helped found the Communist Party of Mexico.[39]

Roy declared the American Constitution "an instrument of bourgeois domination." Most Indian American activists, by contrast, claimed that their work embodied American ideals. Their praise for the United States was galvanized by the desire to court American support. It was strategic flattery that inspired the editors of the *Independent Hindustan* to declare in 1921, only a few years after the Hindu Conspiracy Trial, that "the heart of America always goes out to those struggling for life and liberty and light." Former Ghadar activists had learned from the calamity of being branded treasonous. At times, their praise for America took the form of genuine gratitude for the support offered by specific Americans. When Taraknath Das spoke before the United Textile Workers of America, delegates from Canada, loyal to the empire, stood up and interrupted. But the president of the union ruled them out of order, in the words of the *Independent Hindustan*, "on the ground that real America stood for freedom of speech and freedom of thought." The First Amendment had not protected Ghadar activists during the war, but the *Independent Hindustan* had legitimate reasons to praise the American commitment to freedom of speech, at least in the context of that particular incident. More often, however, Indian American praise for the United States glossed over American injustice and imperialism, as when *Young India* praised American rule in the Philippines in order to attack British tyranny in India.[40]

In December 1921, a group of American congressmen, mayors, ministers, and other public officials published an open letter of support for

Indian independence. The letter stated, "The United States has never failed to extend sympathy and support to all peoples who struggle for freedom." Such a declaration ignored American imperialism in the Philippines, Latin America, and elsewhere, as well as the racism that confronted Indian Americans. As with the pro-America rhetoric common among Indian American activists, we can understand such declarations as a form of strategic patriotism, a way to goad Americans to live up to their ideals. But we should not discount the fact that some pro-India activists saw the United States as a model of democracy, if only in part. Strategic patriotism cannot alone explain why the *Independent Hindustan* was renamed the *United States of India*. An editorial in July 1923 proclaimed, "Our aim has been and now is the attainment for India of a form of government such as America has, with some modification befitting India. We want to have the United States of India."[41]

By praising American democracy, Indian Americans envisioned their own nation. In the pages of the *Independent Hindustan* and the *United States of India*, a distinctly transnational nationalism emerged. One article declared, "Indian Nationalism is not a narrow thing that admits only a tiny stream of humanity into it." Tolerant and pluralistic, Indian nationalism contained space "for any and every kind of worker, no matter what his race or religion." As a model for such a pluralist society, the *Independent Hindustan* again turned to America. "As in America, so in India," the article stated, "no Nationalism can be erected upon the foundations of identical religious or racial customs or origins." The *Independent Hindustan* went so far as to suggest that Indian independence was only a temporary goal on the way to world unity. Such a vision appealed to Indian Americans whose lives had transgressed the borders of the world. A global government would bring relief to persecuted migrants. But first they would have to fight for their rights within the United States. As the 1920s progressed, Indian American activists would have many reasons to reconsider their praise for American democracy.[42]

In the wake of the *Thind* decision, the American government moved to cancel the citizenship of scores of Indian Americans. By December 1926, at least forty-three Indian Americans had been stripped of their citizenship. As United States officials fought to cancel citizenships, they simultaneously began to deport Indian Americans back to India. Many of those targeted for deportation had been active in the Ghadar movement, and thus faced imprisonment or even execution in India.

The FFI mobilized its network in opposition to deportation. Members sent letters and speakers to partner organizations such as the American Federation of Labor. In the summer of 1919, the AFL passed a resolution opposing the deportation of Indian activists. This was a remarkable move for a conservative branch of the labor movement with a history of anti-immigrant xenophobia. The AFL was only one of many labor organizations to oppose the deportation of Indian Americans. As historian Joan Jensen has written, "A glass bottle blowers' local in Pennsylvania, a ladies' kimono and housedress maker's local in New York, and a carpenter's and joiners' local in Oakland protested against the deportation of Indians. The California State Federation of Labor, the American Labor Party . . . the National Civil Liberties Bureau, and senators Frank Norris, William S Kenyon, and George Huddleston—all sent their objections." At least seventy and perhaps as many as one hundred Indian American activists were ultimately deported. But that figure might have been significantly higher if not for the efforts of the FFI and its supporters.[43]

Avoiding deportation was only the first hurdle facing Indian Americans in the wake of the *Thind* decision. In California, the Alien Land Law prevented Indian Americans from owning land. With few legal rights, many Indian Americans fell victim to extortion and other forms of exploitation. Some took desperate measures. In 1925, a Punjabi migrant, Pahkar Singh, killed two white men who had tried to cheat him out of his lettuce harvest. Unlike Singh, most Indian Americans chose legal, nonviolent methods to defend their rights. American supporters rallied to their cause—sometimes by fighting against the racism that targeted all nonwhite immigrants, sometimes by trying to exempt Indians from being seen as nonwhite. In 1928, Representative Emanuel Celler and Senator Royal Copeland introduced legislation that would define "Hindus" as white and thus eligible for American citizenship. They failed. Without the protections afforded by legal whiteness, many Indian Americans struggled to survive in the harsh legal, economic, and psychological landscape of a profoundly racist America.[44]

In 1928, Vaishno Das Bagai rented a small room in San Jose, California, turned on the gas, and took his own life. Bagai had come to America thirteen years earlier with his wife and two children. He learned English, gained U.S. citizenship, and opened a successful business in San Francisco. He was, in his words, "dreaming and hoping to make this land my own." But after the *Thind* decision declared that Indians were no longer able to claim the privileges of whiteness, Bagai lost his citizenship and his right to own land. Before taking his life, Bagai wrote a note addressed to the San Francisco *Examiner*. He asked, "Who is responsible for all this? Me and the American government."[45]

The *Hindustan Times* called Bagai's suicide a "patriotic protest against racial discrimination." That protest was aimed not just at American racism but also at the racism of the British Raj. Bagai had participated in Ghadar. His despair at being rejected by the United States was driven in part by the fact that he had already renounced his identity as a British subject. After losing his American citizenship, Bagai tried to travel to India, but was refused an American passport. He might have returned to India as a subject of the British crown. But as Bagai saw it, that would have entailed rejecting his commitment to Indian independence. In a remarkable note he left his wife before taking his own life, Bagai wrote, "I could not think for a moment to accept the British passport. I have once renounced my British citizenship and can never become a British subject again." Reclaiming his own fate, he crossed out the word *can* and inserted the word *will*: "I have once renounced my British citizenship and will never become a British subject again."[46]

Some Indian Americans successfully defended their rights as American citizens. Sakharam Ganesh Pandit came to the United States in 1909. In the tradition of Vivekananda, he attracted American supporters by offering spiritual lessons from the East. In 1910, he delivered a lecture in Kilbourn, Wisconsin, titled "The Fourth Dimension or a Larger World." A promotional pamphlet featured a glossy image of a bearded, turbaned Pandit, a "High Caste Brahmin Teacher and Lecturer from India," dressed in flowing robes against a celestial background. In 1914, Pandit became a citizen. One American newspaper noted that he was "a high caste Hindu" who had been deemed by the presiding judge to be "of the Caucasian race from the ancient Indo branch." Having achieved citizenship through the courts, Pandit decided to begin a new career as an attorney. He was admitted to the California Bar in 1917 and proudly called himself "the only Hindu lawyer in the United States." In 1920, Pandit married a white American woman. With a successful career and a happy marriage, it seemed as if Pandit was living the American dream. But after the *Thind* decision, the government moved to strip him of his citizenship. If they were successful, Pandit would lose his livelihood and might be deported. In 1924, he argued his own case before a federal court, and

*Figure 3.* Vaishno Das Bagai, Kala Bagai, and their children. The suicide of Vaishno Das Bagai testified to the discrimination faced by Indian Americans. Vaishno Das and Kala Bagai Family Materials, South Asian American Digital Archive, Philadelphia. Courtesy of Rani Bagai.

won. The case went to the Supreme Court. On March 14, 1927, the Court ruled in Pandit's favor, effectively blocking government efforts to revoke the citizenship of Indian Americans.[47]

If Pandit had lost, his wife might also have found her citizenship in question. That is what happened to Mary Das, the American-born wife of Taraknath Das. Mary Das traced her ancestry back to seventeenth-century English colonists. But when Taraknath's citizenship was declared void, Mary was refused an American passport on the grounds that her husband had been ruled ineligible for citizenship. In a patriarchal legal system, her citizenship depended on his. They both might have become Indian citizens. But Taraknath's Indian citizenship had been compromised when he had become an American citizen. Suddenly, both Taraknath and Mary Das had become stateless. They were not, however, voiceless. They denounced the American government for failing to afford basic rights to Indian American citizens—and their wives. Mary Das wrote, "In America today, as well as in other countries, there exist double standards of international morality—one for the superior Whiteman and the other for the Asiatics."[48]

Despite the overt racism of the *Thind* decision and its aftermath, many Indian Americans managed to remain in America and to thrive. Bhagat Singh Thind himself exemplifies the tenacity of many Indian Americans. After being ruled ineligible for citizenship, Thind stayed in the United States, earned a PhD, and became a renowned spiritual teacher. He published a series of books with titles like *House of Happiness* and *Radiant Road to Reality*. "You must never be limited by external authority," he declared, "whether it be vested in a church, man, or book. It is your right to question, challenge, and investigate." Thind continued to fight against British rule, and the British continued to spy on him. One paid informant reported on lectures Thind gave in Detroit in 1926. Thind "lectures on psychology," the spy wrote, "and when he has his pupils well under control" he then launches an "anti-British attack." In May 1926, Thind was deemed a "notorious Indian seditionist" in a letter from a British spy reporting on his speeches in Omaha. According to the spy, Thind declared, "I am a man without a country for the United States has taken away my citizenship. But it is better to be a man without a country than a citizen of an enslaved country."[49]

Despite the resilience of Indian Americans like Thind, the 1920s would prove a low point for the Indian American struggle. Many of the most dedicated Indian American activists had fled the country or been deported. Even some of their strongest American supporters turned to other causes. In 1920, Agnes Smedley left for Germany, where she lived with the Indian radical Viren Chattopadhyay. The FFI fell apart the following year. The dissolution of the most effective organization working on behalf of Indian Americans might have proven a major setback for Americans who supported India's independence. But even as the FFI collapsed, the rise of a new Indian leader captivated Americans and created fresh opportunities for those sympathetic to the cause of India's freedom.

## Mahatmas and Missionaries

On the day she turned twenty-two, Nilla Cram Cook was baptized in the Ganges by Mahatma Gandhi. Originally from Iowa, Cook had moved into Gandhi's ashram earlier that year after concluding a brief love affair with a prince in Mysore. That affair was the latest in a string of scandalous exploits Cook confessed to the Mahatma, in his words, "omitting not even a twelve-year old kiss in a high-school kissing game." "Her life was one of lewdness, untruth and extravagance," Gandhi later wrote. But after promising to reform her ways and to "live a beggar's life," Cook was admitted into the Mahatma's retinue. "I see my salvation in the teaching of Gandhi," she declared, "whom I regard as the prototype of Christ." She added that Gandhi would be her "guide and father" and she would be "his daughter." But after eight months, Cook abandoned Gandhi and the ascetic life. She made news by driving a car into a ditch and then trying to register at a hotel in New Delhi as the Hollywood actress Janet Gaynor. In January 1934, the Indian government detained Cook in a psychiatric hospital in Calcutta and then deported her. Cook's story is one of the stranger episodes in the history of American fascination with Gandhi, a man some saw as a dangerous radical and others embraced as a saint.[50]

In the wake of the First World War, Gandhi rose to international fame as the protagonist in an epic nonviolent battle against the British Raj. Over time, Gandhi's peaceful methods would come to overshadow the radical nature of his goals. But when he first became well-known in America, it was as a nonviolent leader and as an anticolonial revolutionary. Indian American organizations helped shape both sides of Gandhi's persona in the United States. At its convention, FFI delegates adopted a resolution sending greetings to Gandhi: "Master of yourself, leader of a great people, forger of a new weapon whereby the spirit of a nation may engage in a victorious struggle with the material force of the oppressing stranger . . . may your courage and self-sacrifice continue to inspire the Indian people, and lead them to attain their independence as we attained ours." The phrase "as we attained ours" is telling. While the Ghadar party had been framed as fundamentally Indian, the FFI presented itself as an American organization—its Indian American members proudly Indian and American. It helped that Gandhi's "new weapon"—nonviolent civil disobedience—was less threatening to Americans than the violent methods Ghadar activists had embraced.[51]

Not all Indian Americans were supportive of Gandhi and his nonviolence. Surendranath Karr believed it "immaterial" whether the Indian revolution would be "bloodless" or "bloody." "We shall not hesitate to use physical force," he stressed. The *Independent Hindustan* expressed "grave doubts" about nonviolence. They supported "giving Gandhi a chance," but only until an opportunity arose for a violent uprising. "As soon as the British lay their hands on Gandhi," one article declared, "the Revolutionists-by-Force will get the opportunity they are waiting for."[52]

If Gandhi's methods alienated some Indian American activists, his nonviolence played a crucial role in gaining American supporters. Coupled with his simple dress and ascetic lifestyle, Gandhi's nonviolence positioned him within a role long familiar to American audiences: the prophet from the East. Like Swami Vivekananda, Gandhi became identified as a spiritual leader. Unlike Vivekananda, Gandhi was described with a Christian vocabulary that boosted his appeal to many Americans. The Mahatma became a saint. In 1921, the Unitarian minister John Haynes Holmes told his parishioners that Gandhi was "the Greatest Man in the World Today." "When I think of Mahatma Gandhi," Holmes preached, "I think of Jesus Christ."[53]

Gandhi gained fame in the United States at the same time that the growing prominence of Hindu spiritual teachers challenged how Americans understood and practiced their faith. By 1930, the influence of Indian religion on the United States had grown prominent enough to deserve a book. Wendell Thomas's *Hinduism Invades America,* despite its alarmist title, was sympathetic to Indian religions. Harry Emerson Fosdick, a leading liberal theologian, introduced the book with a defense of religious hybridity. He told his readers, "There is no possibility of Indian religion escaping the influence of Jesus Christ, and there is no possibility of American religion escaping the influence of the great Indian faiths."[54]

Such a pluralist, syncretic approach to the relationship between Christianity and Indian religions found its champion in E. Stanley Jones, perhaps the most renowned missionary of his generation. Born in Baltimore in 1884, Jones left for India in 1907. As the pastor of a large English-language church in Lucknow, he was expected to preach the gospel to the faithful and to save the souls of the heathen. But Jones came to believe that the best way to win more souls was to respect Indian culture and to collaborate across religious divides. In 1925, Jones distilled his radical ideas into a best-selling memoir called *The Christ of the Indian Road*. The book sold more than a million copies. At its core was the idea of a "Christ without Western civilization." Jones told his readers that "the next great spiritual impact upon the soul of the race is due to come by way of India." Only two years later, Katherine Mayo would publish *Mother India*. Unlike Mayo, Jones was respectful of Hinduism as a faith and a culture. He envisioned an inclusive Christianity that he modeled on what he saw as the best attributes of Hinduism. As he explained, "The genius of Hinduism is its all-inclusiveness. Nothing is rejected. Everything finds a place in its ample fold." Such a framing of Hinduism fit Gandhi's understanding of his own faith. Just as Jones celebrated Hinduism, Gandhi actively learned from Christianity and other world religions while remaining a proud Hindu. In 1923, Jones met Gandhi. He asked the Mahatma how to make Christianity "a part of the national life of India" and thus contribute "its power to India's uplift and redemption." Gandhi replied that Christians should "begin to live more like Jesus Christ."[55]

Jones openly supported Gandhi's politics and the larger struggle against British rule. His criticism of the Raj troubled British officials. Their anxiety was heightened by the fact that Jones was not the only anti-colonial American missionary in India. When the viceroy of India, Lord Linlithgow, committed the Indian army and India's resources to the Second World War, four Methodist missionaries responded with a letter of protest. One of the four was Jay Holmes Smith, a close associate of Jones. Like Jones, Smith had become an admirer of Gandhi. Smith advocated a blend of Gandhian *satyagraha* and Christian ethics that he called "Kristagraha." Smith might have directly joined the anticolonial struggle and launched his own "Kristagraha" campaign had he not been recalled from India by Methodist leaders concerned about burning bridges with British authorities.[56]

Smith founded an ashram in Harlem that blended daily Christian worship and Bible study with community activism in opposition to "such problems as war and racial justice." The ashram hosted a stream of Gandhian visitors, including Muriel Lester, a British pacifist, and

A. J. Muste, a renowned advocate of nonviolence. During his visit, Muste relayed the moral and financial support of E. Stanley Jones.[57]

In addition to Smith and Jones, British officials were troubled by Frederick Fisher, one of the highest-profile American missionaries in India. Born in Pennsylvania, Fisher worked his way up the clerical ladder to become the bishop of the Methodist Episcopal Church in Calcutta. But in 1930, Fisher abruptly resigned. He explained that he could not serve Indian parishioners while representing a "foreign power," and told readers of the *Christian Century* that missionaries needed a "complete spiritual emancipation from an ubiquitous imperialism that is racial, political and economic." As early as 1919, Fisher had published a book that supported Indian self-rule. His critique of British imperialism was framed as a defense of unity within the "Aryan" race. If the British would respect Indian autonomy, Fisher suggested, Indians would embrace their Aryan identity and remain committed to the cause of the Aryan world. If the Raj continued to oppress the legitimate desires of the Indian people, however, India would be forced to "throw in her three hundred millions, with all their man power and resources, to become a true Asian among Asiatics." Despite his belief in such a stark racial divide, Fisher defended a global conception of democracy. He wrote, "It will not be possible during the years that lie ahead for the Allies to discriminate in their application of democracy, demanding it for the Occident and denying it to the Orient. It is a world ideal, which knows neither racial nor territorial boundaries."[58]

Not all American missionaries rallied against British rule. Consider the career of Robert Allen Hume. Born in Bombay of missionary parents, Hume attended Yale and Andover Seminary before returning to India to found the Ahmednagar Divinity College. He edited the Anglo-Marathi newspaper, *Dnyanodaya,* joined the Indian National Congress, and raised funds for famine relief. Hume's work with the Congress did not entail embracing the anticolonial cause. On the contrary, Hume opposed Indian independence and turned to American history to explain his support for British rule. "When Americans fought the Revolution they were united, had self-government, were economically well-to-do, and were self-reliant while in India you have the opposite," Hume wrote in 1917. "Before material self-government exists," he argued, "we need more local government, industrialization, and social reform." Hume's use of "we" is as telling as his embrace of the proimperial line.

He spoke as an Indian, even while arguing that India was not ready for self-rule.[59]

By comparing the United States and India, Hume indulged a common strategy on both sides of the anticolonial struggle. One pro-British missionary wrote, "Americans owe India a clear and unvarnished interpretation of American life and methods. There are no social bars in America." By ignoring the many divisions within the United States—the color line, for example—many missionaries presented the United States as a country that had already gained freedom. But as the Indian American community grew and more Indians visited the United States, such a rosy depiction of American life became untenable. Indians began to suggest that American missionaries should work on first Christianizing the United States. According to an article in the *Indian Social Reformer* in 1925, American missionaries should serve "the sixty million Americans who have no religion and whose entire energy is devoted to chasing the omnipotent dollar."[60]

Indians critical of American society found ample evidence in the oppression of the Indian American community. In February 1929, the renowned Indian poet Sarojini Naidu wrote Gandhi about "the unhappy plight of the Indian settlers who after twenty or thirty years of prosperous labours on their own farm lands have by the recent immigration laws been deprived of all right to land and citizenship." Naidu recognized that the plight of Indian Americans was a reflection of India's own lack of freedom. So long as their mother country was under colonial rule, Indian migrants would have no one to protect them. "I have come to the conclusion," Naidu wrote, "that the status of Indian settlers can never be satisfactory anywhere till the status of India is definitely assured among the free nations of the world."[61]

Naidu came to the United States in 1928 to inspire greater sympathy for Indian independence and to counter the influence of *Mother India*. Indian anticolonial leaders had long worked to gain American support. In the early 1920s, Gandhi had requested that the Indian National Congress send Narayan Subbarao Hardikar to North America to report on public opinion and how it could be turned to support the nationalist cause. Hardikar spent years in America, completing a graduate degree in public health from the University of Michigan and working with Lala Lajpat Rai as the secretary of the India Home Rule League. In 1922, Hardikar finished his report, *Publicity Work in America: A New but Permanent*

*Plan.* Hardikar envisioned an overseas propaganda mission directed by the Indian National Congress. Nothing so coordinated was ever developed. But Gandhi did help arrange for several emissaries to visit the United Sates. Especially after the publication of *Mother India,* many Indians felt an urgent need to defend India's reputation in America. Naidu was Gandhi's first choice for that task.[62]

Naidu called herself a missionary for the Mahatma. In a letter from Cincinnati, she referenced Harriet Beecher Stowe, "a very noble woman who dedicated her genius to the deliverance of the Negros from their pitiful bondage." Naidu wrote, "Mine was, like Harriet Beecher Stowe's, also a message of deliverance from bondage—another version for another land." Referring to Gandhi as "the Mystic Spinner" and herself as a "Wandering Singer," Naidu told Gandhi, "The gospel of the Mystic Spinner as interpreted by a Wandering Singer was from first to last, from the initial to the ultimate word, the evangel of *self*-deliverance from *every* kind of personal, national, economic, social, intellectual, political, and spiritual bondage."[63]

Naidu's status as a leading Indian woman was central to her reception in America. The African American newspaper *Chicago Defender* called her India's "greatest woman." A promotional pamphlet lauded her status as "the first woman president of the Indian National Congress." In its efforts to underscore her uniqueness, the pamphlet ignored the breadth of the women's movement in India. Naidu was certainty not "the first woman in India to enter into and to make her efforts effective in meeting the problems of religion, education and sociology of her country." Nevertheless, Naidu's status as a feminist and an anticolonial figure was an important rebuke of one of Katherine Mayo's central arguments—that the subjection of Indian women justified colonial rule.[64]

Like Naidu, Nancy Ann Miller complicated American preconceptions about Indian womanhood—albeit in a very different fashion. In 1928, Miller married the former Maharaja of Indore, and changed her name to Maharanee Sharmishthabal Holkar. Her new husband had been forced to abdicate his throne after being implicated in the murder of one of the "dancing girls" in his palace. His sordid history did not diminish the enthusiasm of the American press for the story of a "regular American girl" becoming an Indian queen. The *Spokane Daily Chronicle* entitled its piece, "Nancy Ann Miller Finds Happiness in Marriage to Rich Indian Prince."

"I consider that my husband and myself have blended the orient and occident," Miller told the paper. "Because my life is much broader," she explained, "it is freer than if I had married an American." Such a statement flew in the face of American arguments that Indian women were backward and oppressed. But it was visits from figures like Naidu that most directly challenged the argument that British rule was necessary to emancipate India's women.[65]

While Naidu believed that Gandhi's message could empower oppressed groups of many kinds, she was especially concerned with the struggles of African Americans. She declared, "It breaks my heart to see the helpless, hopeless, silent and patient bitterness and mental suffering of the educated Negroes." Her adjectives—"helpless, hopeless, silent and patient"—denied African Americans agency in the same way that high-caste reformers, including Gandhi, often viewed Dalits as weak and deserving of pity. Naidu made the race / caste comparison explicit by calling African Americans "the socially and spiritually outcast children of America." But even while underestimating African American activism, Naidu denounced American racism and inspired Indians, including Gandhi, to express solidarity with African American struggles.[66]

In the spring of 1930, Gandhi walked 240 miles from his ashram near the banks of the Sabarmati River to the coastal town of Dandi. His goal was to break the monopoly on the production of salt maintained by the British government. By gathering natural salt from the ocean, Gandhi would break the law and—he hoped—shake the foundation of British rule. By the time Gandhi reached the Arabian Sea, Americans were riveted. Cole Porter sang, "You're the top! / You're Mahatma Gandhi. / You're the top! / You're Napoleon Brandy." Thornton Wilder published a novel whose main character is a disciple of Gandhi. And a group of prominent Americans invited Gandhi to visit the United States. He declined, citing his concern that he would be "exploited, ridiculed and misinterpreted." He did not want to be treated solely "as a curiosity." But he did express his "great affection for the American people," and addressed the American public in a special radio message that was published in the *New York Times*. Gandhi would continue to inspire a range of Americans. Perhaps his greatest impact would be on African Americans. While many Americans came to support Gandhi, it was African American activists who strove to make his methods their own.[67]

## Against Racism

In March 1922, the executive secretary of the NAACP, James Weldon Johnson, described Gandhi as "a prophet and a saint" and declared, "If non-cooperation brings the British to their knees in India, there is no reason why it should not bring the white man to his knees in the South." Two years later, African American sociologist E. Franklin Frazier asked readers of the *Crisis* to imagine that "there should arise a Gandhi to lead Negroes without hate in their hearts to stop tilling the fields of the South under the peonage system; to cease paying taxes to States that keep their children in ignorance; and to ignore the iniquitous disfranchisement and Jim-Crow laws." Whereas Johnson believed that Gandhian techniques might destroy Jim Crow, Frazier offered a darker assessment of the prospects of nonviolent civil disobedience. If African Americans took up Gandhi's methods, Frazier prophesied, "I fear we would witness an unprecedented massacre of defenseless black men and women in the name of Law and Order and there would scarcely be enough Christian sentiment in America to stay the flood of blood."[68]

Beginning in the early 1920s, African Americans debated Gandhi's relevancy. But regardless of whether Gandhian tactics would work in America, one thing was clear: the fight against British rule in India offered hope that the global ascendency of white supremacy would soon end. W. E. B. Du Bois framed Gandhi's noncooperation movement as one front in a global struggle against white rule. He used Gandhi's arrest to offer a sharp criticism of color-coded imperialism:

> White Christianity stood before Gandhi the other day and, let us all confess, it cut a sorry figure. This brown man looked into the eyes of the nervous white judge and said calmly, "It is your business to enforce the law and send me to jail; or if you do not believe that the law is right, it is your business to resign." Can you imagine such a judge resigning? Gandhi is in jail. So is English Christianity.

Like Du Bois, many Indians understood their struggles as part of a global fight for the freedom of people of color. As early as November 1908, an Indian journalist, Saint Nihal Singh, authored a lengthy analysis titled "Colour Line in the United States of America." Published in the Calcutta journal *Modern Review,* Singh's article juxtaposed British imperialism and Jim Crow racism. "The white man metes out the same treatment to coloured people in India and out of India," Singh wrote. "It makes little difference whether the coloured man is an Indian, a Chinese, a Japanese or an Afro-American."[69]

In September 1924, Benarsidas Chaturvedi, the editor of the Hindi-language magazine *Chand,* wrote Du Bois, "I entirely agree with you when you say that the different colored peoples and more especially the Indians and the American Negroes must get into touch and co-operation with each other." Chaturvedi asked Du Bois to contribute a short note "on the colour problem" for a special edition of *Chand.* In his message "To the People of India," Du Bois declared that African Americans were fighting "the same terrible battle of the color bar which our brothers in India are fighting." The claim that Indians and African Americans faced "the same terrible battle of the color bar" ignored the many differences between Indian and African American freedom struggles. But as Du Bois himself demonstrated, colored solidarity could be conceived as a way to unite Indians and African Americans without obscuring their differences.[70]

Du Bois imagined a global solidarity between people of color that respected diversity within what he called "the colored world." He developed a colored cosmopolitanism that simultaneously embraced solidarity while recognizing difference. Du Bois gave his colored cosmopolitanism literary form in *Dark Princess,* a novel he published in 1928. The novel tracks the relationship between an African American medical student and an Indian princess who also happens to be the leader of a secret organization of colored people from throughout the world. Several of the other participants in the movement at first reject the African American student, allowing Du Bois to decry what he calls in the novel "a color line within a color line, a prejudice within prejudice."[71]

His opposition to "prejudice within prejudice" led Du Bois to denounce the class inequality that divided communities of color throughout the world. Many of his Indian admirers did the same. In the summer of 1925, Du Bois received a letter from Abdur Raoof Malik in Gujranwala, Punjab. Connecting antiracism and socialism, Malik praised Du Bois for "liberating the Negroes from the bondage of aristocrats and capitalists." In July 1936, the renowned Indian socialist Rammanohar Lohia wrote Du Bois, "We on our part are equally anxious to establish the closest relations with our Negro comrades of America." Lohia was especially "anxious to learn of the experiences of your people in their fight for freedom and a higher standard of living." Like Du Bois, both Malik and Lohia connected struggles for racial equality and economic justice.[72]

Du Bois was not the only prominent African American leader to position Gandhi's struggle within a global movement against racism. In August 1921, Marcus Garvey welcomed "the news that there is a serious uprising in India." Born in Jamaica, Garvey had moved to the United States and built the world's largest organization of people of African descent, the Universal Negro Improvement Association (UNIA). Garvey warned his thousands of readers that "the English people are marshaling their troops to subdue the spirit of liberty, of freedom, which is now permeating India." Garvey sent Gandhi a series of telegrams expressing his sympathy with the Indian struggle. He told Gandhi, "The Negroes of the world through us send you greetings for [sic] fight for the freedom of your people and country." Gandhi published the telegram in *Young India* under the title "Negroes' Sympathy," and declared, "There is in them no inherent inferiority as is commonly supposed to be the case." Garvey hired Hucheshwar G. Mudgal, an Indian of Caribbean descent, as a contributor to the *Negro World* and *Daily Negro Times*. He also met with several prominent Indian Americans, including Lala Lajpat Rai and a young Gandhian graduate student, Haridas T. Muzumdar. In May 1922, Muzumdar discussed "Gandhi and the Future of India" at the UNIA's Liberty Hall and gave "an illustrated talk on India" the following week. On May 6, 1922, the *Negro World* published an article by Muzumdar entitled, "Gandhi the Apostle of Freedom."[73]

Beginning in the early 1920s, Garveyites began joining the Ahmadiyya movement, a religious community that had begun amongst Muslims in colonial India. Founded by Mirza Ghulam Ahmad, who declared himself to be the promised Mujaddid, or "reformer of the age," the Ahmadiyya movement came to be considered heretical by many Muslims. Despite resistance from other Muslims, the Ahmadiyya movement grew, and in 1920 Dr. Mufti Muhammad Sadiq, an Ahmadi missionary, arrived in Philadelphia to convert Americans to the Ahmadiyya's understanding of Islam. Sadiq was most successful in attracting African American converts. In cities like Detroit, Chicago, and Cleveland, the Ahmadiyya movement recruited many UNIA members, in part because of considerable institutional support between Ahmadis and the UNIA. In 1923, Sadiq gave five lectures at UNIA meetings in Detroit. Sadiq's successor as editor of the Ahmadiyya newspaper, *Moslem Sunrise*, reprinted pro-Muslim excerpts from the *Negro World*, which in turn printed his article "Has Christianity Failed and Has Islam Succeeded?"[74]

The growing popularity of Islam among African Americans created opportunities for connections with Indian American Muslims. But most Indian Americans were either Hindu or Sikh. And within the Indian American community there remained strong pressures to self-identify as white. In February 1921, the *Independent Hindustan* published a response to the infamous racist best seller *The Rising Tide of Color*. The response defended solidarities of color—such as the growing connections between Indians and African Americans—as "a menace to the exploiting imperialists of the white race, not the workers of the white race." But even while attacking racism and imperialism, the article rehashed the Aryan idea by declaring, "India has been the land of aryan culture and civilization long before the English gave up painting their bodies and wearing barks of the trees."[75]

Some Indian Americans refused to claim the privileges of whiteness. When a British official publicly stated, "I do not like black and yellow men," Har Dayal responded in the pages of *Ghadar*, "You do not like us and we do not like you. . . . Take your white carcass to your cold and barren country, and leave our land to us." Taraknath Das also rejected the idea of aligning India with the white world. In his speech at the national convention of the FFI, Das declared that the "freedom of all people is our ideal." Some argued that "a color conflict could be won by the white-skinned men, if the Indian people can be won to the side of the white men." Das rejected such an alliance. "Independent India will not be a tool," he declared, "for those capitalistic, imperialistic nations whose business it is to subject men of another color and creed."[76]

While Indian American leaders like Das spoke up against racism at home and abroad, African Americans continued to turn toward Gandhi for inspiration. In February 1929, Du Bois wrote Gandhi to ask for a message to the "twelve million people who are the grandchildren of slaves." "I know you are busy with your own problems," Du Bois added, "but the race and color problems are world-wide, and we need your help here." Gandhi responded on May 1, 1929, with what he called "a little love message" that Du Bois published in the *Crisis*:

Let not the 12 million Negroes be ashamed of the fact that they are the grand children of the slaves. There is no dishonour in being slaves. There is dishonour in being slaveowners. But let us not think of honour or dishonour in connection with the past. Let us realise that the future is with those who would be truthful, pure and loving. For, as the old wise men have said, truth ever is, untruth never was. Love alone binds and truth and love accrue only to the truly humble.

Gandhi repeated Du Bois's emphasis on slavery, while offering a distinctly Gandhian homily on truth, love, and humility. For the readers of the *Crisis,* Du Bois summarized the message of the Mahatma: "Agitation, nonviolence, refusal to cooperate with the oppressor, became Gandhi's watchword and with it he is leading all India to freedom. Here and today he stretches out his hand in fellowship to his colored friends of the West." While Gandhi meditated on truth and love, Du Bois framed the Mahatma as an antiracist radical. Their differences were more than a matter of style. At stake were larger questions concerning the struggle against racism, casteism, and other forms of inequality and discrimination. How can an oppressed group reclaim the history of that oppression? As Anupama Rao has written, "Dalit history traces the paradoxical manner in which an identity predicated on a future outside or beyond caste was conceived with historical humiliation and suffering as its enabling ground." Such a paradox marks African American history as well.[77]

Gandhi's salt march fueled a surge of interest in Gandhian methods among African Americans—an interest that extended beyond Gandhi's anti-imperialism to his relationship with caste. The African American press covered the salt march closely. An article in the *Chicago Defender* declared, "It is the consensus of opinion here that Gandhi will eventually play the part of Moses and lead all of the darker races from the wilderness of bondage into the light of freedom." By comparing Gandhi to Moses, the *Defender* revealed the religious lens through which many African Americans viewed Gandhi. A religiously motivated commitment to social change inspired several influential black theologians to travel to India to meet with Gandhi.[78]

In 1935, Reverend Howard Thurman and Sue Bailey Thurman traveled to South Asia on a "Pilgrimage of Friendship" funded by the Student Christian Movements of the United States and India. Dean of Rankin Chapel at Howard University, Reverend Thurman was one of America's most prominent African American theologians. Sue Bailey Thurman, a historian by training, had worked for several years on the staff of the Young Women's Christian Association (YWCA). The Thurmans were accompanied by another prominent African American family. Their journey to India would be closely followed in the African American press, in part because of the long history of comparisons between British imperialism and American racism. But the treatment the Thurmans received demonstrated that the "color bar" operated differently in the United States and India. At times, the Thurmans were treated as "Europeans." On their way to Calcutta, the Thurmans checked into a hotel only to discover that an Indian student traveling with them had been turned away because he was a "native."[79]

In February 1936, the Thurmans met Gandhi. Gandhi's secretary later confided to Thurman, "This is the first time in all the years that we have been working together that I've ever seen him come out to greet a visitor so warmly." In the conversation that followed, Gandhi asked probing questions about African American history and American racism. Thurman recalled, "Never in my life have I been a part of that kind of examination: persistent, pragmatic questions about American Negroes, about the course of slavery, and how we have survived it." Thurman remembered Gandhi asking about "voting rights, lynching, discrimination, public school education, the churches and how they functioned." After the meeting, Gandhi declared, "It may be through the Negroes that the unadulterated message of non-violence will be delivered to the world."[80]

When asked why British rule continued, Gandhi blamed untouchability for weakening the Indian cause. He described the segregation of Dalits in ways that left his African American visitors thinking of home. "He was striking close to home with this," Thurman recalled. Before he left for India, Thurman had written that as an African American he could "enter directly into informal understanding of the psychological climate" of India's lowest castes. The suffering of African Americans and Dalits did not "differ in principle and in inner pain." Asked how he envisioned ending caste oppression, Gandhi said that he had adopted a Dalit child and explained that he used the word *Harijan* to avoid the stigma associated with the word *untouchable*. Immodestly, he proclaimed, "I became the spearhead of a movement for the building of a new self-respect, a fresh self-image for the untouchables in Indian society." Importantly,

Gandhi emphasized "self-respect" rather than legal, political, and economic rights. While the Thurmans embraced Gandhi as an anticaste champion, not all African Americans supported Gandhi's approach to ending caste oppression.[81]

Benjamin Mays, the dean of the School of Religion at Howard University, was more critical of Gandhi's approach to caste. Mays traveled to India to attend the 1937 World's Conference of the YMCA. Like Howard Thurman, Mays denounced the racial oppression he witnessed in the Raj. "It is my firm conviction," Mays wrote, "that the British-Indian situation, though greatly aggravated and complicated on account of caste, is further complicated because the Indians are colored people and do not belong to the so-called 'white race.'" Mays described the Raj as "imperialism built on racialism." Like the Thurmans, Mays met with a variety of leading Indians, including Jawaharlal Nehru and Gandhi. Mays challenged Gandhi about the relevance of nonviolence for a minority struggling against an oppressive majority. Gandhi replied that "a minority can do much more in the way of non-violence than a majority." He offered as an example his own history in South Africa. Mays later wrote that Gandhi "did more than any other man to dispel fear from the Indian mind" and concluded, "When an oppressed race ceases to be afraid, it is free."[82]

His admiration for the Mahatma did not prevent Mays from challenging Gandhi's approach to caste. Mays asked Gandhi why he had chosen to attack untouchability but not caste more generally. Mays explained, "Gandhi made it clear to me that he was not fundamentally against caste. He believed in caste." According to Mays, Gandhi saw caste as "an economic necessity" that allowed a useful "division of labor." Mays rejected such a view of caste. He used his own interactions with Dalits to present a sharper critique of caste. In Mysore, the headmaster of a school for Dalits introduced Mays as "an untouchable who had achieved distinction." Mays remembered, "The headmaster told them that I had suffered at the hands of the white men in the United States every indignity that they suffered from the various castes in India and that I was proof that they, too, could be 'somebody worthwhile' despite the stigma of being members of a depressed class." Mays wrote, "At first I was horrified, puzzled, angry to be called an untouchable, but my indignation was short-lived as I realized, as never before, that I was truly an untouchable in my native land."[83]

The imperial white supremacy that coalesced across the globe in the nineteenth century inspired many to envision an equally global struggle against imperialism, racism, and "caste" in all its forms. Movements against imperialism and racism became bound up with other struggles in both India and the United States. Visions of freedom multiplied, expanded, and interacted. It would not be enough to end Jim Crow segregation if African Americans were relegated to the bottom of the economic pyramid. It would not be enough to gain Indian independence if Dalits remained oppressed. Democracy demanded more than grand promises that rang hollow at the core. The First World War had galvanized freedom struggles in both the United States and India, even while calling into question the meaning of freedom itself. It would take another war to again force the hard questions: When would true freedom come? And what would it look like when it arrived?

CHAPTER 4

# Cold Wars

∞

The Allied declaration that the Allies are fighting to
make the world safe for freedom of the individual and
for democracy sounds hollow so long as India and, for
that matter, Africa are exploited by Great Britain and
America has the Negro problem in her own home.
—Mahatma Gandhi to Franklin Delano Roosevelt,
July 1, 1942

O N MARCH 3, 1944, Private Herman Perry shot and killed Lieutenant
Harold Cady on a remote jungle road in the hills of northeastern
India. Both soldiers were in the United States Army. Perry was black and
Cady was white. Their bloody confrontation reveals the sharp divides of
a segregated army, divides that were both deepened and reconfigured
within the context of colonial India. At least two hundred thousand
American soldiers served in India during the Second World War. More
than twenty-two thousand were African American. In a war that was
supposed to be about defending freedom, black soldiers were relegated to
segregated units, paid less than white soldiers, and routinely subjected to
racial discrimination. Treated as second-class citizens at home, African
American men and women labored abroad as second-class soldiers.[1]

They were not alone. Indian soldiers during the Second World War also experienced segregation and discrimination while being told they were fighting to defend liberty. Indian civilians suffered as the nation's resources were siphoned away to support distant armies. Many Indian leaders spent the war in jail or actively struggling against British rule—whether through nonviolent combat or, in the case of the Indian National Army, through a more literal and bloody warfare. Like the African American soldiers who poured into Calcutta, the people of India embodied the hypocrisy of a war fought for freedom by people who were not free.

Herman Perry rebelled against the hypocrisy of the war. The harsh realities of daily life—rotten food, muddy camps crawling with leeches, endless days building roads through malarial jungles—were compounded by the injustice of racial discrimination and the arbitrary rule of imperious white officers. In small ways, Perry rebelled repeatedly. And he was punished repeatedly. Sentenced to ninety days in the stockade, Perry was forced to serve an additional two weeks without explanation. He was barely free when he was charged with yet another minor infraction. Facing imprisonment again, Perry fled camp on foot. It is unclear where he would have gone had Lieutenant Cady not come upon him on that isolated stretch of road. But after killing a white officer, Perry had no choice. He plunged into the jungle.

Stumbling through dense forest, Perry came upon a group of Naga tribesmen. Seen as uncivilized savages by colonial authorities, the Naga were under new pressures now that their ancestral lands were being traversed by multiple armies. They might have seen Perry as yet another foreign oppressor. But using hand gestures, Perry managed to explain himself and his situation, and the Naga welcomed him at their camp. Perry decided to make a new life among the Naga people. He married a Naga woman and had a son with her. "I intended to pass the remaining years of natural life in the jungles," Perry later explained, "and live with the Naga girl who I claim as my wife." But after word leaked out that a black man was living with the Naga, Perry was trapped, arrested, and chained to a log at a military prison in Ledo. He escaped and eluded a special team of military police for months before being recaptured. In the spring of 1945, Herman Perry was hung in India by order of the United States Army. He was twenty-two years old.[2]

Perry's story is unique. But many African American soldiers resisted injustice while forging solidarities with Indians. When a new Red Cross swimming pool in Calcutta was opened on a segregated basis, one black soldier wrote home that the "Master Race" had built a swimming pool while racially segregating its use. A group of African American soldiers organized a boycott. Such protests resonated with Indians who had themselves been denied entry to "European" clubs. In 1944, a confidential army intelligence report warned that "natives of India closely watch any indication of American discrimination against the Negro soldiers."[3]

On July 1, 1942, Mahatma Gandhi told Franklin Delano Roosevelt that "the Allied declaration that the Allies are fighting to make the world safe for freedom of the individual and for democracy sounds hollow so long as India and, for that matter, Africa are exploited by Great Britain and America has the Negro problem in her own home." Like Gandhi, many Indian leaders publicly connected the oppression of African Amer-

*Figure 4.* African American soldiers in Calcutta. Note the advertisement in the background for *Tarzan's New York Adventure.* Courtesy of the U.S. National Archives and Records Administration, College Park, Maryland.

icans to the subjugation of India. African American leaders used Indian opinion to pressure American officials, including President Roosevelt, to support racial equality in the United States. If Americans did not end Jim Crow, Indians would come to see the United States as yet another racist imperial power.[4]

American anxiety about Indian opinion was heightened by the Cold War. After 1947, the threat of losing India to the Communists helped pressure American presidents, Supreme Court justices, and diplomatic officials to counter America's image as a racist country. India's refusal to take sides in the Cold War, a policy that came to be called nonalignment, complicated Indo-American relations. Many Americans came to distrust Indian leaders and Indian policy. In 1954, in a dramatic blow to Indo-American relations, the United States forged a military agreement with Pakistan.[5]

Despite America's embrace of Pakistan, the United States and India did not completely severe ties. Both countries stood to gain from closer relations. American officials hoped that India could be lured away from the influence of the Soviets. And India became increasingly dependent on American aid. That dependence limited the degree to which Indian officials would interfere in what they saw as American domestic affairs, including the struggle against American racism. But even as Indian officials remained muted in their support for civil rights in the United States, African Americans drew upon the legacy of Gandhi to launch a massive wave of nonviolent civil disobedience.[6]

Before Indian independence, before the civil rights movement, African American soldiers and Indian civilians developed their own form of Indo-American relations. Indians did not always see "colored troops" as allies in the struggle against imperialism. American soldiers—white and black—were paid more than their Indian counterparts and vastly more than most Indian civilians. Colonial India had always been defined by inequality, but the sudden arrival of two hundred thousand American soldiers created a new class of privileged elites at a time when many Indians had plunged even further into poverty. The buildup of American troops coincided with one of the worst famines in the history of India, a mass starvation that killed millions. Even those Indians who were protected from starvation suffered as a result of wartime shortages. In the city of Calcutta, where most American soldiers spent time, conflicts between Indians and Americans became commonplace. Many were petty disputes over money, sex, and booze. But there was an additional anxiety that influenced how Indians viewed the Americans in their midst. When the war was over, even if the British were forced to abandon the Raj, would the Americans take their place?

## The Calcutta Key

In December 1944, an American Army newspaper, the *CBI Roundup*, published a poem by Sergeant Elwood Jones:

> "Indian Phonograph"
> An Indian song on a phonograph I heard
> Halted my shadow on the moonlit ground
> I understood the theme, yet not a word,
> As I passed the hut that could not cage the sound.
>
> Wandering fire-flies glimmered here and there
> As the Indian girl's recorded voice rang out
> Along the silver reaches of the air.
> And I knew the ageless theme she sang about.
> For the heart translates the language of a tune.
>
> As I caught her plaintive, lifting melody
> I looked at the silent disc we call the moon
> And I heard the music of a memory.

By celebrating the power of music to transcend the borders of language and culture, Sergeant Jones framed the American military presence in India as an opportunity for cross-cultural appreciation. He demonstrated a respect for Indian culture that military authorities actively cultivated. If American soldiers were disrespectful, they might threaten not only the immediate war effort, but also the future of American relations with soon-to-be independent India. Not every American solider was inspired by the beauty of Indian music to break into verse. But for the first time, the American state actively cultivated pro-India sentiment.[7]

When it came to relations between Indian civilians and American soldiers, Calcutta was ground zero. Significant numbers of American soldiers worked in the port cities of western India, particular Bombay and Karachi. But the majority were concentrated in Bengal and Assam, where they built roads into Burma and supplied the planes that flew provisions "over the hump" into China. With so many Americans stationed in northeast India, Calcutta filled with GIs. The army prevented soldiers from exploring all of the city. Indeed, more than half of Calcutta was off limits to the Americans. The "in-bounds" area stretched south of Bow Bazar Street and west of Lower Circular Road, and was marked by large signs warning Americans to stay within bounds. The army hoped to keep Americans in areas where they were less likely to find or cause trouble. But army leaders knew that spatial segregation would not be enough to prevent American soldiers from getting into dangerous situations. The soldiers themselves had to be taught to behave as ambassadors for their nation. Toward that end, the army produced a remarkable pamphlet entitled *The Calcutta Key*.

*The Calcutta Key* was designed to introduce American soldiers to the city and to keep them from getting into trouble. The army assumed that danger was everywhere, often in female form. "As in any port city in the Orient," the *Key* declared, "Calcutta is riddled with venereal diseases. Studies show that professional prostitutes are 150% infected (half have one and the other half have two)." Reproducing stereotypes of the dangerous Oriental woman, the *Key* ignored the economic distress that forced some Indian women to survive through prostitution. Soldiers were told to focus on their own health, either by abstaining from sex or by visiting one of several dispensaries that offered condoms. In its approach to sex, as with many issues, the *Key* remained silent on the social, political, and economic inequalities of colonial India as well as the ways the United States military exacerbated that inequality.[8]

Soldiers were actively discouraged from discussing politics. In a list of ten recommendations, the first was categorical: "Avoid political discussions." At a time of profound social transformation, when political rebellion convulsed much of India, it proved difficult to convince American soldiers to avoid politics. It was an especially difficult task given that the *Key* encouraged solidarity with the residents of Calcutta and the legions of poor people flooding the city in the midst of the war. In a section entitled "The Laboring Man," soldiers were asked, "Who is he, that somewhat dirty, ill-clothed fellow, that sweating fellow, who hauls you to your destination in a rickshaw, the amazing individual who lugs a load of you-name-it-he'll-carry-it in a basket on his head?" After explaining that many laborers were migrants from Bihar driven into the city "by the famine, by flood, drought, or other causes," the *Key* offered a Dickensian description of human suffering: "Homeless, helpless, hopeless when they reach Calcutta, they fare as men have always fared, in that the able-bodied and the strong among them as usual survive and soon find their way into the immense labor corps around the city—the rest, they soon vanish—some die in the epidemics, others just disappear." The phrase "as men have always fared" positioned the famine as timeless and natural. Nowhere does the *Key* explore the relationship between the famine and the requisitioning of grain for the war, the callousness of the imperial government, or the endemic poverty solidified by generations of colonial rule. Millions would die in the Bengal famine at the height of the American presence in India. The *Key* is remarkably silent on the origins of that mass death. That silence extended from the brutality of colonial rule to the severity of injustice within Indian society. For example, the *Key* assured GIs that "the shackles of caste are slowly but surely falling away." Yet despite its blindness to colonialism and other forms of structural inequality, the *Key* taught its readers to see Indians as human beings and not just strange curiosities or threatening foreigners.[9]

The *Key* argued that American soldiers should respect Indians as allies. Of bearded Sikhs, the *Key* had this to say: "Fierce-looking fellow, isn't he? As a matter of fact he is quite a warrior, as more than one Axis foe has unwillingly learned." In addition to celebrating Indians as allies in the war, the *Key* argued that respect for Indian cultures and traditions was the only way to prevent another war. In a section on "relations with our allies," soldiers were told, "The only way to avoid future wars, and also to end this one more quickly, is to establish good relations between nations." Thus, the *Key* drove home its central message: that the future of Indo-American relations was in the hands of American soldiers. The *Key* ignored the vast discrepancy between the influence of those soldiers and that of the elite powerbrokers who debated India's future in London, Delhi, and Washington.[10]

In April 1942, Jawaharlal Nehru wrote Franklin Roosevelt to ask for American support for Indian independence. In exchange, Nehru offered assistance in the fight against fascism. Five years later, Nehru would become India's first prime minister and Roosevelt would be dead. But in 1942, Roosevelt was one of the world's most powerful men. Nehru reassured Roosevelt that the "sympathies" of India and of the Indian National Congress were strongly "with the forces fighting against fascism and for democracy and freedom." "With freedom in our own country," he continued, "those sympathies could have been translated into dynamic action." The implication was clear. If the United States would pressure the British to give India its freedom, the new Indian government could mobilize its people and resources to support the Allied cause.[11]

As American soldiers poured into India, the American government struggled to understand a country long considered marginal to American foreign policy. Government officials turned to Indophiles like W. Norman Brown, a professor of Sanskrit at the University of Pennsylvania, whose father had served in India as a missionary. Brown was tasked with heading the Indian division of the Office of Strategic Services, the predecessor of the CIA. He hired other scholars of India to advise policymakers on how to prevent Indian opinion from turning against America and American soldiers.[12]

The leaders of the Indian National Congress knew that the Americans worried about the welcome their troops would receive in India. A few months after Nehru wrote Roosevelt, Gandhi also sent a note to the American president. Gandhi assured Roosevelt that he was "a friend and well wisher of the Allies." He pledged that "the Allied troops will remain in India during the war under treaty with the Free India Government that may be formed by the people of India without any outside interference." The Americans need not worry about their troops in an independent India. But if India remained under colonial rule and the Indian National Congress was forced to launch a massive civil disobedience campaign, who knew what might happen to the American war effort?[13]

If Nehru and Gandhi had been alone in lobbying Roosevelt, it is unlikely their appeals would have borne fruit. The British were a vital ally, and Roosevelt did not want to complicate such an important relationship. But when it came to encouraging American support for Indian independence, the Indian National Congress was far from alone. Within the United States, a robust campaign was underway to convince Roosevelt to support Indian independence. At the center of that campaign was a Punjabi-American businessman named Jagjit (J. J.) Singh. Cleanshaven and partial to Western suits, Singh was a disarming face for an Indian American community still seen by many Americans as racially and culturally foreign. He was also an effective organizer. Over the course of the 1930s, Singh emerged as one of the most prominent and politically savvy Indian American leaders. His organization, the India League of America, lobbied for Indian independence and the civil rights of Indian Americans, especially the rights to citizenship and immigration that Indians had lost in 1923 as a result of the *Thind* decision. Those rights were also pursued by the Indian Welfare League, an organization founded in 1937 by Mubarak Ali Khan, an Indian American farmer based in Arizona. Singh, Khan, and other Indian American leaders did not always work together—but collectively they helped forge what has been called the "India lobby," a diverse group of activists and organizations that acted to convince Americans to support Indian independence.[14]

The India lobby benefited from a dramatic change in how Americans viewed the political situation in India. In the nineteenth century, many Americans embraced British rule as a pillar of Anglo-Saxon dominance. But over the course of the 1920s and 1930s, many Americans came to support Indian independence. Organizations like the India Home Rule League and the Friends of Freedom for India had created important networks of support for Indian freedom. Gandhi's growing popularity further swelled the ranks of the India lobby. And American Indophiles did their part as well. In 1930, Will Durant, the popular philosopher and historian, published *The Case for India*. He declared, "The British conquest of India was the destruction of a high civilization by a trading company utterly without scruple or principal." Durant's emphasis on Indian civilization was significant. The strength of the India lobby drew on American interest in Indian culture. India's freedom was an obvious good to Americans like Vida Scudder, a prominent social activist and pacifist, born in India to missionary parents, who celebrated in her memoir the "contemplative wisdom" of the Bhagavad Gita. Whereas figures like Emerson and Thoreau had praised Indian culture while ignoring British oppression, many Americans were coming to embrace both Indian culture and Indian independence.[15]

Perhaps the most influential American Indophile was the renowned novelist Pearl Buck. In March 1942, Buck wrote Eleanor Roosevelt with a warning. If India was not granted its freedom, the anger of the Indian people might yield "revengeful massacres against all white people." FDR read the letter and saved it, despite the fact that Buck had asked for it to be destroyed. In addition to sending private messages to the White House,

Buck advocated publicly for Indian independence, and was offered the honorary copresidency of the India League of America. As a prominent writer, she modeled how other intellectuals could use their pens to support India's freedom. The journalist John Gunther wrote on behalf of Indian independence in his best-selling book *Inside Asia*. And the influential editor of *Time* and *Life* magazines, Henry Luce, offered support to the anticolonial cause. In August 1942, *Time* published a supportive cover of "India's Nehru."[16]

Several members of Congress took up the cause of India's freedom. In 1941, Senator Bob Reynolds of North Carolina read aloud in Congress from a newspaper editorial that declared that India was being held "probably against the will of a majority of its people, and certainly against the will of the followers of Mahatma Gandhi." Reynolds was a notorious isolationist with distinctly anti-Semitic and profascist leanings. But there were more sympathetic voices in support of Indian freedom. One of India's most determined friends in Washington was Congressmen Emanuel Celler who, in his words, cared "passionately" about India's independence. "India must march with the free nations of the world," Celler declared. Equally supportive of Indian independence was Clare Booth Luce, the wife of Henry Luce. Clare Booth Luce worked closely with the India League and J. J. Singh before and after being elected to Congress in 1942. That same year, a representative from Michigan supported a bill that would "provide for the recognition by the United States Government of the National Government of India." And Senators Theodore Green of Rhode Island and George Norris from Nebraska wrote Roosevelt to express their support for India's cause. Wendell Willkie, the Republican presidential candidate in 1940, declared that American ambivalence in India left "millions of Eastern peoples" unsure "whether we really do stand for freedom, or what we mean by freedom."[17]

In the face of broad support for India's freedom, Roosevelt might have publicly embraced Indian independence if not for the opposition of Winston Churchill. A diehard imperialist, Churchill was adamantly opposed to freeing India from colonial rule. As he explained it, the "political, social, racial, and religious conditions of the country in which they live" made it "preposterous" that Indians could create a democracy. Churchill's opposition left Roosevelt in the difficult position of navigating between his most important ally in the war and the powerful pro-India lobby within the United States. That middle course became increasingly treacherous as American troops poured into India and the Indian political situation deteriorated in the spring of 1942.[18]

In April 1942, Roosevelt sent Louis Johnson to India as his personal representative. A former Assistant Secretary of War, Johnson was charged with assessing the preparations for a major increase in American troops. But he also had a more political task—to foster an accord between the British and the Indian National Congress, and thus mobilize more of India's resources for the war. Johnson arrived in India a few days after Sir Stafford Cripps, a high-ranking British official and a personal friend of Nehru. Cripps was eager to make a deal with the Congress. But with Churchill opposed, Cripps found it difficult to create a workable accord. As the Cripps mission ran into trouble, Johnson felt increasing sympathy for the Indian cause. Nehru, Cripps, and Johnson worked together to craft an agreement that would grant real autonomy to India, while guaranteeing Indian support for the war against the Axis.

Roosevelt had good reasons to support Johnson's efforts. Intelligence reports prepared in January 1942 had argued that the United States should "help India unite behind the war and behind a democratic peace." India's support was crucial to the war effort. Moreover, British colonialism in India had become a disgrace to the Allied cause even beyond the subcontinent. The head of the Office of Strategic Services forwarded Roosevelt a letter from the Indian American author Krishnalal Shridharani. For countries throughout Asia, Shridharani warned, India had "become the acid test of the Allied bona fides."[19]

Even before Johnson arrived in India, Roosevelt had pressured Churchill to grant greater freedom to India. On the eve of the Cripps mission, Roosevelt sent a cable to Churchill suggesting a "temporary dominion government" for India. "It is, strictly speaking, none of my business," Roosevelt wrote, "except insofar as it is a part and parcel of the successful fight that you and I are waging." In a strange historical reference, Roosevelt suggested that "perhaps the analogy of some such method to the travails and problems of the U.S. between 1783 and 1789 might give a new slant in India itself." It is unclear why Roosevelt thought a reference to the aftermath of the American Revolution would reassure a dedicated imperialist like Churchill. In any case, Roosevelt's intention was never to force Churchill to concede Indian autonomy. Harry Hopkins, one of Roosevelt's most trusted advisors and his unofficial representative in London, told Churchill that Johnson did not represent FDR. That made it easy for Churchill to scuttle the agreement designed by Cripps, Johnson, and Nehru. After the Cripps mission failed, Roosevelt chastised Churchill for his reluctance to "concede to the Indians the right of self-government." But Roosevelt's intervention, toothless and ill-timed, did nothing to accelerate India's path toward freedom.[20]

On August 8, 1942, the All India Congress Committee called for widespread civil disobedience. Throughout the country, Indians purposefully disobeyed laws and were imprisoned in large numbers. The last major civil disobedience movement in the colonial era, the Quit India Movement, had begun. The British responded by arresting Congress leaders and clamping down on all forms of protest. Meanwhile, American troops continued to arrive in India, and the war raged ever closer.

Unwilling to abandon India to Churchill's unyielding imperialism, FDR sent a new representative to the subcontinent. William Phillips was a distinguished diplomat with decades of experience. Twice undersecretary of state, Phillips had also served as ambassador to Belgium, Italy, and Canada, and as the London chief of the Office of Strategic Services. Phillips had outstanding credentials. But he lacked knowledge of India. Before he left London for New Delhi, Phillips met with dozens of government officials, businessmen, and political figures. Most were British and strongly pro-empire. The most prominent exception was V. K. Krishna Menon, the head of the India League, and one of the most vocal anticolonial figures in London. Even as Phillips deepened his understanding of the situation in India, he remained unclear about how the State Department and President Roosevelt understood America's role in India. In November 1942, just before he left London for India, Phillips received a telegram from Secretary of State Cordell Hull. Hull explained that the United States wanted "freedom for all dependent peoples at the earliest date practicable." Phillips should "in a friendly spirit talk bluntly and earnestly" with colonial officials in India. But he should avoid "objectionable pressure." It remained unclear how Phillips was supposed to avoid being objectionable while pursuing a goal that was anathema to most colonial authorities.[21]

British officials were pleased at first with how Phillips conducted himself in India. The viceroy reported that Phillips "seems to me better really than anything we could reasonably have hoped for." It was "impossible to imagine a greater contrast to Johnson." But such rosy impressions of the new American quickly faded after Phillips told the viceroy that the

British needed to do more to win the support of Indians. When Phillips toured the country, he demanded to meet with a variety of Indians, several of whom were openly critical of the Raj. Especially significant for Phillips was a conversation with Lala Dunichand Ambalvi, an imprisoned anticolonial activist who prepared a special memo defending the cause of India's freedom.[22]

In March 1943, Phillips wrote FDR to suggest an assembly in India "presided over by an American who could exercise influence in harmonizing the endless divisions of caste religion, race and political views." A few months later, Phillips again wrote Roosevelt. "If we do nothing," he warned, "and merely accept the British point of view that conditions in India are none of our business then we must be prepared for various serious consequences in the internal situation in India which may develop as a result of despair and misery and anti-white sentiments of hundreds of millions of subject people." Such instability could directly threaten American military objectives. Phillips made clear what was at stake: "Assuming that India is bound to be an important base for our future operations against Burma and Japan, it would seem to me of highest importance that we should have around us a sympathetic India rather than an indifferent and possibly a hostile India."[23]

Despite the pleas of Louis Johnson and William Phillips, Roosevelt remained unwilling to force Churchill to free India. It would be Indian resistance, British exhaustion, and the war itself that would make Indian independence inevitable. But the American role in the endgame of the British Raj should not be underestimated. American leaders could have actively supported British rule in India as they would the French in Vietnam. Roosevelt felt constrained by the need to work closely with Churchill, but he refused to use American resources to prop up the Raj.[24]

Roosevelt hoped to maintain Indian goodwill. But would Roosevelt's tepid support for Indian independence mitigate the damage American racism caused to Indo-American relations? In January 1943, John Davies, political aide to the commanding general of the China-India-Burma theater of the war, finished an extensive report detailing his meetings with a variety of Indian public figures. Davies found that an awareness of global racial inequality united many Indian leaders and contributed to their distrust of the United States. Dr. Ambedkar, the renowned Dalit leader, was "fully conscious of the color issue and resentful on that score." Pothan Joseph, the editor of the Muslim League's weekly publication

*Dawn,* "mentioned with fierce resentment white domination of the colored peoples of the world." Davies warned that "insofar as color is identified with a condition of economic and political servitude, it can be a powerful emotional factor contributing to a future war."[25]

African American activists used Indian opinion to link the struggle against fascism abroad to the fight against American racism. If American leaders ignored racial inequality, Indians might see the United States as yet another racist imperial power. But would the plight of African Americans influence the way Indian leaders viewed the United States? American State Department officials argued that prejudice against dark skin would prevent Indians from sympathizing with black Americans. Undersecretary of State Sumner Welles wrote Roosevelt that Indian concerns about American racism would be limited "on account of well-recognized racial prejudices on the part of Indian leaders themselves." "Indians, despite their dark complexion," Welles told the president, "do not regard Negroes as their equals." Old analogies between race and caste resurfaced, as NAACP leader Walter White complained that the State Department believed that the "people of India consider American Negroes to be in the same class with India's untouchables."[26]

Color prejudice had deep roots in India. But since the First World War, many prominent Indians had come to see African Americans as partners in a common struggle against white oppression. The Second World War deepened such solidarities. In August 1942, one day before the launch of the Quit India Movement, Gandhi linked American racism to British imperialism. "I do not regard England, or for that matter America, as free countries," he declared. "They are free after their own fashion, free to hold in bondage the coloured races of the earth."[27]

By referencing the "coloured races," Gandhi evoked the colored cosmopolitanism championed by African American activists like Du Bois. During the war, a range of Indian figures advanced their own versions of colored solidarity. In the spring of 1941, Kamaladevi Chattopadhyay repeatedly embraced colored unity during her travels across the American South. Indian Americans also expressed sympathy with the struggles of African Americans. In the spring of 1943, Taraknath Das spoke to a congressional panel about America's "double standards of international morality." Das underscored the hypocrisy of American racial discrimination in the midst of a war against fascism. "Since the American people declared that they did not believe the superior race theory of the

Nazis," Das proclaimed, "there should be no discrimination against any individual because of race, creed or country of origin."[28]

While Indian and Indian American activists supported African American struggles, African American activists championed India's independence. Writing in the *Chicago Defender* in January 1943, Langston Hughes stated, "Now is when all the conquered nations of Europe are asking for freedom. Now is when the Jews are asking for it. Now is when America is fighting to keep it. Now is when Nehru and Gandhi are sitting in jail silently demanding it for India." On February 10, 1943, Gandhi began a three-week fast while imprisoned. Hughes responded with a poem that compared British imperialism and American racism.[29]

No one championed the link between imperialism and racism more effectively than Walter White. As the executive director of the NAACP, White built ties with J. J. Singh and the India League of America. Together, White and Singh lobbied for Indian independence and the civil rights of Indian Americans and African Americans. When Gandhi's son, Devadas, came to America, Singh connected him with White. Devadas was the editor of the influential *Hindustan Times*. White introduced him to the publishers of the three most prominent African American newspapers, facilitating a stream of articles that the African American press published in support of Indian independence.[30]

While White supported Indian independence, leading Indians made clear their opposition to American racism. Vijaya Lakshmi Pandit, Nehru's sister and a prominent Indian diplomat, publicly denounced Jim Crow segregation in 1945. Invited to speak at Baltimore's Lyric Theater, Pandit refused until the segregated space was opened to African Americans. "The happiest moments I have spent in America," Pandit remarked, "were those when I was at dinner in Harlem. I felt that I was at last with my own." Told that "she would injure India's cause if she identified it with the Negro's struggle for freedom," Pandit replied, "I am colored myself and so are my people."[31] Would such antiracist colored solidarity persist after India gained independence?

On August 15, 1947, India threw off the British yoke and emerged on the world stage a free country. That achievement was marred by the persistence of extreme poverty, the inequalities of caste and class, and above all by the division of British India into two antagonistic nations: India and Pakistan. The partition of British India, and the violence that accompanied partition, played a central role in how many Americans viewed that dramatic moment in the history of the subcontinent. "India and Pakistan Become Nations; Clashes Continue," the *New York Times* declared on its cover. The article recognized the achievement of Indian independence, and quoted Nehru's famous words, "At the stroke of the midnight hour when the world sleeps, India will awake to life and freedom." But even while acknowledging the success of the Indian independence struggle, the *Times* focused on the uncertainty surrounding partition. The *Chicago Daily Tribune* offered a similarly mixed assessment in an article entitled, "Mountbatten New Governor of Hindu India; Punjab Riots Rage On; 250 Dead." The *Washington Post* offered a more upbeat headline: "India Achieves Sovereignty Amid Scenes of Wild Rejoicing." But it was the Indian American community that, not surprisingly, viewed Indian independence with the greatest excitement. The Indian Students' Association at the University of Washington printed a greeting card that declared, "Sincerest Greetings on this historic day, August 15th, 1947—India's Independence Day! At the dawn of this new era, let us all resolve to build a better India, stronger India and a prosperous India! Jai Hind." In Hawaii, a department store run by a prominent Indian American family was decorated to celebrate Indian independence. In the store's display window, a sign proclaimed, "To Celebrate India's Independence, August 15, 1947—Friday, The Watumull Store Extends Open House, Refreshments Served, 10% Discount On All Purchases, Entire Proceeds of Today's Business Will Be Donated to Indian Charities."[32]

African Americans also celebrated Indian independence—and wondered what it might mean for them. W. E. B. Du Bois called August 15 "the greatest historical date of the nineteenth and twentieth centuries." His explanation deserves quoting in full:

This is saying a great deal, when we remember that in the nineteenth century, Napoleon was overthrown, democracy established in England, Negro slaves emancipated in the United States, the German Empire founded, the partition of Africa determined upon, the Russian Revolution carried through, and two world wars fought. Nevertheless, It is true that the fifteenth of August marks an event of even greater significance than any of these; for on that date four hundred million colored folk of Asia were loosed from the domination of the white people of Europe.

Du Bois wrote these words in the *Crisis*. Other African American peri-
odicals covered Indian independence with equal enthusiasm. "A Dream
Comes True in India," declared the *Pittsburgh Courier*. Readers learned
that "subjugated, exploited and oppressed colonial peoples everywhere
took heart on Aug. 15 when, after 200 years, the British Government
gave India its freedom in a move unprecedented in history." "Colored
Races Hail India's New Freedom," proclaimed the cover page of the *Chicago Defender*. In an editorial in the *Defender*, Walter White wrote, "the
cause of the colored peoples everywhere has been advanced by what has
happened in India."[33]

Would Indian independence advance the cause of racial equality
within the United States? Much depended on the words and actions of
India's new leaders, especially Jawaharlal Nehru. During Nehru's trip
to the United States in 1949, the State Department limited his interactions with African Americans. He responded by prolonging his stay so
that he could attend a private meeting in New York with a range of prominent civil rights advocates. Nehru accepted a life membership in the
NAACP and toured Harlem. Such gestures were widely reported in the
black press. But Nehru was unwilling to voice his support for civil rights
in any way that might jeopardize Indo-American relations. According
to the Associated Negro Press, Nehru "said he felt it would have been
highly improper for him to come into another country, especially on an
official visit and venture to criticize the internal policies of that country."[34]

Even before independence, there were signs that Indian leaders would
rather work around American racism than directly confront it. In 1942,
J. J. Singh wrote Nehru, "In sending the representatives of India to the
United States, it may be borne in mind that they should not be of too
dark a complexion, because we have the Negro problem in this country."
In January 1947, Nehru sent a secret note to the first Indian ambassadors
to the United States and China. "In the U.S.A. there is the Negro problem,"
Nehru wrote. "Our sympathies are entirely with the Negroes." Nehru
added, however, that representatives of India should "avoid any public
expression of opinion which might prove embarrassing or distasteful to
the Government or people of the country where they serve." How
could Indian ambassadors avoid embarrassing the American government without betraying India's long-standing opposition to racism?[35]

While Indian leaders prioritized diplomacy above antiracist solidarities, they were not entirely silent in the face of American racism. Their

criticisms of American racism, though muted, were amplified in importance by India's strategic significance in the midst of a new global conflict. The Second World War led Americans to worry about Indian opinion, but it was the Cold War that charged those worries with urgency. Nehru's effort to chart a middle course between American and Soviet influence meant that American policymakers were especially sensitive to Indian opinion. But even while investing Indian opinion with greater significance, the Cold War threatened to rupture Indo-American relations—to turn the United States and India from ambivalent friends into unequivocal enemies.

## True Independence

In 1953, the Senate Fact-Finding Committee on Un-American Activities in California probed the connection between the Ghadar movement and international communism. The committee's report branded Ghadar "a conspiratorial, highly disciplined group that was fanatically dedicated to rid India of imperialist domination." Without explaining what was "fanatic" about seeking the end of "imperialist domination," the report made clear its real argument: that Ghadar fit "perfectly with Russia's postwar plans for the Communizing of Asia" and had been infiltrated by "some highly indoctrinated Communists." One year after the committee published its report, the United States signed a military agreement with Pakistan, profoundly complicating American relations with India. Like the persecution of Indian American radicals in California, the military pact between the United States and Pakistan reveals the impact of anticommunism on American society. It was the Cold War that drove American politicians to reassess the communist impact on Ghadar. And it was the Cold War that pushed American policymakers toward a military alliance with Pakistan. For decades, the Cold War fundamentally shaped Indo-American relations, simultaneously advancing, narrowing, and complicating the quest for democracy in both countries.[36]

In October 1949, Jawaharlal Nehru told a joint session of the United States Congress that India's independence was incomplete. "We have achieved political freedom but our revolution is not yet complete and is still in progress," Nehru explained, "for political freedom without the assurance of the right to live and to pursue happiness, which economic progress alone can bring, can never satisfy a people." Although India faced many challenges, ending poverty was Nehru's chief priority. "Our immediate task is to raise the living standards of our people," he declared, "to remove all that comes in the way of the economic growth of the nation." Nehru's focus on growth appealed to American legislators concerned about India's flirtation with the Soviet Union. But Nehru was not entirely reassuring. After decrying "the low standard of living of the masses," he stressed the importance of land reform, which he called the "major problem of India." American history offered more than one example of land reform contributing to democracy. But in the hypercharged climate of the early Cold War, any mention of land reform risked igniting anticommunist outrage. Was Nehru veering toward the kind of economic redistribution favored by the Soviet Union?[37]

Nehru had long been critical of American capitalism and American foreign policy. In 1945, he told the American consul in Calcutta that "it was all very well to talk about the War of Independence and anticolonial traditions, but America itself had for a long time been an imperialist power." Nehru mentioned, as examples, that the United States was actively helping the French and Dutch maintain their empires. Nehru's opinions of America were shaped by his American friends, many of whom were on the left of the political spectrum. Roger Baldwin, for example, the founder of the ACLU, became an important influence on Nehru's thinking about the United States. Nehru met Baldwin in 1927 at the Brussels Congress Against Imperialism. In 1931, Baldwin wrote Nehru that "independence itself means little if the exploitation of the peasants and workers is to continue unchanged." He encouraged Nehru to champion not just a "political revolution" but also "a far-reaching program of land and industrial reform." Like Baldwin, Paul Robeson helped pull Nehru toward the left and a sharp critique of American inequality. A renowned African American singer, actor, and activist, Robeson was also a committed communist. He and Nehru became close friends, although their friendship rose and fell in relation to India's position in the shifting geopolitics of the Cold War.[38]

Despite his criticisms of the United States and his admiration for the Soviet Union, Nehru strove to find a middle ground between the two superpowers. He admired the economic policies of the Soviet Union but simultaneously prized the political freedoms of the United States. In 1946, Nehru wrote Vijaya Lakshmi Pandit that "we have to be on friendly terms with both Russia and America." "Personally," Nehru explained, "I think that in this worldwide tug-of-war there is on the whole more reason on the side of Russia." But, he added, "not always of course." That same year, Nehru told Asaf Ali, the Indian ambassador to the United States, that America was "a great power" and that India needed "to be friendly" with the United States "for many reasons." Still, Nehru made clear, "I should like to make it clear that we do not propose to be subservient to anybody."[39]

What did it mean for India to not "be subservient to anybody"? Nehru labeled such a principled neutrality "nonalignment," but left vague what nonalignment would entail for Indian foreign policy. In a speech at Columbia University in 1949, Nehru defined the "main objective" of Indian foreign policy as "the pursuit of peace, not through alignment with any major power or group of powers, but through an independent approach to each controversial or disputed issue, the liberation of subject peoples, the maintenance of freedom both national and individual; the elimination of racial discrimination; and the elimination of want, disease and ignorance." Nonalignment did not mean passivity. "Where freedom is menaced or justice threatened or where aggression takes place," Nehru declared, "we cannot be and shall not be neutral."[40]

Only two weeks earlier, the emergence of the People's Republic of China made all of Asia seem, from the perspective of Washington, at risk of "falling" into communism. Nehru's decision to recognize the People's Republic deepened American concerns about the future of Indo-American relations. The following year, the outbreak of war in Korea made Asia even more important in American eyes. Yet again, Indian neutrality irked American leaders. In July of that year, Nehru dispatched identical notes to Stalin and Secretary of State Dean Acheson outlining potential steps to peace in Korea. Nehru understood his efforts as nonalignment at its best. By refusing to take sides in the Cold War, India could help create a path toward a lasting peace.[41]

Nehru explained nonalignment by citing American history. "Having achieved independence by breaking off from the British Empire," the United States "avoided being involved in the chaotic situation of Europe." "For a country that has newly attained freedom," Nehru concluded, such a cautious neutrality "is the natural policy to pursue." American leaders did not agree. After returning from his trip to America in 1949, Nehru sent a letter to his chief ministers. "Americans had gone out to welcome me and I am grateful to them for it," he wrote. "But they expected more than gratitude and goodwill and that more I could not supply them."[42]

India's nonalignment alienated American policymakers who saw the Cold War as a battle between good and evil. Secretary of State John Foster Dulles deemed India's stance "obsolete" and "immoral." Vice President Richard Nixon visited India in 1953 and similarly came to view nonalignment as a morally bankrupt isolationism. While attacking nonalignment as a policy, some Americans blamed Nehru's personality for the chill in Indo-American relations. George McGhee, the assistant secretary of state, later wrote, "Nehru came to America with a chip on his shoulder toward high American officials, who he appeared to believe could not possibly understand someone with his background." Many

*Figure 5.* Truman and Nehru shake hands. Also featured is Nehru's daughter and the future prime minister, Indira Gandhi, as well as Nehru's sister and the first Indian ambassador to the United States, Vijaya Lakshmi Pandit. Abbie Rowe, National Park Service, Accession Number 73-3160, Harry S. Truman Library & Museum, Independence, Missouri. Courtesy of the U.S. National Archives and Records Administration.

American leaders were deeply ambivalent about Nehru. In a memo, Secretary of State Dean Acheson said that Nehru was "so important to all of us, that if he did not exist—as Voltaire said of God—he would have to be invented." But in his memoir, Acheson called Nehru "one of the most difficult men with whom I have ever had to deal." John F. Kennedy complained that Nehru's visit was "the worst head-of-state visit I have had."[43]

Nehru's standing among Americans was not helped by his relationship with V. K. Krishna Menon, the Indian figure Americans most loved to hate. Known for his acerbic personality and fierce opposition to imperialism, Menon embodied the left wing of the Indian National Congress. A close friend of Nehru, Menon served the government in a variety of roles, including defense minister. As the historian Paul McGarr has chronicled, State Department officials labeled Menon "venomous," "violently anti-American," and "a tough, poisonous bastard." American newspapers portrayed Menon as "devious," "insufferably arrogant," and "probably the most widely disliked man in India." In February 1962, *Time* magazine published a cover image of Menon, a menacing frown across his face—behind him, a cobra and a snake charmer's flute.[44]

In addition to such orientalist tropes, gender stereotypes also influenced how Americans viewed India and Indian foreign policy. As historian Andrew Rotter has demonstrated, Americans regularly portrayed Indian leaders as weak and effeminate, whereas Pakistanis were associated with manly courage and rectitude. These stereotypes built on older narratives employed by the British, as well as on common American perceptions of Hinduism and Islam.[45]

Pakistan's "manly" commitment to anticommunism attracted increasing American support. In December 1947, the prominent Pakistani leader Malik Feroz Khan Noon issued a public appeal to Harry Truman. Noon promised Truman that Pakistan would never become "communistic" and went so far as to describe Pakistan as the "Eastern bastion" against communism. Would such assurances lead the United States to favor Pakistan over India? During his visit to America in 1949, Nehru was sensitive to Washington's increasingly friendly relations with Islamabad. "The Americans are either very naïve or singularly lacking in intelligence," he declared. "They go through the same routine whether it is Nehru or the Shah or Liaquat Ali." Liaquat Ali Khan, the prime minister of Pakistan, had arrived in America shortly after Nehru. Khan was received warmly—too warmly, as Nehru saw it. Nehru wrote his sister, "It does appear that there is a concerted attempt to build up Pakistan and build down, if I may say, India."[46]

Nehru's worries were justified when, in February 1954, Eisenhower announced a major military aid agreement with Pakistan. Eisenhower wrote Nehru that he would prevent the aid from being "misused." Nehru was understandably skeptical, as were many American supporters of India. The renowned public intellectual Walter Lippmann denounced the deal. He wrote, "We have alienated India and Afghanistan by our meddling and we have not made secure the adherence of Pakistan." In 1959, Senator Albert Gore challenged General Thomas D. White, the chief of staff of the United States Air Force, "whether it was not a fact that Pakistanis really wanted military aid against India." General White responded with a banal generality: "The forces that we are supporting are only those that we feel are necessary in our interest overall on a strategic basis." Senator Gore shot back, "In other words, you give them the aid for one purpose and they accept it for another."[47]

While the United States alienated India by embracing Pakistan, Indian foreign policy continued to upset American leaders. In December 1961, Indian troops surged across the border of Portuguese Goa, the last remaining European colony on the Indian subcontinent. Within days, Goa had been liberated from colonial rule. At least, that is how most Indians viewed what Portugal loudly denounced as an unwarranted invasion of its sovereign territory. Portugal was a staunch American ally in the Cold War, and American leaders responded to the liberation of Goa with dismay. Adlai Stevenson, the U.S. ambassador to the United Nations, was especially critical of India's actions. In response, Nehru sent a long letter to Kennedy deploring "the extraordinary and bitter attitude of Mr. Adlai Stevenson." Kennedy responded, "You have my sympathy on the colonial aspects of this issue. There is, I am sure, a feeling in your part of the world that this is a matter we do not quite understand." To make personal his anticolonial sentiments, Kennedy turned to his Irish American upbringing. "I grew up in a community where the people were barely a generation away from colonial rule," he wrote. Rather than directly criticize India's annexation of Goa, Kennedy emphasized the potential impact on American public opinion. "My major concern was and continues to be," he wrote, "the effect of the action on our joint tasks, especially in terms of its impact on American opinion." India's use of force was "a shock to the majority who have admired your country's ardent advocacy of peaceful methods." Kennedy warned that without broad support among the American people, it would be impossible to convince the American Congress to support aid for India. In retrospect, he need not have worried. American opinion would soon swing back toward India, thanks to a surprise invasion that neither Nehru nor Kennedy saw coming.[48]

At sunrise on October 20, 1962, Chinese soldiers poured across the border with India. Nothing could have brought American politicians closer to India than the Chinese invasion. The Kennedy administration rushed arms to India while also using diplomatic pressure to prevent Pakistan from entering the conflict on the side of the Chinese. Some American officials, including General Maxwell Taylor and Secretary of Defense Robert McNamara, argued that the United States would ultimately need to use nuclear weapons to repel Chinese aggression. Would supporting India lead to nuclear war against China? On April 25, 1963, Kennedy convened a special meeting with his national security team and key advisers on India. Secretary of State Dean Rusk outlined the American dilemma as one of balance. "If we back India against the Chinese, we may drive the Paks off the deep end," Rusk worried. "If we abandon the Indians, they might move toward the USSR and China again." Abandoning India was not an option, at least from Kennedy's perspective. The president told his advisors that "it is hard to see how we can stop the Chinese Communists without India."[49]

Kennedy had long seen India as a bulwark against China. In 1958, in an article entitled "If India Falls," Kennedy celebrated India as the lynchpin of noncommunist Asia. In 1959, he declared, "If China succeeds and India fails, the economic balance of power would shift against us." Like Nehru, Kennedy turned to American history to justify Indian nonalignment. "Let us remember," he wrote, "that our nation also during the period of its formative growth adopted a policy of noninvolvement in the great international controversies of the nineteenth century." India's conflict with China sealed Kennedy's support for India—and offered strong ammunition to others who argued for stronger ties to India. In May 1962, Chester Bowles, the undersecretary of state and a former ambassador to India, told Kennedy that India was the "only major nation that fully shares our immediate concern over the dangers of Chinese expansionism."[50]

Having gained substantial terrain, the Chinese army decided not to push deeper into India. The conflict simmered, prolonging the new warmth in Indo-American relations. When India and Pakistan went to war for the second time in 1965, the United States refused to intervene on behalf of Pakistan, despite the terms of their military pact. Instead, the United States cut off military supplies to both sides. Meanwhile, the "spirit of Gandhi" that Hubert Humphrey had defended made its way into American society. Beginning in the 1940s, civil rights activists, inspired by Gandhi, began to experiment with nonviolent civil disobedience. Their labors would bear fruit in the 1950s and 1960s, as a mass movement for freedom and justice shook the racist hierarchies that oppressed not just African Americans but also Indian Americans.

## Gandhi in Mississippi

In March 1940, Pauli Murray boarded a bus bound for Durham, North Carolina. She was traveling with a friend, Adelene McBean. Both young women were African American. They sat near the back of the bus. But when McBean became ill, they moved up to the middle of the bus. The driver ordered them to move back. They refused, and after a heated debate with the driver and local police officers, both young women were arrested. Murray wrote friends, "We did not plan our arrest intentionally. The situation developed and, having developed, we applied what we knew of *Satyagraha* on the spot." By using the word *satyagraha*, Murray signaled her engagement with Indian freedom struggles. By the time she was arrested, Murray had long pondered how to use Gandhian methods against American racism.[51]

From jail, Murray wired her aunt: "Easter greetings. Arrested Petersburg warrant Greyhound Bus. Don't worry. Contact Walter White." White recognized that Murray and McBean's case might be used to test the constitutionality of segregation on interstate buses. He explored that possibility with leading NAACP attorneys, including Charles Hamilton Houston and Thurgood Marshall. Murray hoped the case would be used to set legal precedent. But the NAACP chose not to pursue the case to the Supreme Court. It would take another six years for the Supreme Court to rule that segregation in interstate travel was unconstitutional. The crucial case, *Morgan vs. Virginia*, also involved a young black woman arrested on a bus in Virginia. Why did the NAACP decline to pursue Murray's case? One explanation concerns a first-person account of Murray's arrest written by a white student and published in the magazine of the National Urban League. The most problematic facet of the story would not have been overlooked by the NAACP despite the fact that the author had no idea that it mattered. The article portrayed Murray as a man.[52]

Murray often passed as a man. She traveled in men's clothes, kept her hair short, and changed her name from Anna Pauline to the more androgynous Pauli. What Murray called her "'boy-girl' personality" was a source of constant struggle throughout much of her life. At a time when public acceptance of her sexual identity was impossible, Murray struggled with what she called the "longstanding emotional and mental conflict, popularly known as homosexuality." She sought in vain for a medical solution. She urged doctors to "experiment" on her "with the male hormone" and underwent an operation in search of hidden male sexual organs. In 1937, she prepared several questions she planned to ask a doctor and, with telling directness, provided her own preliminary answers: "Why the inverted sex instinct—wearing pants, wanting to be one of the men, doing things that fellows do, hating to be dominated by women unless I like them?—answer—glandular." Another question probed her feelings toward others who defied the sexual norm: "Why do many other Homosexuals irritate me instead of causing me a bond of sympathy, particular when I think it is acquired? (Don't know)." Murray's irritation might be easily explained: she lacked patience for those she felt had chosen a life that had been forced upon her. But Murray valorized individual choice in so many spheres of her life that it seems unlikely that the question of choice could alone explain her mixed feelings toward others who did not fit mainstream America's conception of sexual normality. There were larger issues at stake. Murray's irritation and her inability to explain that irritation together speak to the challenge of forging a "bond of sympathy" sufficiently large to include all her many identities, passions, and causes—at least in the United States in 1937. By initiating satyagraha on that bus in Virginia, Murray fought not only against racism, but also against discrimination based on sex, gender, and other forms of difference.[53]

There is a certain inevitability to the story of Gandhian nonviolence in the American civil rights movement. It is a story we all know, with a reassuring conclusion and a familiar cast of characters: Rosa Parks, the noble seamstress tired after a long day of work; Martin Luther King Jr., the heroic young pastor inspired by Gandhi. The standard narrative of the civil rights movement is not entirely wrong, but it is vastly incomplete and often misleading. Rosa Parks was tired when she refused to give up her seat for a white man, but she was also a seasoned activist who had studied Gandhian nonviolence. Martin Luther King did find inspiration in Gandhi, but there were dozens of other civil rights activists who studied Gandhi before King did, and thousands who risked their lives to fight for justice without any thought of the Mahatma.

African Americans had debated the relevancy of Gandhi's tactics for decades. But it was not until the Second World War that civil rights activists began directly experimenting with nonviolent civil disobedience. In June 1940, six students at Antioch College founded Ahimsa Farm just outside Cleveland. Inspired by an Indian sociology professor, the students called for Indian independence and launched a "swim-in" to desegregate a local swimming pool. A few years later, students at the University of Chicago founded the Congress of Racial Equality (CORE), an organization dedicated to using Gandhian strategies to achieve racial equality. CORE activists launched a series of sit-ins at segregated restaurants in Chicago. While Ahimsa Farm would last only a few years, CORE would grow to become a major civil rights organization. But in the 1940s, CORE, Ahimsa Farm, and most other efforts to use civil disobedience against racism were hobbled by the absence of robust connections to African American communities. Gandhian activists tended to be idealistic young people willing to risk their safety for a larger cause, but without the organizational resources of more established civil rights organizations. Only by bridging the divide between Gandhian praxis and the organizational capacity of African American communities could any civil rights organization wield Gandhian nonviolence on a vast scale. In the 1940s, only one organization came close to such a mass-based satyagraha.[54]

In the fall of 1942, A. Philip Randolph announced that his March on Washington Movement (MOWM) was preparing to launch nationwide nonviolent civil disobedience. The founder of the Brotherhood of Sleeping Car Porters, an important African American labor union, Randolph had spent decades building organizational capacity to effect change on a national scale. One month after the outbreak of Quit India, he unveiled plans for a "Negro Liberation Movement" that would combine picketing, marches, and civil disobedience. "Witness the strategy and maneuver of the people of India with mass civil disobedience and non-cooperation and marches to the sea," Randolph proclaimed.[55]

While drawing on Gandhian tactics, Randolph also spoke out in support of Indian independence. He called for an end to "the old Anglo-American empire systems," and told the American Federation of Labor that it was "pure hypocrisy to talk of this war as being fought for democracy while India is continually oppressed by British autocracy." Randolph framed his support for India in terms of colored solidarity. At a YWCA gathering in Chicago, he declared, "Colored people of America, the West Indies, and Africa should support this grim, determined and courageous battle for freedom of the Indian people under the gallant, wise and dauntless leadership of Mohandas K. Gandhi." Indians, he asserted, "constitute one of the great oppressed and exploited sections of the darker races of the world."[56]

Unlike Randolph, many civil rights leaders feared that Gandhian tactics were too radical and would lead to bloodshed. As a professor in a Southern black college explained, "In India, Gandhi is jailed; in Georgia, he'd be lynched." Several African American newspapers opposed civil disobedience. The *Atlanta Daily World* denounced satyagraha as "revolutionary and radical," and the *Pittsburgh Courier* opined that "Gandhi's way" was "not suited to the temperament of the American Negro."[57]

Randolph's plans for mass civil disobedience failed to materialize. But committed Gandhians continued to demonstrate the promise of satyagraha. In April 1947, CORE organized a "journey of reconciliation" that brought sixteen men, eight white and eight black, on a trip into the American South to test compliance with a recent Supreme Court decision that outlawed segregation on interstate travel. One of the African American travelers, Bayard Rustin, was a longtime pacifist who had worked for years to bring Gandhian tactics into the African American struggle. Arrested in North Carolina, Rustin was sentenced to thirty days on the chain gang. Before he served his sentence, he traveled to India, where he was welcomed by leading Indian figures, including Jawaharlal Nehru.[58]

In 1956, Rustin traveled to Montgomery, Alabama, to support the bus boycott sparked by Rosa Parks, the boycott that would make famous a twenty-six-year-old pastor named Martin Luther King Jr. King had encountered Gandhian ideas at Morehouse College, and as a seminary student had attended a lecture on Gandhi given by Mordecai Johnson, the president of Howard University. Johnson's description of Gandhi was "so profound and electrifying" that King immediately "bought a half dozen books on Gandhi's life and works." In the years ahead, dozens of activists and scholars, including Bayard Rustin, would encourage King to learn from Gandhi. Many African American residents of Montgomery had developed their own commitment to nonviolence, inspired equally by Christian precepts and basic common sense. As one woman in Montgomery declared, "Gandhi's all right, but we get this straight from Jesus Christ." But as the spokesman for the Montgomery movement, King found it useful to frame the struggle as Gandhian. Such a narrative attracted liberal whites who admired Gandhi and might be frightened by a struggle that was not explicitly nonviolent. It was not just Gandhi's nonviolence, however, that King found worthy of emulating. Gandhi's anticolonial courage and his use of civil disobedience were equally inspiring. In March 1956, King told a large audience at Brooklyn's Concord Baptist Church that "Gandhi was able to break loose from the political and economic domination by the British and brought the British Empire to its knees. Let's now use this method in the United States."[59]

On February 1, 1960, four African American college freshmen sat down at a "white only" lunch counter in Greensboro, North Carolina. They were refused service, but they did not leave. The next day, there were twenty students "sitting-in" at that lunch counter. By the end of the month, thousands of students and supporters had launched sit-ins, swim-ins, and other protests throughout much of America. A month after the first Greensboro sit-in, a group of students gathered at Shaw University in Raleigh, North Carolina, to discuss how to maintain the momentum of the sit-in movement. The importance of nonviolence to their understanding of the movement became clear in the name of the organization they created, the Student Nonviolent Coordinating Committee (SNCC). James Lawson, a theology student at Vanderbilt, shaped SNCC's understanding of nonviolence. Lawson had spent three years as a Methodist missionary in Nagpur, India. In February 1957, Martin Luther King had invited Lawson to come south to help spread nonviolent resistance in the aftermath of the Montgomery bus boycott. Lawson moved to Nashville and began teaching the fundamentals of nonviolent civil disobedience. Participants in Lawson's workshops read Gandhi and studied the Indian freedom struggle. When protests in Nashville began, John Lewis, a key SNCC leader and a regular participant in Lawson's workshops, added a note to the instructions given to protestors: "Remember the teachings of Jesus, Gandhi, Thoreau, and Martin Luther King Jr."[60]

South Asian visitors helped inspire the growing interest in Gandhian nonviolence. In 1958, Kaka Kalelkar, a close associate of Gandhi and a member of the Indian Parliament, visited Montgomery. Kalelkar spoke at a mass meeting on August 4, and later wrote King, "I have no doubt about the ultimate success of the coloured people. The American constitution is on your side, and so are justice and the spirit of the Times with you. Need I add that the prayers of millions of my country folk are also on your side?" In October 1960, CORE leaders presented Jawaharlal Nehru with a citation celebrating the birthday of Gandhi. While accepting the citation, Nehru stated that he was "all for racial equality" and was "proud" and "pleased" by African American efforts to continue Gandhi's legacy. The Indian ambassador, M. C. Chagla, called racial prejudice "anachronistic" and "antediluvian" while speaking alongside Howard University president Mordecai Johnson. At the University of Kansas, Chagla praised "massive non-violent, non-cooperation" and compared the sit-ins to the Indian struggle for independence.[61]

Indian newspapers and magazines offered sympathetic coverage of African American struggles. In October 1956, the weekly *Mankind* published an article on "civil disobedience in Alabama." The Bombay-based journal *United Asia* praised SNCC for utilizing "the technique of non-violent mass resistance to injustice, oppression, and exploitation which Gandhiji evolved in India." "Gandhi does not live in the pontifical sermons of Indian leaders, nor does he live in the statues of stone," readers learned. "He lives today in the brave non-violent action of American Negroes."[62]

Some Indians traveled to America to offer guidance to civil rights activists. In 1960, Sucheta and Jivatram Bhagwandas (J. B.) Kripalani, both eminent Gandhian activists, led an SNCC training at Morehouse College alongside Martin Luther King and Coretta Scott King. The Kripalanis spoke about their time organizing with Gandhi in the midst of violent riots between Hindus and Muslims. One participant remembered the Kripalanis stressing "how they were absolutely terrified, but did it nonetheless," a sentiment that would have reverberated for young SNCC activists confronting the constant threat of violence. The Kripalanis also met with veteran Gandhians Mordecai Johnson and William Stewart Nelson at a small gathering at the Indian Embassy. Thus, the Kripalanis bridged generations of activists working to bring Gandhian nonviolence into the struggle for American racial equality.[63]

On May 27, 1964, Rammanohar Lohia, a member of the Indian Parliament and a socialist firebrand, was turned away from Morrison's Cafeteria, a "whites only" establishment in Jackson, Mississippi. The following day, dressed entirely in white, Lohia returned to Morrison's to launch his own satyagraha. The manager told him to leave. Lohia replied, "I tell you with greatest humility, I am not leaving." By forcing the police to arrest him, Lohia turned what had been a local story into a global scandal. The State Department sent a formal apology to the Indian ambassador. The American ambassador to the United Nations, Adlai Stevenson, offered his apologies. Lohia replied that the State Department "may go to hell" and added that Stevenson should apologize to the Statue of Liberty.[64]

Lohia understood his protest as part of a global struggle against oppression. In January 1960, Lohia had written a close friend linking color prejudice within India to the oppression of "the Negroes and the coloured peoples." After his arrest, Lohia explained that the problem he was opposing in Mississippi, what he called "the challenge of colour and caste," also existed in India. He told one journalist, "Let me make it perfectly clear that I am not trying to uncover or publicize something foul in American life. Such foul spots exist everywhere—also in India." Lohia revealed the scope of his activism during a long conversation with a dozen African American civil rights activists. He told the group that he would never stop promoting "the seven revolutions," which included "women's rights as well as the problems of caste, and colour which had brought him to Mississippi."[65]

In 1936, twenty-eight years before his arrest in Jackson, Lohia had written W. E. B. Du Bois in the hope of establishing "the closest relations with our Negro comrades of America." In the early 1950s, Lohia worked to build such relations while traveling across the American South. At Fisk University, Lohia lectured on "the Awakening of Asia and Africa." He also spoke at Highlander Folk School, the racially integrated community-organizing center that would later host both Rosa Parks and Martin Luther King. Lohia encouraged his African American audiences to use civil disobedience against racism in America. Several years before the Montgomery bus boycott, Lohia's suggestions were seen by many as radical. But by the time Lohia was arrested in Jackson in 1964, many young Americans had come to see Gandhian nonviolence as insufficiently militant.[66]

In the face of the stubborn brutality of white supremacists and the apathy of federal authorities, many activists came to feel that nonviolent civil disobedience could never undo American racism. After four young girls were killed by the bombing of the 16th Street Baptist Church in Birmingham, SNCC activist Anne Moody told another movement leader, "If Martin Luther King thinks nonviolence is really going to work for the South as it did for India, then he is out of his mind." In Baltimore in 1966, CORE delegates voted to discard a commitment to the "technique of nonviolence in direct action" as a requirement for chapters. Floyd McKissick, CORE's chairman, attacked nonviolence as a "dying philosophy" that had "outlived its usefulness." In 1969, SNCC changed its name to the Student *National* Coordinating Committee.[67]

While African American activists turned away from nonviolence, Indian politics demonstrated the limits of Gandhi's legacy. Since Gandhi's death in 1948, India had amassed one of the world's largest standing armies and had repeatedly fought wars with its neighbors. If India had abandoned Gandhi's legacy, what hope was there for foreign advocates of nonviolence? Even as committed a nonviolent figure as the Catholic monk Thomas Merton became disillusioned. In 1965, Merton published a small edited volume of Gandhi's writings, entitled *Gandhi on Nonviolence*. "The little book on Gandhi came out, at a curious time," Merton wrote, "now that India is swept with war fever." He told a friend, "I am afraid that in the end we will have to admit that non-violence really failed in India, as Gandhi himself saw before he died It asks very much of men: really, true non-violence cannot be carried out except by real saints. In this country there are indeed some really dedicated men in the nonviolent civil rights movement, but a lot of them are anything but saints."[68]

Merton had good reasons to be skeptical concerning the future of nonviolence. But many Indians continued to embrace nonviolence—and its most prominent American advocates. In June 1969, J. J. Singh sent a long letter to his friend Jayaprakash Narayan. A strident critic of the Indian government's failure to reduce poverty, Narayan had been quoted in the press seeming to condone violent opposition to the government. In

1968, Singh had presided over a discussion on "Black Power" at the India International Center in Delhi. In his letter to Narayan, he used the lessons of Black Power to convince Narayan "that man will remain close to the animal so long as he is unable to eschew violence." Singh granted that the threat of violence may have pressured American leaders to respond to the demands of African American protesters. But he added that a broader perspective revealed the superiority of nonviolence. "Martin Luther King kept on talking of non-violence notwithstanding the fact that almost all negroes decried his stand."[69]

It is easy to frame the transnational history of Gandhian nonviolence as a success story. Indian independence shook the foundations of white supremacy and imperial rule. With the help of Gandhian civil disobedience, the civil rights movement delivered another blow to the global system that marginalized people of color. But the structural inequality created by centuries of slavery and imperialism proved resilient. In India, the persistence of inequality based on caste, class, and creed continues to betray Gandhi's hopes for his country. In the United States, the resilience of white supremacy is seen not just in the oppression of African Americans, but also in the racial profiling of South Asian Americans.

Recognizing the persistence of racism should not entail overlooking the victories of the civil rights movement—victories that extended beyond domestic American politics to influence how Americans related to other parts of the world. By breaking down some of the social and cultural constraints of American society, the movement contributed to a renaissance of American interest in other peoples and cultures—including Indian culture. As in the days of Emerson and Thoreau, the flourishing of Indophilia in the 1960s and 1970s ranged from sincere engagement to cheap forms of cultural appropriation. At stake was not just what Americans made of Indian culture, but what Americans and Indians made of culture itself.

## Of Curry and Culture

In 1972, the best-selling cookbook *The Vegetarian Epicure* offered Americans a lesson on Indian culture: "Thousands of years before the rise of Christianity and the onslaught of Western Civilization, a great culture was already flourishing in India. At its best, it was and remains marked by wisdom approaching universal understanding, and a way of life harmonious with universal laws." This tribute to Indian civilization occurs in a section entitled "Curries and Indian Preparations." In her desire to respect Indian culture, the author of *The Vegetarian Epicure,* Anna Thomas, risked flattening India's diversity in much the same way that many Americans gloss the variety of Indian culinary traditions with the generic category "curry." But Thomas dispelled the myth that there is a curry tree, explained that there is no such thing as "curry," and offered a range of different styles and dishes. She celebrated the diversity of Indian food and thus of Indian culture.[70]

It is rarely easy to distinguish narrow forms of cultural appropriation from dynamic examples of cultural engagement. Where is the line between appropriation and cosmopolitanism? Consider perhaps the most renowned Indian cultural form in the United States: yoga. How "Indian" and how "cultural" is contemporary American yoga? As we have seen, yoga arrived in the United States in the nineteenth century as a form of spiritual and philosophical wisdom. Today, many Americans understand yoga primarily as a form of exercise, albeit one with some relationship to Indian and particularly Hindu spirituality. The religious dimensions of yoga have generated controversies in both India and America. In the United States, several Christian pastors have denounced yoga as unchristian. One megachurch leader in Seattle went so far as to declare yoga "demonic." Indians have also debated yoga's religious character. In 2013, India's Supreme Court received a petition to make yoga a compulsory part of the school curriculum. But the court expressed concern given that Indian public schools are supposed to be secular and yoga is associated with Hinduism. A similar debate arose in California when some parents complained after public schools began to introduce regular yoga classes. One school district responded by replacing the Sanskrit names for popular yoga postures with labels like "child-friendly" and with safely "non-Hindu" English names such as "surfer," "washing machine," and "criss-cross apple sauce." In both India and the United States, what is at stake is not just the religious character of yoga, but the secularism of the state at a time when pluralism is under attack from religious extremists who would use faith to divide rather than to unify.[71]

Compared to yoga, classical Indian music has had a less controversial journey to America. In 1966, the renowned Indian classical singer M. S. Subbulakshmi toured America to great acclaim. The *San Francisco*

*Chronicle* called her performances "a series of miracles." The popularity of classical Indian music demonstrates the possibility of transporting a cultural form without significantly changing its contours. But the American encounter with Indian music has involved a considerable amount of cultural blending. Take, for example, the impact that the most famous Indian musician in America, Ravi Shankar, had on the American composer Philip Glass. Meeting Shankar was, in the words of Glass, "like totally clearing all my decks, and overnight I began to write a completely different kind of music."[72]

Before Indian classical music became popular in the United States, jazz had already become a cultural bridge between India and America. In the 1920s and 1930s, jazz artists—many African American—regularly performed in Indian cities. In 1935, the African American jazz violinist Leon Abbey traveled with his "all Negro" band to Bombay for a series of shows at the Taj Mahal Hotel. Abbey's band quickly became a sensation. One Indian fan wrote, "The music went to my head that evening and when Leon started beating up a rumba I left my table and my partner to shake the maracas that were offered me. In those few moments I forgot my whole upbringing, forgot that I was back in the land of my fathers, through which the Ganges flowed." As famous American musicians, African American artists were generally able to sidestep the discrimination faced by many dark-skinned Indians. When the great piano player Teddy Weatherford was asked in the early 1940s whether he enjoyed being in India, he smiled and replied, "They treat us white folks just fine!"[73]

Indian musicians developed their own approach to jazz. Many of India's most prominent jazz artists were Goans who also worked in the film industry in Bombay. They brought jazz into Hindi films. One of the most famous of these Goan jazz musicians, Anthony Gonsalves, later became immortalized in the hit song "My Name is Anthony Gonsalves," a beloved tune from the classic film *Amar Akbar Anthony* (1977). The song's persistent resonance was made clear in 2008 when a new film was entitled *My Name Is Anthony Gonsalves*.[74]

Many prominent American jazz artists made use of Indian instruments and sounds. Yusef Lateef developed a connection to South Asia when he converted to the Ahmaddiya branch of Islam in Detroit. Studying with an Indian flute player and experimenting with a variety of indigenous Indian instruments, Lateef became one of the most prominent musicians to bring Indian music into jazz. Keith Jarrett explored the power

of Indian ragas, as did John McLaughlin and John Mayer. These sorts
of connections were often explicit efforts to investigate Indian music as
a distinct tradition. One of Lateef's tracks is called "India." By contrast,
John Coltrane brought Indian music into American jazz in ways that
often blurred the boundaries between the two.[75]

By the early 1960s, Coltrane had become fascinated with Indian
music. He gathered his own collection of Ravi Shankar's recordings.
"When I hear his music," Coltrane declared of Shankar, "I want to copy
it—not note for note of course, but in his spirit." Coltrane met with
Shankar several times in the 1960s and spent time learning about Indian musical techniques. The admiration was mutual. Shankar heard
Coltrane perform at the Village Gate and declared, "The music was fantastic." Shankar was "much impressed," but also "distressed" by the "turbulence in the music." "Here was a creative person who had become a
vegetarian, who was studying yoga, and reading the Bhagavad-Gita,"
Shankar wrote, "yet in whose music I still heard much turmoil." Shankar
might be accused of a certain cultural self-congratulation, as if yoga and
the Gita automatically bring peace to the soul. Nevertheless, one expects
that Coltrane would have appreciated Shankar's sympathetic reading of
his music and its "turbulence" and "turmoil."[76]

The confluence of jazz and Indian religious traditions reached its
apogee in the work of Alice Coltrane, a renowned pianist long before she
met her husband, John. Alice took the name Turiyasangitananda, Sanskrit for "the bliss of God's most elevated song." In the early 1980s, she
purchased forty-eight acres in Agoura Hills, California, and built the
Shanti Anantam Ashram. There, she blended jazz, blues, and gospel with
rhythmic Vedic chanting. The scholar Franya J. Berkman attended a service at the ashram and left a vivid description of Turiyasangitananda as
a musical and spiritual guru:

> She would make offerings at the altar, take her seat behind the Ham-
> mond B3 organ, and begin to play. First would be a bhajan to Ganesha,
> the elephant deity to whom Hindus traditionally pray before starting any
> religious and worldly endeavor. Alice would depress the pedals, and the
> bass vibrations would pass through the walls and floorboards. Playing
> syncopated chords with her left hand and a soaring, pentatonic melody
> with her right, she would signal the song leader in the men's section to
> start the men singing. The women would respond, and blues-inflected
> devotional music would fill the room.

One doubts that Turiyasangitananda ever considered whether the music she was performing was Indian or American. These were not studio recordings but deeply felt devotionals performed in religious services that combined elements of Hindu worship with the traditions of the black church.[77]

The relationship between spirituality and artistic creation—central to the flow of music between India and America—was equally prominent in the many literary works that gestured across the divide between the two countries. In his novel *The Stoic* (1947), Theodore Dreiser presented India as a mystical haven where one could find "mental and spiritual help, away from the Western world and its crass materialism." The Bhagavad Gita "seemed to condense and epitomize thousands of years of Asiatic religious thought." As with Emerson and Thoreau, many of Dreiser's allusions to Hinduism could be seen as superficial window dressing. Yet it would be a disservice to *The Stoic* to dismiss its generous portrayal of India's spirituality.[78]

A similarly sincere yet thin hybridity marks John Steinbeck's *Cannery Row* (1945) and its repeated references to a poem by the eleventh-century Kashmiri poet Bilhana. The novel ends with a stanza from the poem:

> Even now,
> I know that I have savored the hot taste of life
> Lifting green cups and gold at the great feast.
> Just for a small and a forgotten time
> I have had full in my eyes from off my girl
> The whitest pouring of eternal light

Could Steinbeck have eliminated all references to the poem without substantially changing the novel? Undoubtedly. But rather than diminish the significance of those references, their lack of necessity only heightens their aesthetic richness.[79]

Many modern American authors were deeply influenced by Indian texts and thinkers. We might explain such influences as another instance of modern Americans turning to ancient India. Yet many of the most influential Indian thinkers were contemporary figures whose own lives and thinking were decidedly transnational and transcultural. The novelist Henry Miller admired Jiddu Krishnamurti, a revered thinker who spent much of his life in California. Of Krishnamurti, Miller wrote, "Here is one man of our time who may be said to be a master of reality. He stands alone. He has renounced more than any man I can think of, except the Christ." Miller's comparison between Krishnamurti and Christ reveals the deep reverence many Americans felt for Krishnamurti, but also the pluralist and often distinctly Western contexts in which Krishnamurti's teaching was received and understood. Born in what is now the Indian state of Andhra Pradesh, Krishnamurti settled in Southern California, where he developed his own devoted following.[80]

Treating someone like Krishnamurti as representative of "timeless" Indian wisdom is historically inaccurate and philosophically flattening. But if drawing sharp boundaries between East and West has its limitations, there is also a danger in ignoring the rootedness of spiritual and philosophical traditions, replacing sincere respect and critical engagement with a hollow spiritual tourism. Consider the emergence of what might be called Hippie India. In the 1960s and 1970s, a major cultural shift led many Americans to equate spiritual progress with India, and to frame such progress in terms of the cheap hedonism of the hippie. The rich complexities of Indian society and philosophy became reduced to a permissive embrace of sex and drugs—at least from the perspective of outraged traditionalists.

The hippie emerged as a mythical figure, the source of fascination and fear in both India and America. Of the many writers who contributed to "hippie culture," few had as rich a relationship to India as Allen Ginsberg. We might dismiss Ginsberg's fascination with India as spiritual tourism at its worst. Ginsberg's *Indian Journals*, written in 1962, abound with images of the holy hedonist. His entry from December 17 typifies his experience of India: "sat inside red stone porch with Saddhus & smoked ganja pipe." But Ginsberg's attention to detail saved him from essentializing exotic India. In the following day's journal, he wrote:

Sitting on Harishchandra Ghat—down below a sand slope at the water's edge blackened with ashes, a high pile of firewood ablaze and a man's head bent back blackened nose & mouth unburnt, black fuzzy hair, the rest of the chest belly outlined along down thighs at top of the pyre, feet sticking out the other end—now turned toes down—cry of geese & rabble of white longnecked good goose swan boids pecking in the water's edge a few feet from fire.

Ginsberg's ability to see through the stereotype of India saved him from the spiritual mush that characterized India in the minds of some American hippies. Ironically, the complexities of Ginsberg's relationship with Indian thought are perhaps most evident in his interactions with the most caricatured embodiment of Hippie India, the Hare Krishna movement.[81]

The International Society for Krishna Consciousness (ISKCON) was founded in New York in 1966 by A. C. Bhaktivedanta Swami Prabhupada. Born in Calcutta in 1896, Prabhupada came to the United States in 1965, a sixty-nine-year-old spiritual teacher without a following. The movement he founded would grow to have hundreds of temples and thousands of followers, not just in the United States but also in Europe and India itself. Here is Ginsberg on the remarkable growth of ISKCON: "Swami Bhaktivedanta came to USA and went swiftly to the Archetype Spiritual Neighborhood, the New York Lower East Side and installed intact an ancient perfectly preserved piece of street India. He adorned a storefront as his Ashram and adored Krishna therein and by patience and good humor singing chanting and expounding Sanskrit terminology day by day established Krishna Consciousness in the psychedelic (mind-manifesting) center of America East."

Ginsberg and Prabhupada did not agree on everything. Consider this conversation, which took place in San Francisco in 1967:

> *Prabhupada:* You have not had LSD, Allen?
> *Ginsberg:* I have had it.
> *Prabhupada:* It is dependence, Allen.
> *Ginsberg:* It's like a car—a mental car—to resolve certain inner things.
> *Prabhupada:* Krishna Consciousness resolves everything. Nothing else
> is needed.

Despite rejecting the Swami's views on LSD and other intoxicants, Ginsberg publicly embraced ISKCON. Alongside writers like Gary Snyder and Alan Watts, Ginsberg helped bring Krishna Consciousness to a new generation of Americans. In January 1967, Ginsberg organized a large reception for Swami Prabhupada at the San Francisco Airport. A few weeks later, Ginsberg took the stage at the Mantra-Rock Dance concert at San Francisco's Avalon Ballroom. The event featured the Grateful Dead, Janis Joplin, and Moby Grape. But the headliner was Swami Prabhupada, whom Ginsberg personally introduced.[82]

As in the nineteenth century, American fascination with Indian spirituality earned the scorn of traditionalists in India and America. The omnipresent Hare Krishnas became a joke in both countries. In 1971, the Bollywood legend Dev Anand starred in a critically acclaimed blockbuster entitled *Hare Rama Hare Krishna*. Influenced by the 1968 American film *Psych-Out,* the movie denounced hippie culture as a bastardized form of Eastern spirituality appropriated by drugged-out Westerners. The "hippie trail" had brought large numbers of Westerners to India. Places like Goa and Varanasi filled with foreigners searching for spiritual enlightenment but also for drugs and free love. But not all Indians objected to the surge in hippie tourists. The lead song of *Hare Rama Hare Krishna,* "Dum Maro Dum" (Puff, Take a Puff), aimed to criticize drug use. As the song unfolds, we see a young Indian woman smoking intoxicants in the presence of half-naked Westerners, one of whom has "free love" painted across his back. The song became a massive hit, its popularity speaking to the ambivalence many Indians felt regarding the social and cultural provocations associated with the hippies.

The geography of Hippie India defied national and cultural borders. It matters that ISKCON was founded in New York. Like so much in the counterculture, ISKCON transgressed the border between India and America, East and West. But recognizing the transnational cosmopolitanism of the hippie counterculture does not require overlooking its limitations. Many of the Americans who poured into India in search of what Gita Mehta called "mythological osmosis" found nothing but "the philosophy of the meaningfully meaningless." In her best-selling satire, *Karma Cola,* Mehta describes encountering one infamous hippie charlatan, dressed in an elaborate costume that evoked the American West. He jokes with her, "I look like Chief Crazy Horse, no?" She replies, "Yes. He was in the wrong Indies, but he had the right act."[83]

At its worst, the American fascination with Indian spirituality fed a cult-like conformity: everyone dressed up like an Indian of one kind or another. The problem was not that thousands of Americans were attracted to Hinduism, Buddhism, and other Indian religious traditions. The problem was that such attraction ranged from cheap forms of cultural appropriation to a disturbing devotion to "new-age" religious figures like Bhagwan Shree Rajneesh. Now often known as Osho, Rajneesh developed a large international following in the 1960s and 1970s. In 1981, he moved from India to a utopian community constructed by his followers on a sprawling ranch in rural Oregon. Thousands of American devotees or *sannyasins,* dressed in shades of red, moved to what became known as Rajneeshpuram. They grew their own food, built their own homes, and lined up to watch their guru drive by in one of his many Rolls Royce cars. In 1984, Rajneesh accused his most prominent follower of orchestrating a series of crimes, including a salmonella attack often cited as the first example of bioterrorism on U.S. soil. The movement fractured, and Rajneesh himself was deported a few years later. Like many of the gurus or "godmen" who attract followers in India and the United States, Rajneesh left a complicated legacy. While his writings continue to inspire many, the history of Rajneeshpuram reveals how the promise of spiritual freedom can become its opposite.[84]

In his introduction to Swami Prabhupada's best-selling version of the Bhagavad Gita, Allen Ginsberg meditated on how to transcend cultural appropriation and the dangers of blind devotion. Rather than provide easy answers, Ginsberg revealed his ambivalent relationship to the idea of renunciation as freedom. He wrote, "I grow old and see that renunciation is what happens. The 'action' leads there—calm realization of sense-desire illusoriness in youth, or on deathbed at worst." Ginsberg's use of the passive voice is revealing. *Renunciation is what happens.* It remains unclear whether this happening is to be embraced. Crucially, the path to "sense-desire illusoriness" is not ascetic renunciation. Ginsberg explains, "Even Tantric path (exploration of sensory limits) leads to liberation (relaxation) from sensory grasping (i.e. desire). Because senses are mechanical and repetitious. Infinite in sensation during their apparent minute, in that sense Blakean Eternal." Such fleeting transcendence through sensory hedonism is not the ultimate goal, but neither is it unrelated to the goal. Ginsberg does not reject pleasure even while aiming for a higher spiritual pleasure. He declares, "The personal vibration set up by chanting 'Hare Krishna Hare Krishna Krishna Krishna Hare Hare Hare Rama Hare Rama Rama Rama Hare Hare' is a universal pleasure." Its universality allows Ginsberg to claim such a seemingly Hindu practice as proudly American. He concludes, "This rare fortune (as Thoreau and Whitman our natural-hearted forefathers prophesied) is our heritage, our own truest Self, our own community of selves, our own true America."[85]

With the spiritual as with the cultural, we must avoid two dangers: celebrating "connections" or dismissing them as inauthentic. Some of the most sincere and multifaceted links between India and the United States came in the form of religious dialogue. Ginsberg's relationship with Swami Prabhupada is one example. Another is the impact of Ananda Coomaraswamy, the renowned scholar of Asian art, on Thomas Merton. Merton called Coomaraswamy "the model of one who has thoroughly and completely united in himself the spiritual tradition and attitudes of the Orient and of the Christian West." Coomaraswamy's *The Transformation of Nature in Art* was, Merton later wrote, "decisive in leading me to take the right turn in life and to set my feet upon the spiritual road, which led to the monastery and to the contemplative life." In 1967, Amiya Chakravarty, an Indian poet and scholar, organized a colloquium on Merton at Smith College. Afterward, Chakravarty wrote to Merton that "we were immersed in the silence and eloquence of your thoughts and writings." He added, "The young scholars here realize that the absolute rootedness of your faith makes you free to understand other faiths." Merton responded, "You have seen something that I see to be most precious." "We all recognize each other in this metaphysical space of silence and happiness," Merton wrote, "and get some sense, for a moment, that we are full of paradise without knowing it."[86]

Recognizing the divine across difference, thinkers and teachers like Merton, Ginsberg, and Prabhupada helped create new spiritual bridges between India and America. It would be easy to contrast such intellectuals with the masses of hippies crowding the beaches of Goa. Whereas artists and thinkers probed the complexities of intercultural encounter, the masses smoked ganja, recited empty mantras, and draped themselves with shiny beads. Such a contrast does not hold. At the heart of Hippie India was freedom—religious, cultural, and personal. Freedom from constraint could lead to hollow hedonism. But the same freedom also challenged restrictions of gender and sexuality, as well as the parochial limitations of self-declared defenders of nationally circumscribed cultures. If some drank Karma Cola and were led astray by spiritual commercialism or cult-like obedience, many found their own form of hybrid spiritual truth, their own view of "the whitest pouring of eternal light."

On August 15, 1969, an Indian man with a long white beard sat on a platform in front of half a million young Americans, raised his hands in greeting, and said, "My Beloved Brothers and Sisters: I am overwhelmed with joy to see the entire youth of America gathered here in the name of the fine art of music." Thus, Swami Satchidananda opened the Woodstock Music Festival. Born as C. K. Ramaswamy Gounder in Tamil Nadu in 1914, Satchidananda embraced the ascetic life after the death of his wife. In 1966, he came to the United States and quickly developed a large following. His address at Woodstock shows why so many came to respect and admire him. Satchidananda praised music as "the celestial sound that controls the whole universe." He spoke out against war, encouraged his audience to find peace within themselves, and praised them for reaching beyond the borders of nation, culture, and religion. "The future of the world is in your hands," he told the mass of young Americans—not because they were sitting in the wealthiest country in the world, but because they were willing to learn from anyone, willing to sit together and to listen.[87]

It would be easy to romanticize that moment of intercultural interaction, especially given the fact that August 15 is India's Independence Day. Twenty-two years after India threw off the British yoke, an Indian swami called into being a rebellious gathering of young Americans eager to embrace new ways of living. There is beauty in that moment, a beauty not unlike the deeper, more sustained journey that impelled Alice Coltrane to become Turiyasangitananda, or that led Thomas Merton to revere Ananda Coomaraswamy. Yet to compare Woodstock and Indian independence is to drive home the vast discrepancy between the cultural cosmopolitanism of certain Americans and Indians and the ongoing failures of democracy in both the United States and India. It matters that John Coltrane and Ravi Shankar found resonance and recognition through music. It matters that Allen Ginsberg and Swami Prabhupada could sit down and chant together. But such cultural bridges could not touch the inequalities that continue to divide both the United States and India. Artists, musicians, and other cultural creators still forge their own relationships between the two countries. But the resurgence of xenophobia and cultural chauvinism in both India and America should chasten those who see the increasing globalization of culture as the death knell of racism, casteism, and other forms of narrowness and injustice. Indeed, some cultural flows between India and America reproduced hierarchies of oppression. Consider the strange history of the word *thug*, a word with deep roots in India that has come to have an equally important and controversial position in the United States.

# PART III

# THUG

We white people are merely modified Thugs; Thugs
fretting under the restraints of a not very thick skin of
civilization.
>                  —Mark Twain, *Following the Equator,* 1897

I'm a thug, that's because I came from the gutter, and
I'm still here.
>                  —Tupac Shakur, "Interview Outside of Court," 1994

IN 1836, William Henry Sleeman, an officer of the British East India
Company, published a guide to the language of a secret band of killers
known as "thags" or "thugs." The following year, an exposé titled "History and Practice of the Thugs" familiarized British readers with tales of
highway robberies and ritual murders in the dark corners of India. But
it was not until 1839, with the publication of the novel *Confessions of a
Thug,* that the cult of the thug became a national obsession. Written by
another colonial official, Philip Meadows Taylor, and presented as a
faithful history, *Confessions of a Thug* became a best seller and one of Queen
Victoria's favorite books. The threat of the thug sold books and made
careers. Sleeman earned the rank of colonel for apprehending suspected
thugs, thousands of whom were executed. Within a few years, colonial
authorities celebrated the decimation of the thugs. But the specter of the
thug would persist, a reminder of the need for vigilance throughout the
empire.[1]

In 1993, Tupac Shakur formed the rap group Thug Life. Their first album, *Thug Life: Volume 1,* arrived at a crucial moment in the history of hip-hop. Another new group, Bone Thugs-n-Harmony, had just released an album with the hit single "Thuggish Ruggish Bone." The burgeoning hip-hop industry was discovering the same lesson that Philip Meadows Taylor had learned in Victorian England: thugs sell. To be sure, the "thug life" was far more than a marketing strategy. From its inception, hip-hop provided a platform for young men of color to respond to the violence of inner cities devastated by deindustrialization, white flight, and police brutality. At a time when imprisonment was becoming "the new Jim Crow," many rappers simultaneously glorified and criticized the violence of urban life. Such subtleties were lost on critics of hip-hop, who used the words *thug* and *gangster* to attack what they saw as the celebration of drugs, sex, and violence. In the culture wars of the 1990s, the figure of the thug regained a fame it had not had since the 1830s. The word remains a potent epithet loaded with racial assumptions. In January 2014, Richard Sherman, a player for the Seattle Seahawks football team, was denounced as a "thug" after offering heated comments on national television. Sherman attacked the word *thug* as "an accepted way of calling someone the n-word nowadays."[2]

The thug was, from the beginning, defined by difference. One of the earliest references to the thug occurs in the Delhi-based historian Ziauddin Barani's *History of Firoz Shahi,* written circa 1356. According to Barani, the sultan rounded up all the thugs in Delhi and moved them "into the Lower country" so that they "would not trouble the neighbourhood." Thugs were to be kept at a distance. In the writings of British colonial officials, thugs operated at the edges of the Raj, where they provided a useful justification for the expansion of the empire. Crime existed within colonial cities, of course, but it was conveniently exempted from most accounts of thug networks. Like the thugs of colonial India, the thugs of inner-city America were positioned as dangerous outcastes. Despite the fact that rappers like Tupac Shakur helped to sever the word *thug* from its colonial roots, their invention of "thug life" echoed the interplay between violence and difference that made the thug so familiar and yet so foreign.[3]

Many scholars see the thug as a colonial invention. Despite the efforts of William Henry Sleeman, little evidence exists that a vast network of thugs committed ritual murders. The grand narrative of *thuggee,* the noun used to describe the thugs as a pan-Indian conspiracy, was itself a kind of theoretical violence that obscured the diversity of precolonial India and justified colonial expansion. In the words of historian C. A. Bayly, the thug became "the most celebrated case of orientalist myth-making." Despite the persistent ambiguity surrounding the thugs of India in the 1830s—in part because of that ambiguity—the idea of the thug proved lasting and remarkably mobile.[4]

The mobility of the thug justified the expansion of surveillance regimes, as authorities from California to Calcutta used the threat of the radical criminal to bolster the police state. Like the word *Indian*, the thug came to embody the history of colonialism that connected India and America. Like *caste*, the thug spoke to the systemic inequality that remained even after colonial regimes gave way to formal democracies. But while the words *Indian* and *caste* retained vestiges of the subcontinent, the thug became Americanized, its colonial origins conveniently forgotten. Such forgetting underpinned the democratic triumphalism that buttresses nationalism in both India and America. As the political scientist Jeanne Morefield has written, "nationalist forgetting doesn't just replace one memory with another." Rather, "in ritualistically calling upon the remembering community to forget, it gestures toward the violence of the past and then purges that violence by asking members of the community to dwell deeper in the familial whole that emerged from such fratricidal rage." Such efforts to unify by dividing and then forgetting have marked not only the history of the thug but the journeys of other useful villains: communists, for example, or terrorists, or all those seen as racially different. Black men were the thugs of America long before the word inherited its distinctly racial undertones. It is strangely fitting that Americans have retained the racial connotations of the word *thug* even while forgetting its Indian origins. Even when most Americans associated the thug with India, it was a flashpoint for the ambiguity that marked how Americans understood race in India and America.[5]


## Thugs of the Desert

In 1837, Ralph Waldo Emerson told an audience at Boston's Masonic Temple that the human imagination could cross the borders of nations, cultures, and peoples—but only to a point. Even if we traveled all the world, Emerson warned, we would not be able to inhabit the minds of the people we encountered. About even the most adventurous traveler, Emerson asked, "Will he have seen all? What does he know about the miners of Cornwall or the lumberers of Maine? Is he sure to allow all that is due to the Thugs of the Desert? Does he appreciate Insanity?" To appreciate insanity fully would require being insane. To give all that is due to the thugs of the desert would require becoming a thug. Emerson used the thug to highlight the difficulty of transnational understanding. He strove to inspire awe at the impossibility of bridging the vast divides between the miners of Cornwall and the lumberers of Maine, between the masons of Boston and the thugs of the desert. Like William Henry Sleeman, Emerson appropriated the foreignness of the thug. But unlike Sleeman, Emerson did not demand the eradication of the thug. He preserved the thug as a testimony to radical difference, a lesson in humility rather than a call to conquest.[6]

By the late nineteenth century, the thug had disappeared from the British Raj, but the idea of the thug had become even more prominent in the United States. No American was more fascinated by the thug than Mark Twain. As a boy, Twain heard "vague tales and rumors of a sect called Thugs." Thugs, he learned, "waylaid travelers in lonely places and killed them for the contentment of a God whom they worshipped." Thus, Twain learned as a child the two key features of the thugs: their foreignness (they killed in "lonely places") and their religious fanaticism.[7]

The thug embodied the persistent ambivalence that marked Twain's relationship to the British Raj. In his travel memoir, Twain dedicated dozens of pages to the thug. Relying directly on the writings of William Henry Sleeman, Twain described thuggee as "a bloody terror" and a "desolating scourge." "In 1830," he told his readers, "the English found this cancerous organization imbedded in the vitals of the empire." Fortunately, Twain concluded, "that little handful of English officials in India set their sturdy and confident grip upon it, and ripped it out, root and branch!" But despite his praise for the British, Twain offered a strikingly sympathetic portrayal of the thugs. Take, for example, his treatment of a British document that described the final moments of a thug who was about to be executed. The thug begged his mother to "relieve him from the obligations of the milk with which she had nourished him from infancy, as he was about to die before he could fulfill any of them."

Twain painted a vivid picture of the thug kneeling before his mother and receiving her forgiveness, and concluded, "There is reverence there, and tenderness, and fortitude, and self-respect—and no sense of disgrace, no thought of dishonor." "And yet one of these people is a Thug," he continued, "and the other a mother of Thugs! The incongruities of our human nature seem to reach their limit here." Twain used the thug, like Emerson, to recognize the vast range of human experience. But by linking the thug to "our human nature," Twain moved away from Emerson and toward a conception of the thug that indicted all humanity. "We white people are merely modified Thugs," Twain declared, "Thugs fretting under the restraints of a not very thick skin of civilization."[8]

Twain was not the only late nineteenth-century figure to use the thug to unsettle ethical absolutism and to challenge the moral superiority of the west. Like Twain, Swami Vivekananda used the thug to force Americans to consider their own barbarism. In the winter of 1895, Vivekananda offered a series of lectures in New York City. "In the last century," he told one audience, "there were notorious bands of robbers in India called thugs; they thought it their duty to kill any man they could." Rather than comment on what Emerson deemed the "insanity" of the thug, Vivekananda complicated the moral position with which his audience might judge the thug. "Ordinarily if a man goes out into the street and shoots down another man," Vivekananda continued, "he is apt to feel sorry for it, thinking that he has done wrong." However, the Swami argued, "If the very same man, as a soldier in his regiment, kills not one but twenty, he is certain to feel glad and think that he has done his duty remarkably well." Like Twain, Vivekananda used the thug to blur the lines between civilized and uncivilized forms of violence.[9]

The contrast between the soldier and the thug, between the violence of civilization and the violence of the outlaw, remained central to American representations of the thug. Those representations gained new power in 1939 when the thug stormed into Hollywood via the blockbuster film *Gunga Din*. Based on the poem by Rudyard Kipling, *Gunga Din* follows three British soldiers as they uncover a secret thug sect led by a bloodthirsty madman. Balding and dressed in a loincloth, the chief thug bears a striking resemblance to Mahatma Gandhi, a fact that was not lost on contemporaries. In *Gunga Din*, one Indian magazine declared, "The white man laughed at the man who we worship as a God in our country." Comparing Gandhi with such a bloodthirsty ruler might seem ridiculous—but the idea of the thug was emblematic of the dangers that might befall India if not for the firm hand of the British.[10]

Nine years before *Gunga Din*, Katherine Mayo had employed the thug alongside sati to defend British rule. "The abolition of ancient indigenous horrors," she wrote, "such as the flourishing trade of the professional strangler tribes, the Thugs; the burning alive of widows; the burying alive of lepers, lie to the credit of the Company." By linking thuggee and sati, Mayo contributed to the gendered framing of the thugs, a framing embodied in the figure of the goddess Kali. The horrors of the thugs were often explained as a result of Kali worship. *Gunga Din*, for example, begins with an ominous statement: "The portions of this film dealing with the goddess Kali are based on historical fact." As historian Andrew Rotter has documented, Kali became a touchstone in American perceptions of independent India as dangerously feminine. Contributing to such perceptions, Hollywood continued to juxtapose thuggee and sati. In 1956, the Academy Award for Best Picture went to *Around the World in 80 Days*, a sprawling epic in which a group of thugs threaten to burn a Hindu princess played by Shirley MacLaine.[11]

Kali worship inspired the most infamous Hollywood depiction of the thug. Released in 1984, *Indiana Jones and the Temple of Doom* revolves around the discovery of a secret thug sect. Echoing *Gunga Din*, the film spares no facet of the thug myth. In the most famous scene of the film, the chief thug rips out a man's heart while muttering oaths to Kali and other Hindu deities. Assuming most audiences would have little familiarity with thuggee, the film includes a conversation between Dr. Jones and a British official. Set amidst an unusual dinner party—complete with live baby snakes, eye-ball soup, and monkey's brains—the conversation locates the thugs (and India more generally) in the realm of the grotesquely foreign.

Yet by the 1980s, the word *thug* had become a generic marker of criminality. If not in the context of Indiana Jones, few Americans would associate the thug with India. The Americanization of the thug began as early as 1852, when the *New York Times* published an article entitled "The Thugs of New-York." "In the heart of India," the article began, "there exists a terrible sect of religionists, whose worship is the most hideous in the whole record of false theologies." The article was not focused on India, however. Readers were asked, "In what do the rowdies of New-York differ from the Thugs of India?" Not much, the article concluded.

Between "Thuggism in Hindostan, and Thuggism in America," the *Times* found little difference. In the next few decades, the *Times* would find thugs from Pittsburgh to Sarasota. The word *thug* began to be used without any reference to India. In 1864, a Confederate force raided a train twenty miles from Baltimore. A witness labeled one of the raiders a "Thug." In 1879, the *National Police Gazette* reported on a murder with an article entitled "The Fate of a Thug." Again, no reference was made to India. In 1908, the magazine *Forest and Stream* called an especially troublesome species of fish "The Blue Thugs of the Sea."[12]

The naturalization of the thug was a slow process. While some Americans began to use *thug* in everyday speech, many continued to see the thug as a distinctly foreign and decidedly Indian figure. From Emerson to Twain, many nineteenth-century Americans capitalized *Thug*. Thus, they recognized the distinctness and foreignness of the "Thugs of the desert." But in the first few decades of the twentieth century, the identity of the thug began to shift. Even as Indian Americans were rejected as nonwhite, the thug quietly became a naturalized American. By the late twentieth century, most Americans no longer associated the word *thug* with India. Gone was any link between the thug and the Thugs. But while the word *thug* was losing its connection to India, it was developing a different referent—one just as racially coded as the thugs of old.[13]

In 1993, the Reverend Calvin Butts, pastor of Harlem's Abyssinian Baptist Church, launched a scathing critique of the thug. His target was neither Indiana Jones nor the violence on the streets of Harlem. Instead, Butts attacked the thug as rapper. "We're not against rap," Butts intoned from the pulpit, "We're not against rappers. But we are against those thugs who disgrace our community, our women, who disgrace our culture, and have absolutely nothing of redemptive value to offer, except the legacy of violence and sexual assault and foul language." Butts organized "rap stompings" in which parishioners smashed hip-hop albums with their feet. In one publicity stunt, Butts personally flattened dozens of records with a bulldozer. His crusade earned him top billing in an exposé on "gangsta rap" that aired on NBC nationwide. But it was not the national news that garnered Butts his greatest fame.[14]

Butts was featured in the video of one of the most popular rap singles of the early 1990s, "Thuggish Ruggish Bone," by the group Bone Thugs-n-Harmony. By using Butts to introduce their video, Bone responded to the criticism of the "thug life" that was a prominent facet of the culture wars of the 1990s. The video begins with footage of Butts offering his famous sermon: "We're not against rap. We're not against rappers. But we are against those thugs. . . ." The word *thugs* is drawn out, while the music cuts in and the video shows the young rappers looking alternately scornful, thoughtful, and amused as they watch Butts on a tiny television. Before Butts can finish his thought, the rappers turn their backs on the TV and walk out onto the streets of their native Cleveland. The video uses images of Cleveland to portray the violence from which hip-hop emerged—not just the violence between street gangs, but also the violence of poverty and of police brutality. Instead of the glorification of wealth that would come to be associated with later hip-hop artists, we see the poverty of the rappers and the community they forged despite that poverty. "Not about that mighty dollar," one rapper rhymes, "Roll with the bone, mo' thugs will follow." By reclaiming the word *thug*, Bone contested the dominant meaning given to violence in urban America and rendered visible what Tricia Rose calls "rap's hidden politics."[15]

For many hip-hop artists, the thug was a product of urban life, as well as the most eloquent witness to that life. In tracks like "Thug 4 Life" and "Livin the Thug Life," Tupac Shakur framed his story as a battle for survival. Like Bone, Tupac used rap to comment on the many layers of violence in urban America. Also like Bone, Tupac emphasized the iniquities of the criminal justice system. In "When Thugz Cry," Tupac offered a multilayered critique of mass imprisonment. "How does it feel to lose your life," he asked, "over somethin that you did as a kid?" From the suffering of the individual, he turned to the social context of mass imprisonment: "You all alone, no communication, block on the phone. / Don't get along with yo' pop, and plus your moms is gone / Where did we go wrong?" *Where did we go wrong?* The inclusivity of the question is vital to Tupac's message. In his lyrics and his life, he located the thug within the larger political and economic violence of American society.[16]

The thug emerged as someone who had overcome violence while remaining rooted in the experience of that violence. Consider the definitions of the word *thug* submitted by users of the website urbandictionary .com. "To be a thug or thugs," one contributor explained, "you have to ALWAYS be true to yourself and not be a FAKE." For some, the authenticity of the thug served to distinguish the thug from the gangster. "A 'tru' or 'thug' doesn't mean a gangsta," another post declared, "because

THUG

there are fake gangsters and there are wannabe gangsters." Surviving struggle while remaining authentic became a defining characteristic of the thug. Multiple contributors reproduced a quote from Tupac that has become a motto of thug culture. Usually attributed to an interview with a reporter from the television network BET (Black Entertainment Television), the quote actually comes from one of the darkest moments in Tupac's career. In 1993, Tupac was convicted of sexually assaulting a young woman in a hotel in New York. It was upon leaving the courtroom, amidst a sea of reporters, that Tupac declared, "I'm a thug, that's because I came from the gutter, and I'm still here."[17]

In response to his indictment and later conviction, Tupac spoke out against the equation of the thug with misogyny and violence against women. Questioned on *The Arsenio Hall Show,* Tupac explained that "coming out of a family and a household with just women" it was especially troubling "to have a woman say I took something from her." In his music, Tupac had condemned violence against women. In "Keep Ya Head Up," he rapped, "I wonder why we take from our women / Why we rape our women, do we hate our women?" One of his most popular tracks, "Dear Mama," was inspired by his love for his mother. Despite Tupac's own music and his public comments, his case became a flashpoint for criticism of the way many hip-hop songs portrayed women. Hip-hop artists have long echoed the violence against women prevalent in American society. In the words of bell hooks, "The sexist, misogynist, patriarchal ways of thinking and behaving that are glorified in gangsta rap are a reflection of the prevailing values in our society." Like the thugs who worshipped Kali, the thug rapper became attacked for defying gender norms that were honored but routinely flouted by the dominant culture. In colonial India and contemporary America, it proved easier to condemn thugs than to confront the violence of the prevailing social order.[18]

On February 6, 2015, a suspicious "skinny black guy" was seen prowling the streets of Madison, Alabama. The police received an urgent call from a concerned resident who was afraid to leave his wife alone with such a dangerous character in the neighborhood. Two officers quickly located the suspect and threw him to the ground. Only later did they realize their mistake. The "skinny black guy" turned out to be a fifty-seven-year-old Indian man, Sureshbhai Patel, recently arrived in the United States to help care for his grandson. Slammed face first into the ground, Patel suffered a spinal cord injury that left him partially paralyzed. Video of the assault went viral, galvanizing outrage from Alabama to India. In response, the police chief of Madison and the governor of Alabama both apologized publicly, and the officer in question was fired and charged with assault. But what if Patel *had* been a "skinny black guy"? Contrasting events in Madison with the police killings of unarmed black men—Eric Garner, Michael Brown, Akai Gurley, Walter Scott—reveals the profound divide between the racial and class positions of Indian Americans and African Americans in contemporary America. But as Sureshbhai Patel discovered, that divide is not always visible. No one called Patel a "thug," neither the man who called 911 nor the police officers who threw him to the ground. But the assumption that an unknown "skinny black guy" must be a threat reveals the pervasive racial stereotypes that have long oppressed African Americans and Indian Americans—if not always in the same ways.[19]

Many of the figures in this book were treated as thugs. From abolitionists to Ghadar volunteers to civil rights activists—anyone who questioned the established order was branded a dangerous criminal to be watched, imprisoned, or killed. At a time when the law openly embraced white supremacy and imperial rule, it fell to the thugs to fight for freedom. What does it say about the contemporary world that the thug remains a necessary figure—whether villain or hero or both?

The relationship between the United States and India entered a new phase beginning in the 1960s and culminating in the 1990s. As the next two chapters reveal, the confluence of several factors—the American civil rights movement, the United States Immigration Act of 1965, and the changing fortunes of India's economy—created an environment that was more conducive to high-level diplomatic and economic collaboration between the countries. The improvement in what we might call "elite Indo-American relations" came at the same time that the Indian American community was growing in size and wealth and substantial progress was being made in the struggle for democracy in both countries, at least when measured by access to the ballot in the United States and the decentralization of power in India. It is important to recognize these related achievements: the warmth of elite Indo-American relations, the rise of the Indian American community, and the progress toward a more inclusive democracy in both countries. But many are those who are excluded from this seemingly golden age in the history of "the world's two largest democracies." And many are the threats to democracy itself.

In both India and the United States, the surveillance state continues to grow. Inequality and discrimination track differences of race, caste, and creed. And even some of the most basic foundations of democracy—a free press, for example, or access to the ballot—are under sustained threat. There is a growing gap between the myth of the two largest democracies and the many threats to freedom in both countries. That gap helps to explain the careers of Tupac and other successful "thug" rappers who simultaneously embody the struggles of impoverished African American communities and the success of those lucky few who are able to transcend those struggles. In both the United States and India, we glorify the outlaw and the thug as emblems of success and as rebels against a corrupt establishment. Even Bollywood has embraced the thug. As I write, cinema fans eagerly await the release of a new film, *Thugs of Hindostan*, that will star Aamir Khan and feature Katrina Kaif and Amitabh Bachchan. Although the plot of the film remains mysterious, it appears that Khan will use his star power to revive the thug for a new generation eager for heroes who fight from the margins. Colored cosmopolitanism and other forms of radical democratic solidarity were weakened by the changing political and economic fortunes of the Indian American community and of India itself. But as the next two chapters demonstrate, old freedom struggles have reemerged—like the thug—where no one expected.

# CHAPTER 5

# The Ends of Poverty

∞

The struggle—the great world struggle is to end political,
economic, racial and cultural imperialism so that this
world will give every man an unfettered opportunity to
give the best that is in him for human progress.
—Taraknath Das, 1946

SARGENT SHRIVER came to India on a mission. The brother-in-law of
John F. Kennedy, Shriver had been tasked with creating the Peace
Corps, an ambitious effort to send young Americans to volunteer abroad.
While domestic support for the initiative surged, the international response remained tepid. Governments struggling to attack poverty were
uninterested in hosting young Americans whose idealism outstripped
their technical skills. In lands recently freed from colonial rule, many
suspected that the Peace Corps was another branch of American imperialism. Shriver knew that the Peace Corps could not be foisted upon
foreign countries. He had to sell it. He also knew that no potential recipient was more important than India.

A massive nation with intense poverty but without the kind of violent instability that might threaten young Americans, India seemed an
ideal location for Peace Corps volunteers. And support from Jawaharlal
Nehru, an anticolonial icon throughout much of the Afro-Asian world,

might open doors in other recently decolonized countries. When Shriver sat down with Nehru, he was prepared to argue for how the Peace Corps could help India meet its development goals. But Nehru turned the discussion on its head. He agreed to accept Peace Corps volunteers but stressed that the impact would be on the volunteers themselves. "I am sure young Americans would learn a great deal in this country," he explained, "and it could be an important experience for them." Nehru dismissed the impact of the Peace Corps on India as insignificant. He told Shriver, "I hope you and they will not be too disappointed if the Punjab, when they leave, is more or less the same as it was before they came."[1]

From 1961 to 1975, some 4,325 Americans served in India as Peace Corps volunteers. Their efforts were part of a massive American undertaking to contribute to India's development. In the decades after Indian independence, American aid poured into the subcontinent. For many of those years, more American aid went to India than to any other country. With American money came American development experts. Since the first Yankee missionaries arrived in Calcutta, Americans had been trying to "save" India. From the Peace Corps to USAID, the new missionaries were decidedly secular. But their zeal was still based on faith—faith in technology, money, and above all expertise.

Many of these Americans also believed in India and in Indians. For every expert who thought that India should follow America's path to affluence, there was another who argued that the solution to ending Indian poverty would come from India's villages. Often dichotomized as "modernization theory" versus "community development," these different approaches to ending poverty shared one fundamental assumption— that Americans could and should play a crucial role in helping India develop. Were they right? Or was Nehru's pessimism justified? Would billions of dollars in American aid and thousands of American volunteers and experts leave India "more or less" the same?

One thing is clear: Nehru was right that Americans who came to India were often transformed by their experiences. The idea that India had something to teach America was at the heart of a little-known government program called Volunteers to America (VTA). Essentially a reverse Peace Corps, the VTA brought volunteers to the United States from developing countries—inverting the usual flow of munificent do-gooders. The idea may have originated with Charles Hudson, the first Peace Corps director in India. In 1964, Hudson complained that Americans were too focused on helping India to realize that Indians could help the United States. He called for a more balanced and reciprocal relationship between the countries. "We must find ways to let India help us," Hudson declared. He envisioned "a two-way pattern of giving that restores their pride, lets them accept gracefully what we give since they are paying in the same coin." Only a year later, Hudson would be tasked with starting just such a program. It began small, with five volunteers brought from India to America in the summer of 1965. After teaching Hindi to Peace Corps volunteers, the Indian social workers were split up and placed at different community organizations, like the Henry Street Settlement House in New York and the Central Outreach Program in Cleveland. The staff at these organizations lauded the Indian volunteers for bringing "an insight and enthusiasm that was refreshing." The achievements of the Indian volunteers led Harris Wofford, the associate director of the Peace Corps, to champion the program's expansion. With support from Lyndon Johnson, the VTA was officially launched in 1966.[2]

The VTA was only one way in which India's development experience radiated back to the United States. Many of the methods that were honed through community-development initiatives in India eventually migrated into American cities. Much of Lyndon Johnson's War on Poverty, and especially his controversial Community Action Programs, owed an intellectual debt to India. The history of community development reflected back and forth between the United States and India, blurring the borders between the countries and between the so-called developed and developing worlds.[3]

While supporting community development, Lyndon Johnson inadvertently built an even more important bridge between the United States and India. On October 3, 1965, seated in the shadow of the Statue of Liberty, Johnson signed into law the 1965 Immigration Act, also known as the Hart-Celler Act. By shifting the immigration selection process from quotas based on national origin to criteria based on skills and family ties, the bill paved the way for a rapid increase in the numbers of South Asians entering the United States. By the mid 1970s, the number of South Asians in the United States had approached two hundred thousand. Now, there are over three million.

After 1965, the class composition of the South Asian American community changed dramatically. As a result of the new immigration preference for professionals, a community once dominated by farmers and laborers became defined by engineers and doctors. Working-class South Asians continued to enter the United States. But the public visibility of South Asian professionals helped foster the "model minority myth," the widespread belief that Asian migrants had succeeded through education and hard work, while less enterprising minorities had fallen behind. The model minority myth obscured the many poor and working-class South Asian Americans as well as the fact that the affluence and education of many South Asian Americans derived in part from the dictates of American immigration policy.[4]

Growing rapidly in size and wealth, the Indian American community played an important role in fostering new economic partnerships between the United States and India. For the first quarter century after Indian independence, American engagement in Indian development focused on questions of aid: how much should be given and toward what ends. But in the 1970s, the economic relationship between India and America began to shift toward business partnerships. Indian Americans helped foster those partnerships, as did new communication technologies. The development of the internet opened a new chapter in the economic linkages between India and America. From Infosys to Google, technology companies have transformed recent Indo-American business ties. Such relationships have fed a resurgence of self-congratulatory Indo-American boosterism. But just as in the days when New England merchants plied the Arabian Sea, there are winners and losers in the new age of trade between India and the United States. The question remains whether India's surging economy will do what decades of American aid failed to do: end the extreme poverty that plagues millions of Indians.[5]

## The Expert and The Community

About thirteen miles northeast of Yuma, Arizona, a concrete dam bridges the Colorado River. An engineering feat in its day, the Laguna Dam would be unremarkable now if not for the forty-seven swastikas chiseled into its concrete walls. In 1903, the engineers planning the dam struggled to find a model for how to build a structure over the unusually shifting soil created by the Colorado. Such a dam existed, but it was several thousand miles away on India's Jumna River. After failing to find a closer model, a team of American engineers sailed toward the subcontinent. They would return home with detailed plans for their new bridge, as well as with an idea for how to show their gratitude to their Indian hosts. The swastika is an ancient Indian symbol. Indeed, the word *swastika* comes from the Sanskrit for an auspicious sign. The American engineers thought they were engaging in a form of cultural connection by branding their bridge with such a positive symbol. They had no way of knowing that Adolf Hitler would render the swastika a sign of intolerance and hatred. The story of those swastikas reveals the connections between development efforts in India and America, as well as the unpredictable and often fraught consequences of those efforts.[6]

Fifty years after the Laguna Dam was constructed, a much larger dam was built near a village called Bhakra in the Indian state of Himachal Pradesh. A charismatic American named Harvey Slocum was recruited to oversee what became India's tallest dam. Struggling to complete the task on time, Slocum wrote Nehru that "only God, not Slocum, could build the Bhakra Dam on schedule." But the dam was completed. In July 1954, Nehru opened its sluice gates and declared such massive development projects the "temples" of modern India. Dams produce clean renewable power, help prevent seasonal flooding, and create new opportunities for irrigation. But they also displace people, often thousands of people, while flooding entire valleys. Did India's development require such disruptive megaprojects?[7]

Many American experts argued that India needed to undergo a period of rapid industrialization as had the United States and other "modern" Western economies. The premise that industrialization would drive economic change, that poor countries should follow the developmental stages taken by industrialized countries, came to be known as modernization theory. The two most important advocates of modernization theory, Max Millikan and W. W. Rostow, used India to justify their stage theory of economic development. Another key figure in modernization theory, Edward Shils, also examined India as a case study in the political dimensions of modernization. But whereas many American experts advocated modernization via industrialization, others championed a different path to Indian prosperity. If Harvey Slocum embodied American support for dams and other massive development projects, a city planner named Albert Mayer became the face of an alternative approach known as community development.[8]

Mayer was given the rare opportunity to design a new city, Chandigarh, destined to become the capital of not one but two Indian states. Much of the city would be designed by the renowned French architect Charles-Édouard Jeanneret-Gris, better known as Le Corbusier. But it was Mayer who created Chandigarh's original master plan. Mayer came to India, like many Americans, in the armed forces. During the Second World War, he designed airfields in India's northeast from which supplies could be flown "over the hump" to China. Mayer prided himself on making Indian friends, and was critical of other Americans for their "Anglo-Saxon feeling of superiority and isolationism." In an article he published in *Survey Graphic* in 1947, he lamented that the presence of American soldiers in India had done little to increase real understanding between the two countries. "Too many Americans came back with less sympathy for India, and certainly with less understanding of it, than they had before they went." He was especially critical of the way India's poverty was used to denigrate the country and to create a false dichotomy between India and America. "One got the impression," Mayer wrote, "that Americans had never seen slums until we reached the Far East; that our streets and parks were immaculately clean."[9]

In May 1946, Nehru invited Mayer to return to India to advise the government on "various matters relating to planning, village reconstruction and the ordered development of community life more especially in our rural areas." Mayer accepted the invitation and spent months traveling through rural India, talking with farmers and villagers. With Nehru's support, Mayer launched an ambitious development effort in Etawah, a district in one of the poorest Indian states, Uttar Pradesh. The Etawah Project, as it became known, was modeled on the Tennessee Valley Authority, a multifaceted program of rural uplift. But Mayer went further than most development experts in stressing the importance of grassroots initiatives. At the heart of Mayer's approach to community development was the Gram Sevak (Village Volunteer), who served as a link between the government and the village. The Gram Sevak was not an expert, but a motivator and a facilitator engaged in what Mayer called the "dirty hands" approach to development. While much emphasis was put on understanding the "felt needs" of each village, the Etawah Project also deployed a variety of top-down initiatives, including new agricultural machinery and seeds. The project began with sixty-four villages but expanded to over three hundred by 1951. Its apparent successes—particularly in increasing agricultural output—received praise from President Truman, Eleanor Roosevelt, and a variety of American publications including *Time, Life,* and the *New York Times Magazine.*[10]

After Mayer himself, Etawah's greatest booster was Chester Bowles, then in his first tour as the American ambassador to India. Ambassador Bowles visited Etawah and was impressed by what he saw: "an administrative framework through which modern scientific knowledge could be put to work for the benefit of the hundreds of millions of people who have long lived in poverty." In November 1951, Bowles wrote Nehru with an ambitious proposal—to expand the Etawah model to tackle rural poverty throughout India. Nehru has earned criticism for embracing large-scale, top-down industrial projects. But he also believed in the power of grassroots development initiatives. That was, after all, why he brought Mayer back to India in the first place. Nehru welcomed the Bowles plan, and in January 1952 an Indo-American Technical Agreement created a joint fund of $54 million for supplies and experts from abroad and an equal amount in rupees for local needs.[11]

At the core of community development was the idea that social change had to come from the grassroots. And yet American experts were tasked with organizing and training their Indian counterparts. Aware of that contradiction, Mayer encouraged his American staff to study Indian religious traditions, and suggested that photographs of development successes such as dams be put in temples next to "the Shivas, the Krishnas, the Ganeshas, the familiar pictures of the Hindu pantheon." But even while Mayer tried to Hinduize and Indianize the process of development, Americans continued to pour into rural India. And with them came American dollars.[12]

American philanthropic organizations played a vital role in shaping and funding community development in India. The Ford and Rockefeller Foundations were especially generous and influential. Like Mayer, the leaders of those foundations presented their efforts as support for Indian initiatives. Community development, Douglas Ensminger asserted, "was not a U.S. imposed program." A sociologist who had studied rural development, Ensminger served as the head of the Ford Foundation in India from 1951 to 1970. "The U.S. was not dangling large sums of money in front of India to try and influence her to buy a change of policy," Ensminger declared. The goal was to help India "carry out its own programs and its own commitments to the people."[13]

But which "people" stood to benefit from community development? In 1952, two Gandhian social workers published a strong critique of the Etawah Project in the prominent Indian journal *Economic and Political Weekly*. Their critique was not aimed at the idea of community development, but the gap between the idea and the reality as they witnessed it. Of the Etawah Project, they wrote, "It is neither a plan of the people, nor for the people, nor by the people, but something imposed from above." Many of the projects focused on boosting agricultural outputs, which, in the absence of meaningful land reform, mainly benefited landowners. A prominent member of Mayer's team admitted before the U.S. Senate in 1951 that absentee landlords stood to benefit the most from increases in productivity. Senator Theodore Green warned that the changes would limit land reform. "The more profitable that land becomes for the owner, the less likely he is to agree to any change." There were specific initiatives that targeted underserved portions of the population. But according to one observer, "Programs for the welfare of women, younger people, and the untouchables lacked imagination and failed to make the desired impact." Mayer himself called caste a "calm and stabilizing institution" and did little to engage women in the process of development.[14]

The weaknesses of community development became apparent as the Etawah Project was scaled up. By 1956, the project had reached some 123,000 villages that collectively housed eighty million people. What was the impact of such a massive program? In 1957, Balvantray G. Mehta, a veteran political figure, headed a committee that issued a report critical of the projects for their top-down approach. In the words of historian Daniel Immerwahr, "Conspicuously absent from community council deliberations were any measures that might address some of the structural issues most obviously responsible for the depressed conditions endured by the lower orders: debt, unequal land tenure, caste, and patriarchy." The anthropologist Gerald D. Berreman was not surprised. To expect village elites to undo their own power was "even more unrealistic than to expect rapid, orderly integration of the schools in the southern United States to result from putting responsibility for school integration in the hands of local school boards."[15]

The failure of community development cannot be blamed solely on the recalcitrance of local elites. The topography of community development—its blend of local knowledge, national commitment, and international funding—requires that its failures be shared across geographic boundaries. Indeed, part of the tragedy of community development is that it succeeded so beautifully at connecting the transnational, the national, and the local even while failing so miserably to eradicate poverty. From the American sailors who traded in colonial Madras to the American soldiers who swarmed Calcutta during the Second World War, American engagement with Indian society repeatedly reinforced local hierarchies. But there was something new about community development that deserves recognition and that sharpens the tragedy of its failure, something that comes into focus when we view this history through the lens of a figure rarely associated with international development of any kind: the thug.

The foreignness of the thug was used to justify the expansion of the colonial state. If the thug's violence had been located within British territory, it would have cast suspicion on the power and benevolence of the British themselves. It was crucial that the thug be seen as an outsider. The genius of community development was the idea that the outsider could be brought in—or, put differently, that the rural poor could be empowered to lead a development effort that was being funded from Delhi and Washington. It was not just the belief in rural people that was radical, but the belief that rural people could succeed in collaboration with a massive network of other actors within and beyond India. The "rule of experts" was to be married to the power of the people. Community development, in theory, leveled hierarchies of power in a way that was new to the history of Indo-American relations. It remains to be seen what it would take to actually achieve such a leveling.[16]

While recognizing the mistakes and corruption that marred all levels of the community-development process, we must be careful to avoid condemning all antipoverty efforts as equally misguided and doomed to failure. It is important to criticize the failures of international aid. Yet as the history of community development makes clear, such failures cannot be blamed simply on the hubris of Western governments and NGOs, nor on the corruption or incompetence of local and national governments. Many development initiatives, including community development, had successes as well as failures—and long-term impacts that are hard to parse into such simple categories. Consider an area of development where inaction remains morally inconceivable: the struggle against mass starvation.[17]

## The Politics of Hunger

In 1943, as Bengal descended into famine, Americans debated whether the United Nations Relief and Rehabilitation Administration (UNRRA) should provide assistance. Dean Acheson, then the assistant secretary of state, argued that the UNRRA should operate only in areas liberated from the enemy. As part of the British Empire, Bengal would thus be ineligible for UNRRA aid. On the floor of the House, Congressman Karl Mundt, a Republican from South Dakota, challenged Acheson. "Should Italians who till a few months earlier had been shooting at American soldiers be helped by UNRRA," Mundt asked, "while India with its enormous contribution to the Allied cause be excluded?" On January 21, 1944, Senator Bennett C. Clark, Democrat from Missouri, offered an even more damning argument. "If occupation is the test," Senator Clark declared, "the British have been in hostile occupation of India for nearly two hundred years." Mundt successfully passed an amendment to make India eligible for aid from the UNRRA. But Winston Churchill refused to allow the UNRRA into India. Such international attention might unmask the inequity and instability of British rule.[18]

American Indophiles refused to abandon Bengal to imperial apathy. In 1946, the India Famine Emergency Committee (IFEC) formed, with Pearl Buck as its chair. Support came from Albert Einstein, the presidents of the AFL and the CIO, and former under-secretary of state Sumner Welles. In March 1946, the IFEC published a prominent appeal in the *New York Times*. "Between ten and twenty million people in India are in danger of starving to death in the next few months," the appeal explained. "These are official figures. But these millions need not die."[19]

Under pressure, Harry Truman sent former president Herbert Hoover to investigate the famine. Hoover had organized aid for occupied Belgians during the First World War and for starving Russians in 1921. In April 1946, he met with Gandhi and Nehru to discuss the famine and how Americans might help. The IFEC launched a similar fact-finding mission. But Truman refused to meet with its members. Pearl Buck wrote him to decry the dangers of abandoning the Indian people at such a crucial juncture. "In so far as we willfully alienate the peoples of the East," Buck wrote, "we persuade them toward Russia."[20]

Truman was not convinced. He saw India as a morass of poverty and superstition, "jammed with poor people and cows wandering around streets, witch doctors, and people sitting on hot coals and bathing in the Ganges." He wondered aloud why "anyone thought it was important." But the fall of China to communist forces and the outbreak of the Korean War forced Truman to reassess his views on India. Suddenly, Asia seemed more important and more dangerous, and India began to look like a vital ally.[21]

Anticommunism galvanized support for sending food aid to India. In August 1950, Hubert Humphrey told his fellow senators that food aid was necessary in the battle against communism. Like Humphrey, Chester Bowles argued that only a resurgent India could serve as a bulwark against communism. Bowles stressed the threat of China. In a note to Assistant Secretary of State George McGhee, Bowles declared, "Communist China and an India striving to remain democratic would inevitably be placed in economic competition." Using the threat of communist expansion, Bowles pushed for a Marshall Plan for Asia. But despite the efforts of the India lobby and its congressional supporters, resistance to aiding India was strong. Skeptics pointed to the fact that India was not a consistent American ally. One Congressman huffed, "If there is anybody in the House who has ever seen or heard that Nehru has ever made a statement favorable to the United States, I would like to hear him say so now." It was not just Nehru's criticism of America that rankled American policymakers. India's embrace of state planning was equally troubling. Congressman Lawrence Henry Smith, a Republican from Wisconsin, expressed the skepticism of many when he declared that India had a "planning" government and that its agricultural deficits came from a socialist emphasis on heavy industry.[22]

"This question of socialism is an interesting thing," Douglas Ensminger remembered while reflecting on the difficulty of explaining Indian politics to reluctant American donors. In one telling incident, Ensminger hosted Donald David, a powerful trustee of the Ford Foundation who served as dean of the Harvard School of Business and was also on the boards of GE, the Ford Motor Company, and several other large corporations. Ensminger described David as "a very committed private enterprise man" who arrived in India wary of Nehru's policies. Ensminger responded by showing David a range of economic conditions in India, including a village, steel mills, and a government-operated coach industry, "one of the best managed industries in all of India," according to Ensminger. When David met Nehru, he said, "Mr. Prime Minister, if I were the Prime Minister over here, I would support what you are supporting." "What you're talking about is equality of opportunity," David told Nehru, "that's what socialism means to you." Advocates of aid for India like Ensminger and Bowles argued that India's socialism was vastly preferable to communism, and that feeding India's millions was vital to protect India from communist expansion.[23]

That argument proved successful—at least in part. In the spring of 1951, Harry Truman approved the first major loan of wheat to India. Communist gains in China and Korea drove his change of heart—as did the powerful American farm lobby. Although political leaders were divided, American farmers were united in support of large aid budgets. Food aid provided a way to get rid of grain surpluses and thus to drive up prices and profits. It was a win / win proposition—oppose communism and curry favor with American farmers. Truman was not the last American president to welcome such an opportunity.

In July 1954, Dwight Eisenhower signed the Agricultural Trade Development Act, also known as Public Law 480, or just PL 480—a dramatic shift in American aid policy that was a direct result of the power of the farm lobby and of anticommunism. The law aimed, in Eisenhower's words, to "lay the basis for a permanent expansion of our exports of agricultural products with lasting benefits to ourselves and peoples of other lands." The law clearly aided American exports, but its impact on the "peoples of other lands" was more complex. Free American grain did feed hungry people. But such aid also depressed the prices of those grains, driving local farmers into bankruptcy. Nevertheless, the Indian government saw the deal as valuable. Indian imports of American wheat exploded. In 1960, India received over four million tons of American wheat.[24]

Truman and Eisenhower were reluctant advocates of aid to India. By contrast, John F. Kennedy embraced using American resources to support India and other "developing" countries. Soon after becoming president, Kennedy rebranded PL 480 as "Food for Peace" and located it in the newly created U.S. Agency for International Development. He declared, "Food is strength, and food is peace, and food is freedom, and food is a helping hand to people around the world whose good will and friendship we want." India was a major beneficiary of that helping hand. From 1955 to 1971, India received some fifty million tons of grain, almost 40 percent of all the food distributed under PL 480.[25]

It was politically difficult to send aid to a country whose leadership was openly critical of American foreign policy. In his letter to Nehru after the invasion of Goa, Kennedy raised "the problem of aid appropriations." He stressed that he did not want to make American "assistance to India contingent on her acceptance of our particular wishes in foreign or domestic policy." "We seek to help develop independence, and independence exists to be used," Kennedy added. But Nehru needed to recognize the potential impact of Indian actions on American public opinion. "Each year," Kennedy wrote, "our appropriations to help, not India alone, but also the other developing countries of the world, involve our most difficult political battle." Such aid could "ease the strains and passions that arise from poverty," but only if American congressmen could be convinced to support it.[26]

In Congress, doubts remained as to how much aid the United States should provide India. In 1963, that opposition coalesced in resistance to plans for the United States to help fund a new steel plant at Bokaro, Jharkhand. To prevent embarrassment, India officially withdrew its request for support. Shortly thereafter, the Soviet Union offered its own aid to fund the plan, which the Indian government accepted.[27]

Congressional opposition to supporting India stemmed in part from stereotypes of Indians as hopelessly backward. Such stereotypes were made clear in a conversation between Congressman Otto Passman, a Democrat from Louisiana, and USAID Administrator William Macomber. A long-time critic of foreign aid, Passman questioned the efficacy of support to India. "It is said," he declared, "that the animals and the rats actually consume or destroy more food and fiber than the Indian people consume because of their reluctance to deprive the cows of the access to the fields." He demanded to know if USAID was fencing off farmland to keep out voracious livestock. Macomber tried to turn the conversation away from fencing to the Indian government's response to the spoilage of grains, but Passman persisted, and the conversation descended into the absurd:

*Passman:* They can't train the cattle to stay out of the fields and away
from the crops?

*Macomber:* No they can't, but they do other things too, as you know,
  sir. . . .

*Passman:* You can control the cows with a child and a stick, but how
  can you control the monkeys?

*Macomber:* They are harder to control.

*Passman:* How do you control them? Aren't they also sacred animals?

*Macomber:* That is correct, sir, and I don't think that they are
  controlled.

*Passman:* They have a priority?

*Macomber:* They have assumed a priority.

As this conversation reveals, opponents of foreign aid often reveled in
the idea that "backward" peoples would never climb out of poverty. Why
give Indians money if their strange superstitions would always hold them
back?[28]

It would prove impossible to convince Congress to release aid to India
on anything near the scale that Bowles, Ensminger, and others believed
was necessary. But American aid remained substantial throughout most
of the 1950s and 1960s, a result of anticommunism, the farm lobby, and
the concerted efforts of a range of American Indophiles. Nevertheless,
if the Peace Corps, community development, and food aid had been the
only thrusts of American development efforts, Nehru's prophecy would
have proved accurate. The Punjab would have remained more or less the
same. But by the 1970s another American initiative was already trans-
forming the Punjab in ways that promised to dramatically reduce hunger
throughout India.[29]


## Green Revolutions

In John Updike's best-selling novel *Rabbit, Run*, one character humbles
another by remarking, "How big do you think your little friends look
among the billions that God sees. In Bombay now they die in the streets
every minute." *Rabbit, Run* was published in 1960. Eight years later, another best seller again cast India in the role of hopeless disaster—less
because of its death rate than its birth rate. Biologist Paul Ehrlich's *The
Population Bomb* darkly predicted, "The battle to feed all of humanity is

over. In the 1970s and 1980s hundreds of millions of people will starve to death in spite of any crash programs embarked upon now." The first paragraph of the book transported readers to "one stinking hot night in Delhi a few years ago." Ehrlich remembered, "The streets seemed alive with people. People eating, people washing, people sleeping. People visiting, arguing, and screaming. People thrusting their hands through the taxi window, begging. People defecating and urinating. People clinging to buses. People herding animals. People, people, people, people."[30]

Ehrlich's memories infused old stereotypes of India—hot, stinking, overrun with beggars—with a new urgency. Fears of a population bomb spread widely in development circles and beyond, contributing to what historian Michelle Murphy has called "the economization of life." It was not only outsiders that worried about India's growing population. Many Indians shared Ehrlich's concerns about the dangers of an expanding population. But even as Ehrlich was predicting doom, Indian farmers and agricultural scientists were building an India that would, for the first time in generations, be able to reliably and consistently feed itself.[31]

In the 1940s, a group of agricultural scientists based in Mexico began experimenting with new varieties of wheat. Their work was directed by an American agricultural scientist named Norman Borlaug. In March 1962, a few of Borlaug's wheat varieties were tested at the Indian Agricultural Research Institute (IARI) in New Delhi. The results were encouraging. That spring, Borlaug was invited to visit India at the request of a scientist named Monkombu Sambasivan (M. S.) Swaminathan. After earning his PhD from the University of Cambridge in 1952, Swaminathan had continued his research at the University of Wisconsin. At Swaminathan's urging, Borlaug came to India with some 220 pounds of wheat seeds. After initial trials proved promising, the Rockefeller Foundation supported the widespread introduction of high-yield wheat. During British rule, India had suffered frequent famines. In the first years after independence, India became dependent on food aid, much of it donated by the United States. But high-yield wheat promised to change everything. According to one estimate, yields nearly doubled in five years, soaring from twelve million tons in 1965 to twenty million tons in 1970. What became known as the "green revolution" transformed agriculture in Mexico, India, and throughout much of the world. Borlaug would win the Nobel Peace Prize in 1970, as well as the Padma Vibushan, India's second-highest honor.[32]

The "green revolution" was not, however, especially green. High-yield wheat required more water than traditional grains and thus contributed to water shortages. The new varieties also depended on regular supplies of synthetic fertilizers and pesticides. Scientists and farmers began to worry about the ecological impact of an agricultural system that soaked up huge amounts of water and required blanketing the land with toxic chemicals. Many were also troubled by the degree to which the green revolution widened the divide between small farmers, many of whom lacked the resources to exploit the new technologies, and wealthy farmers and corporations, whose profits soared. The "miraculous" yields produced by new crop varieties have been questioned, as has an even more basic assumption at the heart of the green revolution—that the way to end hunger is to produce more food.[33]

By treating hunger as a problem of supply rather than demand, planners ignored the fact that hunger is rarely a result of the absence of food. Rather, it is the absence of buying power in poor and marginalized groups that leads to mass hunger. People starve when they do not have enough access to food, not necessarily when there is not food to be accessed. Many of the architects of the green revolution were unconcerned by questions of fairness. Borlaug later admitted, "I wasn't worried a damn bit about equity at this point." The persistence of widespread hunger and malnutrition in contemporary India reveals the profound limitations of a policy that emphasized production at the expense of equitable distribution.[34]

The obsession with output is evident in one of the most celebrated development agreements between the United States and India. In November 1965, Orville L. Freeman, the American secretary of agriculture, and C. Subramaniam, the Indian minister of food and agriculture, signed a historic agreement in Rome. The agreement outlined a new direction for Indian agriculture, including greater openness to foreign inputs, especially of fertilizer. John Lewis, the Director of USAID in India, celebrated the agreement as paving the way for "a breakthrough for Indian agricultural expansion." That "breakthrough" involved massive infusions of pesticides and fertilizer, both of which were needed to support the high-yield grains that were being introduced at the same time.[35]

In the late 1960s, many Indians were eager to gain agricultural independence by any means necessary. American aid had helped independent India avoid major famines, but that aid became increasingly unpredictable after Lyndon Johnson became president. While Kennedy had reasoned calmly with Nehru, Johnson butted heads with Nehru's daughter, Indira Gandhi. Enraged by Gandhi's criticism of American foreign policy and of the war in Vietnam in particular, Johnson repeatedly threatened to cut off food aid. Chester Bowles later wrote, "At least five occasions in the critical years of 1965, 1966, and 1967, the President put the Indian government and people through a needless ordeal in regard to food supplies with no valid explanation even to me and my associates."[36]

Like Johnson, Richard Nixon tied aid to India's support for American foreign policy. Even more than Johnson, Nixon was willing to ignore humanitarian disasters in order to win political battles with Indira Gandhi's government. Take, for example, his response to the war that would give birth to Bangladesh. In 1947, Bengal had been torn in two, its western half becoming the Indian state of West Bengal and its eastern half becoming East Pakistan. In 1970, an East Pakistani political party, the Awami League, won a majority of seats in the Pakistani Parliament. But the ruling powers in West Pakistan refused to honor the election. Instead, planeloads of West Pakistani soldiers descended on the East and began a brutal crackdown.[37]

The Nixon administration stood by West Pakistan. A resolute Cold War ally, Pakistan was vital to secret efforts to open relations with China. Yahya Khan, the military leader of Pakistan, was the kind of anticommunist strongman the Nixon administration loved. In March 1971, Kissinger told Nixon that the violence in East Pakistan was "nothing of any great consequence." "Yahya has got control of East Pakistan," he boasted. Kissinger gloated that "all the experts were saying that 30,000 people can't get control of 75 million." But as the West Pakistani crackdown made clear, "The use of power against seeming odds pays off." Nixon agreed. "Hell, when you look over the history of nations 30,000 well-disciplined people can take 75 million any time." To prove his point, Nixon turned to history. "Look what the Spanish did when they came in and took the Incas and all the rest. Look what the British did when they took India." Thus, the leader of the free world held up Spanish conquistadors and British imperialists as role models of good governance. Both Kissinger and Nixon used euphemisms to cloak the brutal subjugation of East Pakistan. Neither referred to West Pakistani soldiers or troops. Instead, they celebrated the seeming triumph of "well-disciplined people." Nixon went so far as to reject the idea that "independence is a virtue." Whether a country is free or not was not what mattered. "The real question is whether anybody can run the god-damn place."[38]

Nixon's response to the crisis in East Bengal echoed his law-and-order approach to the "drug war" within the United States as well as his antipathy toward protesters. In the fall of 1970, Nixon decried the "thugs and hoodlums" who threw rocks at his car in San Jose, California. "As long as I am President," he snarled, "no band of violent thugs is going to keep me from going out and speaking with the American people." Nixon's casual use of the word *thug* demonstrates that most Americans no longer associated the word with India, but also that they could have learned from the similarities between their world and the Raj. The idea of the thug was used to justify state power, whether American, British, or (West) Pakistani.[39]

Nixon and Kissinger remained unmoved by the violence of the Pakistani army. Their cold disregard is especially remarkable given the courageous efforts of local American diplomats. In April 1971, Archer Kent Blood, the American consul general in Dhaka, sent a telegram signed by some twenty members of the staff. "Our government has failed to denounce the suppression of democracy," the telegram declared. "Our government has failed to denounce atrocities." The politics of the government amounted to "moral bankruptcy" in the face of genocide. The telegram was shelved, and Blood was recalled from Dhaka.[40]

Indira Gandhi appealed to Nixon to reign in the Pakistani military. She decried the unfolding refugee crisis as millions of East Pakistanis fled across the border into India. At the White House, Gandhi suggested that Americans "imagine the entire population of Michigan State suddenly converging on New York State and imagine the strain it would cause on the administration and on the services such as health and communications." But the United States government did nothing to check the Pakistani military. On December 3, Pakistan launched a surprise attack against India. While responding with what would prove a decisive show of force, Indira Gandhi simultaneously wrote Nixon to ask the American leader to use his "undoubted influence with the Government of Pakistan to stop their aggressive activities against India."[41]

As it became clear that Indian forces were gaining ground in East Pakistan, Kissinger and Nixon secretly hoped that Indian rule would become repressive, thus justifying American support for West Pakistan. Kissinger predicted that "in six months the liberals are going to look like jerks because the Indian occupation of East Pakistan is going to make the Pakistani one look like child's play." Instead, India withdrew, and independent Bangladesh was born. In response to India entering the war, Nixon threatened to cut off food aid to India. "We told Mrs. Gandhi we're going to cut off that aid and we're going to do it," he told Kissinger. Nixon ordered Kissinger to examine "every other possibility of how we can squeeze India right now."[42]

The Bangladesh war led to a halt in American aid to India, but it was other major developments that turned that halt into a permanent decline. First, Nixon's détente with China removed the most powerful argument for supporting India. No longer was the subcontinent a necessary check on Chinese expansion. "With China no longer a threat," the presidential advisor Lucian Pye explained in 1976, "it was possible to ask in much more realistic terms what had been accomplished in India as a result of nearly $10 billion of American assistance." Had the Punjab remained the Punjab, as Nehru had predicted? In fact, American assistance had helped transform much of India in ways that contributed to the decline in American aid. As the green revolution expanded Indian agricultural outputs, the need for American aid dwindled, and Indo-American economic ties shifted into the realm of business.[43]

For the first few decades after India achieved independence, American businesses struggled to operate in India as the Indian government prioritized the development of indigenous industries. The production of fertilizer reveals India's suspicion of foreign companies. In the early 1960s, India struggled to produce sufficient fertilizer. The U.S. government and the World Bank encouraged the Bechtel Corporation, a large American company, to build a series of fertilizer plants in India. After sending a team to India, Bechtel proposed building ten fertilizer plants. The Indian government rejected the offer. Bechtel and its supporters were, in the words of Douglas Ensminger, "absolutely dumbfounded and amazed." The fertilizer plants would create jobs, produce tax revenue, and boost the supply of fertilizer. Why would India turn down such an opportunity? If they had built ten plants, Ensminger explained, "Bechtel Engineering Corporation would have been in position to control policies with respect to fertilizer in India." The Indian government welcomed American investment but only so far as it did not impinge on Indian autonomy.[44]

While Indians debated how much to let American companies into India, Americans worried that economic globalization would lure jobs overseas. In the 1990s, the word *outsourcing* became a lightning rod for debates about free trade and its impact on American workers. Technically, the term describes any situation in which a business transfers a task to a third-party provider, regardless of whether that outside company is based overseas. Offshoring, by contrast, is when a task is sent overseas—regardless of whether it is being "outsourced" to a different company. To many American workers, it did not matter whether an American company was outsourcing a service or just moving it overseas. What mattered was whether American jobs were at stake.

While some Americans considered offshoring a zero-sum game, in which the question was whether a particular job went to an Indian or to an American, advocates of free trade argued that both economies would benefit from increasing collaboration. Viewed from the perspective of corporate profits, they were right. A strong argument can be made that the economies of both India and the United States benefited from increasing collaboration. But an emphasis on aggregate gains and corporate success obscures the uneven distribution of economic growth. Prophets of the "flat world" obscured the vast distance that separates the captains of industry from those working at the lower levels of the economy, whether in India or the United States. The question is not which country benefited most from Indo-American economic partnerships, but which Indians and which Americans benefited and to what degree. As with the old India trade, we must turn from nation to class to understand who won and who lost as the economies of India and America became increasingly interconnected.[45]

## The Business of Development

In 1928, General Motors opened its first Indian plant, just outside Bombay. The factory produced Chevrolet cars, trucks, and buses. Other American corporations had already invested in India: from Kodak and Westinghouse to more specialized enterprises like the Ludlow Jute Company. In New York, an Indo-American Chamber of Commerce actively fostered such investments. The fact that investment dollars flowed from the United

States to India rather than vice versa reveals the imbalance of wealth between the two lands. Trade offers another marker of the growing economic ties between India and America—as well as the vast difference between their economies. Most of the goods sent from the United States to India were expensive, advanced technologies, including motor vehicles and industrial machinery. By contrast, most of the goods sent from India to the United States were cheap raw materials, including jute, hides, and nuts. Whether investment or trade, the growing economic linkages between India and the United States reproduced vast imbalances of wealth and power.[46]

American diplomats worked to secure opportunities for American businesses. At times, the line between those businesses and the American government was so thin as to be meaningless. Take, for example, the career of the marvelously named Colonel Comfort, who served as consul, vice-consul, and honorary consul-general in Bombay and Calcutta at the end of the nineteenth century. Colonel Comfort's job was to advance the interests of the United States, but he focused on promoting the interests of the Standard Oil Company. For nearly a decade, the Bombay consulate was housed in the Standard Oil building. The relationship was so strong that many of the company's representatives were considered consular employees. Thus, the line between American business and the American government was blurred, as was any distinction between the freedom-loving Americans and the imperialist British. Far from challenging British imperialism, American businessmen and officials like Colonel Comfort worked with colonial officials to extract wealth from India.[47]

As the Raj began to crumble, American corporate leaders rushed to secure opportunities in independent India. In 1942, the economist and businessman Henry F. Grady traveled the subcontinent to foster stronger economic connections between India and America. He met with prominent industrialists and government officials. In September 1944, the American magazine *Amerasia* published an article entitled, "India: New Economic Frontier?" It seemed as if India might become the next major market for American goods. But Indian leaders, wary of replacing one imperial master with another, put in place government controls that would become known as the "license, quota, permit raj." One of the most prominent development experts in the United States, John P. Lewis, wrote sympathetically of such government-controlled development. But while some American economists supported India's planned approach to economic growth, others became increasingly critical of the limits placed on trade and foreign investment.[48]

In 1964, the president of the World Bank, an American named George Woods, commissioned a major study to identify "the critical obstacles to more rapid economic growth in India." The study was directed by an American economist, Bernard Bell, and came to be known as the Bell Mission. After nearly two years of research, Bell and his team submitted a ten-volume report that recommended major changes to the Indian economy, including the devaluation of the Indian rupee and the widespread liberalization of the economy. Two years later, the World Bank presented India with a major aid package: $900 million every year for three years. But there was a catch: India would need to implement the advice of the Bell report by devaluing the rupee and taking concrete steps to liberalize the economy. George Woods made the deal explicit in the first major example of "structural adjustment," a process in which U.S.-backed financial institutions, mainly the World Bank and the International Monetary Fund, used the promise of aid to pressure poor countries to roll back state controls and embrace more "business-friendly" policies. Facing a dire economic situation, Indira Gandhi felt compelled to accept the World Bank's offer. The Indian Finance Minister, T. T. Krishnamachari, remained fiercely opposed to devaluation. But after strong lobbying from Washington, Krishnamachari was replaced and the rupee was devalued.[49]

The basic structures of state control over the economy remained in place, however. It was not until 1991 that a balance-of-payments crisis led the Indian government to break with its state-centered approach to development. The "license, quota, permit raj" would be undone, if slowly and in parts. The new era of Indian economic policy created new opportunities for American businesses, some of which had already developed a major presence on the subcontinent.[50]

In 1989, Jack Welch, the CEO of General Electric, traveled to India to secure a contract for aircraft engines. At a posh New Delhi hotel, Welch sat down with several government officials, including Sam Pitroda, an adviser to the prime minister. Welch made his pitch. Pitroda responded by agreeing to the terms of the agreement, but with one major caveat: he told Welch that GE would need to outsource $10 million worth of software development to India. Welch had come to India to sell jet engines, and now he was being asked to buy IT services. Welch agreed to the terms and closed the deal.[51]

GE was among the first American companies to move software work to India. But others had already begun to offshore other kinds of "back-office" tasks such as payroll and accounting. In addition to GE, key American players included Texas Instruments and American Express. Smaller American companies also began outsourcing work to India. By 2006, the United States accounted for some 80 percent of India's business-process-outsourcing (BPO) market. For an American business looking to outsource, India offered several advantages: widespread knowledge of English, strong secondary training in science and technology, a time zone difference that allowed work to be done in India while Americans were asleep, and—perhaps most importantly—a vast supply of low-cost labor.[52]

While outsourcing takes many forms, perhaps the most well-known and controversial is the call center. Young, educated Indians sitting at computer terminals late into the night field calls from Americans who need help fixing their computers, buying airplane tickets, or understanding their electricity bill. Hiring Indians to perform such tasks offers clear savings for American companies. A call-center employee in India makes approximately $3,000 to $10,000 a year, versus about $27,000 to $55,000 in the United States. GE opened its first call center in India in 1997, and other companies quickly followed suit. As call centers proliferated, they came to symbolize the complexity of outsourcing. Many call-center workers earn more money than they would otherwise. And American businesses certainly benefit. But there is a distinct inauthenticity to the interactions between many call-center workers and their American customers. Call-center workers are often trained to speak with an American accent, and told not to mention that they are in India.[53]

It is not such dishonesty, however, that has fed the American backlash against outsourcing. It is the reality of Americans losing their jobs. In October 2014, Disney fired several hundred IT professionals. One by one, they were called into a conference room and read a script that informed them they had only a few more months of employment. Many were also told that in order to earn their full severance pay, they would be required to train their replacement. Many of those replacements came from India. It is difficult to estimate how many American jobs have been lost as a result of offshoring to India. Companies often keep their offshoring contracts private. And just because an American company hires an IT worker in India does not mean that an American IT worker is out of a job. Advocates of economic globalization argue that offshoring boosts overall economic productivity, ultimately creating jobs not just in countries like India but also in the United States. Nevertheless, outsourcing has remained a potent political issue, as American politicians woo voters by blaming free trade for the loss of American jobs.[54]

The economic dislocations of outsourcing received a comedic twist in the 2006 film *Outsourced*. When his department is offshored, Todd Anderson is informed that he must travel to India to train his replacement. He struggles to navigate an India that is presented as hopelessly inefficient and incompetent. But he falls in love with an Indian woman and slowly learns to love the country as well. Thus, the trauma of economic disruption is hidden behind the sugary veneer of a hackneyed love story.

It would be easy to bring such romance to the story of Indo-American IT partnerships. Consider the rise of Infosys, the Indian IT giant. In 1981, seven Indian engineers launched Infosys with initial capital of barely $250. In 2015, their company was valued at over $42 billion. What makes the success of Infosys especially striking is its dependence on a fundamentally transnational business model. Their first client, Data Basics Corporation, was located in New York. One of the founders of Infosys, S. D. Shibulal, received a master's degree in computer science from Boston University and worked for Sun Microsystems before returning to Infosys in 1997. In 1987, Infosys opened its first overseas office in Boston. The company now has over a dozen offices across America.

More than companies like Infosys, however, it is the movement of Indian IT workers to the United States that has blurred the lines between the two economies—even while reinforcing other divides, particularly those of class. In 1994, American International Group (AIG) fired 130 software programmers in New Jersey and outsourced its operations to a company called Syntel, which in turn hired a new team of programmers in Mumbai. But Syntel also hired a different group of programmers that would work in North Carolina. By passing work between teams, the company was able to work on projects twenty-four hours of the day. Most of the workers in North Carolina were Indians on H-1B visas. The H-1B program allows American employers to temporarily hire foreign workers in particular high-demand occupations such as software engineering. The program is supposed to provide American companies with a way to temporarily fill jobs for which there are not enough trained Americans. But the program has also created a way to employ a low-cost labor force that can operate both in the United States and India. In 1994, Oracle employed over a hundred H-1B programmers, many of them from India. When Oracle opened an R&D center in India, they were able to send home a team of Indian programmers who had been trained in America. The H-1B program does place some limits on the ability of companies operating in the United States to hire foreign workers. In 2013, Infosys paid $34 million to settle a lawsuit alleging that it had illegally employed people on B-1 visitor visas rather than the more stringent H-1B work visas. But even while trying to use other visa categories, Infosys became the fifth-largest employer of H-1B visa workers in the United States. Indian companies hired Indian workers to live in the United States and collaborate with Indians working in India—all to serve a predominantly American customer base.[55]

While a small coterie of successful entrepreneurs has achieved tremendous success, many Indian software engineers—whether in India or the United States—are paid far less for their efforts. By law, companies must pay H-1B workers the same they would pay equally qualified Americans. But empirical studies have found that most H-1B workers receive substantially less. Many H-1B workers feel unable to demand higher salaries, as their immigration status depends on employment. Being fired could mean being deported.[56]

Advocates of increasing business ties between India and America point to the economic gains from such partnerships. The impact of Indo-American collaboration on the Indian economy is not overwhelming but is significant. In 2005, India earned some $17 billion from foreign corporations—American and otherwise. That is only about 1 percent of India's GDP and under 2 percent of annual job creation. India once dominated the global BPO market, commanding some 65 to 85 percent of the market in the years after the millennium. But it has lost significant business to the Philippines, Brazil, and other emerging economies. Nevertheless, relationships with American companies remain an important economic driver, especially in particular sectors of the Indian economy. And those relationships offer more than short-term profit. Azim Premji, the chief executive of Wipro, explained that GE "helped us understand global companies." The former head of Tata Consultancy Services, one of India's largest software companies, similarly praised their relation-

ship with GE. By depriving India of human capital, the migration of educated Indians to the United States could be seen as a form of brain drain.
But the many connections between Indian Americans and India has
meant that the flow of Indians to the United States could also be seen as
a "brain bank." By sending engineers and scientists to the United States,
India created a bridge that facilitated the return flow of technological
knowledge.[57]

While it is easy to prove that Indo-American collaboration has benefited particular companies, it is harder to assess the impact of such
partnerships on the economies of both countries, and even harder to
disaggregate the impact on different socioeconomic strata. One thing is
clear. The influence of Indo-American business ties has done little to
benefit the poorest segments of society in the United States or India. As
in the days of the India trade, those with the greatest power and money
have reaped tremendous rewards, while comparatively little has trickled
down to those in greatest need. If we focus on Indo-American collaborations in the IT sector, one can argue that Indian workers have benefited
and that the overall economic impact on poor Indians has been positive,
if relatively insignificant. But if Indo-American collaborations are seen
more broadly as part of the larger shift toward free trade and economic
liberalization, we must account for the widespread environmental harm,
displacement, and economic exploitation that has devastated poor
communities throughout India.

On December 3, 1984, just after midnight, a cloud of poison gas descended upon the central Indian city of Bhopal, killing thousands as they
slept. The gas, methyl isocyanate, emanated from a pesticide plant owned
by Union Carbide, a multinational company based in the United States.
Over five hundred thousand people were exposed to the gas, and nearly
four thousand were killed, according to official government estimates.
The total number of dead and seriously injured remains contentious, as
does the question of who deserves blame for the disaster. In March 1985,
a variety of labor organizations organized a conference held in Newark,
New Jersey, to create the Citizens' Commission on Bhopal, an advocacy
group that eventually became the Bhopal Action Resource Center. Thus,
an American organization was created to hold accountable an American
company for crimes committed in India. We might celebrate such mo-
bilization as an example of the public sphere rising to confront the dep-
redations of multinational corporations. But many of the survivors of

the Bhopal disaster received nothing for their suffering. And while industrial disasters command attention, if only briefly, the vast inequality
that continues to mark Indo-American economic linkages is easily obscured by the myth of the two democracies.[58]

Recognizing such inequality does not require overlooking the economic advances of both countries—especially India. For decades, India
was the largest recipient of American foreign aid. In the first forty years
after independence, India received over $50 billion in aid, much of it from
the United States. But in 2012, it pledged some $10 billion to the Inter-
national Monetary Fund to help rescue a struggling Europe. In January
of that year, India created its own agency to distribute foreign aid. The
Development Partnership Administration embodies a dramatic reversal
for a country that was once a major destination of aid. The United States
remains considerably wealthier than India, with just over $300,000 in
wealth per person on average, compared to only $4,645 per person in
India. Put differently, the United States is some sixty-five times wealthier
per person than India. The GDP differential is difficult to calculate, but
the American economy is roughly nine times bigger than India's economy
if you look at overall figures, or 2.5 times bigger if you factor in pur-
chasing power parity. But these comparisons obscure the fact that India's rate of growth in the last few decades has brought the two countries
closer in many ways, at least when it comes to money. We must celebrate
India's growing economy, even while refusing to hide the persistence of
poverty and inequality in both countries behind a narrative of national
friendship and economic growth.[59]

The danger of that narrative is evident in the recent economic success
of the Indian American community. In the 1930s, the Indian American
community was poor, and India remained under colonial rule. Now, India's economy is surging, and the Indian American community is among
the wealthiest and most educated ethnic groups in the United States. Yet
just as India's growing economy has failed to benefit all Indians equally,
so the Indian American community is more diverse and divided than
most accounts admit. In both the United States and India, the stereotypical Indian American has become a successful figure—like the internet entrepreneur Vinit Bharara, who earned a fortune through
websites like Diapers.com. The equation of Indian Americans with financial success resonates from Silicon Valley to Bangalore and beyond—
especially among India's aspirational middle class. In the words of Sam

Pitroda, the telecommunications engineer who helped convince Jack Welch to outsource work to India, "The level of success achieved by Indians in Silicon Valley is inspiring the nation." Writing about Indian American computer engineers, Pitroda proclaimed, "The success of these Indians sends out the message that we are not losers; it has restored self-confidence in the nation." By equating the financial success of a small group of people with the fate of one of the world's most populous countries, Pitroda overlooked the degree to which the success of Silicon Valley entrepreneurs coincided with—and contributed to—the growth of inequality in the United States and India.[60]

To be fair, Pitroda had reason to hope that the success of the Indian American community would radiate back to India. Many of the most successful Indian Americans have worked to forge connections between the land of their birth and their adopted home. In 1914, Jhamandas Watumull Ramchandani arrived in Honolulu. His brother Gobindram followed, and the two ran a clothing store that would become one of Hawaii's most successful family businesses. In 1922, Gobindram married an American woman but was denied citizenship because of his ethnicity. His wife, Ellen, lost her American citizenship because of the marriage. But with time, the Watumull name would become an iconic part of Hawaiian life, not just because of the success of their store or the floral-patterned clothes they helped popularize, but also because the Watumulls were generous philanthropists. The Watumull Foundation gave money to American universities to purchase books about India, created an exchange of scholars between the United States and India, and offered scholarships to Indians studying in the United States. They also funded an award through the American Historical Association that recognized an outstanding work of scholarship on the history of India.[61]

In the early 1990s, a group of Indian graduate students at the University of Maryland began gathering to discuss what they could do to help their homeland. From those conversations emerged AID, the Association for India's Development, an NGO driven by nonresident Indians that supports hundreds of antipoverty initiatives across India. The organization strives to create "a more equitable society, using natural resources in a sustainable manner and envisaging a mode of development that doesn't exploit the poor and marginalized, but bridges the gaps between people." Two key figures in AID, Aravinda Pillalamarri and Ravi Kuchimanchi, returned to India to work on antipoverty initiatives, including the development of a pedal-power generator that can be used to light isolated village schools. As the history of AID and of the Watu-mulls demonstrates, many Indian Americans have worked to span the divide between the United States and India. That effort remains a struggle, as many divisions remain even within the Indian American community itself.[62]

## The Model Minority

Lilia didn't understand how Mr. Pirzada was different. Like her parents, he spoke Bengali, ate pickled mangoes, "took off his shoes before en-tering a room, chewed fennel seeds after meals as a digestive, drank no alcohol, for dessert dipped austere biscuits into successive cups of tea." Her father explained that Mr. Pirzada was from Dacca, a city that had been part of India but that had joined Pakistan at the time of partition. Now, Dacca was in turmoil yet again, and would soon become the cap-ital of a new country: Bangladesh. In Jhumpa Lahiri's short story "When Mr. Pirzada Came to Dine," the birth of Bangladesh is seen through the eyes of a young Indian American girl, Lilia, as she struggles to under-stand divisions between Hindu and Muslim, Indian and Pakistani and Bangladeshi. By locating her story in the United States, Lahiri revealed how the South Asian diaspora could transcend the divides of South Asia. Lilia's parents welcome Mr. Pirzada to their home precisely because their similarities matter more than their differences—at least in the United States, where they are all foreigners.[63]

In 1946, the Luce-Celler Act gave Indians the right to become Amer-ican citizens and opened a small annual quota for Indians wishing to emigrate to the United States. In a speech given in New York and later reprinted in the Calcutta weekly the *Modern Review,* Taraknath Das cel-ebrated the Luce-Celler Act as "a partial victory in the long drawn out struggle for freedom of man from bondages created by men and their governments." The ultimate goal was not, Das explained, the inclusion of South Asians within a society that remained divided by race and class. Rather, Indian Americans should fight for a more inclusive America and a more just world. Even as the United States Census began once again to count South Asians as "white," Das encouraged his fellow Indian Americans to reject such a privileged status. "The struggle—the great world struggle," Das declared, "is to end political, economic, racial and cultural imperialism so that this world will give every man an unfettered opportunity to give the best that is in him for human progress."[64]

The expansive anti-imperialism of Taraknath Das defined a generation of Indian American activists. But a persistent dilemma confronted the Indian American community. Should Indians in America align themselves with other oppressed ethnic minorities in order to fight for the rights of all Americans? Or should they exploit their ambivalent racial identity to distinguish themselves from other minorities and thus claim the benefits of whiteness? The ambivalent racialization of Indians in the United States, glaringly evident in the years before the *Thind* decision, was not resolved by the restoration of Indian American naturalization. The law was changed so that no one needed to prove their whiteness in order to become a citizen. But America remained divided by race and color. And so the dilemma remained: where should Indian Americans position themselves in the spectrum of status and identity that was postwar America?

On October 3, 1965, Lyndon Johnson signed into law the 1965 Immigration Act. Johnson portrayed the act as a modest advancement of long-standing American commitments to openness and equality. But there was nothing modest about a law that shifted the immigration selection process from quotas based on national origin to a system based on skills and family ties. Those changes would revolutionize immigration into the United States, paving the way for a rapid increase in the number of South Asians entering the country. Fewer than ten thousand South Asians had been recorded entering the United States before 1965. One estimate puts the number at 7,629 intrepid souls. Now, there are over three million.[65]

Indian Americans settled throughout the United States. Even in the smallest rural towns, it became common to find a motel run by a Gujarati family. But the majority of Indian Americans settled in four areas of high density: the East Coast, especially New York and New Jersey; the West Coast, especially Los Angeles and the Bay Area; the South, especially Atlanta and Dallas; and Chicago. Many cities sprouted "Little Indias," complete with restaurants and sari shops and specialty markets offering Parle G biscuits, Mango Frooti, and other reminders of home.[66]

In 1974, more than half the Indian American population worked in the sciences, engineering, and medicine. Although the community has diversified, it remains among the most affluent and educated in America. In 2008, 69 percent of Indian Americans held bachelor's degrees. The mean household income was $86,615, dramatically higher than the national median income of $52,175. The prominence of South Asian doctors, scientists, and computer engineers contributed to the "model minority myth," the mistaken belief that certain immigrants succeeded because, unlike African Americans and Latinos, they had a culture that prioritized hard work and education. Proponents of the model minority myth ignored the relationship between American immigration policy and the economic success of South Asian Americans. In the United Kingdom, where the immigration system did not discriminate in favor of professionals, a greater percentage of South Asians remain working-class.[67]

Even in the United States, many South Asians do not fit the prevailing stereotype of the affluent, educated, "successful" immigrant. Indian Americans now own half of all American motels, the majority low-budget, family-run operations. Many own and operate convenience stores. Thousands work as taxi drivers or nurses. Working-class South Asians are more prominent in New York than in California or Chicago, but they live throughout the country, if not always within the same social worlds as their more affluent countrymen. As one South Asian American magazine declared in 1994, "The middle-class section of the South Asian immigrant community in North America has long suffered from a particularly virulent disease known as classism."[68]

Class is only one of several divides within the South Asian American community. Perhaps even more significant is language. The remarkable linguistic diversity of India survived the journey to America. In the wake of immigration reform, dozens of linguistically defined Indian American cultural organizations sprouted across the country. From New York's Gujarati Samaj to the Federation of Kerala Associations of North America to the American Telugu Association, the cultural importance of language found organizational form. Kinship networks linked linguistic, religious, and caste-based identities. Malayali Christians, Gujarati Patels, and Bengali Brahmins might all identify as Indian American, but they tended to marry, worship, and socialize within more narrowly defined circles.

Religion has both divided and united South Asian Americans, as different communities have struggled with the relationship between faith, identity, and citizenship. Every major American city now includes populations of Hindus, Muslims, Sikhs, and other Indian faith communities. America is dotted with temples, mosques, gurdwaras, and other houses of worship. During the early years of the Indian American community, the small size of the community and the fierce pressures of American racism tended to blunt the "communal" tensions that led to conflict and violence between faith communities in India itself. But as the South Asian community has grown, religious intolerance has become a major concern and has led to ardent debates within as well as between faith communities.[69]

The rise of Hindu nationalism has divided South Asian Americans as it has divided India. In 2005, the opposition of Indian Americans helped convince the United States government to deny a visa to Narendra Modi. As the chief minister of Gujarat, Modi had failed to stop brutal anti-Muslim riots that killed thousands. Modi's critics accuse him of actively stoking the riots. After Modi became India's prime minister, he was allowed into the United States, where he was greeted by crowds of adoring fans. In addition to raising funds to support Hindu nationalist organizations in India, some Indian Americans also work to defend the rights of Hindus within America and to oppose what they see as insults to the Hindu faith or to India's history. In California, for example, a group of Indian Americans challenged the depiction of caste in the state's textbooks, leading to a prolonged fight with scholars who defended the accuracy of the textbooks. Advocates of a more tolerant and inclusive Hinduism point to the irony that some Hindu nationalists fight for their rights as minorities within the United States while attacking minorities in India.[70]

Religious and linguistic divides call into question the very idea of a South Asian America. Many Indian Americans feel a stronger cultural bond with India than they do with the more abstract geographic term *South Asia*. Yet others have found meaning in simultaneously embracing their Indian identity and the larger category South Asian. In the winter of 1992, the inaugural issue of *SAMAR* (*South Asian Magazine for Action and Reflection*) promised "to reflect the full complexity of 'South Asian.'" That promise reveals one of the attractions of South Asia as an idea: its ability to embrace multiple identities—national, religious, linguistic, and political. The term *South Asian* also recognizes the degree to which everyone from the subcontinent faces similar forms of racial profiling

in the United States. "In North America as in South Asia," the editors of
*SAMAR* wrote, "we see the growing institutionalization of bigotry of race
and religion, class and caste, gender and sexual orientation." The idea
of South Asia offered a way to seek harmony and to oppose a variety of
oppressions.[71]

Debates about the idea of South Asia overlap with strong generational
divides within the Indian American community. Parents who were born
in India sometimes struggle to understand their American-born children.
A similar gap exists between those who have recently arrived from India
and Indian Americans born in the United States. These differences have
become a source of humor, particularly on college campuses, where the
two groups interact most directly. Indian Americans born and raised
in the United States are sometimes known dismissively as ABCDs or
American-Born Confused Desis (compatriots), versus more recent
arrivals or FOBs (Fresh off the Boat). Such divides are the stuff of low-
budget films, and they mask the degree to which the younger generation of Indians—whether in India or America—are separated less by
country of origin than by differences of class and the social and political
orientations of their families and communities.[72]

In the decades before Indian independence and the Luce-Celler Act,
Indian American organizations focused on lobbying for India's freedom
and for civil rights for Indian Americans. Those struggles culminated
in 1946 and 1947, as Indian Americans regained citizenship rights and
India gained independence. The rising fortunes of the Indian American
community gained a political dimension in 1956 when Dalip Singh Saund
was elected to the United States Congress, the first Indian American
to be so honored. Fittingly, Saund was elected to represent a district in
California that had a long history of Indian American labor and of
anti-Indian bias. Saund's victory testified to the shifting perceptions of
Indian Americans, as well as to the relatively small size of the Indian
American community—small enough to no longer be seen as a threat
by white workers.

Their small numbers rendered Indian Americans something of a
harmless curiosity within mainstream (white) American culture. Consider the remarkable career of Kuldip Singh. In 1956, the same year that
Dalip Singh Saund was elected to Congress, Singh—a twenty-one-
year-old medical student at UCLA—competed on a popular quiz show,
Groucho Marx's *You Bet Your Life*. With light skin and wavy hair, Singh

*Figure 6.* Dalip Singh Saund, the first United States congressional representative of Indian descent. Courtesy of the D. S. Saund Family Archives.

looked a bit like Desi Arnaz—foreign but not too foreign. In front of a national audience, he spoke in clear, if at times halting English as he explained that he was from the "beautiful, romantic valley of Kashmir." His lighthearted jokes went over well with the audience, but what launched his career was his decision to sing the popular hit "A Woman in Love." His performance earned thousands of fan letters, apparently five of which included offers of marriage. As the scholar Manan Desai writes, "Kuldip Singh fan clubs had formed across the country, and Singh soon received multiple offers, including an invitation to appear on the George Gobel Show, a call from 20th Century-Fox, a recording contract from RCA-Victor, and a profile in Life magazine." Singh's success resulted from his ability to speak (and sing) across divides. "I sing to everybody," he told *Life* magazine. Like today's "reality TV" stars, Singh projected himself as a common man despite his exotic origins—a common man living the American dream. But when American immigration authorities learned of his success, they moved to have him deported on the grounds that his student visa was no longer valid given that he had dropped out of school to pursue his musical career. Singh was forced to leave the country. He later returned on a visitor's visa, but his career never fulfilled its promise. Singh's moment in the spotlight makes clear the challenges facing Indian Americans in the 1950s and early 1960s.[73]

After 1965, as the Indian American population exploded in size, Indian American organizations also grew and diversified. Many championed particular communities of professionals. Among the largest is the American Association of Physicians of Indian Origin, founded in 1984. Others include the American Society of Engineers of Indian Origin, the Indo-American Pharmaceutical Society, the Indian American Bar Association, and the South Asian Journalists Association. Regional or religious identify often overlap with profession. The India Diamond and Colorstone Association, for example, is predominantly a Jain organization. Similarly, Patidars from Gujarat constitute the vast majority of the Asian American Hotel Owners Association. This flowering of professionally based organizations might be understood as the fracturing of a once-united Indian American community. Compared to the India League of America or the Friends for the Freedom of India, the sudden emergence of dozens of distinct organizations does reveal certain centrifugal forces within the Indian American community. At the same time, however, several organizations emerged to provide national cohesiveness to Indian American politics. The Association of Indians in America was founded in 1967, and other national umbrella organizations soon followed. These organizations worked to create a unified Indian American community and to give that community an effective political voice. In 1982, the Indian American Forum for Political Education was established to encourage Indian American political participation. Despite the 1965 immigration act and the victories of the civil rights era, many social and political issues remained that concerned all Indian Americans.[74]

The new generation of South Asian immigrants entered the United States at a time of turbulent shifts in the racial landscape. The 1964 Civil Rights Act and the 1965 Voting Rights Act helped end officially sanctioned Jim Crow segregation. But the struggle for racial equality continued in the North as well as the South. South Asian migrants strove to negotiate the country's rapidly evolving racial dynamics. Consider, for example, how the United States Census classified Indian Americans. Between 1920 and 1940, a box labeled "Hindu" was used to identify anyone from India. Beginning in 1950, residents of Indian descent were identified as "Other Race" and treated as "Caucasian," but the word

"Hindu" continued to be written in as a pan-Indian racial category. In 1970, Asian Indians became "White," a remarkable achievement, at least from the perspective of those who had suffered in the wake of the *Thind* case. In 1974, however, the Association of Indians in America (AIA) began to advocate for an alternative racial label for South Asians in the United States. Attracted by affirmative action programs, the AIA campaigned to have South Asians classified as Asian Americans in the 1980 census. The AIA campaign hinged on the historic exclusion of South Asians and the discrimination South Asians had faced and continued to face in the United States. Ironically, the *Thind* decision, long seen as a setback for South Asian Americans, suddenly became an evidentiary boon, as the Supreme Court's decision came to embody the racially based exclusion that South Asians had faced. The AIA campaign succeeded in identifying South Asians as "Asian / Pacific Islander" in the 1980 census. The United States government had decided, once again, that South Asians were not "Caucasian." After continued lobbying, South Asians also won designation as a "socially disadvantaged group" and thus attained the right to be considered for affirmative action programs.[75]

As one of the wealthiest and best-educated minorities in the United States, South Asians might seem a surprise choice for a "socially disadvantaged group." It is important to remember, however, that affirmative action benefits were granted at a time when the South Asian community had yet to complete the demographic transition initiated by immigration reform. Even today, as we have seen, South Asian Americans are not uniformly middle class. Still, it required a considerable amount of historical amnesia to frame South Asian demands for affirmative action as a form of solidarity with the struggles of African Americans. At a speech to the United States Department of Justice in May 1990, the first South Asian American Commissioner of the Equal Employment Opportunity Commission (EEOC), Joy Cherian, referenced the relationship between Gandhi and Martin Luther King Jr. while discussing the creation of the EEOC. He defended South Asian claims for affirmative action by establishing a lineage of struggle between South Asians and African Americans. Such a lineage could inspire meaningful collaboration against racism. But in defense of affirmative action benefits for South Asians, the history of Afro-Asian solidarity could also obscure the different histories and contemporary circumstances that distinguished South Asian Americans and African Americans.[76]

Tellingly, South Asian demands for affirmative action in the work-force were not joined by calls for similar affirmative action programs in education. Such a targeted approach to affirmative action is not surprising given the success young South Asians have had in gaining admission to American institutions of higher education. In October 1986, at the Asian American Voters Coalition National Leadership Banquet in Dallas, Joy Cherian stated, "We need our children to reach excellence in education without facing problems from quota systems, backed by unwritten rules established in certain centers of higher learning." Cherian failed to mention that affirmative action programs often support African Americans and Native Americans, communities that have faced a history of American racism unique in the extent of its brutality.[77]

In critically assessing South Asian claims for affirmative action, it is important to not overlook the racism many South Asians have encountered and continue to encounter in the United States. Even before the *Thind* decision, Indian migrants faced overt legal racism. While such legalized discrimination was largely eliminated by the 1950s, anti-Indian bias experienced a resurgence as the South Asian community became more visible in the 1970s and 1980s. A wave of anti-Indian attacks roiled New Jersey in the 1980s and early 1990s. The attacks followed the publication in a Jersey City newspaper of a threatening letter by a group calling itself the "dot-busters," a reference to the colored dot, or bindi, that some Hindu women wear on their forehead. Such overtly anti-Hindu attacks have been eclipsed, since September 11, 2001, by attacks on South Asians perceived to be Muslim.[78]

The terrorist attacks of 9/11 accelerated a shift in the racialization of South Asians that had begun in the 1980s and 1990s as Americans became increasingly concerned about "Islamic" radicalism. Before 9/11, South Asians were often assumed to be Hindu and, at times, mocked for their faith, as in the case of the notorious *Simpsons* character Apu Nahasapeemapetilon. Post-9/11, the most prominent South Asian stereotype became that of the Muslim terrorist. Amina Mohammad-Arif noted this shift in regard to South Asian Muslims in New York City. "Pakistanis, Bangladeshis and Indian Muslims, before 11 September," she wrote, "were in a more comfortable position than Arabs in that they were often taken for Hindus, who have a good reputation in the United States." After 9/11, however, "All those who come from the subcontinent tend to be seen as Muslim, even Hindus and Sikhs. Discrimination (especially violent discrimination) may therefore be aimed at any South Asian, regardless of their religion." Only days after 9/11, Balbir Singh Sodi, a Sikh American gas station owner, was gunned down in Mesa, Arizona. His killer had announced he was going to go out and "shoot some towel-heads." In 2012, six Sikh worshippers were fatally shot at a gurdwara in Wisconsin. The attacker had close ties to white-supremacist organizations.[79]

In the face of such religiously tinged racial violence, South Asian Americans have debated the same dilemma that confronted earlier generations struggling against anti-Asian bias: whether to claim the mantle of patriotism and whiteness and strive to assimilate, or to join antiracist solidarities forged among those rejected by prevailing systems of oppression. Writing in *SAMAR* in 1995, Arvind Rajagopal declared that the phrase "model minority" may "ostensibly refer to Asian Americans, but the unspoken reference is to African-Americans; it is they who are the 'model' and archetype of the 'minority': dark, unassimilated and unassimilable." In the pages of *SAMAR* and among South Asian activists, an alternative model was formed—what might be called the radical minority. Take, for example, the story of Vanita Gupta, the young Indian American lawyer who defended forty-six African Americans who had been convicted in a drug case that hinged on the testimony of a single white police officer in the small town of Tulia, Texas. Gupta proved that the officer had perjured himself on multiple occasions. In 2003, she secured the release of all forty-six defendants. "I feel my identity as a South Asian is closely linked to my identity as a person of color," Gupta told a reporter for the South Asian web portal *Rediff.com*. Gupta declared, "We have a duty to take on issues that affect all communities of color."[80]

South Asian American hip-hop artists have advanced solidarities of color. Artists like Chee Malabar link the racism faced by brown-skinned immigrants to the discrimination faced by African Americans. Malabar's repeated play on the word *brown* echoes the long history of colored cosmopolitanism, while tapping into a common practice on the part of many young, politically active South Asian Americans who have embraced a language of "brownness." That language transcends the boundaries between racial minorities within the United States, calling into question the racial logic of the model minority myth.[81]

Grassroots social-justice organizations have also redefined what it means for South Asians to succeed in America. While championing the civil rights of all South Asians, organizations like South Asian Americans Leading Together (SAALT) focus on the struggles of South Asians often marginalized: women, the poor, and LGBTQ communities. SAALT directs the National Coalition of South Asian Organizations (NCSO), an umbrella group that brings together smaller, community-based social-justice organizations like Sakhi in New York and Maitri in the San Francisco Bay Area, both of which work to combat domestic violence. While SAALT helps coordinate existing South Asian American activism, organizations like Bay Area Solidarity Summer and the East Coast Solidarity Summer work to train a new generation of South Asian American activists. They strive to foster "solidarity" not only within South Asian American communities, but also between South Asians and other communities of color. These two forms of solidarity—internal and external—have long been linked. Consider the ongoing struggles of LGBTQ South Asians, struggles that have opposed multiple oppressions both within and beyond South Asian America.[82]

In 1994, New York's Indian Community poured into the streets for the fourteenth annual Indian Day parade. But not all Indian Americans were welcome at the parade. The city's most renowned South Asian LGBT organization had been excluded. SALGA, then known as the South Asian Lesbian and Gay Association, had applied a month in advance. But event organizers rejected their application, arguing that SALGA was South Asian and not Indian. In 1995, SALGA participated in New York City's Pride Parade. A flyer called for "saris for the queens, salwar kameez for the kings, dupattas for the ambivalent, and shorts / t-shirts for those who don't know what we're talking about." The flyer demonstrated the power of colored solidarity to offer alternative forms of community for those rejected by organizations that try to police the borders of the Indian American community. The SALGA flyer proudly noted, "We will be marching with other queer people of color groups."[83]

While some South Asian Americans allied themselves with other racial minorities, several prominent politicians embraced the opportunities afforded by the model minority myth. In 2004, Bobby Jindal, an Indian American born in Baton Rouge, won a seat in the United States House of Representatives. In 2007, he was elected governor of Louisiana. In 2010, Nikki Haley, another rising Indian American politician, was elected governor of South Carolina. Both Jindal and Haley won office in the American South, in states with long traditions of white supremacy.

Their successes reveal the achievements of the civil rights movement in creating a racial climate in which Indian Americans can succeed not just economically but also in the realm of American politics. Yet their successes are also a testament to the long history in which some Indian Americans have advanced by evading racism rather than confronting it. Both Jindal and Haley changed their birth names and religious affiliations before winning public office. Would Piyush Jindal or Nimrata Randhawa have been as successful as Bobby Jindal and Nikki Haley? Both Jindal and Haley have resisted efforts to confront racial discrimination and inequality. In January 2011, Benjamin Jealous, the president of the NAACP, appealed to Haley as South Carolina's "first governor of color" to stop flying the Confederate flag. Jealous did not know that Haley, when asked to identify her race on South Carolina's official voter registration card, had checked the box for "White."[84]

In 2016, a cluster of new Indian American politicians was elected. After winning the race to represent Washington's Seventh Congressional District, Pramila Jayapal became the first Indian American woman to be elected to the House of Representatives. A veteran civil rights activist who spent years fighting for the rights of immigrants and wrote a book about her connection to India, Jayapal stands in stark contrast to both Nikki Haley and Bobby Jindal. Promising to champion the rights of immigrants and ethnic minorities, Jayapal is politically akin to Rohit "Ro" Khanna, Raja Krishnamoorthi, and the most renowned Indian American political figure to win in 2016, Kamala Harris. The first Indian American to be elected to the United States Senate and a strong advocate for civil rights, Harris embodies the long history of connections between Indian Americans and other racial minorities. Her mother is a doctor from Chennai; her father a Jamaican American economist. In her success as a political figure as well as in her own life story, Harris has expanded what it means to be Indian American.[85]

Much has changed in the years between the *Thind* decision and the election of Kamala Harris. Yet it remains painfully obvious that Indian Americans continue to face racism in the United States. The same year in which Harris was elected, Donald Trump became the president of the United States. One month after Trump's inauguration, two Indian engineers were shot in a bar in Kansas. One of them, Srinivas Kuchibhotla, was killed. Their assassin bragged that he had killed two Iranians. Many linked the killing to a surge in anti-immigrant and anti-Muslim hate

*Figure 7.* Kamala Harris, United States senator from California. In her success as a political figure as well as in her own life story, Harris has expanded what it means to be Indian American. Renee Bouchard, U.S. Senate Photographic Studio. Courtesy of the U.S. Senate Historical Office Photo Collection.

crimes stoked by Trump's campaign rhetoric. A prominent Indian actor tweeted, "Trump is spreading hate. This is a hate crime! RIP #SrinivasKuchibhotla." The father of one of the shooting victims declared, "The situation seems to be pretty bad after Trump took over as the US President. . . . I appeal to all the parents in India not to send their children to the US in the present circumstances." Regardless of whether the death of Srinivas Kuchibhotla should be linked to the words of Donald Trump, anyone who cares about American democracy or the image of the United States in the world should be troubled that millions of Indians were told that the United States was no longer safe for anyone who looked like an immigrant, a Muslim, or any other category of "thug" currently under suspicion. What is at stake is not just Indo-American relations, but the future of American democracy.[86]

In our post-9/11 world, and especially after the election of Donald Trump, anyone with brown skin risks being branded a thug. Within India, discrimination based on class, caste, and especially religion threatens to echo American xenophobia. Both countries are struggling to advance democracy in an age in which the threat of terrorism has provided a powerful excuse for further encroachments on basic civil liberties. Consider the transnational legacy of one of the worst terrorist attacks in the history of India.

The Taj was on fire. While smoke engulfed the ornate domes of Mumbai's landmark hotel, armed men roamed the halls, stoking the flames, shooting and killing. Other terrorists were launching simultaneous attacks throughout the city: at the Victorian railway station, a Jewish community center, the Leopold Café, a maternity hospital, an art deco movie theater. At least 164 people would die and hundreds more were wounded. The coordinated attacks of November 26, 2008, became known as 26/11, a numerical shorthand that linked India's worst terrorist attack with the tragic events of 9/11. Mumbai and New York are both cosmopolitan cities that came under assault by terrorists acting in the name of Islam. In the wake of 26 / 11, the threat of terrorism created new opportunities for collaboration between the United States and India. But the potential for a new Indo-American solidarity hit a snag when it emerged that the Mumbai attacks were largely planned by an American citizen with ties to the United States Drug Enforcement Agency (DEA) and other branches of American intelligence.

David Coleman Headley was born Daood Sayed Gilani in Washington, DC, in 1960. His father was a Pakistani diplomat. His mother was from a wealthy Philadelphia family. Soon after the birth of their child, the family moved to Pakistan. Headley grew up in his father's land, only returning to the United States when he was seventeen. A troubled young man, Headley became hooked on heroin. To finance his addiction, he began working as a drug smuggler. At the age of twenty-eight he was arrested. Rather than complete a long prison term, Headley became a DEA informant. Here the story becomes murky. For years, Headley made trips to Pakistan to meet with leaders of Lashkar-e-Taiba, the Army of the Righteous, a terrorist group bent on taking control of Kashmir, a contested region of the subcontinent divided between India and Pakistan. Whether Headley was working for a branch of the American government during these trips remains unclear. In January 2013, a US federal court convicted Headley of helping to mastermind the Mumbai attacks and sentenced him to thirty-five years in prison. But Headley's conviction did little to mollify Indians troubled by Washington's ties with Pakistan.[87]

Both the United States and India face the threat of radical violence committed in the name of Islam. Both countries struggle with how to protect civil liberties while maintaining security. In India, Muslims face police harassment and unlawful "encounter" killings. In America, racial profiling targets those who wear turbans, long beards, or happen to speak Arabic on an airplane. In both countries, the demonization of Muslims continues a long history in which marginalized communities were tarred as dangerous thugs. But despite the racial profiling of Muslims within India, American discrimination against Muslims has complicated ties to India—most famously when India's biggest movie star claimed to have been mistreated while trying to enter the United States.[88]

# CHAPTER 6

# Bollywood / Hollywood

∞

Main yeh nahin maanta ki hamara desh duniya ka
sabse mahaan desh hai . . . lekin yeh zaroor manta
hoon ki hummein kabiliyat hai, taakat hai, is desh ko
mahaan banaane ki.
(I don't believe our country is the greatest in the
world . . . but I do believe that we have the capacity,
the power, to make this country great.)
—Shah Rukh Khan as Mohan Bhargava in *Swades*

IN AUGUST 2009, the renowned Indian actor Shah Rukh Khan was detained at Newark International Airport. According to Khan, his Muslim surname led American immigration officials to question him for over two hours. The purpose of Khan's visit was to publicize a movie in which a character named "Khan" is falsely accused of being a terrorist. Khan was racially profiled while publicizing a movie about racial profiling. The purpose of Khan's visit raised suspicions that his detention was purposefully triggered or, at the least, exaggerated for dramatic effect. In any case, news spread quickly that one of India's best-loved celebrities, the man the *Los Angeles Times* called "perhaps the world's biggest movie star," had been detained at an American airport. The American ambassador to India quickly released a statement that read, "Shah Rukh Khan, the actor and global icon, is a welcome guest in the United States." But the damage had been done.[1]

The film that Khan had arrived to promote, *My Name Is Khan*, culminates in a speech by an African American president modeled on Barack Obama. While the crowd cheers, the film concludes with the Hindi version of the classic civil rights ballad "We Shall Overcome." Even in India, Obama's election inspired hopes that the United States had finally overcome its long history of racial discrimination. Yet Khan's treatment, both in the film and in real life, suggested that American racism had survived Obama's election. In the film, Khan loses his son in a racially charged anti-Muslim attack in the wake of 9/11. Distraught, he wanders the country until he is adopted into an African American family in rural Georgia. The matriarch of the family, Mama Jenny, has also lost a son, and the film makes a point of connecting the two tragedies. Khan attends a memorial service at the local black church and places his son's picture next to the photo of Mama Jenny's child. That moment encapsulates *My Name Is Khan*—an earnest but heavy-handed gesture toward solidarity in the struggle against racism. Yet even as the film attacks racism, it reproduces crude racial stereotypes, as in the resemblance of Mama Jenny to Aunt Jemima, and Khan's repeated references to a black child as "funny-haired." Such hackneyed jokes betray the film's message of tolerance, a message that is just as important in India as in America.

*My Name Is Khan* could have been set in India. Like the United States, India faces a terrorist threat linked to radical Islam. Like the United States, India has struggled to protect both national security and civil liberties. It was a choice to locate *My Name Is Khan* in the United States. That choice reveals the importance of America within Indian public culture and within the Indian film industry in particular. As *My Name Is Khan* makes clear, such cinematic connections have often reproduced misconceptions and stereotypes. Like the old trade in elephants and ice, movies have bound together India and America by selling difference even while creating connections across difference.[2]

Hollywood and Bollywood—the names themselves tell a complicated story of connection and disconnection. The name "Bollywood" makes it seem that the Indian film industry is a junior partner, merely an echo of Hollywood. But more films are made in Mumbai every year than in Los Angeles—and Mumbai is only one of many film hubs in India. Still, to contrast Bollywood and Hollywood misses the point. Like India and America, Bollywood and Hollywood have long been interconnected. Dadasaheb Phalke, often described as "the father of Indian cinema," held up Hollywood as his most significant inspiration. Phalke's *Raja Harish-chandra,* often credited as the first film made in India, was inspired by the American epic *Life of Christ.* Phalke saw *Life of Christ* in 1910 in a Bombay theater that regularly screened Hollywood films, a theater significantly named America-India. By 1939, sixty-four Americans were working in the film industry in Bombay. And both United Artists and Universal Pictures had investments in the growing Indian film industry. Those links only grew stronger with time. The renowned Indian film-maker Satyajit Ray praised American cinema, which, in his words, "taught me almost everything I knew about filmmaking at the time when I decided to take my plunge into this profession." As Ray's films make clear, the cinematic links between India and America extend well beyond the Hindi film industry. Ray produced his films in Bengali. From Bengal to Tamil Nadu to Kerala, many non-Hindi Indian films have their own links to America. Nevertheless, it is still useful to speak of the relationship between Hollywood and Bollywood, not just because of the size of the Hindi film industry, but also because the very name *Bolly-wood* has its own fraught history.[3]

The origins of the word *Bollywood* remain mysterious. The scholar Madhava Prasad has uncovered a clue in the form of an article by Wilford E. Deming, an American film engineer who claimed to have worked on India's first talkie. In a 1932 article in the *American Cinematographer,* Deming refers to a telegram he received just after leaving India: "Tollywood sends best wishes happy new year." Deming explained that "Tollywood" was what his colleagues had come to call the studios in Tollygunge, a suburb of Calcutta. "After studying the advantages of Hollygunge we decided on Tollywood," he explained. As the Indian film industry shifted toward Bombay, it seems only natural that the name would be reinvented as Bollywood. But there is nothing natural about the name *Bollywood.* In the words of Prasad, "It is a strange name, a hybrid, that seems at once to mock the thing it names and celebrate its difference." Still, by 1976, the word had made its way into a detective novel, *Filmi, Filmi, Inspector Ghote.* And by the 1990s, the term had become the standard label for the most popular genre of Indian film. For many Americans, Bollywood became synonymous with all of Indian cinema.[4]

Just as Indian films offer unique windows into how Indians view the United States, Hollywood movies offer telling portraits of India. In both directions, the views afforded by the movies are replete with stereotypes and misunderstandings, as *My Name Is Khan* makes clear. But even while demonstrating the persistent distance between India and America, movies themselves bridged that distance. Music, talent, and storylines flowed between Hollywood and Bollywood, necessitating what Nitin Govil has called "more nuanced formulations of proximity and distance." The connections between Bollywood and Hollywood were emblematic of the long relationship between India and the United States, a strange mixture of warmth and distrust, respect and misunderstanding, connection and distance.[5]

If this book were a movie, perhaps this chapter could be its happy ending. All the loose ends would be tied together—villains vanquished, heroes lauded, the greater good triumphant. It would be a crowd-pleaser. An epic saga. Two nations, born in revolt against empire, emerge as triumphant democracies and allies on the world stage. Indian Americans, once persecuted because of their color, rise to become one of the most successful ethnic communities in the United States. And like the heroes of old, movie stars come together to create new bridges between distant peoples. Even while xenophobic racists erect new walls between nations, Hollywood and Bollywood converge to demonstrate the power of interconnection, hybridity, and polycultural pluralism.[6]

The problem with such a narrative is not just that Indo-American relations remain fraught with misunderstanding and inequalities of power and knowledge—as the very word *Bollywood* makes clear. The problem is not that both India and the United States remain divided and unequal. Such inequalities can be contained within a narrative of gradual improvement. The real problem is that narratives of connection as progress can distract us from confronting inequality by equating freedom with the transnational flow of certain cultural forms. The recent history of India and the United States can be seen as a great coming together—of economies, peoples, and cultures. But while we recognize the growing relationship between "the world's two largest democracies," we must not overlook the disconnections that remain and all those undemocratic inequalities that are cast into shadow when we reify connection as the essence of freedom. As the history of Hollywood / Bollywood makes clear, arrogant transnationalism can be just as dangerous as xenophobic nationalism—especially when yoked to the romance of the movies.

## Bollywood's America

Shah Rukh Khan sings "Pretty Woman" in front of a giant American flag. Neither a statement of Indo-American solidarity nor a sarcastic spoof of American patriotism, Khan's performance in the critically acclaimed hit *Kal Ho Na Ho* (Tomorrow May or May Not Come), reveals that what America offers Bollywood is what Bollywood offers India and perhaps what the movies have always offered everywhere—a way to get beyond the ordinary, a passport to a new world. The literary scholar Priya Joshi has described the Bollywood tradition of dancing in foreign settings as a kind of "reverse colonization." Rather than white bodies exploring the subcontinent, we see brown bodies prancing in front of the Swiss Alps, Big Ben, or Times Square. All these settings are equally foreign to most Indian audiences. But as *Kal Ho Nah Ho* makes clear, Bollywood's romance with America is a love affair of a very particular sort. Unlike the pristine shots of European mountains that mark Bollywood films of a certain era, Bollywood's America is a place of aesthetic, moral, and racial mixture, a place where you can break the rules and mix things up, but also where you need to be careful not to lose yourself—and your Indian identity.[7]

It is the liberating potential of America that emerges from *Kal Ho Na Ho*. The film's creators might have opted to locate just one song in an American setting, but instead chose to set the entire film in New York. The repeated shots of famous icons—the Statue of Liberty, Times Square, Wall Street, Central Park—add a foreign flair to the restless energy at the heart of the film's plot. Naina Kapur is an MBA student who lives with her widowed mother. She has a few devoted friends, including another MBA student named Rohit. But her life remains hard and depressing until Shah Rukh Khan's character, Aman, moves in next door. Aman helps Naina find more passion for life by helping her experience the passion of New York. She falls in love with him. But Aman is terminally ill, and so convinces Naina that her true love is Rohit. In the title song, Khan sings on the Brooklyn Bridge, the city skyline behind him, as he reminds the audience that tomorrow is never guaranteed.

As American cities became icons for Indian audiences, Indian producers paid extra for an American setting. Recent Indian movies filmed in the United States include *Dhoom 3*, filmed in Chicago; *Dostana*, set in Miami; *Kites*, shot in New Mexico; *Kurbaan*, filmed in Philadelphia and Brooklyn; *Anjaana Anjaani*, shot in New York, Los Angeles, Las Vegas, and San Francisco; and the Tamil hit *Jeans*, filmed in Los Angeles, Las Vegas, New York, and the Grand Canyon. As *Jeans* makes clear, South Indian cinema has also recognized the power of America. As early as 1987, the Telugu thriller *America Abbayi* was filmed in New York, Detroit, and Chicago. Three years later, the Malayalam comedy *Akkare Akkare Akkare* was shot largely in the United States. More recent South Indian films set in America include the 2006 Tamil crime story *Vettaiyadu Villaiyadu*, and the 2011 Malayalam comedy *Akkarakazhchakal: The Movie*.

Compared to *My Name Is Khan*, most of the Indian films shot in America could easily have been set in India. Take *Anjaana Anjaani*, for example, a 2010 romantic comedy about two people who fall in love while trying to kill themselves. Why not set the film in Mumbai or Delhi? There is nothing distinctly American about suicide. Indeed, *Anjaana Anjaani* drew inspiration from a 2001 Telugu film that was located in India. One might argue that for an Indian audience the moral uncertainties of *Anjaana Anjaani* fit an American setting—and New York City in particular. Where better for two suicidal characters to meet than on the George Washington Bridge, the vast "amoral" metropolis of Manhattan behind them? It is true that several Bollywood films portray the United States as a land of moral danger. But many of the Bollywood films located in America make no such assumption. A safer generalization would be that the United States provides Indian filmmakers with a location that is simultaneously exotic and immediately recognizable. Like the calico cloth that drove the India trade, American settings sell because they are simultaneously foreign and familiar.

No American city is better known to Indian audiences than New York. The appeal of the Big Apple results, in part, from the large Indian diaspora in the city. That diaspora makes it easy to hire Indian extras, and also makes for realistic plotlines. It is not surprising to an Indian audience for a variety of Indians to be passing through New York. But even while a large Indian American community makes New York an attractive destination, the non-Indian population of New York is perhaps even more important. Diversity is an important advantage of filming in New York. Note the extras who dance behind Khan in that "Pretty Woman" routine. White, black, Indian—the crowd is a testament to the multiracial character of New York. Or consider the 2005 film *Jo Bole So Nihaal* (Whoever Utters Shall Be Fulfilled), in which a similarly diverse crew dances in Times Square. Of course, the presence of a few black faces is a shallow form of diversity, fraught with the potential for stereotypes. But in several Indian films the diversity of America goes well beyond a few extras.

In 2012, the hit comedy *English Vinglish* used the ethnic diversity of New York to make a point about gender equality. The renowned actress Sridevi is a housewife whose husband and daughter mock her lack of English. She comes to New York for a family wedding, and secretly enrolls in an English-language course with students from throughout the world. Befriended by her classmates and courted by a Frenchman, she learns to respect herself and thus garners the respect of others—most importantly, her husband and daughter. The film portrays America as an international crossroads defined by diversity, variety, and equality.

Unlike *My Name Is Khan*, many Bollywood films envision the United States as a haven for foreigners. In *English Vinglish*, neither Sridevi nor any of her foreign friends encounter racism. In *Love at Times Square*, two young Indian men, both working in America, fall in love with the same woman, an Indian student and budding reporter who also happens to be the daughter of a billionaire. Written and directed by the legendary Bollywood actor Dev Anand, *Love at Times Square* repeats many of the plot elements common to Bollywood films. Anand plays the loving father. The effect is to make the film's setting feel more familiar than foreign. It helps that the America on-screen is familiar to most Indian audiences. The film is framed by New Year's Eve celebrations in Times Square, among the most iconic of American settings. The United States appears to be a land of opportunity, welcoming to immigrants. There is even a high-ranking American politician who speaks fluent Hindi. The attacks of 9/11 cast a brief pall, but Anand's character writes a check to Rudy Giuliani for a million dollars, and the film ignores the hostility and suspicion faced by Indian Americans suspected of being terrorists.

The absence of xenophobia in *Love at Times Square* and *English Vinglish*—and in many Bollywood portrayals of America—is especially striking given that Indian society continues to struggle with the challenge of confronting terrorism while maintaining tolerance and protecting civil liberties. Take the history of anti-Sikh violence, for example. In *Jo Bole So Nihaal,* Nihaal Singh (Sunny Deol), a Sikh policeman in India, happens to inadvertently help a dangerous terrorist. Nihaal is recruited by the FBI to travel to America to help find the terrorist. Such a plot obscures the fact that Sikh Americans have suffered racist attacks because their beards and turbans have become associated with terrorism, as the killing of Balbir Singh Sodhi made tragically clear. Sikhs have faced targeted violence in India as well. In 1984, anti-Sikh riots took the lives of thousands. It would be asking too much to expect a film like *Jo Bole So Nihaal* to examine such histories in detail. But it is telling that so few Bollywood films acknowledge the legacy of xenophobia and discrimination that continues to haunt both America and India.

Perhaps the most notable exception is the film *New York.* Released in 2009, *New York* tracks the impact of 9/11 on the lives of three South Asian Americans. At the heart of the story is Sameer "Sam" Shaikh (John Abraham), a Muslim man wrongly arrested and tortured at Guantanamo Bay. The critique of torture and racial profiling at the heart of the film is complicated by the fact that Sam decides, as a result of his torture, to launch a terrorist attack in revenge. But overall the film humanizes figures seen by the state as nothing but "Muslim terrorists." Contrast *New York* with *Kurbaan* (2009), another Bollywood take on the dangers of terrorism. In *Kurbaan,* Avantika Ahuja (Kareena Kapoor) lives in New York but returns home to Delhi when her father has a heart attack. In Delhi, she falls in love with Ehsaan Khan (Saif Ali Khan), a Muslim scholar. Despite her father's reservations regarding Ehsaan's faith, they marry and return together to New York. After various twists and turns, Avantika discovers that Ehsaan is involved in a terrorist ring. Her father's fears are justified, as is the broader suspicion of Islam shared by many Indians and Americans.

Although different in their approach to racial profiling, both *New York* and *Kurbaan* reinforce the connection between Islam and terrorism. That connection was further strengthened by the 2013 blockbuster *Vishwaroopam,* a spy thriller released in both Tamil and Hindi and dubbed into other Indian languages as well. Like *New York* and *Kurbaan, Vishwaroopam* concerns the threat of terrorism committed in the name of Islam. All three films are set in part in New York. All three suggest that state surveillance of Muslims is justified—a point as dangerous in India as it is in the United States. In the face of these films, *My Name Is Khan* emerges as a vital corrective, a testament to racial and religious inclusivity, despite its recourse to racial stereotypes of African Americans.

In regard to racial stereotypes, *My Name Is Khan* is far from the extreme. Compare it to *Kambakht Ishq,* a 2009 romantic farce in which the lead character, played by Akshay Kumar, wears blackface. In another scene, he is taken out of an airport security line and searched by an overweight African American woman, a grotesque Mammy-like caricature. Or consider the Malayalam comedy, *Akkare Akkare Akkare,* in which the two leading characters pretend to be African American. Their efforts at blackface are meant to be funny. When their disguises fail and they are asked if they are Indian, one responds defensively that they are "original negroes, black negroes." Such humor might be explained as mere insensitivity to American racial etiquette, if not for the fact that antiblack racism and colorism are rampant in India as well as America.[8]

While criticism of American racism remains rare in Bollywood, America is often associated with other forms of moral turpitude. In 1997, *Pardes* (Foreign Land) offered Indian audiences a parable about the dangers of America and the redeeming power of Indian values. Kishorilal, a wealthy businessman, returns to India from the United States and decides to marry his son Rajiv to the daughter of a good friend. The daughter in question is the embodiment of traditional India and is appropriately named Ganga, the Hindi name for the river Ganges. But will Rajiv agree to the marriage? Aware that his son has become Americanized and might reject his father's wishes, Kishorilal turns to his foster son, the loyal Arjun (played by Shah Rukh Khan). Predictably, Arjun himself falls in love with Ganga, but still fulfills his duty, going so far as to cover up for Rajiv's failings by claiming them as his own. It is only when she comes to America that Ganga discovers the real Rajiv, a dissolute playboy who embodies the moral failings of the West. After Rajiv tries to rape her, Ganga flees with Arjun back to India, where everything works out in the end.

In *Pardes,* the Americanized Rajiv cannot be redeemed, but several Indian films offer hope that Indian values can reclaim even the most Americanized prodigal son. Such redemption is at the heart of the 2013 Telugu family drama, *Greeku Veerudu* (Greek Hero), which was tellingly dubbed *America vs. India* when translated into Hindi. Chandu (played by the actor Nagarjuna) is a selfish and hedonistic businessman in New York who runs into trouble financially. He sees an opportunity to save himself when his extended family asks him to visit India. Chandu plans to use the trip to mooch funds from his family. Instead he falls in love with a woman who embodies traditional Indian values and who works as a volunteer with terminally ill children. Inspired by his new love, Chandu puts his selfish ways behind him. The film equates family and commitment with India, money and hedonism with America.

Not all Indian films offer such black-and-white dichotomies between India and America. Moral ambivalence is at the heart of one of the most renowned Indian films set in New York. *Kabhi Alvida Naa Kehna* (Never Say Goodbye) revolves around two couples: Maya (Rani Mukerji) who is engaged to her childhood friend, Rishi (Abhishek Bachchan), and Dev (Shah Rukh Khan), a soccer player who lives in New York with his wife, Rhea (Preity Zinta). Dev meets Maya just before she is to marry Rishi, and the two feel an instant connection. They eventually have an affair even while trying to save their marriages. The American setting, and New York in particular, fits the ambiguous morality at the heart of the film. But *Kabhi Alvida Naa Kehna* rejects simple moral allegories that distinguish between Indian and American values.

Many Indian films play on the idea of the United States as a place of moral uncertainty. One common storyline might be called the American interlude. The action begins in India, shifts to America, where the main characters confront dangers, and then returns to India, where all is happily resolved. *Pardes* features an American interlude, but an even better example is the film *Aa Ab Laut Chalen* (Come, Let's Go Back Now). That line is uttered by the hero, Rohan (Akshaye Khanna), to the heroine, Pooja (Aishwarya Rai), at the climax of the film. Both Rohan and Pooja traveled to America with high hopes, invited by Indians who they expected would help them. Both discovered that their Indian contacts had been corrupted by American greed. After struggling to survive, Rohan eventually convinces Pooja to return to India, where they live happily ever after.

An American interlude also features in the 2006 romantic comedy *Jaan-E-Mann* (Beloved). The film opens with Suhaan (Salman Khan) learning that his ex-wife, Piya (Preity Zinta), wants a divorce settlement of 5 million rupees. Suhaan has spent almost all his money, and he convinces Agastya (Akshay Kumar), who has long loved Piya, to woo her so she won't need the settlement. Piya has moved to New York, and Suhaan and Agastya follow her there. Like a modern Cyrano de Bergerac,

Suhaan feeds lines to Agastya using wireless technology. But even as Suhaan succeeds in getting Piya interested in his puppet suitor, he discovers that Piya still loves him. And he loves her. After ruminating on the pain of love in Times Square, Suhaan manages to win Piya back. They return to India and to happiness together.

American-interlude films like *Jaan-E-Mann, Pardes,* and *Aa Ab Laut Chalen* all present the United States as a place of moral danger. They might be contrasted with Bollywood films like *English Vinglish* or *Love at Times Square* that present an overly rosy image of the United States. But even most American-interlude films fail to acknowledge the depth of American inequality and injustice, and instead focus on common stereotypes of America as a land of materialism and immorality. Films like *My Name Is Khan* and *New York* are rare in their focused attention on the failures of American democracy.

The paucity of Indian films that critically engage America is in part a result of timing. Most of the Indian films set in America were produced after 1990. They testify to the growing prominence of America in the Indian consciousness, as well as to the growing size and wealth of the Indian American community. They also speak to the preoccupations of mainstream Bollywood cinema at a particular moment in time—and the silences that resulted from those preoccupations. Why do so many Bollywood films use America as a setting without engaging the racism, sexism, and class inequality that plague American society? Part of the answer is that Bollywood has turned away from those problems in Indian society as well. It should not be surprising that even the few Bollywood films that do turn a critical eye on America tend to focus on the corrupting power of American modernity. Simple dichotomies between tradition and change, morality and immorality, have come to flatten many Bollywood plotlines. Of course, Indian cinema extends beyond Bollywood, and even within Bollywood many films defy such stagnant tropes. But the fact remains that even while increasing numbers of Bollywood films are set in the United States, it remains rare for an Indian film to probe the limitations of American democracy.[9]

Long before Bollywood took a strong interest in America, Hollywood had ventured to India. Whereas many Bollywood films shot in the United States could have been located in India, American films set in India are invariably driven by plot elements inseparable from the setting of the film. One might argue that Hollywood has thus done a better job of actually engaging India. Dozens of Bollywood movies have been set in America, but they are dominated by Indian actors, with American extras, like the streets of New York, portrayed merely as an exotic backdrop. By contrast, most Hollywood films about India have at least one, if not several, Indian characters. But the India that is featured in many Hollywood films—especially those produced before Indian independence—is an imaginary India that ultimately says more about American myths than about the subcontinent itself.

## Hollywood's India

In 1939, as war erupted in Europe, American audiences were offered a disaster story set in India. *The Rains Came* is the story of an earthquake which triggers a flood which unleashes an epidemic of cholera. Yet somehow the film manages to be optimistic about the future of India. Based on a novel published in 1937, the story follows Lady Edwina Esketh (played by Myrna Loy) as she falls in love with an energetic Indian doctor, Major Rama Safti (played by the very un-Indian Tyrone Power, originally from Cincinnati). A remake of the film was released in 1955 under the name *The Rains of Ranchipur*, with Lana Turner playing Lady Esketh and Richard Burton playing Major Safti. Although the two films differ in several ways, both present Major Safti as a hopeful embodiment of India's future. If not a full-throated critique of colonial rule, both films offer at least some reason to believe in an India free from British rule.[10]

Contrast *The Rains Came* with what may still be the most influential Hollywood depiction of India, *Indiana Jones and the Temple of Doom*. Released in 1984, long after India had emerged from colonial rule, the second episode of the Indiana Jones trilogy finds Dr. Jones in a mythical Indian kingdom. As we have seen, that kingdom—like the film as a whole—is dominated by a secretive Thuggee cult. Even though the British are not portrayed in a flattering light, it is the film's Indian villain, the thug priest, who dominates the screen. Despite the ultimate triumph of Dr. Jones, American audiences were left to pity a hopelessly benighted India, awash with brutal rituals, abject suffering, and wicked thugs. The centrality of the thug deserves emphasis, as does the fact that Indiana Jones is a scholar who fights not just for goodness but for truth and knowledge. Yet again the thug was used to demonstrate the triumph of Western knowledge over the dangerous and the foreign.[11]

Most of the early films about India that were shown to American audiences were closer to *Indiana Jones* than to *The Rains Came*. Many were produced with British partners. The majority offered a decidedly imperial view of the subcontinent, a dangerous land overrun with thugs of one kind or another. These "empire films" romanticize the exploits of white men subduing an alluring but also dangerous country—a country often embodied by a sultry seductress. An early example of the genre, *The Black Watch* (1929), was directed by John Ford, who would later make critically acclaimed Westerns. The film follows a British army captain on a secret mission to save British prisoners in India. Myrna Loy, an American actress from Montana, plays the enticing Yasmani. American viewers must not have been bothered by such casting. Loy became famous for impersonating Asian women. But not all viewers were impressed by the film's generic portrayal of the exotic Asian beauty. "Miss Loy does fairly well," wrote the reviewer for the *New York Times,* despite the jarring fact that "she is a heroine of the Mohammedan hill people who is meticulous about her facial make-up and the inextensiveness of her attire."[12]

While characters like Yasmani embodied the dangerous allure of the subcontinent, the subordination of Indian women allowed American directors to underscore the barbarity of traditional Indian society. One of the only American films to deal directly with the creation of the British Empire, *Clive of India* (1935), traces the career of Robert Clive, renowned for winning the Battle of Plassey and thus giving the British their first substantial territory in the subcontinent. The film begins with a caption that frames British expansion as a humanitarian act at a time when "a madman sat on the throne of Northern India." When an emissary of Clive comes to that "madman" to ask for the release of English prisoners, the depraved king is found cracking his whip at a courtyard full of terrified and scantily dressed dancing girls. By opposing such barbarity, Clive emerges as a hero, and the rise of the British Empire becomes, in the words of the film's closing captions, "a monument to one man's courage."

Many American-made empire films focused on the conflict between the British and Muslim rulers, often presented as ruthless bandits roaming the foothills of the Himalayas. Religious antipathy toward Islam fit nicely within narratives that celebrated fair-skinned heroes conquering the swarthy masses. No wonder Adolf Hitler was a fan of the genre. One of the most celebrated American films about India, *Lives of a Bengal Lancer* (1935), was one of the Führer's favorite films. The film follows a team of British soldiers (one played by Gary Cooper) courageously defending their camp against a horde of dangerous Muslims. In 1937, Hitler told the British Foreign Secretary that he had seen *Lives of a Bengal Lancer* three times. "I like this film because it depicted a handful of Britons holding a continent in thrall," he explained. "That is how a superior race must behave and the film is compulsory viewing for the SS." The production of the film spoke to America's own history of conquest. The studio sent a team to shoot in India, but much of the film was destroyed by heat, and many scenes had to be reshot in the hills surrounding Los Angeles. The producers hired members of the Paiute tribe as extras. These Indians were once again confused with those Indians, and the line between British and American imperialism was washed away.[13]

Many American films placed India within a generic romanticized East. Take, for example, the first American film to address India—in fact, one of the first American films of any kind—Thomas Edison's three-minute-long *Hindoo Fakir.* Produced in 1902, the film conveys the magic of moving pictures by showing a magician, the eponymous "Hindoo Fakir," levitating a woman in midair before making her disappear. A stereotypical Eastern spirituality played a central role in several early American films about India, films like *Oriental Mystic* (1909), *The Bombay Buddha* (1915), *The Soul of Buddha* (1918), and *The Green Goddess,* made as a silent film in 1923 and remade with sound in 1930. Sometimes Indian imagery was used to further orientalize films that had nothing to do with India. If not for such generic orientalism, it would be hard to explain why *Arabian Nights* (1942), a film that has no plot link to India, begins with an opening shot of a harem with the Taj Mahal in the background. The universality of empire, its portability across time and space, was portrayed yet again in *The Charge of the Light Brigade* (1936), a film based around the suicidal cavalry charge depicted in the famous poem by Alfred Lord Tennyson. That charge occurred during the Crimean War. But the commercial success of *Lives of a Bengal Lancer* convinced Warner Brothers to start the film in India. In order to make such a setting seem less far-fetched, they borrowed plotlines from the siege of Cawnpore (now Kanpur) during the Rebellion of 1857, a conflict that had nothing to do with Crimea and that occurred well after the famous charge had become history.

The empire film reached its apex in 1937 with *Wee Willie Winkie*, a Shirley Temple comedy directed by John Ford. Based on a Rudyard Kipling story, the film follows a little girl, Priscilla, to a remote British fort on the northwestern frontier of India. Priscilla's grandfather, Colonel Williams, is stationed at the fort. His greatest antagonist, the rebel Pashtun chief, Khoda Khan, is captured early in the film, and Priscilla befriends him during his captivity. When he escapes, it is up to Priscilla to convince him to lay down his arms and embrace the peace made possible by British hegemony. Even while validating British rule, *Wee Willie Winkie* presents Khoda Khan as a noble figure. Shirley Temple calls him a "nice gentleman." When she appears at his mountain hideout, he treats her with kindness, offering her food and answering her questions:

> *Priscilla:* "Don't you think it's awful silly to be mad all the time and fighting when you don't have to?"
> *Khan:* "Why don't you ask your grandfather that question?"

Priscilla replies that her grandfather, the commanding British officer, told her that "the Queen wants to protect all her people and make them happy and rich." Khan laughs, but then suddenly grows serious: "Between your people and mine, little one, there can be only war." Khan's pessimism hides a noble heart. But it is the idealism of the little girl and the benevolence of the British Empire that emerge triumphant.[14]

Also triumphant is the idea that white men are destined to rule the world. Although Shirley Temple is the heart of the film, and Khoda Khan remains a noble figure, it is the fair-minded rulers of the British Empire who serve as the ultimate arbiters of power—and the only guarantee of a lasting peace. And not just in India. The film offers a portable defense of white hegemony, in part through its mountainous setting, which lacks architectural elements distinctive to India, and in part by portraying Khan and his people as racially ambivalent. Khan was played by the Cuban American actor Cesar Romero; the unctuous servant Mohammed Dihn was played by the Chinese American actor Willie Fung.[15]

Two years after *Wee Willie Winkie*, another American film celebrated the potential for the British Empire to bring peace—in this case, however, only by crushing the opposition violently. Based on a poem by Rudyard

Kipling, *Gunga Din* follows three British soldiers as they uncover a secret band of thugs. We have already seen how the film juxtaposed the thug leader with Mahatma Gandhi. Whether or not the appearance of the thug chieftain was designed to subvert Gandhi's image, the film's overall message was clearly sympathetic to the empire. The title character, the loyal Gunga Din, wants nothing more than to become a soldier of the queen. By sacrificing himself to defeat the thugs, he dies for the empire he lived to serve.[16]

Well after Indian independence, the British Raj continued to fascinate American audiences. Films like *Bhowani Junction* (1954), *Bengal Brigade* (1954), and the remake of *The Rains Came* (1955) continued to dramatize the heroism of empire. But these later versions of the empire film genre approached the imperial project with greater ambivalence. In *Bhowani Junction,* for example, Ava Gardner stars as a mixed-race Anglo-Indian torn between nations and lovers. The film is set in 1947, with Indian independence imminent. Ava Gardner's character, Victoria Jones, having been raised by an Indian mother and English father, does not know what the future holds for her or her native land. Attacked by a dissolute British officer, Jones fights back and kills the officer with a steel rod. An Indian man, Ranjit Kasel, finds her badly injured and takes her home to care for her. She decides to marry Kasel and thus to commit her life to India, but she changes her mind at the last minute. Meanwhile, a shadowy Indian revolutionary has been arousing the masses against British rule. Jones becomes pulled into the political unrest as she becomes close to the film's two other key figures: another Anglo-Indian whom Jones knew as a child, and a British officer desperately trying to maintain order. Suddenly, there are three men in her life, each representing a different future for her and for India—the British, the Indian, and something in between. In the novel from which the film was based, she chooses her fellow Anglo-Indian. But in the film, it is the British officer who wins her heart, even as the British Raj crumbles all around them. The tension between East and West, the conflict at the heart of *Bhowani Junction,* would shape Hollywood's India long after the lure of the empire began to fade.

But even as the East / West divide remained resilient, its significance changed. Older Hollywood films portrayed the divide between East and West as a source of existential angst. By contrast, most contemporary American films see cultural diversity less as a problem than as an opportunity. Compare Ava Gardner's character in *Bhowani Junction* to the

American woman played by Julia Roberts in *Eat Pray Love* (2010). Both are located at the junction of multiple nations and cultures. But for Julia Roberts, such diversity is liberating.

In *Eat Pray Love*, the main attraction of India is spirituality. The film typifies a strain of Hollywood films that star a curious American exploring the mysterious East. Spiritual India abounds as Julia Roberts learns to pray, or Steve Jobs wanders the subcontinent in the biopic *Jobs*. Wes Anderson's 2007 comedy, *The Darjeeling Limited*, parodies the genre. The film follows three brothers as they complete what the oldest brother, played by Owen Wilson, repeatedly calls a "spiritual journey." But their efforts at spiritual experiences are halfhearted and tangential to the real action. If the brothers seek an otherworldly India, what they find is something all too mundane, and at times tragic. The film is less about India as a land of spirituality than about the humanity that cuts across the false divides that keep nation from nation, brother from brother.

The "spiritual India" genre deserves parody because it reinforces a related and even more pernicious stereotype—what we might call the "incompetent India" trope. Incompetent-India films involve an American trying to get something done in a chronically dysfunctional India. Consider Disney's *Million Dollar Arm* (2014), a feel-good movie about a sports agent who travels to India to find promising recruits for major-league baseball. The agent is a hard-driving workaholic who arrives in India to discover that none of his plans have been put into action. His conversation with a local Indian administrator is telling:

> *Indian Administrator:* "First of all, I am happy to inform you that all our plans are running smoothly and on time."
> *American Agent:* "Great. Can I see the flyers?"
> *Administrator:* "The flyers are not here yet. They are at the printers. We are trying to get them."
> *Agent:* "OK. How about the T-shirts?"
> *Administrator:* "They are at the warehouse. We are trying to get them too."

And thus it goes. Although the agent ultimately learns from his Indian recruits, and is humanized in the process, Indian society remains unredeemed. *Million Dollar Arm* is far from alone in contrasting a dysfunctional India with an effective America. *Outsourced* (2006) plays on such stereotypes repeatedly. Even *Darjeeling Limited,* a film that focuses its parody on its American stars and tries to present a multifaceted India, still slips into the stereotype of the incompetent subcontinent. After their train stops unaccountably, the brothers are told that the train is lost:

> *Jack:* What did he say?
> *Peter:* He said the train is lost.
> *Jack:* How can a train be lost? It's on rails.

Of course, many Indian films also mock the failures of public transit or the incompetence of bureaucrats, whether public or private. But it is one thing to mock such failures in your own home, and something different to mock them abroad.

By highlighting India's spiritual heritage at the expense of its material success, Hollywood films return to the old dichotomies between East and West offered by Emerson and Thoreau. Even films that parody India's "spiritual" image can reinforce the limitations of that image. *Darjeeling Limited* manages to compensate for its reproduction of the incompetent-India genre. The same cannot be said for *The Love Guru,* a painfully unfunny effort starring Mike Meyers. While sparing no stereotype about the Indian guru, the film manages to import tropes usually reserved for maharajahs: unctuous servants, voluptuous women, and a team of elephants. Of course, there is a difference between a film that mocks a stereotype—however unsuccessfully—and a film that treats such stereotypes as real. There is a difference between *The Love Guru* and *Indiana Jones and the Temple of Doom.* But regardless of whether the guru or the thug is a source of comedy, drama, or history, such stereotypes maintain a cultural distance between India and the United States.

That cultural distance can also be a form of racial distance. While most Bollywood films that engage America ignore racism entirely, many American films perpetuate racist stereotypes of the Indian. The 1968 cult classic *The Party* features Peter Sellers as a hapless Indian actor who is accidentally invited to a fancy Hollywood dinner party. With little plot, the film unfolds as a series of slapstick routines. Sellers bungles his way through one gaffe after another, the clumsy foreigner serving as the butt of all jokes. The racial undertones of the film would be less troubling if Sellers had not appeared in brownface.

Not all Hollywood films recycle old stereotypes of India. Several American action films have reveled in a more modern India. *The Bourne Supremacy* (2004) begins in Goa. Rather than repeat hackneyed qualities associated with India—ancient, mysterious, unknowable—the film begins in a bustling beach town full of foreigners. Similarly, *Mission Impossible 4* (2011) involves a car chase through a refreshingly modern Mumbai. The old monuments are obscured by the bright lights of a global city. *The Bourne Supremacy* and *Mission Impossible 4* both portray contemporary India as complex and dynamic—no longer the benighted land of the thugs, nor the enlightened land of the guru. Such an update to India's image reveals the cultural impact of India's growing economy—and the growing prominence of Bollywood itself. With glamourous celebrations of wealth, many Bollywood films stand in sharp relief with the old Hollywood portrayal of an impoverished India. Of course, Bollywood's India is itself a fabrication, one that often overlooks the poverty that continues to afflict millions of Indians. But for American audiences, it is a useful corrective to see Bollywood stars dancing through glitzy sets that defy the old stereotypes of India.

In addition to India's growing economy, the success of the Indian American community has changed how Americans understand India through film. While Hollywood has long portrayed an imaginary India, and Bollywood has offered stories about Indians in America, a distinct genre has emerged, driven by low-budget independent films that explore the diversity of the Indian American experience. These films are not without their own stereotypes. Many repeat a hackneyed story of assimilation in which the distance between India and America is overcome by the tenacity of an ideal immigrant. But if the model minority myth has been featured on the big screen, many of the films that examine the Indian American experience are more attuned to the complexity of what it has meant to be both Indian and American.

## Filming Diaspora

Mina and Demetrius fall in love across racial lines in a place long known for policing such boundaries: Mississippi. Theirs is not a story of black and white, but of a different racial fault line—the line between

Indian Americans and African Americans. Released in 1991, Mira Nair's *Mississippi Masala* probes similarities between the Indian American experience and the struggles of other people of color, even while revealing that those similarities have not always led to solidarity. As Mina (Sarita Choudhury) and Demetrius (Denzel Washington) fall in love, the anti-black prejudice of Mina's family becomes increasingly apparent. That prejudice was sharpened but also complicated by the family's experience of being forced out of Uganda by Idi Amin. In Mississippi, the family's prejudice evokes old fears of black men as sexual predators. In one scene, a friend of Demetrius comments, "United we stand, divided we fall. Ain't that a bitch! Yeah, but if you fall in bed with one of their daughters, your ass is gonna swing." In the background, we hear the classic Hindi film song "Mera Jutaa Hai Japani":

> Mera Jutaa Hai Japani
> Yeh Patloon Anglastani
> Sar pe lal topi rusi
> Phir bhi dil he Hindustani
>
> (My shoes are Japanese
> These pants are English
> The red hat on my head is Russian
> But my heart is Indian)

While the song suggests a resilient Indian identity that can survive globalization, the film complicates such a cosmopolitan vision. Mina's family members seem driven less by overt racism than by a desire to maintain their Indian identity by asserting control over the female body. Like many an old Hollywood film about India, racial difference is embodied by an alluring woman—although in this case, it is not the imperial power of white men that comes to the rescue, but the possibility that a new generation will privilege love over the boundaries of race, culture, and nation.[17]

In 2006, the Public Broadcasting Service screened an independent film made by a young South Asian director that dramatizes the need for antiracist alliances. In the film, entitled *American Made,* car troubles leave a Sikh family stranded by the side of a road during a trip to the Grand Canyon. The bearded and turbaned father is optimistic. Someone will stop to help his family. But as car after car drives by, his hopes sink, and his teenaged son says pointedly, "Dad, no one is going to stop for us, because you look like a terrorist." The family eventually gets help from a dark-skinned man whose ethnicity remains vague. He concludes the film by telling the family that he knows what it is like to not have anyone stop for him. Such a moment of antiracist solidarity stands in sharp relief to the model minority myth, revealing the impact of 9/11 on how South Asian Americans—and especially Sikh Americans—are racialized in contemporary America.

The arc of recent South Asian racialization is evident in the career of Kal Penn, one of the actors in *American Made,* and one of the best-known American-born actors of Indian descent. Penn began his career playing the stereotypical Indian immigrant, heavily accented and the butt of jokes. As he gained fame and the South Asian community grew in size, Penn was able to explore South Asian American identity with greater nuance. But after 9/11, new stereotypes threatened to erase that nuance. Contrast Penn's role in the screen adaptation of Jhumpa Lahiri's best-selling novel *The Namesake* with the covert terrorist he played on the television show *24.* Penn himself criticized the *24* role. He explained, "I have a huge political problem with the role. It was essentially accepting a form of racial profiling. I think it's repulsive." Perhaps Penn's best-known character, Kumar, is one of the leads in a series of films that confront racial profiling, albeit in a comic light. While the first *Harold and Kumar* film included an African American man arrested solely for being black, the second one found Kumar and his Korean American counterpart arrested on suspicion that they were part of the "Axis of Evil."[18]

Despite their differences, *Harold and Kumar, American Made,* and *Mississippi Masala* are similar in their exploration of Indian American connections to other people of color. The majority of films on the Indian American experience, by contrast, focus more on links between Indian Americans and white America. Many of these films are romantic comedies in which the romance is both international and intercultural. *Cosmopolitan* (2003) revolves around a middle-aged Indian American man who becomes increasingly obsessed with his free-spirited white American neighbor. With a spoof Bollywood song-and-dance routine in Hindi, *Cosmopolitan* tries to bring a comic touch to the Indian origin of its main character. The production of the film itself demonstrates the growing artistic salience of the Indian diaspora in America. The film was directed by Nisha Ganatra, who was born in Canada and raised in California. The lead actor, Roshan Seth, was born in India but has made his career primarily acting in British and American films. The film was based on an acclaimed short story by the Indian American writer Akhil Sharma. The screenplay was written by Sabrina Dhawan, who was born in England and raised in India and who lives in New York. The film's diasporic credentials are striking, but not unique. Neither is the idea of romance across national lines. Independent romantic comedies based on the Indian American experience include *Lonely in America* (1990), *Flavors* (2003), *Bicycle Bride* (2010), *The Other End of the Line* (2008), and *Walkaway* (2010). Most of these films play on romance as a metaphor for intercultural connection, but ultimately the love between man and woman overshadows the more complicated relationship between India and America.

A darker take on Indian American identity launched the career of M. Night Shyamalan, one of the best-known Indian Americans in Hollywood. Shyamalan's suspenseful ghost movie, *The Sixth Sense,* has overshadowed his first film, *Praying with Anger* (1992), in which a second-generation Indian American, played by Shyamalan, travels to Chennai to study abroad. The first question everyone asks is whether he knows Michael Jackson. He has a positive interaction with a swami, and heroically intercedes between an angry mob and its victim. But whereas *The Namesake* connects generations and thus India and America, *Praying with America* offers a more unsettling meditation on the elusiveness of home.

Many low-budget films find humor in that elusiveness. *American Desi* (2001) follows a college freshman, Krishnagopal Reddy, or Kris as he prefers to be called. In his choice of name, Kris distances himself from his Indian roots. To his chagrin, Kris learns that all his college roommates are Indian. He feels trapped in the world of his parents, despite the fact that his new roommates are far from homogenous. Ajay (Kal Penn) savors hip-hop and hangs a poster of Malcolm X. In some ways, he is just like Kris: an Indian American who does not want to be Indian. But while Kris tries to be just another (white) American, Ajay embraces black culture. The other two roommates are more traditional, a fact that repels Kris until he falls for an Indian woman who is deeply committed to Indian culture. Other films that explore the travails of young Indian Americans include *American Chai* (2001), *Dude, Where's the Party? aka Where's the Party Yaar?* (2003), and *Indian Cowboy* (2004).

The commonality of certain Indian American genres—the family reunion drama, the coming-of-age comedy—can obscure the diversity of South Asian America. A corrective of sorts came in the documentary *Not a Feather, but a Dot* (2011), which dispels stereotypes and recognizes the diversity of the Indian American community. Feature films have explored aspects of that diversity as well. *Chutney Popcorn,* released in 1999, reminded audiences that LGBTQ South Asians have their own struggles at the intersection of racial, national, and sexual difference. The film revolves around a mother and her two daughters, Reena and Sarita. When Sarita discovers that she is infertile, Reena offers to be a surrogate mother. Her decision complicates her relationship with her white American girlfriend. Ultimately, Reena delivers the child and is reunited not just with her girlfriend but also with her mother—who had previously disapproved of her daughter's sexuality.

Class disparities within the South Asian American diaspora have also made it onto the big screen. *Chintakayala Ravi . . . Software Engineer,* a 2008 Telugu romantic comedy, offers a working-class spin on the classic story of the Indian migrant. Chintakayala Ravi journeys to America to become a software engineer. Instead, he ends up working in a bar. When his mother tells the entire village that her son is a successful software engineer, Ravi cannot bring himself to tell her the truth. His lies unravel when his family arranges his marriage, forcing Ravi to rethink the nature of success, and challenging the audience to remember the many working-class South Asians in America.

Twenty years earlier, a different Telugu film offered an alternative perspective on East / West relations. *Padamati Sandhya Ragam* (Evening Raga of the West), released in 1987, follows three generations of Indian Americans. The patriarch of the family, Adinarayana (Gummaluri Sastry), relocates to America along with his wife and daughter, Sandhya (Vijaya Shanti). Sandhya attracts the attention of a white American neighbor named Chris (Thomas Jane), whom she eventually decides to marry. But Adinarayana is too traditional to accept his daughter marrying a foreigner, and Sandhya and Chris must elope in order to be married. When Sandhya and Chris have a daughter, Adinarayana takes her back to India, where he hopes she will be free from the dangers of the West and will avoid the path her mother took. The granddaughter grows up believing that it was her father, Chris, who poisoned family relations.

But when Adinarayana dies and Chris and Sandhya visit India, they are able to reclaim their daughter. The happy family then returns to the United States. Between 1987 and 2008, between *Padamati Sandhya Ragam* and *Chintakayala Ravi . . . Software Engineer,* the Indian American community boomed in size and affluence. But as these films make clear, the complexity of the South Asian American experience—especially in regard to race and class—has remained a constant.

Fans of South Indian cinema might be tempted to argue that movies produced in Telugu, Tamil, Malayalam, or Kannada present a richer and more complex portrait of America than their Hindi counterparts. But a more striking comparison is between independent American films made about the Indian American experience and films made in India about that experience. Most Indian films—regardless of where in India they are produced—focus on first-generation migrants. They often say more about India than America.

While films like *Chintakayala Ravi . . . Software Engineer* portrayed the challenges that still face migrants from India to America, the film industry was creating its own connections between the two countries. As with the rise of IT partnerships, it is tempting to celebrate such connections as a form of transnational collaboration, yet another way in which creativity knows no bounds. But as with the India trade of old, partnerships between Hollywood and Bollywood have been marked by inequality, not so much between the two industries as between the investors, producers, directors, and stars, who have grown fabulously rich, and the masses of humble fans, who idolize a lifestyle they will never know.

## Singing in the Rain

Two friends race through rural India on a motorcycle. They swerve through banyan trees, compete for the attention of a woman, and their motorcycle careens out of control. But the two remain jovial, confident that their friendship will survive even greater trials. All the while, they sing a catchy tune, proclaiming their friendship to the world. This scene from *Sholay,* one of the most beloved Hindi films, embodies many of the trademarks of Bollywood: triumphant music, elaborate choreography, heavy emotion. Those same traits once marked many Hollywood films as well. It is telling that the greatest cinematic paean to Bollywood, *Om Shanti Om*, echoes the classic Hollywood musical *Singin' in the Rain*. In both, an aspiring actor falls in love on a film set. In both, the film-within-a-film genre reminds viewers that movies have their own reality, a reality that has blurred the boundaries between fact and fiction and between India and America.

The connections between cinema in the United States and India are part of a global circuit of ideas, forms, and methods. Take *Sholay*, for example. The film drew upon the tropes of the American Western and of *The Magnificent Seven* in particular. Both films concern a small group of heroic tough guys who defend an isolated community against a gang of villains. Such crosscurrents of influence have linked many Indian films to Hollywood. *Gun Sundari* was based on *Why Husbands Go Astray*. *Zanjeer* echoed *Dirty Harry*. *Ta Ra Rum Pum* borrowed from *Days of Thunder* and *Talladega Nights*. *Deewane Huye Paagal* is a remake of *There's Something about Mary*. *Dostana* was partly inspired by *I Now Pronounce You Chuck and Larry*. It would be wrong to dismiss these films as cheap imitations. *Sholay* is much more than a remake of *The Magnificent Seven*—and not just because the plots are distinct in many ways. Both films echo Akira Kurosawa's *The Seven Samurai*. Like *Sholay* and *The Magnificent Seven*, many films in both India and America reveal the creative power that results when filmmakers draw upon ideas and techniques from throughout the world.[19]

These connections extend beyond the world of film. Raj Kapoor's 1973 hit, *Bobby*, was inspired by the classic American comic book series Archie Comics. As Kapoor explained it, "I came across a sentence . . . spoken by Archie himself, something like, 'Seventeen is no longer young—we have a life of our own too and we are aware of it!' This really got me. I felt, here is something very profound—and thinking about this resulted in my making Bobby." It is a cliché, of course, to declare that art defies borders. It is important to recognize the degree to which Indian films—even those that draw upon outside inspiration—remain Indian. And we must resist the temptation to celebrate the links between Bollywood and Hollywood as revelatory of a larger freedom. Still, it matters that the last scene of *Bobby* echoes the famous yellow-brick-road scene from *The Wizard of Oz*. Such cinematic transnationalism does not reveal a world without walls, but it does point to the ways in which those walls have long been surmounted.[20]

In addition to plotlines, other cinematic elements have crossed between Hollywood and Bollywood—in both directions. The use of elaborate dance routines is returning to Hollywood, inspired in part by the success of Bollywood. Take, for example, the musical *Moulin Rouge!*, directed by Baz Luhrmann. Luhrmann credited Indian cinema with helping to inspire his approach to the genre. Other musicals or biopics of musicians—films like *Chicago, Ray, Dreamgirls,* and *La La Land*—may not have been explicitly inspired by Bollywood, but nevertheless demonstrate a convergence of technique. On the other end of the spectrum, many Hindi films are dispensing with musical routines, increasing the use of sophisticated special effects, and turning from melodrama toward a greater realism that evokes Hollywood. Films like *Chak de India, Kahaani,* and *Rajneeti* employ a style more associated with Hollywood.[21]

The line between Hollywood and Bollywood has begun to blur—and not just on-screen. In 2007, Columbia Tristar released *Saawariya,* the first Bollywood film distributed by a major Hollywood company. As *Saawariya* reveals, the links between Bollywood and Hollywood must be understood as a form of globalization, not just of pop culture but also of corporate power. An Indian film adapted from a Russian story is distributed by a Hollywood studio owned by a Japanese conglomerate. Such multinational corporate links are increasingly common in film production as well. The title song in *Ta Ra Rum Pum* features a lengthy animated sequence cocreated by Disney and Yash Raj Films. Yash Raj Films would partner with Disney yet again in 2008 on *Roadside Romeo,* an animated comedy starring an ambitious dog. *The Other End of the Line* (2008) brought together the Hollywood giant MGM with the Indian production house Adlabs. Coproduced by the Indian American producer Ashok Amritraj, the film follows an employee at an Indian call center who flies to California to be with a man she meets over the phone. The film's tagline is "Two countries. Two cultures. One chance at love." Such a saccharine tale of love's triumph over difference—a tale in which corporate globalization is celebrated as a source of romance—is well suited to the ambiguities of a film that reveals the coming together of two of the world's most powerful film industries.

Filmmakers in the United States and India have long learned from each other, and it would be wrong to frame recent Hollywood / Bollywood ties as entirely new. It would be equally misguided to suggest that such ties portend a complete convergence of the two industries. There remain significant aesthetic differences between Bollywood and Hollywood. As Stephen Alter puts it, "Hollywood and Bollywood speak different languages—not just the actors' dialogues but the visual vocabulary as well." What we are seeing is not a blending of the two languages, but an uptick in a long process of mutual translation. That translation has often reinforced the differences between the industries. As Madhava Prasad has written, "The successful commodification of Indian cinema as Bollywood in the international market is based on the idea of an unchanging essence that distinguishes it from Hollywood." Such a belief in Bollywood's inherent difference from Hollywood was on display when Shah Rukh Khan discussed the hit film *Chennai Express,* coproduced by Khan's company, Red Chillies Entertainment, and Disney-UTV (a product of Disney's purchase of the Indian media company UTV). Khan declared, "I think that it's fantastic that the Hollywood studios are here. At first the studios wanted to popularize Hollywood films here but our cinema is deeply rooted in Indian culture. So it's good to see them producing Indian films."[22]

Such national contrasts can obscure the similarities between industries that thrive in the age of neoliberal globalism. In 2009, one of India's wealthiest men, Anil Ambani, invested several hundred million dollars in Steven Spielberg's DreamWorks production company. A Wharton MBA, Ambani had already become a major player in India's media scene through his control of Reliance Entertainment. The partnership with Spielberg created a new bridge between major Indian and American film companies. In 2015, Spielberg and Ambani announced the creation of Amblin Partners, a new media production company that draws upon the resources of Reliance Entertainment and DreamWorks. As with the ties between Infosys and GE, it would be easy to celebrate corporate convergence as a form of national friendship. Yet the collaboration between Ambani and Spielberg is not the coming together of India and America but of the wealthy elite who own and control the film industries of both countries.[23]

As Indian films are shot in America and American films in India, the physical confluence of Hollywood and Bollywood reveals the ambiguities of inclusion at the heart of cinema. Consider the filming of *Kabhi Alvida Naa Kehna.* The script required Shah Rukh Khan, Preity Zinta, and Saif Ali Khan to be filmed at Grand Central Station. The New York police, accustomed to protecting American movie stars, were unprepared for the hundreds of diehard Indian American cinema fans who showed up to catch a glimpse of their favorite Bollywood stars. The crowd was peaceful, and its size alone would not have been a problem. Grand Central is often crowded. But the director wanted to capture a typical New York crowd, and instead was faced with a mob composed almost entirely of eager Indian faces. There is something touching but also unsettling about the love between cinema fans and the stars they adore. In crowding Grand Central Station, those desi fans were demonstrating the basic fact that film production involves selectively including and excluding—and that being a fan often means being included only at the periphery.[24]

Such ambiguity has marked the growing roster of Indian actors in Hollywood. Anupam Kher gained fame by playing key supporting roles in such Bollywood classics as *Dilwale Dulhania Le Jayenge* (The Courageous Will Win the Bride) and *Kuch Kuch Hota Hai* (Something Is Happening). But American audiences know him from his role in the TV series *ER* and as the psychiatrist in *Silver Linings Playbook*. Perhaps the most famous actor to have connected the industries is Irrfan Khan. Khan has played key roles in a variety of Hindi-language films, including the 2003 adaptation of Shakespeare's Macbeth, *Maqbool*; the 2007 hit *Life in a Metro*; and the 2013 biopic *Paan Singh Tomar*. Khan's Hollywood career includes his role as a Pakistani policeman in the 2007 film *A Mighty Heart*, and his captivating performance as the father figure in *The Namesake*. Khan had a small but powerful role in *Darjeeling Limited*, a larger role in *Slumdog Millionaire*, and a starring role in *Life of Pi*. He also played Dr. Ratha in *The Amazing Spider-Man*.

Such circuits of fame are not always examples of cultures coming together. Indeed, actors that cross borders can embody the distance between India and America, and the misconceptions that thrive in that distance. Amrish Puri played the father figure, Kishorilal, in *Pardes*. But he also played the evil thug priest in *Indiana Jones and the Temple of Doom*. In one film, he is a loving patriarch; in the other, an evil ruler who tears out the beating hearts of his victims. The first Indian actor to build a career in Hollywood embodied such limiting stereotypes. Born in Mysore in 1924, the actor known as Sabu (sometimes identified as Sabu Dastagir) gained fame as Mowgli in the 1942 version of *Jungle Book*. He played a similar "tropical" role in films like *White Savage* (1943) and *Cobra Island* (1944). In 1944, Sabu joined the U.S. Air Force, served as a tail gunner, and was awarded the Distinguished Flying Cross. But Hollywood

Figure 8. Sabu, also known as Sabu Dastagir, in *Jungle Book* (1942). An Indian American actor, Sabu was repeatedly portrayed as having a special relationship with animals, like the giant snake, Kaa, featured here. Alexander Korda Films, Inc. / United Artists.

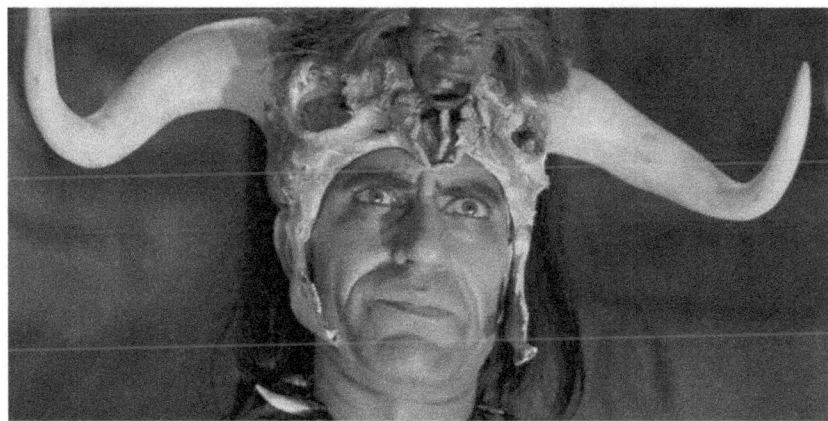

Figure 9. Thug priest Mola Ram, as played by Amrish Puri in *Indiana Jones and the Temple of Doom* (1984). Lucasfilm Ltd. / Paramount Pictures.

continued to cast him as a foreigner in films like *Man-Eater of Kumaon* (1948) and *Jaguar* (1956). Sabu's last film, *A Tiger Walks* (1964), released three months after his death, portrays him as a tiger trainer. The 2012 blockbuster *Life of Pi* might be seen as an update on the Sabu character. Shipwrecked in the middle of the sea, Piscine Molitor "Pi" Patel survives by sharing a lifeboat with a Bengal tiger. Yet again, Western audiences marveled at a strapping young Indian man taming wild creatures.

While Sabu never broke the bounds of typecasting, many Indian film stars have become icons of border crossing—both on- and offscreen. Despite Shah Rukh Khan's travails, most Bollywood stars have no trouble coming to America. Like those of their Hollywood peers, their worlds are defined more by class than by country. The discrepancy between the lives of film stars and of most people in India and America should caution us against celebrating the transnational cosmopolitanism of the movies. Film stars are icons, and their movements on-screen—whether in character or not—allow audiences to imagine a more global world and, if only briefly, to escape the limitations of their own reality. But what does it mean for a Bollywood film to be set in America if the majority of Indians will never have the chance to make such a journey themselves?

Even for those Indians who have journeyed to America—and the millions of Indian Americans who call the United States home—the confluence of Hollywood and Bollywood should not be seen as inherently transformative. A profound gap separates film stars in both countries from the fans who idolize them and their global lifestyles. Recognizing that gap should not entail discounting the significance of the shift from Sabu to Shah Rukh Khan. While we must be wary of using the movies to glorify a certain kind of globalization, it matters that India's film stars have risen to global prominence. Second- and third-generation Indian Americans are finding new icons amidst a new generation of Indian American celebrities such as Aziz Ansari, Sakina Jaffrey, Mindy Kaling, Hari Kondabolu, Hasan Minhaj, and Aparna Nancherla. Many of these figures are comedians who use their status as "hyphenated Americans" to mock the image of American society as a "postracial" melting pot. Whereas Kal Penn was forced to grapple with being typecast as a terrorist thug, many actors are now calling such stereotypes into question through a deliberate practice of what Parama Roy, in an article on the history of thuggee, calls the "problem of impersonation / mimicry." Just as the thug was revalued within American hip-hop, many Indian American stars are remaking what it means to be Indian and what it means to be Indian American.[25]

We must bring such a skeptical lens to the narrative of film as transcendent, a narrative that has made its way into several low-budget movies that imagine the filmmaking process as itself a way to connect India and America. In *Happy Ending*, a 2014 Hindi-language romantic comedy set largely in Los Angeles, the main character makes money copying Hollywood movies into Bollywood movies. In *Marigold*, a 2007 romantic comedy, an American actress travels to India to make a film. Director Willard Carroll hoped the film would bridge "the gap between Indian and American cinema." The actress, Marigold Lexton (Ali Larter), finds herself alone in Goa, stumbles upon the set of a Bollywood musical, and manages to land a small role and a relationship with the choreographer. In the same year *Marigold* was released, another romantic comedy, *Americanizing Shelley*, told a similar story but in reverse. Instead of an American woman traveling to India, an Indian woman journeys to America, where a Hollywood producer (played by Beau Bridges) tries to "Americanize" her in order to make her a movie star. Rather than recognize the exclusion and violence that defined much of the history of the Indian American community, *Americanizing Shelley* hides such violence behind a saccharine tale of love as border crossing.

Like *Mississippi Masala*, several films have explored the violence that can accompany border crossing, whether the borders in question are national or racial or cultural. In *Kites*, a 2010 film, the Bollywood heartthrob Hrithik Roshan stars opposite the Mexican actress Barbara Mori. Roshan plays Jai, an Indian American dance teacher in Las Vegas, who moonlights as a husband-for-hire, helping immigrant women who need green cards. One of his "wives," a Mexican woman named Natasha (played by Mori), falls for a violent hooligan named Tony. Roshan's character, Jai, becomes enmeshed in a dangerous situation, and he and Natasha have to flee to Mexico. The movie reveals the violence that often accompanies the border, as well as the way in which such violence is often directed at controlling women and their bodies.

Like the borders of nations, gender norms have been both challenged and reinforced within Indo-American cinema. In Gurinder Chadha's adaptation of Jane Austin's *Pride and Prejudice*, clumsily called *Bride and Prejudice*, we follow a romance between an American man and an Indian woman played by Aishwarya Rai. Their courtship is fraught with tension

and misunderstanding, not unlike the history of Indo-American relations. In one scene, Rai confronts the hapless American's misconceptions concerning the "backward" nature of arranged marriage. And yet
the film as a whole does little to question the centrality of marriage to
a woman's sense of identity—and of heteronormative love to the
romantic-comedy storyline. Rai's next American film was *The Mistress
of Spices,* an adaptation of a popular novel by Indian American author
Chitra Banerjee Divakaruni. Rai plays Tilo, the owner of a spice store
who uses the spices to magically help her customers achieve their wishes.
Set in San Francisco, the film highlights the ethnic diversity of California.
Rai again falls for a white American man, but her character's magical
powers—and the diversity of the supporting cast—carry *The Mistress of
Spices* a bit further toward a critique of conventional racial and gender
norms.[26]

The irony and self-reflectivity of some films make it unclear whether
gender norms are being transgressed or reinscribed. Consider the strange
career of the porn star turned Bollywood actress Sunny Leone. Born in
Canada as Karenjit Kaur Vohra, Leone moved to the United States as a
teenager. In 2001, at the age of twenty-one, she launched a successful
career as a porn actress. In 2003, she was named Penthouse Pet of the
Year. In 2012, she made her Bollywood debut in the erotic thriller *Jism
2,* going on to star in *Jackpot, Ek Paheli Leela,* and *Ragini MMS 2.* In the
latter film, an erotic horror film, Leone plays a former porn star named
Sunny Leone. Does such a role reinforce the objectification of women
as sex toys? Or is Leone's character an opportunity for women to claim
their own sexuality as a source of power?[27]

Contrast Leone's on-screen persona with Persis Khambatta's portrayal
of Lieutenant Ilia in *Star Trek: The Motion Picture.* Khambatta, a former
Miss India, was required to shave her head for the role. But her lack of
hair did nothing to diminish the charged sexuality that her character
embodied. Khambatta plays a Deltoid, a native of the planet Delta IV, a
species with such intense sexual energy that they are required to take
an oath of celibacy before being allowed to serve in Starfleet. With her
shaved head and vow of celibacy, Khambatta might be seen to embody
the Gandhian strand of American perceptions of India. Yet her sexuality remains overpowering, even after she is killed by a mysterious ro-
botic probe. When she returns as a kind of cyborg, her sexual appeal
returns with her, sharpened by the danger she now personifies. She is

the alluring yet threatening woman of the East. Of course, most American viewers did not see Lieutenant Ilia as Indian or even Asian. But in her foreignness and her dangerous sexuality, she replayed old tropes associated with Hollywood's India.

Sunny Leone and Persis Khambatta embody dangerous sexuality in ways that simultaneously empower and constrain them as women and as actresses. The ambiguity of sexuality as liberation and limitation is at the center of Mira Nair's *Monsoon Wedding* (2001), one of the top-grossing Indian films in the United States. Whereas Nair's earlier film, *Mississippi Masala*, probes an illicit love, *Monsoon Wedding* concerns an arranged marriage between an Indian girl and an Indian American boy—a marriage that has been approved by both families. The wedding plans begin to unravel when the girl admits that she has been having an affair. By first complicating and then reaffirming the power of love, *Monsoon Wedding* could be seen to fit smoothly into old cinematic narratives. But the film offers a more complicated understanding of how romantic relationships work—and how sex can be an instrument of oppression and repression. The girl's uncle, the villain of the story, lives in the United States, as does one of the film's heroes, the girl's cousin. When it emerges that the uncle had abused the cousin when she was a child, the family is forced to confront the reality of sexual abuse.

By grappling with a subject often ignored in Indian and American cinema, *Monsoon Wedding* challenges the dominance of facile love stories in Bollywood and Hollywood. That challenge is more powerful because the film still celebrates the power of love—not just between husband and wife (there are two weddings, in the end) but also between generations separated by time and distance. We see a family come together across multiple continents and even more profound divides. The style of the film contributes to this coming together by blending cinematic techniques from Hollywood and Bollywood. *Monsoon Wedding* dispenses with the normal Bollywood dance routines. But the film includes extended dance sequences that feature the "global" dance music that can be heard in New York and Los Angeles, as well as Mumbai and Delhi. In its music, as well as in other elements of its style, the film bridges film industries and cultures.[28]

The sound of Bollywood has long transgressed the line between East and West. Most early Indian films made use of classical Indian music. By the end of the 1950s, however, Western orchestral music had become a key element of Bollywood's sound. Jazz also infused many Bollywood soundtracks. The hit song "Eena Meena Deeka" from the 1957 film *Aasha* combined a swinging beat, a big-band sound, and the meaningless wordplay known as scat. While some Bollywood films were infused with jazz, others rocked and rolled. Chubby Checker must have been proud when the 1965 film *Bhoot Bangla* featured the hit "Aao Twist Kare" (Come and Do the Twist). More recently, Hindi film songs have borrowed from hiphop. "Chammak Challo," a song from the 2011 Bollywood hit *Ra.One*, was performed by the hip-hop star Akon. In 2008, Snoop Dogg had a cameo in the title song of the comedy *Singh Is Kinng* [*sic*]. Many years of cultural flows and migration patterns paved the way for Snoop Dogg to open a Bollywood song-and-dance routine: "Yo, what up? This is the big Snoop Dogg. Represent that Poon-jabi."

While Bollywood has borrowed from Western music, inspiration has flowed in the opposite direction as well. Note the Britney Spears hit "Toxic," or the collaboration between Jay-Z and Punjabi MC. A variety of American pop stars have made use of sounds associated with Bollywood and the Indian-inspired fusion music known as bhangra. As Indians consume hip-hop and Americans dance to bhangra, the lines between these musical forms blur, raising again the question of when cultural appropriation becomes a more robust and meaningful form of cultural connection and collaboration. Like the role of the Hindu classics for Emerson and Thoreau, there are clear instances in which American pop stars have used Indian cultural forms without recognizing or respecting their context. Selena Gomez drew criticism for performing "Come and Get It" while wearing a Bindi at the MTV Awards in 2013. Her response to the criticism did not help. "The song kind of has that almost Hindu feel, that tribal feel," Gomez explained. "Plus, I've been learning a lot about my seven chakras and bindis and stuff. I've learned a lot about the culture, and I think it's beautiful."[29]

Film is one of many cultural bridges between the United States and India, bridges that call into question the meaning of culture and of "connections" between cultures. From blue jeans to rock music to Kentucky Fried Chicken—American cultural forms have proliferated across much of India. At the same time, Indian cultural forms, from yoga to curry, have become equally prominent in the United States. Such cultural flows have long been decried as appropriation or globalization. While Americans bastardize Indian cuisine, Pizza Hut invades India. But the history of India and America defies neat dichotomies between *their* culture and *our* culture. While Americans make yoga their own, Indians go to McDonalds to eat McAloo Tikki Burgers. Rather than a history of cultural exchange, the history of Bollywood / Hollywood is part of a larger process of translation, in which both Indian and American "cultures" have been reinterpreted, blended, and made new. Like the specter of the thug, many cultural forms have been disconnected from their roots even while reinforcing pernicious dichotomies between inside and outside, ours and theirs. But from yoga to curry to Bollywood and Hollywood, cultural traditions and artifacts have also defied the borders of nations and cultures—like all translations, bearing a legacy of loss as well as creation.[30]

Cultural traditions have defied borders because people have defied borders. The growth of the Indian American community after 1965 played an important role in expanding connections between Hollywood and Bollywood. The Indian American community created a market for Bollywood films in the United States. First came small art theaters and satellite TV companies geared toward Indian films. In July 1988, Asian Variety Show offered viewers access to Bollywood. Ten years later TV Asia entered the market. And in July 2005, MTV launched a station that aimed to appeal to the Indian diaspora. MTV-Desi was only available with DirecTV's Hindi Direct package, which also included five other Indian channels. It failed after eighteen months, in part because fans of Indian cinema were finding many ways to gain access to Bollywood films. In 2007, an Indian movie-theater chain called Big Cinemas acquired more than two hundred screens across the United States and repurposed them for Indian movies. Mainstream cinemas also began to play Bollywood films. Indian movies now earn millions of dollars in American theaters. The action hit *Dhoom 3*, for example, earned some $3.3 million in just one weekend. Its success in America was fitting, given that most of the film was set in Chicago.[31]

Diasporic audiences have driven the rise of diasporic characters in Bollywood. In the words of the anthropologist Purnima Mankekar, "There is no question that the preoccupation with NRIs [nonresident Indians] in Hindi films such as DDLJ was the result of the fact that Indian diasporas represent a crucial segment of their market." There is money to be made in doing what Mankekar has called "the affective work of representing the diaspora to itself." Bollywood is also representing the diaspora to Americans. It is telling that a major exhibition on South Asian Americans at the Smithsonian Natural History Museum was called *Beyond Bollywood*. Bollywood shapes not just how Americans think of Indian film, but also how they think of India and of Indian Americans. There is a sense that what Meheli Sen says about Bollywood is especially true of Bollywood in America: "Bollywood remains a dehistoricized, reified category whose very ubiquity tends to evacuate it of meaning." Is the same true of Hollywood in India?[32]

While more and more Bollywood films are screened in the United States, Hollywood films have become big moneymakers in India. In 2014, action blockbusters like *Transformers 4: Age of Extinction* and *The Amazing Spider-Man 2* earned over 2 billion Indian rupees. In the first half of 2015, Hollywood produced three of the five biggest hits in India. *Jurassic World* and *Furious Seven*, both big-budget action films, each earned more than a billion rupees. *Furious Seven* received one of the biggest releases any Hollywood film has garnered in India, playing on some twenty-eight hundred screens across the country.

Is this the culmination of the long history of Indo-American relations: *Dhoom 3* earns millions in America while *Furious Seven* sweeps India? It is tempting to dismiss such developments as nothing more than the triumph of a certain kind of cheap globalization. From calico cloth to yoga, Indo-American cultural relations have long been commercialized and, in some ways, homogenized. But despite the pressures of the market, artists have found inspiration in Indo-American cultural connections. And far from being passive consumers, audiences have also contributed to the richness of Indo-American cultural exchange. One doubts whether *Dhoom 3* or *Furious Seven* inspired significant amounts of cross-cultural understanding or cosmopolitan tolerance, but the increasing overlap in the market for Hollywood and Bollywood has, at the least, expanded the basic cultural familiarity that grounds Indo-American relations. And there are successful films that encourage audiences in both India and America to grapple with their shared legacy of democracy.

Consider the critically acclaimed 2004 film *Swades*. Like *The Namesake*, *Swades* follows an Indian American who confronts an identity crisis. Unlike *The Namesake*, however, the main character was born and raised in India. Mohan Bhargava (Shah Rukh Khan), a successful NASA scientist, decides to return to India to care for an elderly woman who had

*Figure 10.* Shah Rukh Khan playing a NASA scientist in *Swades*
(2004). Ashutosh Gowariker Productions / UTV Motion Pictures.

served his family while he was growing up. After encountering rural
poverty, he sets about to help the villagers overcome their problems. He
falls in love with his country—and, of course, also with a woman. But
even while celebrating Indian patriotism, *Swades* defines patriotism as
fundamentally cosmopolitan and humble.

*Swades* rejects the myth of the two democracies and the triumphant
nationalism that myth supports. The subtitle of the film makes a reference to the preamble of the constitution of India, a reference that also
gestures toward the United States: *We the People of India.* Whereas the film
mostly contrasts Indian poverty with American affluence, one crucial
scene connects both countries within a common struggle for progress.
When a group of villagers asks Mohan about life in America, he replies
that the United States provides basic necessities to its citizens. One elder
huffs, "But we have something they do not have and will never have:
culture and tradition." "Ours is the greatest country in the world," he
proclaims. Mohan disagrees. He says that India is not the greatest country
in the world, but it has the potential to become great. "America has progressed on its own strengths," he explains. "It would be wrong," he lectures the villages, "to claim that their culture, tradition, and beliefs are
inferior and ours are laudable." One villager says that she has heard that

there is discrimination in America. Mohan confirms the reality of American discrimination, but counters that Indians also discriminate based on caste. Rather than use the race / caste comparison as a shield to hide domestic wrongs, Mohan uses American racism as a mirror to turn attention to India's own problems.

*Swades* begins with a quote from Gandhi: "Hesitating to act because the whole vision might not be achieved, or because others do not yet share it, is an attitude that only hinders progress." With its title, *Swades* evokes the legacy of the Indian anticolonial movement and of the Swadeshi Movement in particular. Indians fought British rule by rejecting the material possessions of the West and reclaiming their own country—the literal meaning of the word *swades*. Such a rejection did not entail a close-minded xenophobia. To "move beyond the East-West binary," Aakash Singh Rathore has written, requires "a dialectical process during which we recognize the otherness within ourselves, acknowledging both the identity and the difference." Gandhi embodied such a process of (self)recognition as he crafted his own conception of freedom, of *swaraj*. In line with Gandhi's legacy, *Swades* rejects the dichotomy between nationalism and internationalism and instead embraces a self-critical cosmopolitanism which entails, in the words of Sudipta Kaviraj, "the acceptance in advance of the possibility that your own culture can be inadequate." As Shah Rukh Khan's character declares, "Main yeh nahin maanta ki hamara desh duniya ka sabse mahaan desh hai . . . lekin yeh zaroor manta hoon ki hummein kabiliyat hai, taakat hai, is desh ko mahaan banaane ki." "I don't believe our country is the greatest in the world . . . but I do believe that we have the capacity, the power, to make this country great." Such a blend of humility and ambition, of global awareness and national pride, inspired many of the figures in this book to advance the struggle for democracy in the United States and India. If the history of that struggle is our shared heritage, its future is our shared burden. Democracy is not a gift but a dream, a dream that must be continually realized and—in the spirit of the movies—reimagined.[33]

# Conclusion

## The Tragedy of Democracy

∞

The spirit of democracy cannot be imposed from
without. It has to come from within.
—Mahatma Gandhi, 1934

I N SEPTEMBER 1947, one month after India gained its independence,
Mahatma Gandhi turned to Abraham Lincoln to define the future of
Indian democracy. Echoing the Gettysburg Address, Gandhi declared,
"Government of the people, by the people and for the people cannot be
conducted at the bidding of one man, however great he may be." During
his education in London and his twenty years in South Africa, Gandhi
had developed a distinctly global perspective on the nature of democracy. But even while he learned from Americans like Lincoln and Thoreau, Gandhi scorned the idea that Indians should see the United States
as a model of democratic achievement. "Western democracy, as it func-
tions today, is diluted Nazism or Fascism," he asserted. "At best it is merely
a cloak to hide the Nazi and the Fascist tendencies of imperialism."[1]

Do the United States and India deserve to be called democracies? "In
America," Malcolm X declared, "democracy is hypocrisy." "We don't see
any American dream," he told one audience, "we've experienced only

the American nightmare. We haven't benefited from America's democracy; we've only suffered from America's hypocrisy." B. R. Ambedkar similarly denounced democratic hypocrisy when he stated, *"Democracy in India is only a top dressing on an Indian soil, which is essentially undemocratic."* After decades of fighting caste oppression, Ambedkar had good reason to be dismissive of India's democratic pretensions. But his view of Indian democracy was not always so withering. He was, after all, one of the key drafters of India's constitution. Once the new constitution went into effect, he warned, "We are going to enter a life of contradictions. In politics we will have equality and in social and economic life we will have inequality." Ambedkar predicted that such a contrast could not survive: either Indian democrats would find a way to achieve social and economic equality or their failure would put "our political democracy in peril."[2]

Ambedkar's warning hangs ominously over the future of democracy in both India and the United States. In the last century, both countries have become increasingly democratic—at least by some measures. Voting rights expanded in the United States as women gained the ballot in 1920 and the civil rights movement removed some of the barriers facing voters of color. In India, universal suffrage was granted at the time of independence. But democracy is about more than elections. There are many freedoms necessary to what Lala Lajpat Rai called "real democracy": freedom of speech, an independent judiciary, due process of law—and also freedom from poverty, discrimination, and police harassment. In both the United States and India, many of these freedoms are limited or under threat. The historian Ramachandra Guha has called India a "fifty-fifty democracy." His assessment could be applied to the United States as well.[3]

In both the United States and India, the gap between rich and poor continues to grow. Economic ties between the two countries have tended to benefit disproportionately those at the top of the economic spectrum. There are now some ninety Indian billionaires, as measured in American dollars. The Indian middle class is booming. And the country has taken on many of the attributes of a wealthy nation—from a space program to a high-profile cricket league that attracts talent from throughout the world. Still, India contains a third of the world's poorest people. In the nineteenth century, some Indian nationalists expressed greater concern with poverty than with the poor. They wanted a wealthy country even if, like the United States, it contained masses of poor people. That is what India is becoming—a wealthy country with a third of the world's poor. That is what the United States remains—a wealthy country with some forty-five million poor people.[4]

In both India and the United States, poverty is compounded by the persistence of discrimination. In the United States, the civil rights movement advanced democracy, but persistent racial segregation, the mass imprisonment of people of color, and growing economic inequality all undermine democracy. In India, the hegemony of the social and political elite has been weakened by the rise of regional political parties and the growing economic and political power of once oppressed castes and communities. But old forms of oppression, especially anti-Dalit and anti-Muslim prejudice, remain rampant. In both India and the United States, the surveillance state has swelled, as in the days of Ghadar, threatening democratic values and demonizing those seen as outsiders—whether based on race, caste, or religion.[5]

If Indians and Americans are to achieve the full promise of their democratic aspirations, they must recognize the limitations of their democracies even while continuing to believe in a better future. Here is where the uncertainties of our present world may prove salutary. The multiple challenges facing both the United States and India offer a fertile environment for what Jim Kloppenberg has called "an ethic of reciprocity grounded on restraint and doubt." Such an ethic, so vital to democracy, thrives when searching self-criticism is married to an audacious faith in a better future. As the histories of India and the United States make clear, democracies are stronger when their internal diversity fosters connections to other democracies, when national diversity becomes a source of transnational solidarity.[6]

Such progress depends on a critical awareness of the limitations of the current order. As the political theorist Timothy Mitchell has written, the many threats to democracy call upon us "not simply to defend existing democratic rights or extend them to others, but to re-democratise the forms of democracy." In both the United States and India, the achievements of democracy have been co-opted by politicians who hide ruthless oppression behind a rhetoric of freedom and democracy. Unless connected to an honest assessment of the pervasive inequalities that plague both countries, celebrating India and America as "the world's two largest democracies" is worse than hypocrisy—it is an act of rhetorical violence.[7]

Despite the many limitations of democracy in the United States and India, there are reasons to be hopeful. For decades after 1947, commentators confidently predicted the imminent collapse of Indian democracy. "When Nehru goes," Aldous Huxley predicted in 1961, "the government will become a military dictatorship." In 1967, the *London Times* declared, "The great experiment of developing India within a democratic framework has failed." Why was Indian democracy doomed to failure? Modernization theorists argued that countries needed to be rich in order to be democratic. With over a third of the world's poor, the argument went, India was bound to devolve into dictatorship. Other "experts" claimed that Asian culture is inherently undemocratic, due to its emphasis on respect for authority, continuity, and tradition. If its poverty did not destroy India's democracy, its Asian culture surely would. Finally, many suggested that India was too diverse to succeed as a democracy. The Indian state would never be able to maintain the integrity of the nation. Yet despite its problems, India remains, in the words of Sunil Khilnani, a "bridgehead of effervescent liberty." While recognizing the many ways in which Indian liberty remains corrupted by imbalances of wealth and power—not unlike American liberty—it would be foolish to overlook the achievements of Indian democracy.[8]

Consider what was perhaps the greatest threat to democracy in the history of postindependence India: what came to be known simply as "the emergency." In June 1975, the prime minister, Indira Gandhi, suspended the constitution and claimed dictatorial powers. Thousands of prodemocracy activists were arrested and held without trial. Journalists were terrified into silence or were arrested. Unable to publish any direct criticism of Indira Gandhi's rule, the *Times of India* managed to sneak a protest into the obituaries section: "D'Ocracy—D.E.M, beloved husband of T. Ruth, loving father of L. I. Bertie, brother of Faith, Hope, Justice, expired on 26th June." Indians living in the United States had more freedom to express dissent—and many did. At the University of Chicago, Indian students organized a protest against "Indira Gandhi's Subversion of Democracy in India." A broadsheet by a group calling itself Indians for Political Freedom demanded that the Indian government "release political prisoners immediately," "end torture and repression of dissenters," and "observe civil liberties and democratic rights of Indian citizens." In Oakland, the journal *India Forum* published a special edition on "political repression and social trends" in what they called "fortress India." On August 15, 1975, India's Independence Day, an ad in the *New York Times* declared, "Today is India's Independence Day. Don't Let the Light Go Out on Indian Democracy."[9]

One of the most prominent Indian American critics of the emergency was Shrikumar Poddar, a businessman based in Lansing, Michigan. As a visiting student in the United States in the early 1960s, Poddar had started a magazine subscription service, which grew to earn over $2 million annually. When the emergency was declared, he dedicated his time and money to generating opposition within the United States. Another key figure was Anand Kumar, a student at the University of Chicago. Kumar traveled the country speaking at universities and town halls, trying to garner support for the prodemocracy movement in India. Kumar, Poddar, and others formed an umbrella organization called Indians for Democracy. The group launched a journal, *Indian Opinion*, the same title Gandhi had used for his newspaper in South Africa. They also organized a twelve-day march, or *padyatra*, from Freedom Park in Philadelphia to the headquarters of the United Nations in New York. The Walk for Democracy attracted the support of thousands of Indian Americans. Indians for Democracy hosted prominent anti-emergency Indians who toured the United States, such as Ram Jethmalani (head of the Bar Council of India), the filmmaker Anand Patwardhan, the artist Devi Prasad, and the author and activist C. G. K. Reddy. They also served as a conduit between prodemocracy activists in India and international NGOs based in the United States, such as Amnesty International and War Resisters International.[10]

The Indian government worked covertly to undermine the opposition in the United States. Anand Kumar's government scholarship was revoked, and at least four Indians had their passports cancelled. On September 16, 1976, Shrikumar Poddar denounced this harassment before the Subcommittee on International Organizations of the House Committee on International Relations. In April 1977, *India Forum* declared, "The fact that such strong arm tactics should be used in India by the Indian government is repugnant, but the fact that they should be used on American soil cannot be tolerated by freedom-loving people anywhere." As in the days of Ghadar, many anti-emergency activists recognized that the United States had its own problems with democracy. Such recognition led *India Forum* to declare, "the 1975 state of 'emergency' will certainly stand as one of the blackest phases of India's history, and Mrs. Gandhi will take her place in history along with the likes of Yahya Khan and Richard Nixon."[11]

It was fitting to compare Indira Gandhi and Richard Nixon—two figures who despised each other and yet similarly disregarded democratic norms in order to maintain their own power. If the emergency revealed the fragility of democracy in India, the United States had its own history of antidemocratic efforts. In 1975, the same year the emergency was launched, the authoritarian strand of American discourse came to the fore in a notorious report entitled *The Crisis of Democracy.* Written by eminent political scientists Michel Crozier, Samuel P. Huntington, and Joji Watanuki, the report was subtitled *On the Governability of Democracies.* They concluded that governability suffered as a result of what Huntington, in his section, called "an excess of democracy." The solution was "a greater degree of moderation in democracy." As Huntington put it, "Marginal social groups, as in the case of the blacks, are now becoming full participants in the political system." Rather than fully embrace the weakening of white supremacy, Huntington worried that the increasing political participation of "marginal social groups" would risk "overloading the political system with demands." African Americans, Indian Americans, and all other minority groups had to be kept "marginal" if "democracy" was to function properly.[12]

It is important to avoid personalizing the distortion of democracy—to blame our woes on easy targets like Nixon and Indira Gandhi. The subversion of democracy in the name of freedom has a long history in both countries. Equally storied is the use of dangerous outsiders—thugs of one kind or another—to justify inequality and oppression. As the history of the Indian American community makes clear, much will depend on the borders of democracy, on who is allowed in and who is relegated to the realm of the thugs. Bhagat Singh Thind was denied citizenship not because he was not white (it was whiteness, after all, that was in question) but because his anti-imperial activism made him seem to be a thug, and because policing the borders of whiteness was a way to protect the status quo and those who benefited from it. Now that the Indian American community has risen to affluence and growing prominence, what will its relationship be with those who continue to be marginalized?

We must celebrate our democracies even while interrogating their failures and continuing to ask what democracy can and should mean. "Is democracy a sufficient instrument of emancipation?" The political scientist Rajni Kothari answered his question with a call to rethink democracy. "The emancipatory thrust of democracy calls for a change in its very definition and the diverse contents—social and cultural, local, national and global—through which it finds expression." We must not equate democracy and freedom—certainly not if by "democracy" we mean only regular elections. If I have at times used the words *freedom* and *democracy* interchangeably, it is because so many of the figures in this book saw both as radical terms that should be used together to fight injustice and oppression. They would be horrified to witness the trappings of democracy used to defend oppression. What Pratap Bhanu Mehta has called "the burden of democracy" and Aishwary Kumar has called "the risk of democracy," I prefer to call the tragedy of democracy: the way in which the idea of democracy has come to hide its promise. By positioning the neoliberal state as the defender of democracy and freedom, our leaders accomplish what Kumar calls the "sacrifice of equality in the very name of an ethical and political community." Juxtaposing the struggle for democracy in the United States and India can free us from the tragedy of democracy by allowing us to remember and thus to reclaim the struggles of the past.[13]

Such remembering must defy the borders of the nation, but without reifying the transnational at the expense of more meaningful forms of emancipation. The story of India and America is full of examples of transnational "connections" that served to reproduce and strengthen existing inequalities. The reason that American sailors, Transcendentalists, and missionaries all failed to denounce colonial rule was not just that their own country was undemocratic, but also that they all had something to get from India—whether money, knowledge, or souls. From the eighteenth century to the twenty-first, many of the links between India and America were less connections than conquests. As in the days of the India trade, we must be wary of profiteering masquerading as emancipation.

We must also be wary of the colonial motivations that lurk behind many efforts to spread democracy across the globe. Any account of democracy in the United States must grapple with the fact that American military and intelligence agencies have repeatedly intervened in the democratic affairs of other nations. One wonders what George Washington would have thought—or Lord Cornwallis for that matter—had they seen the United States assert its own form of empire on every continent on the planet. Like the British Raj, American imperial adventures have been routinely defended as selfless efforts to defend the welfare of others. During the Cold War, it was under the aegis of freedom and democracy that the United States supported dictators across the globe. Today, the United States continues to provide money and arms to governments that are openly autocratic or dominated by military or security agencies. From the vantage point of India, the most relevant example is, of course, Pakistan. It must trouble all those who believe in the promise of American democracy that American presidents have repeatedly gone to war in the name of democracy. The ongoing relationship between American democracy and American militarism should caution us against presenting the long history of Indo-American relations as the story of democracy spreading across the globe.

At the heart of this book is the relationship between two kinds of freedom: the freedom of the nation from foreign rule, and the freedom of the people from the nation and the state. African Americans, Dalits, and other minorities looked with profound skepticism on the supposed triumph of national independence. What good was swaraj if the poor remained poor and the chains of the past were left unbroken? Still, it would be a mistake to paint the story of democracy in the United States and India as nothing more than a clever subterfuge for exploitation. Indian independence and the American civil rights movement both altered the balance of power and led to an expansion of rights for millions of people. Yet it is equally obvious that neither country has achieved the kind of society Du Bois envisioned a century ago, a democracy that includes everyone, "a freedom that does not involve somebody's slavery."[14]

Does freedom always depend on somebody else's slavery? The historical and philosophical necessity of slavery for freedom poses a problem for Du Bois, a problem the sociologist Orlando Patterson framed succinctly. After chronicling the relationship between slavery and freedom across the world, Patterson asked, "Are we to esteem slavery for what it has wrought, or must we challenge our conception of freedom and the value we place upon it?" As Saidiya V. Hartman has argued, the "vexed genealogy of freedom" is bound up in "the complicity of slavery and freedom." In Hartman's words, "The entanglements of bondage and liberty shaped the liberal imagination of freedom, fueled the emergence and expansion of capitalism, and spawned proprietorial conceptions of the self."[15]

There is good reason to reject the rhetoric of freedom so popular in both India and the United States, especially when that rhetoric is used to defend the status quo. And there is also good reason to look beyond the promise of a democratic nation-state to align the interests of the oppressed with an explicitly transnational and perhaps even global conception of redemption. As Ambedkar declared, "The socio-religious disabilities have dehumanized the Untouchables and their interests at stake are therefore the interests of humanity." Many of the patriots who fought to redeem democracy in the United States and India simultaneously embraced a cosmopolitan vision of a just and free world. Consider the courage of Pauli Murray and Kamaladevi Chattopadhyay, the two women to whom this book is dedicated.[16]

In the spring of 1940, Murray created a diagram in her journal that outlined the differences between the Indian independence movement and the African American freedom struggle. Her diagram offered three reasons why Gandhian nonviolence would not work for African Americans. First, Indians were a majority in their country, while African Americans were a minority in the United States. Second, Gandhi led a "well-disciplined movement," something African Americans lacked. Finally, India boasted a relatively "unified labor movement," while American workers were divided between "dual Jim-Crow unions." With straight lines and clear contrasts, Murray separated two distinct struggles. Yet that very month Murray courted arrest on a bus in Virginia and launched her own satyagraha against Jim Crow. She recognized the difficulty of using Gandhian nonviolence against American racism, and then went ahead and did it anyway.[17]

One year later, Kamaladevi Chattopadhyay boarded a segregated train traveling across the American South. Unlike Pauli Murray, Kamaladevi sat in the "whites only" section of the train. Like Murray, she resisted when ordered to move. Kamaladevi began by demanding to know why she should move. The train conductor replied, "That is the rule and you better obey it or you will regret it." She did not move. The conductor stormed away. After a few minutes, he returned to interrogate her again. Kamaladevi might have declared that she was a renowned advocate of Indian independence and the rights of Indian women. She could have told the conductor about her recent visit to the White House as the guest of Franklin and Eleanor Roosevelt. Instead, when prompted to tell the man "from which land she came," Kamaladevi replied, "It makes no difference. I am a colored woman obviously and it is unnecessary for you to disturb me for I have no intention of moving from here." The conductor muttered, "You are an Asian," but he did not trouble her again.[18]

By calling herself "colored," Kamaladevi expressed solidarity with the millions of African Americans who suffered the brutalities of segregation. She linked the struggles of Indians, African Americans, and other "colored peoples" throughout the world. Words were equally important to Pauli Murray. Two years after she was arrested, Murray published an article on the Indian independence movement, in which she quoted Jawaharlal Nehru demanding "full and equal freedom for all the countries of Asia" and "the recognition of Indian independence." Murray told her readers to "change the word 'Asia' to 'Negro' and the word 'independence' to 'equality.'" She used words like *freedom, independence,* and *equality*—like *satyagraha*—to advance the solidarities she made evident on that bus in Virginia.[19]

Murray and Kamaladevi were both seen as dangerous radicals by authorities who defended racism, imperialism, sexism, and other forms of injustice under the banner of law and tradition. Anyone who opposed the prevailing order risked being labeled a thug, and dealt with accordingly. At a time of surging authoritarianism, it is good to be reminded that the struggle for democracy has long entailed breaking the law. But we must not be overly sanguine about the potential of nonviolent civil disobedience in all contexts. Rather, the key lessons Murray and Kamaladevi offer us are the necessity of relentless dissatisfaction with the status quo—and the power of reaching across borders to resist multiple injustices simultaneously.

The struggles of Murray, Kamaladevi, and other freedom-loving "thugs" were complicated by the fierce opposition of those in power, and by the challenge of building bridges across disparate struggles, cultures, and contexts. It is important to recognize the limitations of their efforts—and their failures. But it is also important to acknowledge that many risked their lives for an expansive freedom they knew would remain beyond their reach. They put faith in future generations—as well as in other people who were toiling halfway around the globe, people they would never meet, never know by name.

Amidst the carnage of the twentieth century, the rise of democracy remains a hopeful story. The decolonization that followed the Second World War created a wave of new democracies. Among some three dozen newly freed postcolonial nations—from Indonesia and the Philippines to Ghana and Nigeria—India was the most populous and also one of the most successful. Many postcolonial democracies faltered, wracked by the poverty and divisions left by colonial powers and consumed by the machinations of Cold War superpowers. But another wave of democratization began in the 1970s and continued through the 1990s. Democracy falteringly returned to dozens of countries from Portugal and Spain to Argentina and Chile to Taiwan and South Korea. With the fall of the Soviet Union, much of Eastern Europe turned toward democracy. The United States and India, proud rebels against the British Empire, seemed to embody a future in which all countries would be free of imperial rule.[20]

Now democracy is under attack on many fronts: the increasing power of China, the resurgence of authoritarian rule in Russia, the near total failure of the Arab Spring, and the rise of nativist xenophobia in the era of Brexit, Hindutva, and Donald Trump. For millennia, governments have built walls to repel unwanted people and ideas. They have failed, some more slowly than others. But the act of dividing the world into hostile camps, if ultimately futile, has exacted a bloody price. War after war has made clear the disastrous consequences of ethnocentric nationalism. Yet today the lessons of the past are being forgotten. As new walls rise to divide nation from nation, it remains to be seen what will happen to the kind of tolerant, inclusive democracy championed by many of the figures in this book—from Kamaladevi Chattopadhyay and Pauli Murray to Taraknath Das and W. E. B. Du Bois. The connections between India and the United States have pushed both countries closer to achieving their democratic principles. But nothing guarantees that such progress will last. Cornwallis is dead, but the revolution continues. "We have frequently printed the word Democracy," Walt Whitman wrote, "yet I cannot too often repeat that it is a word the real gift of which still sleeps, quite unawakened." What will it take to awaken democracy?[21]

# NOTES

## Book epigraph

Walt Whitman, *Poetry and Prose,* ed. Justin Kaplan (New York: Library of America, 1996), 984.

## Introduction

1. Ranajit Guha, *A Rule of Property for Bengal: An Essay on the Idea of Permanent Settlement,* 3rd ed. (Durham, NC: Duke University Press, 1996); Philip Lawson, *The East India Company: A History* (London and New York: Routledge, 1993), 129–143; Franklin and Mary Wickwire, *Cornwallis: The Imperial Years* (Chapel Hill: University of North Carolina Press, 1980).
2. Franklin and Mary Wickwire, *Cornwallis: The American Adventure* (Boston: Houghton Mifflin, 1970); R. Adams, "A View of Cornwallis's Surrender at Yorktown," *American Historical Review* 37, no. 1 (October 1931): 25–49.
3. We should not draw too sharp a line between the British Empire in America and in India. As David Armitage has noted, "Historians of the eighteenth-century British Empire have protested against any easy separation between the 'First' and 'Second' British Empires on the grounds that the two overlapped in time, that they shared common purposes and personnel, and that the differences between the maritime, commercial colonies of settlement in North America and the military, territorial colonies of conquest in India have been crudely overdrawn." As Chapter 1 makes clear, the British

conquest of India was in many ways an extension of the British presence in the Americas. David Armitage, *The Ideological Origins of the British Empire* (Cambridge, UK: Cambridge University Press, 2000), 2; Peter James Marshall, "The First and Second British Empires: A Question of Demarcation," *History* 49 (1964): 13–23; Peter James Marshall, *The Making and Unmaking of Empires: Britain, India, and America, c. 1750–1783* (Oxford, UK: Oxford University Press, 2005).

4. Irfan Habib, *Confronting Colonialism: Resistance and Modernisation under Haider Ali and Tipu Sultan* (London: Anthem Press, 2002); Kate Brittlebank, *Tipu Sultan's Search for Legitimacy: Islam and Kingship in a Hindu Domain* (Delhi: Oxford University Press, 1997).

5. Robert Parkinson has convincingly argued that the revolution contributed to racial oppression, as colonial leaders strove to use antiblack and anti-Indian sentiment to create a "common cause" among whites. See Robert G. Parkinson, *The Common Cause: Creating Race and Nation in the American Revolution* (Chapel Hill: University of North Carolina Press, 2016); Ira Berlin, *Many Thousands Gone: The First Two Centuries of Slavery in North America* (Cambridge, MA: Belknap Press, 2000), 256–262; Gary B. Nash, *Race and Revolution* (Lanham, MD: Rowman and Littlefield, 1990).

6. W. E. B. Du Bois, *Darkwater: Voices from within the Veil* (New York: Harcourt, Brace, and Howe, 1920), 207.

7. Many scholars have explored the relationship between diversity and democracy. See Earl Lewis and Nancy Cantor, eds., *Our Compelling Interests: The Value of Diversity for Democracy and a Prosperous Society* (Princeton, NJ: Princeton University Press, 2016); Aishwary Kumar, *Radical Equality: Ambedkar, Gandhi, and the Risk of Democracy* (Stanford, CA: Stanford University Press, 2015); K. Shankar Bajpai, ed., *Democracy and Diversity: India and the American Experience* (New Delhi: Oxford University Press, 2007); Charles Tilly, *Democracy* (Cambridge, UK: Cambridge University Press, 2007); Rajni Kothari, *Rethinking Democracy* (New Delhi: Orient Longman, 2005); Pratap Bhanu Mehta, *The Burden of Democracy* (New Delhi: Penguin India, 2003); Judith Green, *Deep Democracy: Community, Diversity, and Transformation* (Lanham, MD: Rowman and Littlefield, 1999). Also see Partha Chatterjee, *The Nation and Its Fragments: Colonial and Postcolonial Histories* (Princeton, NJ: Princeton University Press, 1993).

8. Paul Kramer, "Power and Connection: Imperial Histories of the United States in the World," *The American Historical Review* 116, no. 5 (December 2011): 1348–1391; "On Transnational History," *American Historical Review* 111, no. 5 (December 2006): 1440–1464; Thomas Bender, ed., *Rethinking American History in a Global Age* (Berkeley: University of California Press, 2002).

9. As H. L. Mencken noted in 1947, "The right of Americans to be so called is frequently challenged, especially in Latin-America." While I use *America* and *the United States* interchangeably, as is common in India and elsewhere, the imperial arrogance that has long led Americans to ignore other parts of the

Americas is an important theme in this text. See H. L. Mencken, "Names for Americans," *American Speech* XXII, no. 4 (December 1947): 241.

10. On the history of the word *swaraj,* see Ananya Vajpeyi, *Righteous Republic: The Political Foundations of Modern India* (Cambridge, MA: Harvard University Press, 2012); Aakash Singh Rathore, *Indian Political Theory: Laying the Groundwork for* Svaraj (New York: Routledge, 2017); Mohandas Karamchand Gandhi, *Hind Swaraj* (Madras: S. E. S. Ganesan, 1921). On keywords, see Raymond Williams, *Keywords: A Vocabulary of Culture and Society* (New York: Oxford University Press, 1976), and Daniel Rodgers, *Contested Truths: Keywords in American Politics since Independence* (New York: Basic Books, 1987). Also see Eric Foner, *The Story of American Freedom* (New York: Norton, 1998), and James Kloppenberg, *Toward Democracy: The Struggle for Self-Rule in European and American Thought* (New York: Oxford University Press, 2016).

11. Angus Burgin, *The Great Persuasion: Reinventing Free Markets since the Depression* (Cambridge, MA: Harvard University Press, 2012).

12. "Inscription on Lord Cornwallis' Monument at Ghazepore, Bengal," *Selections from the Asiatic Journal and Monthly Register for British India* (Madras: Higginbotham, 1875), 625.

## Keyword: *Indian*

Epigraph: Timothy Pickering, "Addressing the Grand Council of the Six Nations of the Iroquois Confederacy," reel 60, page 86, Timothy Pickering Papers, Massachusetts Historical Society, Boston, Massachusetts. I am grateful to Francis G. Hutchins for first drawing my attention to this remarkable speech. See Francis G. Hutchins, *Tribes and Citizenship in the United States* (West Franklin, NH: Amarta Press, 2010), 49.

1. Pickering, "Addressing the Grand Council of the Six Nations of the Iroquois Confederacy," 86; Edward H. Phillips, "Timothy Pickering at His Best: Indian Commissioner, 1790–1794," *Essex Institute Historical Collections* 102 (July 1966): 163–202.

2. Romila Thapar, *A History of India: Volume 1* (New York: Penguin, 1990); Diana Eck, *India: A Sacred Geography* (New York: Three Rivers Press, 2012), 61–70; Simon Keynes and Michael Lapidge, trans., *Alfred the Great: Asser's Life of King Alfred and Other Contemporary Sources* (New York: Penguin Classics: 1984), 219–220 and 266; "Epistola Christofori Colom . . . de insulis Indie supra Gangem," April 1493, www.gilderlehrman.org/history-by-era/exploration/resources/columbus-reports-his-first-voyage-1493.

3. "The Term Hindoo," *New York Daily Times,* May 29, 1855; Tyler G. Anbinder, *Nativism and Slavery: The Northern Know Nothings and the Politics of the 1850s* (Oxford, UK: Oxford University Press, 1994), 81–82; Michael F. Holt, *The Rise and Fall of the American Whig Party: Jacksonian Politics and the Onset of the Civil War* (Oxford, UK: Oxford University Press, 2003), note 107, p. 1162.

4. George Drach and Calvin F. Kuder, *The Telugu Mission: Of the General Council of the Evangelical Lutheran Church in North America: Containing a Biography of the Rev. Christian Frederick Heyer, M.D.* (Philadelphia: General Council Publishing House, 1914), 16–17, 41–47, 81; J. William Allen Lambert, *Life of Rev. J. F. C. Heyer, M.D.* (Philadelphia: Prepared for the Father Heyer Missionary Society of the Lutheran Theological Seminary at Mount Airy, 1903).

5. *People v. Hall*, 4 Cal. 399 (1854).

6. H. Richards, "Sati in Philadelphia: The Widow(s) of Malabar," *American Literature* 80, no. 4 (2008): 647–675; Marie A. Dakessian, "Envisioning the Indian Sati: Mariana Starke's 'The Widow of Malabar' and Antoine Le Mierre's 'La Veuve du Malabar,'" *Comparative Literature Studies* 36, no. 2 (1999): 110–130; Lata Mani, *Contentious Traditions: The Debate on Sati in Colonial India* (Berkeley: University of California Press, 1998); Wendy Doniger, *The Hindus: An Alternative History* (New York: Penguin Press, 2009), 610–635.

7. Uma Chakravarty, "The Myth of 'Patriots' and 'Traitors': Pandita Ramabai, Brahmanical Patriarchy and Militant Hindu Nationalism," in *Embodied Violence: Communalising Women's Sexuality in South Asia,* eds. Kumari Jayawardena and Malathi di Alwis (London: Zed, 1996), 196–239; Pandita Ramabai, *American Encounter: The Peoples of the United States* (1889), trans. and ed. Meera Kosambi (Bloomington: Indiana University Press, 2003).

8. Clementina Butler, *Pandita Ramabai Sarasvati: Pioneer in the Movement for the Education of the Child-Widow of India* (New York: Fleming H. Revell, 1922), 19, 25, and 44–45; Pandita Ramabai, *The High-Caste Hindu Woman* (Philadelphia: J. B. Rodgers, 1888), 118–119.

9. Ramabai to Manoramabai, letter no. 116, January 8, 1888, in Pandita Ramabai, *The Letters and Correspondence of Pandita Ramabai,* comp. Sister Geraldine, ed. A. B. Shah (Bombay: Maharashtra State Board for Literature and Culture, 1977), https://msblc.maharashtra.gov.in/pdf/newpdf/next20/The%20Letters%20and%20Correspondence%20of%20Pandita%20Ramabai.pdf; Anupama Arora, "The International Colour Line Has Been Challenged," in *Historic Engagements with Occidental Cultures, Religions, Powers,* eds. Anne R. Richards and Iraj Omidvar (New York: Palgrave Macmillan, 2014), 145–165.

10. Ramabai, *American Encounter,* 64, 115.

11. Ibid., 72, 115–116.

12. Ibid., 72, 227.

13. Sunrit Mullick, *The First Hindu Mission to America: The Pioneering Visits of Protap Chunder Mozoomdar* (New Delhi: Northern Book Centre, 2010), 64–65, 69.

14. Ramabai, *American Encounter,* 70.

15. Paulin Ismard, *Democracy's Slaves: A Political History of Ancient Greece,* trans. Jane Marie Todd (Cambridge, MA: Harvard University Press, 2017).

16. Lisa Lowe, *The Intimacies of Four Continents* (Durham, NC: Duke University Press, 2015), 3; Steve Inskeep, *Jacksonland: President Andrew Jackson, Cherokee Chief John Ross, and a Great American Land Grab* (New York: Penguin, 2016).

17. "From Slave to College President," *Indian Opinion*, September 10, 1903, *Collected Works of Mahatma Gandhi* (CWMG) Electronic Book (New Delhi: Government of India, 1999); Romain Rolland, "Booker T. Washington and His Work," *East and West* 2, part 2 (September 10, 1903): 893–903. There are significant problems with the electronic version of the CWMG, but it remains the easiest to access for most readers.

18. "Interview to N. G. Ranga," October 29, 1944, CWMG.

19. Lala Lajpat Rai, *The United States of America: A Hindu's Impressions and a Study* (Calcutta: Brahmo Mission Press, 1916), 1–3; Nancy Shoemaker, "How Indians Got to Be Red," *American Historical Review* 102 (June 1997): 624–644; Alden T. Vaughan, "From White Man to Redskin: Changing Anglo-American Perceptions of the American Indian," *American Historical Review* 87, no. 4 (October 1982): 917–953.

20. *United States v. Balsara* 180 Fed. 694 (C.C.A. 1910).

21. "Ourselves," *Young India* 1, no. 1 (1918): 4. Also see Kenneth Jones, *Arya Dharm: Hindu Consciousness in 19th-Century Punjab* (Berkeley: University of California Press, 1976); Lala Lajpat Rai, *The Arya Samaj: An Account of Its Origin, Doctrines, and Activities, with a Biographical Sketch of the Founder* (London: Longmans, Green, 1915); Rai, *The United States of America*, 1–3.

22. Nayan Shah, *Stranger Intimacy: Contesting Race, Sexuality, and the Law in the North American West* (Berkeley and Los Angeles: University of California Press, 2011), 75–78.

23. Letter, *Bombay Chronicle*, August 28, 1921, quoted in Earl Robert Schmidt, "American Relations with South Asia 1900–1940" (PhD diss., University of Pennsylvania, 1955), 326.

24. Excerpts from Naidu's letter were reprinted by Gandhi in his newspaper. See Mahatma Gandhi, "From and About Sarojini Devi," *Young India*, May 30, 1929, CWMG.

25. Ibid.

26. Cedric Dover, "Intergroup Relations and the Coloured World," *Asia: Asian Quarterly of Culture and Synthesis* (September 6, 1952), 193.

27. Kamaladevi Chattopadhyay, *Inner Recesses, Outer Spaces: Memoirs* (New Delhi: Navrang, 1986); Kamaladevi Chattopadhyay, *America: The Land of Superlatives* (Bombay: Phoenix Publications, 1946), iv, 270–271, 281, 284, 294.

28. Joseph M Marshall III, *The Day the World Ended at Little Bighorn: A Lakota History* (New York: Penguin, 2007), xiii–xiv.

29. Campbell Gibson and Kay Jung, "Historical Census Statistics on Population Totals by Race, 1790 to 1990, and by Hispanic Origin, 1970 to 1990, for Large Cities and Other Urban Places in the United States," footnote 6, United States Census, www.census.gov/population/www/documentation/twps0076/twps 0076.html; Julie L. Davis, *Survival Schools: The American Indian Movement and Community Education in the Twin Cities* (Minneapolis: University of Minnesota Press, 2013); Dennis Banks with Richard Erdoes, *Ojibwa Warrior: Dennis Banks and the Rise of the American Indian Movement* (Norman: University

of Oklahoma Press, 2005); Paul Chaat Smith and Robert Allen Warrior, *Like a Hurricane: The Indian Movement from Alcatraz to Wounded Knee* (New York: The New Press, 1997).

30. Richard H. Davis, *South Asia at Chicago: A History,* foreword by Milton Singer, COSAS New Series, no.1 (April 1985), https://southasia.uchicago.edu/sites /southasia.uchicago.edu/files/A%20History%20by%20Richard%20Davis .pdf; Nicholas Dirks, "South Asian Studies: Futures Past," *Autobiography of an Archive: A Scholar's Passage to India* (New York: Columbia University Press, 2015), 265–292.

31. Alpa Shah, *In the Shadows of the State: Indigenous Politics, Environmentalism, and Insurgency in Jharkhand, India* (Durham, NC: Duke University Press, 2010); Indra Munshi, ed., *The Adivasi Question: Issues of Land, Forest, and Livelihood* (New Delhi: Orient BlackSwan, 2015); Megan Moodie, *We Were Adivasis: Aspiration in an Indian Scheduled Tribe* (Chicago: University of Chicago Press, 2015).

32. Vine Deloria Jr., *Custer Died for Your Sins: An Indian Manifesto* (New York: Macmillan, 1969), 5–6.

33. See Jace Weaver, "Indigenousness and Indigeneity," in *A Companion to Postcolonial Studies,* eds. Henry Schwarz and Sangeeta Ray (Malden, MA: Blackwell Publishing, 2000), 224; Jodi A. Byrd, *The Transit of Empire: Indigenous Critiques of Colonialism* (Minneapolis: University of Minnesota Press, 2011), 74.

34. Byrd, *The Transit of Empire,* xx; Pekka Kalevi Hämäläinen, *The Comanche Empire* (New Haven, CT: Yale University Press, 2009), 1–2; Aileen Moreton-Robinson, *The White Possessive: Property, Power, and Indigenous Sovereignty* (Minneapolis: University of Minnesota Press, 2015); Glen Sean Coulthard, *Red Skin, White Masks: Rejecting the Colonial Politics of Recognition* (Minneapolis: University of Minnesota Press, 2014); Paul Chaat Smith, *Everything You Know about Indians Is Wrong* (Minneapolis: University of Minnesota Press, 2009), 10.

35. Pickering, "Addressing the Grand Council of the Six Nations of the Iroquois Confederacy," 86.

36. Gerald H. Clarfield, *Timothy Pickering and the American Republic* (Pittsburgh: The University of Pittsburgh Press, 1980), 128; G. Peter Jemison and Anna M. Schein, eds., *Treaty of Canandaigua 1794: 200 Years of Treaty Relations between the Iroquois Confederacy and the United States* (Santa Fe, NM: Clear Light Publishers, 2000); Doniger, *The Hindus,* 637–638.

## Chapter 1: Elephants and Ice

Epigraph: Henry David Thoreau, *Walden: Or Life in the Woods* (New York: T. Y. Crowell, 1899), 313.

1. Logbook for the ship *America,* Wednesday, 17 February 1796, log 3003 (O.S.), p. 36, at Helena Roads, Phillips Library, Peabody Essex Museum; George G. Goodwin, "The Crowninshield Elephant: The Surprising Story of Old Bet,

the First Elephant Ever to Be Brought to America," *Natural History* (October 1951), www.naturalhistorymag.com/editors_pick/1928_05-06_pick .html.

2. Goodwin, "The Crowninshield Elephant."

3. Jacob Crowninshield letters, November 1794 and January 1796, folder 1, box 4, series IV, John Crowninshield Papers, Crowninshield Family Papers, Peabody Essex Museum, Salem, MA; Hiram Waring to Huggnagel, April 21, 1834, in Correspondence, 1835, William C. Coles Jr. Collection, Historical Society of Pennsylvania, Philadelphia; James R. Fichter, *So Great a Profit: How the East Indies Trade Transformed Anglo-American Capitalism* (Cambridge, MA: Harvard University Press, 2010), 103–105.

4. Joyce Chaplin, "Race," in *The British Atlantic World, 1500–1800,* eds. David Armitage and M. J. Braddick (New York: Palgrave, 2002), 154–174; Edmund Morgan, *American Slavery, American Freedom: The Ordeal of Colonial Virginia* (New York: Norton, 1975).

5. On the Civil War in American memory, see David W. Blight, *Race and Reunion: The Civil War in American Memory* (Cambridge, MA: Belknap Press of Harvard University Press, 2001). Also see Rajmohan Gandhi, *A Tale of Two Revolts* (New York: Viking, 2009).

6. Dadabhai Naoroji, *Poverty and Un-British Rule in India* (London: Sonnenschein, 1901); Sven Beckert, *Empire of Cotton: A Global History* (New York: Knopf, 2014).

7. Laurence Bergreen, *Columbus: The Four Voyages, 1492–1504* (New York: Penguin, 2012); S. C. Welch, *India: Art and Culture, 1300–1900* (New York: Metropolitan Museum of Art, 1985); P. C. Keller, "Emeralds of Colombia," *Gems and Gemology* 17, no. 2 (1981): 80–92.

8. Alfred W. Crosby, Jr., *The Columbian Exchange: Biological and Cultural Consequences of 1492* (Westport, CT, Greenwood Press, 1972); Charles C. Mann, *1493: Uncovering the New World Columbus Created* (New York: Alfred A. Knopf, 2011).

9. Jonathan Eacott, *Selling Empire: India in the Making of Britain and America, 1600–1830* (Chapel Hill: University of North Carolina Press, 2016), 14; Marcus Rediker, *Between the Devil and the Deep Blue Sea: Merchant Seamen, Pirates and the Anglo-American Maritime World, 1700–1750* (Cambridge, UK: Cambridge University Press, 1989); Aaron Jaffer, *Lascars and Indian Ocean Seafaring, 1760– 1860* (Woodbridge, UK: Boydell, 2015).

10. Hiram Bingham, *Elihu Yale, The American Nabob of Queen Square* (New York: Dodd, Mead, 1939); Diana Scarisbrick and Benjamin Zucker, *Elihu Yale: Merchant, Collector and Patron* (London: Thames and Hudson, 2014); www.yale .edu/about/history.html.

11. Eacott, *Selling Empire,* 87; H. V. Bowen, "Perceptions from the Periphery: Colonial American Views of Britain's Asiatic Empire, 1756–1783," in *Negotiated Empires: Centers and Peripheries in the Americas, 1500–1820,* eds. Christine Daniels and Michael V. Kennedy (New York: Routledge, 2002), 284–295; Fichter, *So Great a Profit,* 18–25.

12. Thomas Paine, "The Crisis," a letter to William Howe, March 21, 1778, available at www.ushistory.org/paine/crisis/c-05.htm; Eacott, *Selling Empire*, 168–226; Amartya Sen, *Poverty and Famines: An Essay on Entitlement and Deprivation* (Oxford, UK: Oxford University Press, 1981), 39.

13. *United States* (Ship) logbook and journal, Historical Society of Pennsylvania, Philadelphia; Holden Furber, "The Beginnings of American Trade with India, 1784–1812," *New England Quarterly* 11, no. 2 (June 1938): 235–265.

14. Holden Furber, "The Beginnings of American Trade with India, 1784–1812."

15. Ibid.

16. Freeman Hunt, *Lives of American Merchants* (New York: Office of Hunt's Merchants Magazine, 1856), I, xv; G. Bhagat, *Americans in India, 1784–1860* (New York: New York University Press, 1970), ix and xxii; Samuel Eliot Morison, "The India Ventures of Fisher Ames, 1794–1804," *American Antiquarian Society* (April 1927): 14–23; Raj Kumar Gupta, *The Great Encounter: A Study of Indo-American Literature and Cultural Relations* (New Delhi: Abhinav, 1986), 6; Eacott, *Selling Empire*, 362.

17. Ram Krishna Tandon, "European Adventurers and Changes in the Indian Military System," in *Responding to the West: Essays on Colonial Domination and Agency*, ed. Hans Hägerdal (Amsterdam: Amsterdam University Press, 2009), 40.

18. *United States* (Ship) logbook and journal, Historical Society of Pennsylvania, Philadelphia; Journal of the ship *Belisarius*, 1799–1800, Peabody Essex Museum, Salem, MA; Linda Colley, *Britons: Forging the Nation, 1707–1837* (New Haven, CT: Yale University Press, 2009); Carl Nightingale, "Before Race Mattered: Historical Geographies of the Color Line in Early Colonial Madras and New York," *American Historical Review* 113, no. 1 (2008): 48–71.

19. Journal of a voyage of the ship *Tartar* to India, 1817–1818, Peabody Essex Museum, Salem, MA; William Duane Notebooks, vol. 2, collection 3114, Historical Society of Pennsylvania, Philadelphia; *Biographical Memoir of William J. Duane* (Philadelphia: Claxton, Remsen, and Haffelfinger, 1868); Nigel Ken Little, "Transoceanic Radical: The Many Identities of William Duane" (PhD diss., Murdoch University, 2003).

20. On the complexities of Jefferson's own claim to be the champion of liberty, see Annette Gordon-Reed, *The Hemingses of Monticello: An American Family* (New York: Norton, 2009). Also see David Brion Davis, *Inhuman Bondage: The Rise and Fall of Slavery in the New World* (Oxford, UK: Oxford University Press, 2008).

21. John Gibaut to E. H. Derby, September 20, 1791, Derby Family Manuscripts, XIV, Peabody Essex Museum, Salem, MA.

22. Benjamin Joy to Thomas Jefferson, 20 January 1793; Thomas Jefferson to Benjamin Joy, 12 March 1793; available at http://founders.archives.gov/search/Correspondent%3A%22Joy%2C%20Benjamin%22%20 Correspondent %3A%22Jefferson%2C%20Thomas%22.

23. Tandon, "European Adventurers and Changes in the Indian Military System," 40.

24. John Crowninshield to his father, June 1, 1796, Crowninshield Family Papers; Benjamin W. Crowninshield to his wife, Mary, November 28, 1816, box 5, Crowninshield Family Papers; Log of ship *America,* Peabody Essex Museum, Salem, MA; Bhagat, *Americans in India,* 59 and 72.

25. Benjamin W. Crowninshield to his wife, Mary, November 28, 1816, box 5, Crowninshield Family Papers; Bhagat, *Americans in India,* 116.

26. Bhagat, *Americans in India,* 56, 63, and 71.

27. Paul Boyer and Stephen Nissenbaum, *Salem Possessed: The Social Origins of Witchcraft* (Cambridge, MA: Harvard University Press, 1974).

28. Eacott, *Selling Empire,* 110–111.

29. Edward Gray, *William Gray of Salem, Merchant: A Biographical Sketch* (Boston: Houghton Mifflin, 1914), 13–14; Ralph Waldo Emerson, "Indian Superstition," edited with a dissertation on Emerson's Orientalism at Harvard by Kenneth Walter Cameron (Hanover, NH: Friends of the Dartmouth Library, 1954), 64; Eacott, *Selling Empire,* 66–67.

30. Goodwin, "The Crowninshield Elephant"; "Setting the Record Straight on Old Bet," *American Heritage* 25, no. 3 (April 1974).

31. Amasa Delano, *A Narrative of Voyages and Travels in the Northern and Southern Hemispheres* (Boston: E. G. House, 1817), 213–216, 245.

32. William Bentley, "The Diary of William Bentley, DD, Pastor of the East Church, Salem, Massachusetts," vol. 1, April 1784–December 1792 (Salem, MA: The Essex Institute, 1905), 228.

33. Francis Hutchins, *Mashpee, The Story of Cape Cod's Indian Town* (West Franklin, NH: Amarta Press, 1979), 80.

34. Joan Jensen, *Passage from India: Asian Indian Immigrants in North America* (New Haven, CT: Yale University Press, 1988), 12–13. Also see James Duncan Phillips, *Salem and the Indies: The Story of the Great Commercial Era of the City* (Boston: Houghton Mifflin, 1947), 364; Walter Muir Whitehill, *The East India Marine Society and Peabody Museum of Salem* (Salem, MA: Peabody Museum, 1949), 34–39.

35. Richard O. Cummings, *The American Ice Harvests: A Historical Study in Technology, 1800–1918* (Berkeley and Los Angeles: California University Press, 1949); David G. Dickason, "The Nineteenth-Century Indo-American Ice Trade: An Hyperborean Epic," *Modern Asian Studies* 25, no. 1 (1991): 55–89; Gavin Weightman, *The Frozen Water Trade: How Ice from New England Lakes Kept the World Cool* (London: Harper Collins, 2003), 200; P. C. F. Smith, "Crystal Blocks of Yankee Coldness," *Essex Institute Historical Collections* (July 1961): 232.

36. Henry David Thoreau, *Walden,* 312–313.

37. Emerson to Thomas Carlyle, 1844, in *The Correspondence of Emerson and Carlyle,* ed. Joseph Slater (New York: Columbia University Press, 1964), 359;

Emerson, "Poetry and Imagination," http://transcendentalism-legacy.tamu
.edu/authors/emerson/essays/poetryimag.html.

38. Emerson, "Brahma," http://www.poetryfoundation.org/poem/175138.

39. Emerson, *The Complete Works of Ralph Waldo Emerson, IX, Poems* (Boston:
Houghton Mifflin and Company, 1904), 467.

40. "A More Excellent Way," *The Quarterly Christian Spectator* 6, no. 9 (September 1824): 472; Adrienne Moore, *Rammohun Roy and America* (Calcutta:
Satis Chandra Chakravarti, 1942); Spencer Lavan, *Unitarians and India: A
Study in Encounter and Response* (Boston: Beacon Press, 1977); J. P. Rao Rayapati, *Early American Interest in Vedanta: Pre-Emersonian Interest in Vedic Literature and Vedantic Philosophy* (New York: Asia Publishing House, 1973); Alan D.
Hodder, "Emerson, Rammohan Roy, and the Unitarians," in *Studies in the
American Renaissance,* ed. Joel Myerson (Charlottesville: University Press of
Virginia, 1988).

41. John Adams to Thomas Jefferson, May 26, 1817, https://www.loc.gov/item
/mtjbib022867/; Wilhelm Halbfass, *India and Europe: An Essay in Understanding*
(Albany: State University of New York Press, 1988); Edward Said, *Orientalism*
(New York: Vintage, 1978).

42. Benjamin Silliman, *Letters of Shahcoolen: A Hindu Philosopher Residing in Philadelphia to His Friend El Hassan an Inhabitant of Delhi* (Boston: Russell and
Cutler, 1802), 13, 22–28, 90, 101.

43. "Brownson's Writings," a review of *Charles Elwood; or the Infidel Converted.
By O. A. Brownson* in *The Dial* 1, no. 1: 26; James Elliot Cabot, "The Philosophy of the Ancient Hindoos," *Massachusetts Quarterly Review* I (September 1848); "Veeshnoo Sarma," *The Dial* 3 (July 1842): 82–85; Umesh
Patri, *Hindu Scriptures and American Transcendentalists* (Delhi: Intellectual Book
Corner, 1998); Arthur Versluis, *American Transcendentalism and Asian Religions*
(New York: Oxford University Press, 1993); Carl T. Jackson, *The Oriental Religions and American Thought: Nineteenth-Century Explorations* (Santa Barbara,
CA: Greenwood Publishing Group, 1982); Dale Riepe, *The Philosophy of India
and Its Impact on American Thought* (Springfield, IL: Thomas Press, 1970); Arthur Christy, *The Orient in American Transcendentalism: A Study of Emerson, Thoreau, and Alcott* (New York: Columbia University Press, 1932).

44. Emerson, "Indian Superstition," 64; Margaret Fuller, *The Great Lawsuit* (Raleigh, NC: Hayes Barton Press, 2007), 19–20; Thoreau, *Walden,* 13; "Manners
and Customs of India," *North American Review* 9 (June 1819): 36–58.

45. Henry David Thoreau, *A Week on the Concord and Merrimack Rivers* (Boston
and Cambridge: James Munroe and Company, 1849), 146; Emerson, *Journals VII,* 291, available at http://www.perfectidius.com/Volume_7_1845–
1848.pdf; Emerson, "Race," in *The Prose Works of Ralph Waldo Emerson,* vol.
2 (Boston: Fields, Osgood, 1870), 181.

46. Emerson, "Plato; Or, the Philosopher," in *Representative Men,* reprinted in *The
Works of Ralph Waldo Emerson: Comprising His Essays, Lectures, Poems, and Orations,* vol. 1 (London: George Bell and Sons, 1883), 293; Emerson, "Hama-

treya," in *The Works of Ralph Waldo Emerson*, 414–415; Emerson, *The Journals and Miscellaneous Notebooks of Ralph Waldo Emerson, Volume IX*, eds. Ralph H. Orth and Alfred R. Ferguson (Cambridge, MA: Belknap Press of Harvard University Press, 1971), 321; Thoreau, *Walden*, 92 and 283; Thoreau, *A Week on the Concord and Merrimack Rivers*, 146; Gupta, *The Great Encounter*, 41.

47. "Thoreau's Journal II," *Atlantic Monthly* 95, no. 2 (February 1905): 232; Thoreau, *A Week on the Concord and Merrimack Rivers*, 116; Arthur Christy, *The Orient in American Transcendentalism* (New York: Columbia University Press, 1965), 242.

48. Gupta, *The Great Encounter*, 41; Arthur Versluis, *American Transcendentalism and Asian Religions*, 51–118; Walter Harding, *The Days of Henry Thoreau: A Biography* (New York: Dover, 2011), 130; Frederic Ives Carpenter, *Emerson and Asia* (New York: Haskell House Publishers, 1968).

49. Henry Wadsworth Longfellow, "King Trisanku," in *The Poetical Works of Longfellow* (London: Griffith and Farran, 1890), 581; Wendy Doniger, *The Hindus: An Alternative History* (New York: Penguin Press, 2009), 250–251.

50. Protap Chunder Mozoomdar, "Emerson as Seen from India," in *The Genius and Character of Emerson: Lectures at the Concord School of Philosophy*, ed. Franklin Benjamin Sanborn (Boston: James R. Osgood, 1885), 365–371; Bipin Chandra Pal, *Memories of My Life and Times*, vol. II (Calcutta: Yugayatri Prakashak, 1951), 132; Mahatma Gandhi, "Letter to Manilal Gandhi," March 25, 1909, *Collected Works of Mahatma Gandhi* (CWMG) Electronic Book (New Delhi: Government of India, 1999); Gandhi, "My Inconsistencies," *Young India*, February 13, 1930, CWMG; Gandhi, "Peace amidst Strife," *Young India*, March 29, 1928, CWMG; Gandhi, "Speech on Birth Centenary of Tolstoy," *Navajivan*, September 16, 1928, CWMG; Gandhi, "God Is," *Young India*, November 15, 1928, CWMG.

51. Gandhi, "Duty of Disobeying Laws [1]," and "Duty of Disobeying Laws [2]," *Indian Opinion*, September 7 and 14, 1907, translated from Gujarati, CWMG; Gandhi, "Address to Ashram Inmates," March 18, 1918, CWMG.

52. Geoffrey C. Ward, *A Disposition to Be Rich: How a Small-Town Pastor's Son Ruined an American President, Brought on a Wall Street Crash, and Made Himself the Best-Hated Man in the United States* (New York: Knopf, 2012), 10–11; Clifton J. Phillips, *Protestant America and the Pagan World: The First Half Century of the American Boards of Commissioners for Foreign Missions, 1810–1860* (Cambridge, MA: Harvard University Press, 1969), 52.

53. Nathaniel Ames, *A Mariner's Sketches* (Providence, RI: Cory, Marshall, and Hammond, 1830), 40 and 56; Bhagat, *Americans in India*, 116; Ward, *A Disposition to Be Rich*, 10.

54. Letter from Rev. John Higginson to his son Nathaniel Higginson, August 31, 1698, Electronic Text Center, University of Virginia Library, http://salem.lib .virginia.edu/letters/higginson_letter.html.

55. "Instructions, Given by the Prudential Committee of the American Board of Commissioners for Foreign Missions, to the Missionaries to the East, Feb. 7,

1812," *Report of the American Board of Commissioners for Foreign Missions* (Boston: Samuel T. Armstrong, 1812), 12; *First Ten Annual Reports of the American Board of Commissioners for Foreign Missions* (Boston: Crocker and Brewster, 1834), 92–104; Anima Bose, *Higher Education in India in the 19th Century: The American Involvement, 1883–1893* (Calcutta: Punthi Pustak, 1978), 87–91.

56. Earl Robert Schmidt, "American Relations with South Asia 1900–1940" (PhD diss., University of Pennsylvania, 1955), 25; Richard H. Davis, *South Asia at Chicago: A History,* foreword by Milton Singer, COSAS New Series, no.1 (April 1985): 7, available at https://southasia.uchicago.edu/sites/southasia .uchicago.edu/files/A%20History%20by%20Richard%20Davis.pdf

57. "Instructions, Given by the Prudential Committee of the American Board of Commissioners for Foreign Missions, to the Missionaries to the East, Feb. 7, 1812," 12; Samuel A. Nott Jr., *A Sermon on the Idolatry of the Hindoos* (Norwich, CT: Hubbard and Marvin, 1817), 21–22; J. R. Campbell, *Missions in Hindustan with a Brief Description of the Country and the Moral and Social Condition of the Inhabitants* (New York: Board of Missions of the Reformed Presbyterian Church, 1852), 108; Ward, *A Disposition to Be Rich,* 35 and 43.

58. Gerald H. Anderson, *Biographical Dictionary of Christian Missions* (Grand Rapids, MI: Wm. B. Eerdman, 1991), 727; *Proceedings of the Baptist Convention for Missionary Purposes* (Philadelphia, 1814), 65, 112; *The Reformer* 4 (April 2, 1823): 73–79. Also see Eliza F. Kent, *Converting Women: Gender and Protestant Christianity in Colonial South India* (Oxford, UK: Oxford University Press, 2004); Elizabeth Elbourne, "Gender, Colonialism, and Faith," *Journal of Women's History* 25, no. 1 (Spring 2013): 182–194.

59. Private Journal of Horace B. Putnam, Horace B. Putnam Papers, Peabody Essex Museum, Salem, MA; "The Late George Bowen," *Christian Advocate,* July 22, 1888, 220; obituary of George Bowen, *The Dinbandhu,* February 12, 1888, and other obituaries in *The Voice of India* (March, 1888), 183–184.

60. William Allen Lambert, *Life of Rev. J. F. C. Heyer, M.D.* (Prepared for the Father Heyer Missionary Society of the Lutheran Theological Seminary at Mount Airy, Philadelphia, 1903); George Drach and Calvin F. Kuder, "The Telugu Mission: Of the General Council of the Evangelical Lutheran Church in North America: Containing a Biography of the Rev. Christian Frederick Heyer, M.D." (Philadelphia: General Council Publishing House, 1914), 41–47, 81.

61. "Religion: A Family Tradition," *Time* (February 16, 1953); Jennifer Georgia, *Legacy and Challenge: The Story of Dr. Ida B. Scudder* (Saline, MI: McNaughton and Gunn, 1994).

62. John Jackson, *Mary Reed: Missionary to the Lepers* (London: Marshall Brothers, 1899), 37–38.

63. John Demos, *The Heathen School: A Story of Hope and Betrayal in the Age of the Early Republic* (New York: Knopf, 2014); *First Ten Annual Reports of the American Board of Commissioners for Foreign Missions* (Boston: Crocker and Brewster, 1834), 200–201; Schmidt, "American Relations with South Asia," 371.

64. Amanda Smith, *An Autobiography: The Story of the Lord's Dealings with Mrs. Amanda Smith, The Colored Evangelist* (Chicago: Christian Witness, 1893), iv–viii, 300, 311, 318–319.

65. "Asians and Pacific Islanders in the Civil War," March 2015, website of the National Park Service, www.nps.gov/civilwar/upload/More-Info-on-Asians-Pacific-Islanders-in-the-Civil-War-Alphabetically-by-Name.pdf; Gomez letters to Beecher, Ephemera of Henry Ward Beecher, collection 128, Billy Graham Center Archives, Wheaton, Illinois.

66. *Francis C. Assisi and Elizabeth Pothen,* "Historic Saga of South Asians in US Civil War," originally posted on indolink.com here: www.indolink.com/displayArticleS.php?id=092005073252, and referenced in a blog post titled "Glory," published by the user named "Abhi," and posted on September 14, 2005, here: http://sepiamutiny.com/blog/2005/09/14/glory_1/.

67. Beckert, *Empire of Cotton,* 251–253, 292–93; Schmidt, "American Relations with South Asia," 15.

68. "An American View of the Indian Mutiny," *Weekly Journal,* October 7, reprinted in *Hobart Won Daily Mercury,* January 11, 1858; *New York Times,* November 27, 1857; "The Indian Mutiny," *New York Times,* August 25, 1857, 4.

69. Arthur Christy, "Orientalism in New England: Whittier," *American Literature* 1, no. 4 (January 1930): 372–392; "An American View of the Indian Mutiny"; *New York Times,* November 27, 1857; "The Indian Mutiny."

70. Marx's views on British imperialism in India were complex. He decried the barbarity of British rule. But he also argued that "England has to fulfill a double mission in India: one destructive, the other regenerating—the annihilation of the old Asiatic society and the laying of the material foundations of western society in Asia." Karl Marx, "The Indian Revolt," *New York Daily Tribune,* September 16, 1857; Marx, "The Revolt in India," *New York Daily Tribune,* October 23, 1857; Doniger, *The Hindus,* 197. Also see Ashutosh Kumar, "Marx and Engels on India," *Indian Journal of Political Science* 53, no. 4 (October–December 1992): 493–504.

71. Frederick Douglass, "If There Is No Struggle, There Is No Progress," speech delivered at Canandaigua, New York, on August 3, 1857, available at BlackPast.org, http://www.blackpast.org/1857-frederick-douglass-if-there-no-struggle-there-no-progress.

72. Gupta, *The Great Encounter,* 112; Roosevelt to Lee, February 7, 1908, Roosevelt Papers, Series 1, Library of Congress; Roosevelt to Morley, December 1, 1908, Roosevelt Papers, Series 2, Library of Congress; Paul Kramer, "Empires, Exceptions, and Anglo-Saxons: Race and Rule between the British and United States Empires, 1880–1910," *Journal of American History* 88, no. 4 (March 2002): 1315–1353; Rudyard Kipling, "Take Up the White Man's Burden," *McClure's* (February 1899); Teddy Roosevelt, "The Expansion of the White Races," in *The Works of Theodore Roosevelt, National Edition,* vol. 16 (New York: Charles Scribner's Sons, 1925), 258–278; Thomas G. Dyer, *Theodore Roosevelt and the Idea of Race* (Baton Rouge, LA: LSU Press, 1980); Frank Ninkovich,

"Theodore Roosevelt: Civilization as Ideology," *Diplomatic History* 10 (Summer 1986): 221–245.

73. William Jennings Bryan, "British Rule in India," reprinted from *India*, July 20, 1906, South Asian American Digital Archive (SAADA), www.saada .org/item/20101015–123.

74. Bayard Taylor, *A Visit to India, China, and Japan in the Year 1853* (New York: G. P. Putnam, 1855), 194 and 271; Caleb Wright, *India and Its Inhabitants* (Cincinnati, OH: J. A. Brainerd, 1858); William Henry Seward, *Travels around the World* (New York: D. Appleton and Company, 1873); Louis Rousselet, *India and Its Native Princes: Travels in Central India and in the Residencies of Bombay and Bengal* (New York: Scribner, Armstrong, 1876); Hezekiah Butterworth, *Zig-Zag Journeys in India* (Boston: Estes and Lauriat, 1887); Jensen, *Passage from India*, 17; Diwarkar Prasad Singh, *American Attitude toward the Indian National Movement* (New Delhi: Munshiram Manoharlal, 1974), 18–19; Jayanta Sengupta, "Through Albion's Looking Glass? Constructions of India in American Travel Writing, c. 1850–1910," in *Different Types of History*, ed. Bharati Ray (Delhi: Centre for Studies in Civilizations, 2009), 333–358; Grant to Michael John Cramer, March 20, 1879, *Letters of Ulysses S. Grant to his Father and his Youngest Sister*, edited by Jesse Grant Cramer (New York: G.P. Putnam's Sons, 1912), 152.

75. Mark Twain, *Following the Equator: A Journey around the World*, vol. 2 (New York and London: Harper and Brothers, 1897 and 1899), 28, 23, and 63; Twain, *The Autobiography of Mark Twain*, ed. Charles Neider (New York: Perennial Library, 1975), 314; Albert Bigelow Paine, ed., *Mark Twain's Letters* (New York: Harper, 1917), 629; Mohamed Elias, "Mark Twain and Indian History," *Journal of Indian History* 56 (April 1978): 140.

76. Twain, *Following the Equator*, 29, 469, 514.

77. Mark Twain, *Mark Twain's Notebook* (New York: Harper, 1935), 270–271, 276; Twain, *Following the Equator*, 149, 301, 469, 514, 626.

## Chapter 2: The Color of Freedom

Epigraph: Joan M. Jensen, *Passage from India: Asian Indian Immigrants in North America* (New Haven: Yale University Press, 1988), 39.

1. Annette Thackwell Johnson, "'Rag Heads': A Picture of America's East Indians," *The Independent* 109, no. 3828 (1922): 234.

2. Karen Leonard, *Making Ethnic Choices: California's Punjabi-Mexican Americans* (Philadelphia: Temple University Press, 1994).

3. Vivek Bald, *Bengali Harlem and the Lost Histories of South Asian America* (Cambridge, MA: Harvard University Press, 2013).

4. Amitava Kumar, *Passport Photos* (Berkeley: University of California Press, 2000), 63; Jensen, *Passage from India*, 13; Gaiutra Bahadur, *Coolie Woman: The Odyssey of Indenture* (Chicago, University of Chicago Press, 2013); Sukanya

Banerjee, *Becoming Imperial Citizens: Indians in the Late-Victorian Empire* (Durham, NC: Duke University Press, 2010); Madhavi Kale, *Fragments of Empire: Capital, Slavery, and Indian Indentured Labor Migration in the British Caribbean* (Philadelphia: University of Pennsylvania Press, 1998).

5. Jensen, *Passage from India*, 14; "Sikhs Allowed to Land," *The San Francisco Chronicle*, April 6, 1899, 10.

6. Bald, *Bengali Harlem;* Rajani Kanta Das, *Hindustani Workers on the Pacific Coast* (Berlin: W. de Gruyter, 1923), 109–116.

7. Nayan Shah, *Stranger Intimacy: Contesting Race, Sexuality, and the Law in the North American West* (Berkeley and Los Angeles: University of California Press, 2011).

8. Frederick Jackson Turner, "The Significance of the Frontier in American History," presented at the meeting of the American Historical Association, Chicago, July 12, 1893, http://xroads.virginia.edu/~HYPER/TURNER/; Richard White, *"It's Your Misfortune and None of My Own": A History of the American West* (Norman: University of Oklahoma Press, 1991); Patricia Nelson Limerick, *The Legacy of Conquest: The Unbroken Past of the American West* (New York: Norton, 2006).

9. Swami Vivekananda, "To the Fourth of July," July 4, 1898, *The Complete Works of Swami Vivekananda* (CWSV), available at www.ramakrishnavivekananda .info/vivekananda/complete_works.htm; Sister Nivedita, *Notes of Some Wanderings with Swami Vivekananda* (Calcutta: Udbodhan Office, 1922), 76–77.

10. Swami Virajananda, *Life of Swami Vivekananda* (Almora, India: Advaita Ashrama, 1924–1928), II, 279; Pravrajika Vrajaprana, *A Portrait of Sister Christine* (Calcutta: Ramakrishna Mission Institute of Culture, 1996); Prabuddha Pravrajika, *Saint Sara: The Life of Sara Chapman Bull, the American Mother of Swami Vivekananda* (Calcutta: Shri Sarada Math, 2002); Stephen Prothero, "Hinduphobia and Hinduphilia in U.S. Culture," in *The Stranger's Religion: Fascination and Fear*, ed. Anna Lannstrom (Notre Dame, IN: University of Notre Dame Press, 2004), 13–37.

11. Earl Robert Schmidt, "American Relations with South Asia 1900–1940" (PhD diss., University of Pennsylvania, 1955), 275; "American Professor Attends Congress Session," *Modern Review*, March 1926, 346.

12. "History," http://sfvedanta.org/the-society/history/; *Voice of Freedom* 7, no. 11 (February 1916): 216; Swami Trigunatita, "How to See God," *Voice of Freedom* 7, no. 2 (May 1915): 22–23; Carl T. Jackson, *Vedanta for the West: The Ramakrishna Movement in the United States* (Bloomington: Indian University Press, 1994), 57–61.

13. Schmidt, "American Relations with South Asia," 17–18; David Shavit, "Ballantine, Henry," *The United States in Asia: A Historical Dictionary* (Westport, CT: Greenwood Press, 1990); Henry Ballantine, *On India's Frontier; or Nepal, the Gurkhas' Mysterious Land* (New York: J. Selwin Tait and Sons, 1895).

14. Wendell Thomas, *Hinduism Invades America* (Boston: Beacon Press, 1930), 219–220; Kirin Narayan, "Refractions of the Field at Home: American

Representations of Hindu Holy Men in the 19th and 20th Centuries," *Cultural Anthropology* 8, no. 4 (1993): 476–509; Bald, *Bengali Harlem*, 17; John Patrick Deveney and Franklin Rosemont, *Paschal Beverly Randolph: A Nineteenth-Century Black American Spiritualist, Rosicrucian, and Sex Magician* (New York: State University of New York Press, 1996); Alexander Rocklin, "'A Hindu Is White Although He Is Black': Hindu Alterity and the Performativity of Religion and Race between the United States and the Caribbean," *Comparative Studies in Society and History* 58, issue 1 (January 2016): 181–210.

15. Raj Kumar Gupta, *The Great Encounter: A Study of Indo-American Literature and Cultural Relations* (New Delhi: Abhinav, 1986), 152–153.

16. Peter Bernard, "Tantrik Worship: The Basis of Religion," *International Journal of the Tantrik Order* 5, no. 1 (1906): 71; Thomas, *Hinduism Invades America*, 219–220; Prothero, "Hinduphobia and Hinduphilia in U.S. Culture," 13–37; Nik Douglas, *Spiritual Sex: Secrets of Tantra from the Ice Age to the New Millennium* (New York: Pocket Books, 1997), 195; Hugh B. Urban, "The Omnipotent Oom: Tantra and Its Impact on Modern Western Esotericism," http://www.esoteric.msu.edu/VolumeIII/HTML/Oom.html, accessed April 2018.

17. Protap Chunder Mozoomdar, "Emerson as Seen from India," in *The Genius and Character of Emerson: Lectures at the Concord School of Philosophy*, ed. Franklin Benjamin Sanborn (Boston: James R. Osgood, 1885): 365–371, 367; Philip Goldberg, *American Veda: From Emerson and the Beatles to Yoga and Meditation: How Indian Spirituality Changed the West* (New York: Harmony, 2010), 40; V. Meenakumari, "Thoreau's India: An Outsider's View," *Indian Review of World Literature in English* 7, no. 2 (July 2011); Joseph S. Alter, *Gandhi's Body: Sex, Diet, and the Politics of Nationalism* (Philadelphia: University of Pennsylvania Press, 2000), 57 and 64.

18. William Walker Atkinson, *The Hindu-Yogi Science of Breath: A Complete Manual of the Oriental Breathing Philosophy of Physical, Mental, Psychic, and Spiritual Development* (Chicago: Yogi Publication Society, 1905); Atkinson, *Hatha Yoga; or, The Yogi of Physical Well Being, with Numerous Exercises* (Chicago: Yogi Publication Society, 1905).

19. Thomas, *Hinduism Invades America*, 134; Alter, *Gandhi's Body*, 66; Stefanie Syman, *The Subtle Body: The Story of Yoga in America* (New York: Farrar-Straus, 2010); Lola Williamson, *Transcendent in America: Hindu-Inspired Meditation Movements as New Religion* (New York: New York University Press, 2010).

20. "Namaste," *The Theosophist* 1, no. 1 (October 1879): 1–3; *The Theosophist* 1, no. 8 (May 1880): 196 and 213; "What's in a Name?" *Lucifer* 1, no. 1 (September 1887).

21. Sunrit Mullick, *The First Hindu Mission to America: The Pioneering Visits of Protap Chunder Mozoomdar* (New Delhi: Northern Book Centre, 2010), 51–60.

22. Ibid., 57, 60, 64, 69; *Christian Register*, September 27, 1883.

23. Marie Louise Burke, *Swami Vivekananda in America: New Discoveries* (Calcutta: Advaita Ashrama, 1958), 47, 166; Gupta, *The Great Encounter*, 119; Carl T. Jackson, *Vedanta for the West*.

24. *The Life of Swami Vivekananda by His Eastern and Western Disciples,* 6th ed. (Calcutta: Advaita Ashrama, January 1989), 406–407, 456, 467; "Dear Alasinga," July 1, 1895, CWSV, vol. 5; "To Miss Josephine MacLeod," September 1895, CWSV, vol. 8; "Sayings and Utterances," CWSV, vol. 9; Sister Nivedita, *The Complete Works of Sister Nivedita* vol. 1 (Calcutta: Advaita Ashrama, 1982), 153.

25. John R. Wunder, "South Asians, Civil Rights, and the Pacific Northwest: The 1907 Bellingham Anti-Indian Riot and Subsequent Citizenship and Deportation Struggles," *Western Legal History* 4 (1991): 59–68.

26. Jensen, *Passage from India,* 140–141.

27. Jodi A. Byrd, *The Transit of Empire: Indigenous Critiques of Colonialism* (Minneapolis: The University of Minnesota Press, 2011), 201; Audra Simpson, *Mohawk Interruptus: Political Life across the Borders of Settler States* (Durham, NC: Duke University Press, 2014), 115–116.

28. Jensen, *Passage from India,* 19–34, 52, and 101; Mae Ngai, *Impossible Subjects: Illegal Aliens and the Making of Modern America* (Princeton, NJ: Princeton University Press, 2004), 18 and 37; "Memorial of the Legislature of Missouri on the Subject of the Central Pacific Railroad," January 3, 1850, Congressional Series of United States Public Documents, vol. 563, (Washington, DC: U.S. Government Printing Office, 1850), 25; Adam McKeown, *Melancholy Order: Asian Migration and the Globalization of Borders* (New York: Columbia University Press, 2011).

29. Jensen, *Passage from India,* 54–55; Shah, *Stranger Intimacy,* 37.

30. Joan M. Jensen, "Apartheid: Pacific Coast Style," *The Pacific Historical Review* 38, no. 3 (August 1969): 340.

31. Bald, *Bengali Harlem;* Lala Lajpat Rai, *The United States of America: A Hindu's Impressions and a Study* (Calcutta: Brahmo Mission Press, 1916), 416; Bharatan Kumarappa, *My Student Days in America* (Bombay: Padma Publications, 1945), 3–7, 81, 84–85.

32. Jensen, *Passage from India,* 140–141; "Turn Back the Hindu Invasion," *San Francisco Call* 107, no. 63 (February 1, 1910), http://cdnc.ucr.edu/cgi-bin/cdnc ?a=d&d=SFC19100201.2.70.1.

33. Seema Sohi, *Echoes of Mutiny: Race, Surveillance, and Indian Anticolonialism in North America* (Oxford, UK: Oxford University Press, 2014), 26–37.

34. Shah, *Stranger Intimacy,* 206–208.

35. Ngai, *Impossible Subjects,* 18 and 37; Sohi, *Echoes of Mutiny,* 15 and chapter 4; Shah, *Stranger Intimacy,* 203–205.

36. Shah, *Stranger Intimacy,* 223–227. Also see Martha Gardner, *The Qualities of a Citizen: Women, Immigration, and Citizenship, 1870–1965* (Princeton, NJ: Princeton University Press, 2005).

37. Jensen, *Passage from India,* 158.

38. Schmidt, "American Relations with South Asia," 218–220.

39. Saint Nihal Singh, "The Picturesque Immigrant from India's Coral Strand," *Out West* (1909): 43–54.

40. Jensen, *Passage from India*, 39; Nico Slate, *Colored Cosmopolitanism: The Shared Struggle for Freedom in the United States and India* (Cambridge, MA: Harvard University Press, 2012), 28.

41. Bruce Baum, *The Rise and Fall of the Caucasian Race: A Political History of Racial Identity* (New York: New York University Press, 2006), 73–94; Thomas R. Trautmann, *Aryans and British India* (Berkeley: University of California Press, 1997); Romila Thapar, "The Image of the Barbarian in Early India," *Comparative Studies in Society and History* 13, no. 1 (October 1971): 408–436.

42. Pardaman Singh, *Ethnological Epitome of the Hindustanees of the Pacific Coast* (Stockton, CA: Pacific Coast Khalsa Diwan Society, 1922); Godha Ram, *Who Are These Mysterious Hindus (Hindustanees)? Interesting Facts About an Interesting People* (1922), South Asian American Digital Archive (SAADA), https://www.saada.org/item/20121211-1144.

43. Saint Nihal Singh, "Colour Line in the United States of America," *Modern Review* (November 1908); "Explosion of Asia as Menace to Peace," *New York Evening Post*, September 22, 1917, 14; Dohra Ahmad, "'More Than Romance': Genre and Geography in Dark Princess," *ELH* 69, no. 3 (2002): 775–803; Lajpat Rai, *The United States of America*, iii, 89, 104, 389; Joginder Singh Dhanki, *Perspectives on Indian National Movement: Selected Correspondence of Lala Lajpat Rai* (New Delhi: National Book Organisation, 1998), 99–101.

44. Jensen, *Passage from India*, 248.

45. *In Re Akhay Kumar Mozumdar* 207 F (E.D. Wash. 1913); *US v Mohan Singh*, 257 Fed. 209 (1919).

46. Jennifer C. Snow, *Protestant Missionaries, Asian Immigrants, and Ideologies of Race* (New York: Routledge, 2007), chapter 5; Doug Coulson, "British Imperialism, the Indian Independence Movement, and the Racial Eligibility Provisions of the Naturalization Act: United States v. Thind Revisited," *Georgetown Journal of Law and Modern Critical Race Perspectives* 7 (2015): 1–42.

47. *United States v. Bhagat Singh Thind*, 261 U.S. 204 (1923); "Court Rules Hindu Not a 'White Person,'" *New York Times*, February 20, 1923.

48. Ian Haney Lopez, *White by Law: The Legal Construction of Race*, rev. ed. (New York: New York University Press, 2006), 64–65.

49. "Indians Not Eligible for American Citizenship," *Modern Review* 33 (March 1923): 407; K. Natarajan, "Reciprocity Bill," *Indian Social Reformer* (March 10, 1926): 418; Schmidt, "American Relations with South Asia," 351.

50. F. Fisher and Others, "B. Singh Case," *Indian Social Reformer* (August 18, 1923): 827; "Indian Rights in the United States," *Nation* 117 (October 17, 1923): 447.

51. Harman Singh Chima, "Why India Sends Students to America" (orig. pub. 1907) in Tilak Raj Sareen, *Select Documents on the Ghadr Party* (New Delhi: Mounto Publishing House, 1994), 4; Diwaker Prasad Singh, "American Official Attitudes toward the Indian Nationalist Movement, 1905–1929" (PhD diss., University of Hawaii, 1964), 172–173, 182; Jensen, *Passage from India*, 94–95.

52. Lajpat Rai, *The United States of America*, 403–405, 407–408.

53. Sarangadhar Das, "Information for Indian Students Intending to Come to the Pacific Coast of the United States," *Modern Review* 10 (December 1911): 602–612.

54. Ibid., 604 and 610; "An Appeal," Association for the Promotion of Education of the People of India, SAADA, https://www.saada.org/item/20120831 -1087.

55. "One Tenth of Student Body Are Foreigners," *The Tech,* January 23, 1922, 1–2; Bharatan Kumarappa, *My Student Days in America* (Bombay: Padma Publications, 1945), 82–83; Nihal Singh, "The Picturesque Immigrant from India's Coral Strand," 52; Saint Nihal Singh, "Indian Students in America," *Modern Review* (August 1908); Sudhindra Bose, "American Impressions of a Hindu Student," *Forum* 53 (February 1915): 251; J. S. S. Paul, "Indian Students," *Modern Review* (February 1922): 255.

56. Sudhindra Bose, "Our Aims," *Bulletin of the Hindusthan Association of U.S.A.* 1 (August 1913): 5, SAADA, https://www.saada.org/item/20110930-387.

57. Har Dayal, "Hindusthanee Students," *Bulletin of the Hindusthan Association of U.S.A.* 1 (August 1913): 8, SAADA, https://www.saada.org/item/20110930 -387.

58. Sayad Muhammad Khuda Box, "The Need of Hindusthanee Co-Eds," *Bulletin of the Hindusthan Association of U.S.A.* 1 (August 1913): 12, https://www .saada.org/item/20110930-387; "A Hindu Co-Ed in America," *Bulletin of the Hindusthan Association of U.S.A.* 1 (August 1913): 23, SAADA, https://www .saada.org/item/20110930-387

59. T. N. Das, "Our Nation Day Celebration in California," *Modern Review* 13 (February 1913): 210–212; Jensen, *Passage from India,* 172; "Hindu Students in America for Boycotting the British," *The Independent Hindustan* 1, no. 6 (February 1921): 137. Lajpat Rai, *The United States of America,* 407; Ramachandra Guha, "How the Congress Lost the Diaspora," *Hindustan Times,* September 28, 2014.

60. Sarangadhar Das to Swami Trigunatita, July 16, 1911, Library and Archives Canada, RG7-G-21, vol. 201, file 332, vol. 5 (a), http://komagatamarujourney .ca/node/11731

61. Bailey Millard, "Rabindranath Tagore Discovers America," *The Bookman* 44 (November 1916): 247; Stephen Hay, "Rabindranath Tagore in America," *American Quarterly* (1962): 439–463; Gupta, *The Great Encounter,* 136.

62. Ramachandra Guha, "Travelling with Tagore," published as the introduction to Rabindranath Tagore, *Nationalism* (New Delhi: Penguin Classics, 2009), http://ramachandraguha.in/archives/traveling-with-tagore-penguin -classics.html.

63. Tagore to Myron N. Phelps, in *Selected Letters of Rabindranath Tagore,* eds. Krishna Dutta and Andrew Robinson (Cambridge, UK: Cambridge University Press, 1997), 74–77.

## Keyword: *Caste*

Epigraph: "The Freedom March," unsigned editorial, *United Asia* 15, no. 9 (September 1963): 600–602.

1. Nicholas Vachel Lindsay, "A Vision, Called: 'Lincoln in India,'" *The English Journal* 16 (September 1927): 495–509.

2. Lajpat Rai, *The United States of America: A Hindu's Impressions and a Study* (Calcutta: Brahmo Mission Press, 1916), 397.

3. Jotirao Phule, *Selected Writings of Jotirao Phule,* ed. G. P. Deshpande (New Delhi: Leftword, 2002), 222; Jotirao Govindrao Phule, *Slavery in the Civilised British Government under the Cloak of Brahmanism,* trans. P. G. Patil (Bombay: Education Dept., Govt. of Maharashtra, 1991); Gail Omvedt, "Jotirao Phule and the Ideology of Social Revolution in India," *Economic and Political Weekly* (11 September 1971); Rosalind O'Hanlon, *Caste, Conflict, and Ideology: Mahatma Jotirao Phule and Low Caste Protest in Nineteenth-Century Western India* (Cambridge, UK: Cambridge University Press, 1985).

4. Charu Gupta, *The Gender of Caste: Representing Dalits in Print* (Seattle: University of Washington Press, 2016); Sukhadeo Thorat and Katherine S. Newman, eds., *Blocked by Caste: Economic Discrimination and Social Exclusion in Modern India Hardcover* (Oxford, UK: Oxford University Press, 2010).

5. Nico Slate, "Translating Race and Caste," *Journal of Historical Sociology* 24, no. 1 (March 2011): 62–79; Daniel Immerwahr, "Caste or Colony? Indianizing Race in the United States," *Modern Intellectual History* 4, no. 2 (2007): 275–301; Balmurli Natrajan and Paul Greenough, eds. *Against Stigma: Studies in Caste, Race and Justice Since Durban* (Hyderabad: Orient Blackswan Press, 2009); Kamala Visweswaran, *Un / common Cultures: Racism and the Rearticulation of Cultural Difference* (Durham, NC: Duke University Press, 2010).

6. Ralph Waldo Emerson, *Indian Superstition,* ed. Kenneth Walter Cameron (Hanover, NH: The Friends of the Dartmouth Library, 1954), 64.

7. Emerson, "Brahma," website of the Poetry Foundation, http://www.poetry foundation.org/poem/175138; Thoreau, "The Laws of Menu," *Dial* 3, no. 3 (January 1843): 331; Henry David Thoreau, *A Week on the Concord and Merrimack Rivers,* (Boston and Cambridge: James Munroe and Company, 1849), 154–155; Charles R. Anderson, *The Magic Circle of Walden* (New York: Holt, Rinehart and Winston, 1968), 167.

8. T. R. Rajasekharaiah, *The Roots of Whitman's Grass* (Madison, NJ: Fairleigh Dickinson University Press, 1970); Nathaniel H. Preston, "Whitman's 'Shadowy Dwarf': A Source in Hindu Mythology," *Walt Whitman Quarterly Review* 15 (Spring 1998): 185–186; Nathaniel Preston, "Walt Whitman's Use of Indian Sources: A Reconsideration," http://www.ritsumei.ac.jp/acd/cg/lt /rb/627/627PDF/Preston.pdf.

9. Oliver Wendell Holmes, "The Brahmin Caste of New England" *Atlantic Monthly* 5, no. 27 (1860).

10. "The British Empire in the East, Part II," *Hunt's Merchant's Magazine and Commercial Review* 20 (May 1849): 481.

11. I am grateful to Daniel Immerwahr for uncovering the significance of caste for antislavery activists. See Immerwahr, "Caste or Colony? Indianizing Race in the United States," *Modern Intellectual History* 4, no. 2 (2007): 275–301; "Petition to Congress for the Abolition of Slavery in the District of Columbia," *Liberator* (1 January 1831): 1; P. H., "The Colored Population of the United States, No. 1," *Liberator* (8 January 1831): 1–2; Frederick Douglass, *My Bondage and My Freedom*, (New York: Miller, Orton and Mulligan, 1855), xx and 399; Horace Greeley, *The American Conflict* (Hartford, London: O. D. Case, 1866), 749; Theodore Parker, *Speeches, Addresses, and Occasional Sermons*, vol. 2 (Boston: Horace B. Fuller, 1867), 149; Horace Mann, *Slavery: Letters and Speeches* (Boston: B. B. Mussey, 1853), 175; William E. Channing, *The Works of William E. Channing*, 17th ed., vol. 2 (Boston: American Unitarian Association, 1866), 86.

12. Charles Sumner, "The Question of Caste" (Boston: Wright and Potter, 1869), 4, 6–10, 31. Also see Debjani Ganguly, *Caste, Colonialism and Counter-Modernity: Notes on a Postcolonial Hermeneutics of Caste* (New York: Routledge, 2005); Nicholas Dirks, *Castes of Mind: Colonialism and the Making of Modern India* (Princeton, NJ: Princeton University Press, 2001); Susan Bayly, *Caste, Society, and Politics in India from the Eighteenth Century to the Modern Age* (Cambridge: Cambridge University Press, 1999).

13. Charles Sumner, *The Question of Caste* (Boston: Wright and Potter, 1869), 4, 6–10, 31.

14. Joan M. Jensen, *Passage From India: Asian Indian Immigrants in North America* (New Haven: Yale University Press, 1988), 153; Sarangadhar Das, "Information for Indian Students Intending to Come to the Pacific Coast of the United States," *Modern Review* 10 (December 1911): 612.

15. Saint Nihal Singh, "The Picturesque Immigrant from India's Coral Strand," *Out West* (1909): 43–54.

16. Shridhar V. Ketkar, *History of Caste in India* (Jaipur: Rawat Publications, 1979), 11, 77–78, 100–115, 143, 169. See also Shridhar V. Ketkar, "Radical Defects of Ethnology," *American Anthropologist*, New Series, 11, no. 2 (1911): 321–322.

17. "Science on Mixture of Races," *Independent Hindustan* 1, no. 11 (July 1921), South Asian American Digital Archive (SAADA), https://www.saada.org/item/20120809-1034; "The Story of the Hindustan Gadar Party," *Independent Hindustan* 1, no. 9 (May 1921), 4, SAADA, https://www.saada.org/item/20120807-1031.

18. Dhan Gopal Mukerji, *Caste and Outcaste* (1923), eds. Gordon H. Chang, Purnima Mankekar, and Akhil Gupta (Stanford, CA: Stanford University Press, 2002), 17, 45–46, 223.

19. Katherine Mayo, "Mahatma Gandhi and India's 'Untouchables'" (1930), in *The Americanization of Gandhi: Images of the Mahatma*, ed. Charles Chatfield (New York: Garland Publishing, 1976), 250. Also see Harry H. Field, *After*

*Mother India* (New York: Harcourt, Brace, 1929), 250; Katherine Mayo, *Mother India* (London: Jonathan Cape, 1927); Mrinalini Sinha, *Specters of Mother India: The Global Restructuring of an Empire* (Durham, NC: Duke University Press, 2006); Andrew J. Rotter, *Comrades at Odds: The United States and India, 1947–1964* (Ithaca, NY: Cornell University Press, 2000), 1; *A Statement by American Residents in India: Is India a Menace? A Reply to Miss Mayo* (Madras: Methodist Mission Press, 1927).

20. C. S. Ranga Iyer, *Father India: A Reply to Mother India* (London: Selwyn and Blount, 1927), 90; Dhan Gopal Mukerji, *A Son of Mother India Answers* (New York: E. P. Dutton, 1928), 62; Kanhaya Lal Gauba, *Uncle Sham: Being the Strange Tale of a Civilisation Run Amok* (Lahore: The Times Publishing Company, 1929), 36–41; Dalip Singh Saund, *My Mother India* (Stockton, CA: Pacific Coast Khalsa Diwan Society, 1930).

21. "Interviews with Foreigners," before March 1, 1929, *Collected Works of Mahatma Gandhi* (CWMG) Electronic Book (New Delhi: Government of India, 1999).

22. Lala Lajpat Rai, *Unhappy India* (Calcutta: Banna Publishing, 1928), lix, 87, 113, and 124.

23. Bhimrao Ramji Ambedkar, "Which Is Worse? Slavery or Untouchability?" in *Dr. Babasaheb Ambedkar: Writings and Speeches,* vol. 12 (Bombay: Government Central Press, 1989), 741–759. Also see *Dr. Babasaheb Ambedkar: Writings and Speeches* vol. 5, 9–18 and 75–88.

24. W. Lloyd Warner, "American Caste and Class," *American Journal of Sociology* 42 (1936): 234–237; John Dollard, *Caste and Class in a Southern Town* (New Haven, CT: Yale University Press, 1937); W. Lloyd Warner and Allison Davis, "A Comparative Study of American Caste," in *Race Relations and the Race Problem: A Definition and an Analysis,* ed. Edgar T. Thompson (Durham, NC: Duke University Press, 1939), 231–233.

25. E. Franklin Frazier, *Negro Youth at the Crossways: Their Personality Development in the Middle States* (New York: Schocken Books, 1967), 91; Frazier, "Sociological Theory and Race Relations," *American Sociological Review*12, no. 3 (June 1947): 265–271; Charles S. Johnson, "The Conflict of Caste and Class in American Industry," *American Journal of Sociology* 42 (1936): 55–65; Charles S. Johnson, *Growing Up in the Black Belt: Negro Youth in the Rural South* (Washington, DC: American Council on Education, 1941), 325, 327; Oliver Cromwell Cox, *Caste, Class, and Race: A Study in Social Dynamics* (New York: Modern Reader Paperbacks, 1948), ix, 21, 83, 332, 426, 453, 468, and 502.

26. Gerald D. Berreman, "Caste in India and the United States," *American Journal of Sociology* 66 (1960): 120–127; Gerald D. Berreman, "Stratification, Pluralism and Interaction: A Comparative Analysis of Caste," in *Caste and Race: Comparative Approaches,* eds. Anthony de Reuck and Julie Knight (London: J. and A. Churchill, 1967), 45–73; Oliver C. Cox, "Berreman's 'Caste in India

and the United States,'" *American Journal of Sociology* 66 (1960): 511; Harold R. Isaacs, *India's Ex-Untouchables* (New York: John Day, 1964), 49.

27. Sidney Verba, Bashiruddin Ahmed, and Anil Bhatt, *Caste, Race, and Politics: A Comparative Study of India and the United States* (Beverly Hills, CA: Sage Publications, 1971), 74.

28. Quoted in Mary L. Dudziak, *Cold War Civil Rights: Race and the Image of American Democracy* (Princeton, NJ: Princeton University Press, 2000), 34.

29. Quoted in Helen Laville and Scott Lucas, "The American Way: Edith Sampson, the NAACP, and African American Identity in the Cold War," *Diplomatic History* 20, no. 4 (October 1996): 572; Carl T. Rowan, *The Pitiful and the Proud* (New York: Random House, 1956), 33, 76–77, 79, 82, and 154–156.

30. George Schuyler, "Views and Reviews," *Pittsburgh Courier,* August 26, 1950, 21; Schuyler, "Views and Reviews," *Pittsburgh Courier,* September 30, 1950, 15.

31. B. R. Ambedkar, *What Congress and Gandhi Have Done to the Untouchables* (Bombay: Thacker, 1946), 281–283; B. R. Ambedkar, *Address Delivered on the 101st Birthday Celebration of Mahadev Govind Ranade* (Bombay: Thacker, 1943); Ambedkar to Du Bois, circa July 1946, reel 58, W.E.B. Du Bois Papers, Special Collections and University Archives, University of Massachusetts Amherst Libraries; D. C. Ahir, *Dr. Ambedkar and the Indian Constitution* (Lucknow: Buddha Vihara, 1973) and B. R. Ambedkar, *States and Minorities: What Are Their Rights and How to Secure Them in the Constitution of Free India* (Bombay: Thacker, 1947).

32. C. Rajagopalachari, *Ambedkar Refuted,* 2d ed. (Bombay: Hind Kitab, 1946), 15; Consulate General, Bombay, to Secretary of State, May 4, 1949, Record Group 59, 811.4016/5–449, United States National Archives, quoting *Blitz,* April 23, 1949.

33. Bharatan Kumarappa, *My Student Days in America* (Bombay: Padma Publications, 1945), Preface and 78–81.

34. "The Freedom March," *United Asia* 15, no. 9 (September 63): 600–602.

35. Martin Luther King Jr., "My Trip to the Land of Gandhi," July 1959, *The Papers of Martin Luther King, Jr.,* Vol. 5, *Threshold of a New Decade, January 1959–December 1960,* ed. Clayborne Carson, Tenisha Armstrong, Susan Carson, Adrienne Clay, and Kieran Taylor (Berkeley: University of California Press, 2005), 236; King, "Statement upon Return from India," March 18, 1959, *Papers* Vol. 5, 143; King, "The Rising Tide of Racial Consciousness," September 6, 1960, *Papers* Vol. 5, 499–508; King, *Why We Can't Wait* (New York: Signet Classic Edition, 2000), 125, and note 4 to King, "Address at the Religious Leaders Conference," May 11, 1959, *Papers* Vol. 5, 197–198.

36. Taylor Branch, *Parting the Waters: America in the King Years, 1954–63* (New York: Simon and Schuster), 824.

37. King, *Papers* Vol. 5, 262.

38. Dalit Panthers Manifesto, in *Untouchable! Voices of the Dalit Liberation Movement*, ed. Barbara Joshi (London: Zed Books, 1986), 145; Lata Maurugkar, *Dalit Panther Movement in Maharashtra: A Sociological Approach* (London: Sangam Books, 1991); Vijay Prashad, "Afro-Dalits of the Earth, Unite!," *African Studies Review* 43 (2000): 189–201; Maurugkar, *Dalit Panther Movement in Maharashtra*, 44 and 237; K. P. Singh, "Liberation Movements in Comparative Perspective: Dalit Indians and Black Americans," in *Dalits in Modern India: Vision and Values*, 2d. ed., ed. S. M. Michael (New Delhi: Sage, 2007), 162–178; Sanjay Paswan and Pramanshi Jaideva, eds. *Encyclopaedia of Dalits in India*, Vol. 2, *Struggle for Self Liberation* (Delhi: Kalpaz Publications, 2002), 106.

39. Ravikumar, "A Grasp of the Past," *Tehelka* (December 15, 2007): 57; Eleanor Zelliot, *From Untouchable to Dalit: Essays on the Ambedkar Movement*, 2d. ed. (New Delhi: Manohar Publications, 1996), 280–281 and 299; Anupama Rao, *The Caste Question: Dalits and the Politics of Modern India* (Berkeley: University of California Press, 2009), 182–216.

40. Michelle Alexander, *The New Jim Crow: Mass Incarceration in the Age of Colorblindness* (New York: The Free Press, 2010), 5; "Upper Caste Men Lynch Dalit in Bihar," *Indian Express*, November 15, 2010, http://indianexpress.com/article/news-archive/web/upper-caste-men-lynch-dalit-in-bihar/.

41. Rao, *The Caste Question*, 4; Anand Teltumbde, *The Persistence of Caste: The Khairlanji Murders and India's Hidden Apartheid* (London: Zed Books, 2010); Chandra Bhan Prasad, *Dalit Diary, 1999–2003: Reflections on Apartheid in India* (New Delhi: Navayana, 2004); Ambedkar, *The Annihilation of Caste*, section 12, paragraph 4, available here: http://ccnmtl.columbia.edu/projects/mmt/ambedkar/web/readings/aoc_print_2004.pdf;

42. Ramnarayan S. Rawat, *Reconsidering Untouchability: Chamars and Dalit History in North India* (Bloomington: Indian University Press, 2011), 22; Cedric Dover, "Notes on Coloured Writing," *Phylon* 8, no. 3 (3rd Quarter, 1947): 222; Nico Slate, *The Prism of Race: W. E. B. Du Bois, Langston Hughes, Paul Robeson and the Colored World of Cedric Dover* (New York: Palgrave Macmillan, 2014).

43. On intersectionality, see Kimberlé Crenshaw, "Mapping the Margins: Intersectionality, Identity Politics, and Violence against Women of Color," *Stanford Law Review* 43, no. 6 (1991): 1241–1299; Evelyn Brooks Higginbotham, "African-American Women's History and the Metalanguage of Race," *Signs: Journal of Women in Culture and Society* 17, no. 2 (Winter 1992): 251–274; Leslie McCall, "The Complexity of Intersectionality" *Signs: Journal of Women in Culture and Society* 30, no. 3 (2007): 1771–1800. Also see Kamaladevi Chattopadhyay, *America: The Land of Superlatives* (Bombay: Phonix Publications, 1946), 209.

44. W. E. B. Du Bois, "To the Nations of the World" (1900), in *The Oxford W. E. B. Du Bois Reader*, ed. Eric J. Sundquist (New York: Oxford University Press, 1996), 625, and Du Bois, *The Souls of Black Folk* (New York: Penguin Books, 1989), 13.

## Chapter 3: Rebellions

Epigraph: Ram Chandra, "What Young India Has in Mind," *New York Times,* July 8, 1916, reprinted in Ram Chandra, *India against Britain,* November 1, 1916, p. 23, available at the South Asian American Digital Archive (SAADA), https://www.saada.org/item/20110525-194.

1. Maia Ramnath, *Haj to Utopia: How the Ghadar Movement Charted Global Radicalism and Attempted to Overthrow the British Empire* (Berkeley and Los Angeles: University of California Press, 2011); T. R. Sareen, *Indian Revolutionary Movement Abroad* (New Delhi: Sterling, 1979).

2. Seema Sohi, *Echoes of Mutiny: Race, Surveillance, and Indian Anticolonialism in North America* (Oxford, UK: Oxford University Press, 2014), 27; Joan M. Jensen, *Passage from India: Asian Indian Immigrants in North America* (New Haven: Yale University Press, 1988), 180; Ramnath, *Haj to Utopia,* 33.

3. Jensen, *Passage from India,* 191 and 217.

4. Michael O'Dwyer, *India as I Knew It, 1885–1925* (London: Constable, 1925), 195–198; Jensen, *Passage from India,* 206–210; Douglas T. McGetchin, "Indo-German Connections, Critical and Hermeneutical, in the First World War," *The Comparatist* 34 (2010): 95–126.

5. Sohi, *Echoes of Mutiny.*

6. Harish K. Puri, *Ghadar Movement: Ideology, Organisation & Strategy* (Amritsar: Guru Nanak Dev University Press, 1983), 39–51; Sohi, *Echoes of Mutiny,* 36–38 and 95.

7. Tapan K. Mukherjee, *Taraknath Das: Life and Letters of a Revolutionary in Exile* (Kolkata: National Council of Education, 1998); Sohi, *Echoes of Mutiny,* 35; Gobind Behari Lal, "Dr. Taraknath Das in Free India," *Modern Review* 91–92 (July 1952): 36–38; Jensen, *Passage From India,* 165–170; Ronald Spector, "The Vermont Education of Taraknath Das: An Episode in British-American-Indian Relations," *Vermont History* 48 (Spring 1980): 89–95.

8. Har Dayal to Van Wyck Brooks, September 30, 1922, SAADA, https://www.saada.org/item/20111127-487; Emily Clara Brown, *Har Dayal: Hindu Revolutionary and Rationalist* (Tucson: University of Arizona Press, 1975); Har Dayal, "India in America," *Modern Review* 10 (July 1911): 2.

9. Sohi, *Echoes of Mutiny,* 54–56.

10. Sohi, *Echoes of Mutiny,* 35, 82, 105; Ram Chandra, *India against Britain.*

11. Jensen, *Passage from India,* 187–191.

12. Thomas G. Fraser, "Germany and Indian Revolution: 1914–18," *Journal of Contemporary History* 12, no. 2 (April 1977): 255–272; Sohi, *Echoes of Mutiny,* 167.

13. French Strother, *Fighting Germany's Spies* (Garden City, NY: Doubleday, 1918), 223–224; Sohi, *Echoes of Mutiny,* 165, 184–186.

14. Sohi, *Echoes of Mutiny,* 190; D. Malceiplannal, "American Impressions," *Indian Social Reformer* (November 6, 1937): 153; Erez Manela, *The Wilsonian*

*Moment: Self-Determination and the International Origins of Anticolonial National-ism* (Oxford, UK: Oxford University Press, 2007); Michael Adas, "Contested Hegemony: The Great War and the Afro-Asian Assault on the Civilizing Mission Ideology," *Journal of World History* 15, no. 1 (2004): 31–63.

15. "Call Bryan to Give Testimony in Big Hindu Conspiracy Trial," *Spokane Daily Chronicle,* April 8, 1918.

16. Ramnath, *Haj to Utopia,* 92; French Strother, *Fighting Germany's Spies.*

17. Ramachandra Guha, *Gandhi before India* (New York: Knopf, 2014); Sukanya Banerjee, *Becoming Imperial Citizens: Indians in the Late-Victorian Empire* (Durham, NC: Duke University Press, 2010); Maureen Swan, *Gandhi: The South African Experience* (Johannesburg: Ravan Press, 1985).

18. Letter from Bhagwan Singh Gyanee to Jagjit Sing, June 18, 1956, SAADA, https://www.saada.org/item/20120805-916.

19. Ramnath, *Haj to Utopia,* 122; J. Daniel Elam, "Echoes of Ghadr: Lala Har Dayal and the Time of Anticolonialism," *Comparative Studies of South Asia, Africa and the Middle East* 34, no. 1 (2014): 9–23; Jensen, *Passage from India,* 177–178.

20. "University for Women in Punjab," *Independent Hindustan* 1, no. 7 (March 1921): 158, SAADA, https://www.saada.org/item/20120806-1021; "The Story of the Hindustan Gadar Party," *Independent Hindustan* 1, no. 9 (May 1921): 4, SAADA, https://www.saada.org/item/20120807-1031; "The Women of India," *Independent Hindustan* 1, no. 9 (May 1921): 16, SAADA, https://www.saada .org/item/20120807-1031; "The World Through [*sic*] Eyes of a Young Indian," *Independent Hindustan* 1, no. 10 (June 1921): 4, SAADA, https://www .saada.org/item/20120809-1033.

21. Jensen, *Passage from India,* 190; Gerald Barrier, *Banned: Controversial Literature and Political Control in British India* (New Delhi: Manohar, 1974), 104–107; Sarangadhar Das, "Information for Indian Students Intending to Come to the Pacific Coast of the United States," *Modern Review* 10 (December 1911): 612.

22. Mark Juergensmeyer, *Religion as Social Vision: The Movement against Untouchability in Twentieth-Century Punjab (*Berkeley: University of California Press, 1985): 42–44 and 283–289.

23. Tilak Raj Sareen, *Select Documents on the Ghadr Party* (New Delhi: Mounto Publishing House, 1994), 70; Sohi, *Echoes of Mutiny,* 54–57 and 97; Ved Prakash and Sylvia Vatuk, "Protest Songs of East Indians on the West Coast, U.S.A." *Folklore* 7 (October 1966): 370–382; Gerald Barrier, *Banned,* 104–107.

24. Sohi, *Echoes of Mutiny,* 56–57 and 97.

25. Basanta Koomar Roy, "Doing England's Dirty Work," *Independent Hindustan* 1, no. 2 (October 1920): 27, 29, 39, SAADA.

26. Sailendranath Ghose, "India's Challenge to American Radicals," *Young Democracy* (June 1, 1919), SAADA.

27. Janice R. MacKinnon and Stephen R. MacKinnon, *Agnes Smedley: The Life and Times of an American Radical* (Berkeley: University of California Press,

1988); Ruth Price, *The Lives of Agnes Smedley* (Oxford, UK: Oxford University Press, 2005).

28. "National Convention of the Friends of Freedom for India," *Independent Hindustan* 1, no. 5 (January 1921): 113–115, https://www.saada.org/item /20120806-1019; Vivek Bald, *Bengali Harlem and the Lost Histories of South Asian America* (Cambridge, MA: Harvard University Press, 2013), 146–147; Jensen, *Passage from India*, 236.

29. Diwaker Prasad Singh, "American Official Attitudes toward the Indian Nationalist Movement, 1905–1929" (PhD diss., University of Hawaii, 1964), 172–173, 182, quoted in Jensen, *Passage from India*, 95.

30. Aravind Ganachari, *Nationalism and Social Reform in a Colonial Situation* (Delhi: Kalpaz Publications, 2005), 137–141.

31. Matthew Plowman, "Irish Republicans and the Indo-German Conspiracy of World War I," *New Hibernia Review* 7, no. 3 (Autumn 2003): 80–105; Ramnath, *Haj to Utopia*, 104 and 223; Eamon Devalera, *India and Ireland* (New York: Friends of Freedom for India, 1920); Thomas R. Trautmann, *Aryans and British India* (Berkeley: University of California Press, 1997).

32. Aravind Ganachari, *Nationalism and Social Reform in a Colonial Situation* (Delhi: Kalpaz Publications, 2005), 149–154; Rabindranath Tagore, *Selected Letters of Rabindranath Tagore*, eds. Krishna Dutta and Andrew Robinson (Cambridge, UK: Cambridge University Press, 1997), 73–79.

33. Sunderland Diary, January 1, 1896, Bentley Historical Library, University of Michigan, Ann Arbor; Spencer Lavan, *Unitarians and India: A Study in Encounter and Response* (Boston: Beacon Press, 1977), 162; J. T. Sunderland, *India, America, and World Brotherhood* (Madras: Ganesh, 1924), 2; J. T. Sunderland, *India in Bondage: Her Right to Freedom* (Calcutta: R. Chatterjee, 1928), iii and 1–2; J.T. Sunderland, "The Cause of Indian Famines," *New England Magazine* 23, no. 1 (September 1900): 60.

34. "Ourselves," *Young India* 1, no. 1 (1918): 4; Jensen, *Passage from India*, 230; Maritsa V. Poros, "Asian Indians and Asian-Indian Americans, 1870–1940," in *Immigrants in American History: Arrival, Adaptation, and Integration*, ed. Elliott Robert Barkan (Santa Barbara, CA: ABC-CLIO, 2013).

35. "The National Convention of the Friends of Freedom for India," *Independent Hindustan* 1, no. 5 (January 1921): 100, SAADA, https://www.saada.org/item /20120806-1019; Surendranath Karr, "India's Fight for Independence," *Independent Hindustan* 1, no. 5 (January 1921): 102–105, SAADA, https://www .saada.org/item/20120806-1019; Robert Morss Lovett, "America and India," *Independent Hindustan* 1, no. 5 (January 1921): 101, SAADA, https://www .saada.org/item/20120806-1019; Taraknath Das, "International Aspects of the Indian Question," *Independent Hindustan* 1, no. 5 (January 1921): 109, SAADA, https://www.saada.org/item/20120806-1019.

36. "India's Independence Movement Supported by Illinois Labor," *Independent Hindustan* 1, no. 4 (December 1920): 92, SAADA, https://www.saada .org/item/20120111-577; "California Labor Stands for Freedom of India,"

*Independent Hindustan* 1, no. 3 (November 1920): 72, SAADA, https://www
.saada.org/item/20120111-576.

37. "The Story of the Hindustan Gadar Party," *The Independent Hindustan* 1, no. 9
(May 1921): 4, SAADA, https://www.saada.org/item/20120807-1031; "The
League of the Oppressed Peoples," *Independent Hindustan* 1, no. 2 (October 1920): 27, SAADA, https://www.saada.org/item/20120111-575; "Independent Hindustan, an Organ of the Plain People," *Independent Hindustan* 1,
no. 10 (June 1921): 3, SAADA, https://www.saada.org/item/20120809-1033;
MacKinnon and MacKinnon, *Agnes Smedley,* 40–52; Agnes Smedley, *Daughter
of the Earth* (New York: Coward McCann, 1929); Jensen, *Passage from India,* 273;
Lala Lajpat Rai, "The New Internationalism," *Young India* 1 (April 1918): 11.

38. Jayaprakash Narayan, "Evolution of My Own Thinking," in *Jayaprakash Narayan: A Centenary Volume,* ed. Sandip Das (New Delhi: Mittal, 2005), 4–5;
Ramachandra Guha, *India after Gandhi: The History of the World's Largest Democracy* (New York: HarperCollins, 2007), 145, 311, 408, 477–485.

39. "The League of the Oppressed Peoples," SAADA; Kris Manjapra, *M. N. Roy:
Marxism and Colonial Cosmopolitanism* (New York: Routledge, 2010); Samaren
Roy, *M. N. Roy: A Political Biography* (Hyderabad: Orient Longman, 1997), 16;
Sohi, *Echoes of Mutiny,* 80–81; Narayan, "Evolution of My Own Thinking,"
4–5.

40. M. N. Roy, "The Foundation of Democracy: The American Experience," *The
Masses of India* 1 (September 1925): 7–9; "United Textile Workers of America for India's Independence," *Independent Hindustan* 1, no. 3 (November 1920):
72, https://www.saada.org/item/20120111-576; "The Story of the Hindustan
Gadar Party," SAADA; "Editorial," *Independent Hindustan* 1, no. 11 (July 1921),
SAADA, https://www.saada.org/item/20120809-1034; "The World Through
[*sic*] Eyes of a Young Indian," SAADA; "The Interest of America" and "Embroiling America," *Independent Hindustan* 1, no. 8 (April 1921), SAADA,
https://www.saada.org/item/20120807-1030; "The Fourth of July," *Independent Hindustan* 1, no. 11 (July 1921): 14, SAADA, https://www.saada.org/item
/20120809-1034; "India and the Philippines," *Young India* 3, no. 2 (November 1920): 244, SAADA, https://www.saada.org/item/20111031-440.

41. "A Christmas Message," *Independent and the Weekly Review* (February 18, 1922):
171; Jensen, *Passage from India,* 244; Ramnath, *Haj to Utopia,* 133 and 138;
Sohan Singh Josh, *Hindustan Gadar Party: A Short History* (New Delhi: People's
Publishing House, 1977), 245; "Editorial," *Independent Hindustan,* vol. 1, no. 11
(July 1921).

42. "Can India Trust 'Naturalized Englishmen'?" *Independent Hindustan* 1, no. 11
(July 1921): 8, SAADA, https://www.saada.org/item/20120809-1034; "The
Interest of America" and "Embroiling America," SAADA.

43. Jensen, *Passage from India,* 238–240, 245, and 263–264; Gary Hess, "The
'Hindu' in America: Immigration and Naturalization Policies and India,
1917–1946," *Pacific Historical Review* 38 (1969): 59–79.

44. Karen Leonard, "The Pahkar Singh Murders: A Punjabi Response to California's Alien Land Law" *Amerasia* 11 (1984): 75–87; Min Song, "Pahkar Singh's Argument with Asian America: Color and the Structure of Race Formation," in *A Part, Yet Apart: South Asians in Asian America,* eds. Lavina Dhingra Shankar and Rajini Srikanth (Philadelphia: Temple University Press, 1998), 79–104; Karen Leonard, "Punjabi Farmers and California's Alien Land Law," *Agricultural History* (1985), 549–562; "Bill Would Admit Hindus as Citizens," *Negro World* (February 11, 1928): 3.

45. Erika Lee, *The Making of Asian America* (New York: Simon and Schuster, 2016), 156–159.

46. I am grateful to Rani Cardona, the granddaughter of Vaishno Das Bagai, for providing me access to Bagai's final note to his wife, as well as the *Hindustan Times* article, "An Indian Merchant's Suicide in U.S.," *Hindustan Times* (May 22, 1928).

47. US v. Sakharam Ganesh Pandit, 15 f.2d. 285 (1926); "Hindu is Granted U.S. Citizenship," newspaper clipping from unknown source, SAADA, https://www.saada.org/item/20130128-1266; "Sakharam Pandit: High Caste Brahmin Teacher and Lecturer from India" (1910), SAADA, https://www.saada.org/item/20111208-530; "Advertisement for S. G. Pandit, B.A.," SAADA, https://www.saada.org/item/20130121-1230; Raymond Eugene Chase and S.G. Pandit, *An Examination of the Opinion of the Supreme Court of the United States Deciding against the Eligibility of Hindus for Citizenship* (Los Angeles: Parker, Stone, and Baird, 1926).

48. Mary K. Das, "A Woman without A Country," *Nation* 123, no. 3187 (August 4, 1926): 105–106; Nancy Cott, "Justice for All? Marriage and Deprivation of Citizenship in the United States," in *Justice and Injustice in Law and Legal Theory,* eds. Austin Sarat and Thomas R. Kearns (Ann Arbor: University of Michigan Press, 1996), 77–78; Mukherjee, *Taraknath Das*; Jensen, *Passage from India,* 260–261 and 268.

49. The following sources come from the website of Dr. Bhagat Singh Thind Spiritual Science Foundation: Letter from British Intelligence Agent in Surveillance on Dr. Thind's Detroit Lectures, February 1926, website of www.bhagatsinghthind.com/popup_bi_13.html; Letter from British Intelligence Agent in Surveillance on Dr. Thind's Omaha Lectures, May 6, 1926, www.bhagatsinghthind.com/popup_bi_17.html; Letter from British Intelligence with Excerpts of Dr. Thind's speech in Detroit, February 1927, Part 2, www.bhagatsinghthind.com/popup_bi_20.html.

50. The range of American impressions of Gandhi mirrors the way in which Indians imagined their own Gandhi. See Shahid Amin, "Gandhi as Mahatma: Gorakhpur District, Eastern UP, 1921-2," in *Selected Subaltern Studies,* eds. Ranaji Guha and Gayatri Chakravorty Spivak (Oxford, UK: Oxford University Press, 1988), 288–348. Also see Nilla Cram Cook, *My Road to India* (New York: Lee Furman, 1939); Martin B. Green, *Gandhi: Voice of a New Age*

*Revolution* (Mount Jackson, VA: Axios Press, 1993), 329–336; "Nilla Cram Cook, 74, a Writer and Linguist," *New York Times*, October 13, 1982.

51. "National Convention of the Friends of Freedom for India," *Independent Hindustan*, 114, SAADA.

52. Karr, "India's Fight for Independence," 102–105; "Gandhi! The Greatest Man in the World," *Independent Hindustan* 1, no. 11 (July 1921): 5, SAADA; "Independent Hindustan, an Organ of the Plain People," 3; "Mr. Gandhi's New Revolution," *Independent Hindustan* 1, no. 10 (June 1921): 3, SAADA; "Life Sketch of M. K. Gandhi," *Independent Hindustan* 1, no. 9 (May 1921): 8, SAADA; Taraknath Das, "An American Attitude to Non-Violent Non-Cooperation," *Modern Review* 34 (December 1923): 751.

53. Holmes, "Who Is the Greatest Man in the World Today?," 1921 sermon, quoted in Carl Hermann Voss, *Rabbi and Minister: The Friendship of Stephen S. Wise and John Haynes Holmes* (New York: World Publishing Company, 1964), 198.

54. Harry Emerson Fosdick, "Introduction," in Wendell Thomas, *Hinduism Invades America* (Boston: Beacon Press, 1930), 9.

55. E. Stanley Jones, *The Christ of the Indian Road*, 6th ed. (London: Hodder and Stoughton, 1925), 3, 13, 15, 118; Susan Haskell Khan, "The India Mission Field in American History: 1919–1947" (PhD diss., University of California, Berkeley, 2006); E. Stanley Jones, *Along the Indian Road* (London: Hodder and Stoughton, 1939), 4.

56. "Methodists v. Viceroy," *Time* (April 22, 1940), and "Non-Political Missions," *Time* (November 25, 1940); David Bundy, "The Theology of the Kingdom of God in E. Stanley Jones," *Wesleyan Theological Journal* 23, nos. 1 and 2 (Spring / Fall 1988): 58–80.

57. Joseph Kip Kosek, *Acts of Conscience: Christian Nonviolence and Modern American Democracy* (New York: Columbia University Press, 2009), 185–186; Paul R. Dekar, *Creating the Beloved Community: A Journey with the Fellowship of Reconciliation* (Telford, PA: Cascadia Publishing House, 2005), chap. 3; David Scott Cooney, "A Persistent Witness of Conscience: Methodist Nonviolent Activists, 1940–1970" (PhD diss., Illiff School of Theology, 2000); Jay Holmes Smith, "A Memorandum Concerning a New York Ashram," box 13, series A-3, Correspondence of A. J. Muste, Section II, FOR Papers, Swarthmore College Peace Collection; Smith, "Ministers and the Revolution," box 4, series A-3, Correspondence of A. J. Muste; Muste to Jones, July 3, 1942, box 4, series A-3, Correspondence of A. J. Muste.

58. Frederick Fisher, *India's Silent Revolution* (New York: Macmillan, 1919), 7 and 192; Khan, "The India Mission Field in American History: 1919–1947," 158.

59. R. A. Hume, "The Mayflower," *Calcutta Review*, September 1917, 593; "Hume, Robert Allen," website of Boston University School of Theology, accessed March 2018, http://www.bu.edu/missiology/missionary-biography/g-h/hume -robert-allen-1847-1929/; K. Natarajan, "Fifty Years of Work of R. A. Hume," *Indian Social Reformer* (November 1929): 194.

60. Editor, "The American in India," *Indian Witness* (September 24, 1924): 615; V. M. Nair, "Religion in America," *Indian Social Reformer* (June 20, 1925): 665.

61. Mahatma Gandhi, "From and about Sarojini Devi," *Young India,* May 30, 1929, *Collected Works of Mahatma Gandhi* (CWMG) Electronic Book (New Delhi: Government of India, 1999).

62. Ramachandra Guha, "How the Congress Lost the Diaspora," *Hindustan Times,* September 28, 2014.

63. Sarojini Naidu, *Selected Letters: 1890s to 1940s,* ed. Makarand Paranjpe (New Delhi: Kali for Women, 1996), 212–216.

64. "Sarojini Naidu," Redpath Chautauqua Collection, University of Iowa, http://digital.lib.uiowa.edu/cdm/ref/collection/tc/id/35165; Mrinalini Sinha, *Specters of Mother India: The Global Restructuring of an Empire* (Durham: Duke University Press, 2006), 103.

65. "Nancy Ann Miller Finds Happiness in Marriage to Rich Indian Prince," *Spokane Daily Chronicle,* January 27, 1932.

66. Naidu, *Selected Letters: 1890s to 1940s,* 212–216.

67. "Gandhi May Make Visit to America," *Ludington Daily News,* October 8, 1931; Thornton Wilder, *Heaven's My Destination* (New York: Harper and Brothers, 1935); Joseph Kip Kosek, *Acts of Conscience: Christian Nonviolence and Modern American Democracy* (New York: Columbia University Press, 2009), 88; Joseph Kip Koseck, "Selling Gandhi," website of History News Network, George Washington University, March 15, 2009, http://historynewsnetwork.org/article/67719.

68. A. L. Jackson, "Mahatma Gandhi," *Chicago Defender,* December 24, 1921, 16; James Weldon Johnson, "Gandhi a Prisoner," *New York Age,* March 25, 1922, in *The Selected Writings of James Weldon Johnson,* vol. 1, *The New York Age Editorials (1914–1923),* ed. Sondra Kathryn Wilson (New York: Oxford University Press, 1995), 243; Lala Lajpat Rai, "Gandhi and Non-Cooperation," *A.M.E. Church Review* 39 (October 1922): 80–81; E. Franklin Frazier, "The Negro and Non-Resistance," *Crisis* 27, no. 5 (March 1924): 213–214; E. Franklin Frazier, "The Negro and Non-Resistance," *Crisis* 28, no. 2 (June 1924): 58–59.

69. "WP-Enemy Propaganda," subject file, 1911–1927, Naval Records Collection, Record Group 45, United States National Archives, College Park, Maryland; "Talking Points," *Crusader* 2, no. 11 (July 1920): 7; "Black and Brown Races," *Crusader* 4, no. 4 (June 1921): 6; "Liberating Africa," *Crusader* 4, no. 6 (August 1921): 8; "Overseas Correspondence," *Crusader* 2, no. 8 (April 1920): 31; A. L. Jackson, "The Onlooker," *Chicago Defender* 25 (March 1922): 12; "The Mystic Gandhi Imprisoned," *Norfolk Journal and Guide* (April 1, 1922): 4; Du Bois, "Opinion," *Crisis* 23 (April 1922): 247; Du Bois, "Opinion," *Crisis* 24 (May 1922): 7; Saint Nihal Singh, "A Negro Educator's Unique Ideals and Successful Methods," *Modern Review* (1908); Saint Nihal Singh, "Colour Line in the United States of America," *Modern Review* (November 1908).

70. Du Bois, "The Outer Pocket," *Crisis* (June 1925): 93–94; Chaturvedi to Du Bois, January 19, 1925, and September 15, 1925, reel 15, W.E.B. Du Bois

Papers, Special Collections and University Archives, University of Massachusetts Amherst Libraries.

71. W. E. B. Du Bois, *Dark Princess: A Romance* (New York: Harcourt, Brace, 1928), 22. Also see Bill Mullen, "Du Bois, Dark Princess, and the Afro-Asian International," *Positions: East Asia Cultures Critique* 11, no. 1 (Spring 2003): 217–239.

72. Du Bois, "The Outer Pocket," *Crisis* (June 1925): 94; Abdur Raoof Malik to Du Bois, reel 22, Du Bois Papers; Rammanohar Lohia to Du Bois, July 20, 1936, reel 45, Du Bois Papers.

73. Robert A. Hill, ed., *The Marcus Garvey and Universal Negro Improvement Association Papers* (MGUNIA), Vol. 2 (Berkeley: University of California Press, 1983), 500 and 502; MGUNIA 3: 734–36. See also MGUNIA 4: 267, 523–525, 891: 601–603 and 636; MGUNIA 5: 645; H. C. [*sic*] Mudgal, "Who Will Help?" *Negro World*, February 1, 1930, 4; Hucheshwar G. Mudgal, *Marcus Garvey: Is He the True Redeemer of the Negro* (New York: African Publication Society, 1932); Sudarshan Kapur, *Raising Up a Prophet: The African American Encounter with Gandhi* (Boston: Beacon Press, 1992), 21–22 *Negro World,* May 6, 1922, 2; Haridas Muzumdar, "Gandhi the Apostle of Freedom," *Negro World,* May 6, 1922, 2l; and Gandhi, "Negroes' Sympathy," August 21, 1924, CWMG.

74. Spencer Lavan, *The Ahmadiyah Movement: A History and Perspective* (Delhi: Manohar Book Service, 1974); Richard Brent Turner, "The Ahmadiyya Mission to Blacks in the United States," *Journal of Religious Thought* 44, no. 2 (Winter / Spring, 1988): 50–67; Richard Brent Turner, *Islam in the African American Experience,* 2d ed. (Bloomington: Indiana University Press, 2003), 127; Tony Martin, *Race First: The Ideological and Organizational Struggles of Marcus Garvey and the Universal Negro Improvement Association* (Westport, CT: Greenwood Press, 1976), 75–76.

75. "The Rising Tide of Anti-Imperialism," *Independent Hindustan* 1, no. 6 (February 1921): 127, SAADA.

76. Sohi, *Echoes of Mutiny,* 99; "International Aspects of the Indian Question," *Independent Hindustan* 1, no. 6 (February 1921): 130–131, SAADA.

77. Du Bois to Gandhi, February 19, 1929, Du Bois Papers; Mahatma Gandhi, "To the American Negro," *Crisis* 36, no. 7 (July 1929): 225; "Message from Gandhi Published in Crisis," *New York Amsterdam News,* July 19 1929, 20; Anupama Rao, *The Caste Question: Dalits and the Politics of Modern India* (Berkeley: University of California Press, 2009), 1.

78. "Hail Gandhi a 'Second Moses' in U.S," *Chicago Defender,* October 17, 1931, 13; see Kapur, *Raising Up a Prophet,* 82–100.

79. Howard Thurman, "What We May Learn from India," in *A Strange Freedom: The Best of Howard Thurman on Religious Experience and Public Life,* edited by Walter Earl Fluker and Catherine Tumber (Boston: Beacon Press, 1998), 206, and 209–210; Kapur, *Raising Up a Prophet,* 83.

80. Howard Thurman, *With Head and Heart* (New York: Harcourt Brace Jova-
    novich, 1979), 128 and 131–135; Mahadev Desai, "With Our Negro Guests,"
    *Harijan* (March 14, 1936); Kapur, *Raising Up a Prophet*, 91–93.
81. See Howard Thurman to Miss Mabel E. Simpson, India Miscellaneous File,
    box 65, Howard Thurman Papers, Boston University; Kapur, *Raising Up a
    Prophet*, 82; Thurman, *With Head and Heart*, 131–135.
82. Benjamin E. Mays, "The Color Line Around the World," *Journal of Negro Ed-
    ucation* 6, no. 2 (April 1937): 134–143; Benjamin E. Mays, *Born to Rebel: An
    Autobiography* (New York: Scribner, 1971), 153–155; "Interview to Professor
    Mays," CWMG, extracted from Mahadev Desai, "A Discourse on Nonvio-
    lence," *Harijan* (March 20, 1937).
83. Mays, *Born to Rebel*, 156–159.

## Chapter 4: Cold Wars

Epigraph: Gandhi to Franklin Roosevelt, July 1, 1942, *Collected Works of Mahatma Gandhi* (CWMG) Electronic Book (New Delhi: Government of India,
1999).

1. Eugene B. Vest, "Native Words Learned by American Soldiers in India
   and Burma in World War II," *American Speech* 23, no. 3/4 (October–
   December 1948): 223–231; Charles F. Romanus and Riley Sunderland, *Stil-
   well's Mission to China* (Washington, DC: Office of the Chief of Military
   History, Department of the Army, 1953), *Stilwell's Command Problems*
   (Washington, DC: Office of the Chief of Military History, Department of the
   Army, 1956), and *Time Runs Out in CBI* (Washington, DC: Office of the Chief
   of Military History, Department of the Army, 1959); "Participation of Negro
   Troops in the Post-War Military Establishment," from the Headquarters of
   the India Burma Theater to the Adjutant General, August 29, 1945, War Department, box 57, file 291.1, National Archives of the United States (NAUS),
   Washington, DC.
2. Deton J. Brooks, "U.S. Soldier Hangs in India," *Chicago Defender*, April 7, 1945,
   10; Brendan I. Koerner, *Now the Hell Will Start: One Soldier's Flight from the
   Greatest Manhunt of World War II* (New York: Penguin Press, 2008); Wil Hay-
   good, "The Jungle of a Life," *Washington Post*, June 4, 2008.
3. Deton J. Brooks, "Negro GIs Jim Crowed in India; Red Cross Worker Quits
   in Protest," *Chicago Defender*, July 14, 1945, 1; and Deton J. Brooks, "Negro
   GIs Snub U.S. Jim Crow Pool in India; Swim with British Troops," *Chicago
   Defender*, July 28, 1945, 5; "4155th Quartermaster Truck Company," 4, "Base
   Section," 7, and "Report of the Headquarters," 18–19, all in "Participation
   of Negro Troops"; Evelio Grillo (AFC/2001/001/13404), Veterans History
   Project, American Folklife Center, Library of Congress; "U.S. Negro Troops
   in Calcutta," Technical Intelligence Report, December 6, 1944, Army Service

Forces Office of the Commanding General, RG 107, Assistant Secretary of War Civilian Aide, box 265, NAUS.

4. Gandhi to Franklin Roosevelt, July 1, 1942, CWMG; interview to Preston Grover, June 21, 1942, CWMG. Also see Thomas Guglielmo, *Race War: World War II and the Crisis of American Democracy* (New York: Oxford University Press, forthcoming); Gerald Horne, *Race War: White Supremacy and the Japanese Attack on the British Empire* (New York: New York University Press, 2004).

5. Mary L. Dudziak, *Cold War Civil Rights: Race and the Image of American Democracy* (Princeton: Princeton University Press, 2000); Thomas Borstelmann, *The Cold War and the Color Line: American Race Relations in the Global Arena* (Cambridge, MA: Harvard University Press, 2001).

6. Carol Anderson, *Eyes off the Prize: The United Nations and the African American Struggle for Human Rights, 1944–1955* (Cambridge, UK: Cambridge University Press, 2003).

7. Elwood Jones, "Indian Phonograph," *The CBI Roundup* III, no. 16 (December 28, 1944), http://www.cbi-theater.com/roundup/roundup122844 .html.

8. *The Calcutta Key*, Information and Education Branch, United States Army Forces in India—Buram, http://www.cbi-theater.com/calcuttakey/calcutta _key.html.

9. Madhusree Mukerjee, *Churchill's Secret War: The British Empire and the Ravaging of India during World War II* (New York: Basic Books, 2011); Srinath Raghavan, *India's War: World War II and the Making of Modern South Asia* (New York: Basic Books, 2016); "The Bengal Famine," *New York Review of Books,* December 24, 2011, www.nybooks.com/articles/2011/02/24/bengal-famine/.

10. *The Calcutta Key*, Information and Education Branch, United States Army Forces in India—Buram, http://www.cbi-theater.com/calcuttakey/calcutta _key.html.

11. Jawaharlal Nehru to Franklin Roosevelt, April 12, 1942, *Foreign Relations of the United States* (FRUS) I (1942): 635–637.

12. Richard H. Davis, *South Asia at Chicago: A History.* University of Chicago, Committee on Southern Asian Studies, New Series, No.1 (April, 1985), 18, available at https://southasia.uchicago.edu/sites/southasia.uchicago.edu/files /A%20History%20by%20Richard%20Davis.pdf.

13. Gandhi to FDR, July 1, 1942, CWMG.

14. Harold A. Gould, *Sikhs, Swamis, Students, and Spies: The India Lobby in the United States, 1900–1946* (New Delhi and Thousand Oaks, CA: Sage Publications, 2006).

15. Vida Scudder, *On Journey* (New York: Dutton, 1937), 17, 34, 363, 433; Will Durant, *The Case for India* (New York: Simon and Schuster, 1930).

16. Pearl Buck to Eleanor Roosevelt, March 7, 1942, container 55, India, President's Secretary's Files, Roosevelt Papers, FDR Presidential Library and Museum, Hyde Park, NY; Peter Conn, *Pearl S. Buck: A Cultural Biography* (Cambridge, UK: Cambridge University Press, 1998), 282; John Gunther,

*Inside Asia* (New York: Harper and Bros., 1942); "India's Nehru," *Time* (August 24, 1942).

17. *Congressional Record,* 1941, Appendix, p. A843; *Congressional Record,* 1942, p. 6003; Willkie quoted in *New York Times,* October 27, 1942; Emanuel Celler, "Justice to Our Ally, India—Repeal Exclusion of Her Nationals," April 17, 1944, quoted in Iftikhar H Malik, *US-South Asian Relations 1940–47: American Attitudes toward the Pakistan Movement* (New York: Palgrave Macmillan, 1991), 301.

18. Winston Churchill, *India: Speeches and an Introduction* (London: T. Butterworth, 1931), 30, 77, 136, 588.

19. Office of Strategic Services (OSS), British Empire Section, special memorandums #24, January 7, 1942, and #25, January 15, 1942, *Office of Strategic Services / State Department Intelligence and Research Reports, Part III: China and India,* microfilm, University Publications of America, Bethesda, MD; Krishnalal Shridharani to Conyers Read, January 21, 1942, in William J. Donovan to Franklin D. Roosevelt, February 11, 1942, President's Secretary's File, 164, OSS, Donovan Reports, Roosevelt Papers.

20. President Roosevelt to the British Prime Minister (Churchill), March 10, 1942, FRUS I (1942): 615–616; Kenton J. Clymer, "Franklin D. Roosevelt, Louis Johnson, India, and Anticolonialism: Another Look," *Pacific Historical Review* 57, no. 3 (August 1988): 261–284; The Acting Secretary of State to the Ambassador in the United Kingdom (a letter from Roosevelt to Churchill), April 11, 1942, FRUS I (1942): 633–634.

21. Kenton Clymer, "The Education of William Phillips: Self Determination and American Policy toward India, 1942–1945," *Diplomatic History* VIII (1984): 13–35; Hull telegram quoted in Kenton J. Clymer, *Quest for Freedom: The United States and India's Independence* (New York: Columbia University Press, 1995), 132–133; William Phillips, *Ventures in Diplomacy* (Boston: Beacon Press, 1952).

22. Phillips to Secretary of State, February 19, 1943, in FRUS IV, *The Near East and Africa* (1943): 196–197; Clymer, "The Education of William Phillips."

23. Phillips report to FDR, March 3, 1943, in FRUS IV (1943): 205–207; Phillips to Roosevelt, May 14, 1943, FRUS IV (1943): 220–222.

24. A. Hope Guy, *America and Swaraj: The U.S. Role in Indian Independence* (Washington, DC: Public Affairs Press, 1968); Gary Hess, *America Encounters India, 1941–1947* (Baltimore: Johns Hopkins University Press, 1972); Clymer, *Quest for Freedom.*

25. Phillips to Secretary of State, February 19, 1943, in FRUS IV; John Davies, "The Indian Problem: Fall and Winter 1942–43," 8–10, 17, 29–31, January 23, 1943, Joseph Stilwell Papers, box 52, folder 14, Hoover Institution Archives, Palo Alto, CA.

26. Sumner Welles to Roosevelt, May 22, 1942, folder 14, box 151, Welles Papers, Franklin D. Roosevelt Presidential Library and Museum, Hyde Park, NY; White to Buck, June 5, 1942, "India 1942, June-Dec.," box A320, NAACP Papers, Library of Congress, Washington, DC.

27. Speech at A.I.C.C. Meeting, August 7, 1942, CWMG.

28. Nico Slate, "'I Am a Colored Woman': Kamaladevi Chattopadhyay in the United States, 1939–41," *Contemporary South Asia* 17, no. 1 (March 2009): 7–19; "Radio Today," *New York Times,* April 7, 1941; 76th Congress, "Hearings on Repeal of Chinese Exclusion Act, House Committee on Immigration and Naturalization," May 19–June 3, 1943, pp. 33–42, quoted in Tapan K. Mukherjee, *Taraknath Das: Life and Letters of a Revolutionary in Exile* (Calcutta: National Council of Education, Bengal, 1997), 207–208.

29. Langston Hughes, "Here to Yonder," *Chicago Defender,* January 30, 1943, 14; "Gandhi Is Fasting," *The Collected Poems of Langston Hughes,* ed. Arnold Rampersad, assoc. ed. David Roessel (New York: Knopf, 1994), 578.

30. White to Singh, June 27, 1944, subject file 35, JJ Singh Papers, Nehru Memorial Museum and Library (NMML), New Delhi; JJ Singh to Vijaya Lakshmi Pandit, August 23, 1944, JJ Singh Papers; Walter White, "The Work of the India League," *Chicago Defender,* February 24, 1945, 11; Hemendra K. Rakhit to White, September 5, 1945, box A378, NAACP Papers; Walter White to JJ Singh, June 9, 1947, JJ Singh Papers; Ralph Izard, "Gandhi's Son Asks Negro Aid for People of India," *Chicago Defender,* May 18, 1946, 1 and 6, and "Gandhi's Son in U.S.," *Chicago Defender,* May 25, 1946, 13. Singh and Walsh to White, May 20, 1946; White to John Sengstacke, Ira F. Lewis, and Carl Murphy, all June 3, 1946; Edmondson to *Chicago Defender,* June 3, 1946— all in box A378, NAACP Papers. See also Frenise A. Logan, "Racism and Indian-U.S. Relations, 1947–1953: Views in the Indian Press," *Pacific Historical Review* 54 (February 1985): 71–79.

31. Vijaya Lakshmi Pandit, *The Scope of Happiness: A Personal Memoir* (New York: Crown Publishers, 1979), 191–192; Toki Schalk, "Madame Pandit, Indian Leader, Found Happiest Hour in Harlem," *Pittsburgh Courier,* April 14, 1945, 5; Walter White, "People, Politics and Places," *Chicago Defender,* June 30, 1945, 13.

32. Robert Trumball, "India and Pakistan Become Nations; Clashes Continue," *New York Times,* August 15, 1947; "Mountbatten New Governor of Hindu India; Punjab Riots Rage On; 250 Dead," *Chicago Daily Tribune,* August 15, 1947; "India Achieves Sovereignty amid Scenes of Wild Rejoicing," *Washington Post,* August 15, 1947; "Letter from Indian Students' Association," August 15, 1947, South Asian American Digital Archives (SAADA), www.saada.org/item/20141107-3974; "Store Window Decorated for Indian Independence," SAADA, www.saada.org/item/20110712-233.

33. W. E. B. Du Bois, "The Freeing of India," *Crisis* 54 (October 1947): 301–304, 316; "A Dream Comes True in India," *Pittsburgh Courier,* August 23, 1947, 6; "Colored Races Hail India's New Freedom," *Chicago Defender,* August 23, 1947; Walter White, "Britain Moves Out of India," *Chicago Defender,* August 30, 1947, 15; Kumar Goshal, "As An Indian Sees It: Existence of Two Indian States Charged against Great Britain; Duty Is to Work for Merger of Two Nations Soon," *Chicago Defender,* August 30, 1947.

34. "Prime Minister Nehru Gets First Hand Briefing on Problem; Dr. Bunche, Walter White Serve as Chairmen of Meeting," *Atlanta Daily World*, November 9, 1949, 1; Brenda Gayle Plummer, *Rising Wind: Black Americans and U.S. Foreign Affairs, 1935–1960* (Chapel Hill, NC: The University of North Carolina Press, 1996), 219; "Nehru Presented Life Membership in NAACP," *Atlanta Daily World*, November 11, 1949, 2, and "Jawaharlal Nehru Joins the NAACP," *New York Amsterdam News*, November 12, 1949, 1; Robert Shelby, "Nehru Shook My Hand," *Chicago Defender*, November 5, 1949, 6.

35. J. J. Singh to Jawaharlal Nehru, April 10, 1942, JJ Singh Papers; Nehru, Note for Asaf Ali and K. P. S. Menon, January 22, 1947, K. P. S. Menon Papers, NMML.

36. Maia Ramnath, *Haj to Utopia: How the Ghadar Movement Charted Global Radicalism and Attempted to Overthrow the British Empire* (Berkeley and Los Angeles: University of California Press, 2011), 140; T. R. Sareen, *Indian Revolutionary Movement Abroad* (New Delhi: Sterling, 1979), 94; Senate Fact-Finding Committee, *Seventh Report on Un-American Activities in California* (Sacramento: California Senate Printing Office, 1953). Also see Paul M. McGarr, *The Cold War in South Asia: Britain, the United States and the Indian Subcontinent, 1945–1965* (Cambridge, UK: Cambridge University Press, 2013); Robert J. McMahon, *The Cold War on the Periphery: The United States, India, and Pakistan* (New York: Columbia University Press, 1994).

37. Jawaharlal Nehru, "Speech to the U.S. Congress," October 13, 1949, website of Yuvasena Youth Association, www.yuvasena.com/nehru_congress _oct_13_1949.html; "The Prime Minister of India, Pandit Jawaharlal Nehru, Addressed a House Reception," October 13, 1949, website of the U.S. House of Representatives, accessed March 2018, http://history.house.gov/Historical Highlight/Detail/36630?ret=True. Also see Jawaharlal Nehru, *Visit to America* (New York: John Day, 1950).

38. Roger Baldwin to Jawaharlal Nehru, April 29, 1931, in *A Bunch of Old Letters: Being Mostly Written to Jawaharlal Nehru and Some Written by Him*, ed. Jawaharlal Nehru (London: Penguin, 1958), 100–101; Robert M. Crunden, ed. *The Traffic of Ideas between India and America* (Delhi: Chanakya Publications, 1985), 15–16; Kenton Clymer, "Jawaharlal Nehru and the United States, the Preindependence Years," *Diplomatic History* 14 (Spring 1990): 143–161; Nico Slate, *The Prism of Race: W.E.B. Du Bois, Langston Hughes, Paul Robeson and the Colored World of Cedric Dover* (New York: Palgrave Macmillan, 2014), 85–112.

39. Kux, *India and the United States: Estranged Democracies, 1941–1991* (Thousand Oaks, CA: Sage Publications, 1994), 51.

40. Jawaharlal Nehru, "Speech to the U.S. Congress"; "The Prime Minister of India, Pandit Jawaharlal Nehru, Addressed a House Reception"; Nehru, "The Pursuit of Peace: Armaments Will Not Solve Basic Problems," speech at Columbia University, October 17, 1949, published in Jawaharlal Nehru, *Speeches from 1949–1953* (New Delhi: Publications Division, Government of India, 1954), 402.

41. Srinivas M. Chary, *The Eagle and the Peacock: U.S. Foreign Policy toward India since Independence* (Westport, CT: Greenwood Press, 1995), 81–82.

42. Kux, *India and the United States*, 72; Sarvepalli Gopal, *Jawaharlal Nehru: A Biography*, Vol. 2, 1947–1956 (Cambridge, MA: Harvard University Press, 1980), 60–61; Chary, *The Eagle and the Peacock*, 64 and 74; L. S. Srivastava and V. P. Joshi, *International Relations: From 1914 to Present Day* (Meerut: GOEL, 2005), 210.

43. "Dulles Declares Neutrality Pose Is Obsolete Idea," *New York Times*, June 10, 1956; Attar Chand, *Nuclear Policy and National Security* (New Delhi: Mittal, 1993), 123; Acheson quoted in Dennis Merrill, "Indo-American Relations, 1947–50: A Missed Opportunity in Asia," *Diplomatic History* 11, no. 3 (July 1987); Dean Acheson, *Present at the Creation* (London: Hamish Hamilton, 1970), 333–335 and 420; George McGhee, *Envoy to the Middle World: Adventures in Diplomacy* (New York: Harper and Row, 1983), 52.

44. *Time*, February 2, 1962; Paul M. McGarr, "'India's Rasputin'?: V. K. Krishna Menon and Anglo-American Misperceptions of Indian Foreign Policy-making, 1947–1964," *Diplomacy and Statecraft* 22, no. 2 (2011), www.tandfonline.com/doi/full/10.1080/09592296.2011.576536.

45. Andrew J. Rotter, *Comrades at Odds: The United States and India, 1947–1964* (Ithaca: Cornell University Press, 2000).

46. Kux, *India and the United States*, 72; Gopal, *Jawaharlal Nehru*, 2:60–61; Chary, *The Eagle and the Peacock*, 74.

47. Eisenhower to Nehru, February 25, 1954, OF8-F, Eisenhower Papers, Dwight D. Eisenhower Presidential Library and Museum, Abilene, Kansas; U.S. Senate, "The Mutual Security Act of 1959," 86th Congress, 1st Session, Committee on Foreign Relations, Hearings (Washington, DC: Government Printing Office 1959), 1:205; Chary, *The Eagle and the Peacock*, 103.

48. Nehru to Kennedy, December 29, 1961, Countries File, box 118, President's Office Files (POF), John F. Kennedy Presidential Library and Museum (JFKL), Boston; Kennedy to Prime Minister Nehru, January 18, 1962, FRUS XIX (1961–1963), South Asia, Document 95.

49. Memo for record by Bundy, "The President's Views on India as Expressed at 25 April Meeting," April 26, 1963, National Security Council (NSC) Meetings and Memoranda, box 314, "NSC Meetings," no. 514, JFKL; FRUS XIX (1961–1963), South Asia, 563–584; "Summary Record of National Security Council Meeting," May 9, 1963, NSC Meetings and Memoranda, box 314, JFKL.

50. Kennedy, "If India Falls," *Progressive* (January 1958): 8–11; John F. Kennedy, *The Strategy of Peace* (New York: Harper & Brothers, 1960), 142–143; Arthur Schlesinger, *A Thousand Days: John F. Kennedy in the White House* (Boston: Houghton Mifflin, 1965), 522; Memo from Bowles to Kennedy, "U.S. Policy Toward India," May 4, 1963, NSC Meetings and Memoranda, box 314, "NSC Meetings, 1963, no. 154, 4/25/63," JFKL.

51. Pauli Murray, *Song in a Weary Throat: An American Pilgrimage* (New York: Harper and Row, 1987), 138 and 144; Glenda Gilmore, *Defying Dixie: The Radical Roots of Civil Rights, 1919–1950* (New York: Norton, 2008), 287–288 and 315–329; "Murray to Jean and Pan," April 2, 1940, and "Petersburg Bus Incident," file 86, box 4, Pauli Murray Papers (PMP), Schlesinger Library, Radcliffe Institute, Cambridge, MA.

52. Murray to Dame, March 24, 1940, "Petersburg Bus Incident," file 85, box 4, PMP; Robert H. Cooley Jr. to Murray and McBean, April 8, 1940, "Petersburg Bus Incident," file 85, box 4, PMP; Harold Garfinkel, "Color Trouble," *Opportunity* (May 1940): 144–151; Gilmore, *Defying Dixie,* 287–288 and 315–329.

53. Murray, "Interview with Dr. ____," pp. 1–2, December 16, 1937, file 71, box 4, PMP; Joanne J. Meyerowitz, *How Sex Changed: A History of Transsexuality in the United States* (Cambridge, MA: Harvard University Press, 2002), 37; Doreen M. Drury, "Love, Ambition, and 'Invisible Footnotes' in the Life and Writing of Pauli Murray," in *Black Genders and Sexualities,* eds. Shaka McGlotten and Dána-Ain Davis (New York: Palgrave Macmillan, 2012), 73; Dayo Gore, *Radicalism at the Crossroads: African American Women Activists in the Cold War* (New York: New York University Press, 2011); Jennifer Terry, *An American Obsession: Science, Medicine, and Homosexuality in Modern America* (Chicago: University of Chicago Press, 1999); Anne Fausto-Sterling, *Sexing the Body: Gender Politics and the Construction of Sexuality* (New York: Basic Books, 2000); Nancy Ordover, *American Eugenics: Race, Queer Anatomy, and the Science of Nationalism* (Minneapolis: University of Minnesota Press, 2003).

54. See "History / Beginnings" and Allen Bacon's "Recollections of Ahimsa Farm," May 4, 1989, Ahimsa Farm papers, Swarthmore College Peace Collection, Swarthmore College, Swarthmore, PA; August Meier and Elliott Rudwick, *CORE: A Study in the Civil Rights Movement, 1942–1968* (New York: Oxford University Press, 1973).

55. Art Preis, "Permanent Organization Established," *Militant* (October 3, 1942), in *Fighting Racism in World War II,* ed. Fred Stanton (New York: Pathfinder, 1980), 261; Nico Slate, *Colored Cosmopolitanism: The Shared Struggle for Freedom in the United States and India* (Cambridge, MA: Harvard University Press, 2012).

56. "Randolph Makes Plea for India," *Chicago Defender,* October 24, 1942, 8; "Urge Race to Support India," *Baltimore Afro-American,* August 22, 1942.

57. "On Mr. Randolph's Proposal for Negro Action," *Atlanta Daily World,* January 19, 1943; "Citizens Repudiate Non-Violence Program: Feel Gandhi's Way Is Not Comparable to U.S. Situation," *Pittsburgh Courier,* April 24, 1943, 4. Also see "Civil Disobedience," *Pittsburgh Courier,* January 23, 1943, 6; James Farmer, ed., "Civil Disobedience: Is It the Answer to Jim Crow?" *Non-Violent Action News Bulletin,* nos. 2 and 3, undated, file 400, box 18, PMP.

58. John D'Emilio, *Lost Prophet: The Life and Times of Bayard Rustin* (New York: Free Press, 2003); and Daniel Levine, *Bayard Rustin and the Civil Rights Movement* (New Brunswick, NJ: Rutgers University Press, 2000).

59. Martin Luther King Jr., *Stride toward Freedom: The Montgomery Story* (New York: Harper and Row, 1958), 96; "The Ghost of Gandhi Walks Montgomery Streets," *New Republic* (March 12, 1956); "Attack on the Conscience," *Time* (February 18, 1957); Dr. Samuel Dubois Cook to King, March 23 1956, *The Papers of Martin Luther King, Jr. Volume III: Birth of a New Age, December 1955-December 1956*, eds. Clayborne Carson, Stewart Burns, Susan Carson, Peter Holloran, and Dana L.H. Powell (Berkeley: University of California Press, 1997), 203–204; J. Martin England to King, April 29, 1956, King Papers, vol. III, 232; "King Speaks at Big Rally in Brooklyn," *Montgomery Advertiser*, March 26, 1956; Stanley Rowland Jr., "2500 Here Hail Boycott Leader," *New York Times*, March 26, 1956, 27; Harris Wofford, *Of Kennedys and Kings: Making Sense of the Sixties* (New York: Farrar, Straus, Giroux, 1980), 118–123.

60. David J. Garrow, *Bearing the Cross: Martin Luther King, Jr. and the Southern Christian Leadership Conference* (New York: Vintage Press, 1988), 89–90, and Wesley C. Hogan, *Many Minds, One Heart: SNCC's Dream for a New America* (Chapel Hill: University of North Carolina Press, 2007), chapter 1.

61. Kaka Kalelkar and Sarojini Nanavati to King, September 9, 1958, in King Papers vol. IV, 493–494; "Nehru 'Pleased' by Sit-In Movement," *New York Amsterdam News*, October 15, 1960, 8; Rosemary Donihi, "Non-Violence Is Best Route Out," *Washington Post*, April 28, 1960, subject file 61, MC Chagla Papers, NMML; "Coexistence Theme Urged by an Envoy," *Kansas City Star*, May 10, 1960, and "Chagla Tells KU Coexistence Best," *Lawrence Daily Journal World*, May 10, 1960, subject file 61, MC Chagla Papers.

62. "Correspondence Carried Out with the Foreign / Indian Contributors to Do articles for World Satyagraha Number of 'Mankind,'" subject number 753, Socialist Party Papers, NMML; "Non-Violent Struggle in America," *United Asia* 14, no. 10 (October 1962): 550. Also see K. T. Narasimha Char, "Mahatma Gandhi's Concept of Passive Resistance and Its Efficacy at the Present Day," *United Asia* 20, no. 5 (September / October 1968): 265; and J. Shaffer, "Satyagraha's Twenty-Fifth Anniversary in the United States," *United Asia* 17, no. 1 (January / February 1965): 5–7.

63. Their trip was planned by the American Friends Service Committee. David Gale to Acharya Kripalani, May 16, 1960, in "Tour of the USA," subject file 66, Sucheta Kripalani Papers, NMML; "Wife Gives Him Two Votes," *Washington Post*, April 18, 1960, subject file 61, MC Chagla Papers, NMML; email correspondence from Jaswant Krishnayya and Ahmed Meer to the author.

64. "Mississippi Oust Indian Politician from a Cafeteria," *New York Times*, May 29, 1964; "U.S. Plans an Apology," *New York Times*, May 29, 1964; "Jackson, Miss., Hit by Indian Socialist," *New York Times*, May 30, 1964; Edwin King, "Lohia and the American Civil Rights Movement," *Gandhi Marg* 59 (1971): 270–277; "Color Arrest Pleases Man from India," *Chicago Daily Defender*, June 3, 1964.

65. Rammanohar Lohia to Roma Mitra, January 28, 1960, Rammanohar Lohia Papers, NMML; Edwin King, "Lohia and the American Civil Rights Movement."

66. Rammanohar Lohia to Du Bois, July 20, 1936, reel 45, W.E.B. Du Bois Papers, Special Collections and University Archives, University of Massachusetts Amherst Libraries; Wofford, *Of Kennedys and Kings,* 110; Wofford to Lohia, May 1952–December 1952, Correspondence Received, subject number 86, Socialist Party Papers, NMML.

67. Anne Moody, *Coming of Age in Mississippi* (New York: Dial Press, 1968); Meier and Rudwick, *CORE,* 414–415; Simon Wendt, *The Spirit and the Shotgun: Armed Resistance and the Struggle for Civil Rights* (Gainesville: University Press of Florida, 2007), 140; Timothy B. Tyson, *Radio Free Dixie: Robert F. Williams and the Roots of Black Power* (Chapel Hill: University of North Carolina Press, 1999).

68. *Gandhi on Nonviolence,* ed. Thomas Merton (New York: New Directions, 1965); Merton to Sister Therese Lentfoehr, September 28, 1965, in *Thomas Merton: A Life in Letters,* eds. William H. Shannon and Christine M. Bochen (Notre Dame, IN: Ave Maria Press, 2008), 97–98.

69. Singh to Jayaprakash Narayan, February 23, 1968 and June 16, 1969, JJ Singh Papers.

70. Anna Thomas, *The Vegetarian Epicure* (New York: Vintage, 1972), 251–253. Also see Rachel Laudan, *Cuisine and Empire: Cooking in World History* (Berkeley: University of California Press, 2013); Krishnendu Ray and Tulasi Srinivas, eds., *Curried Cultures: Globalization, Food, and South Asia* (Berkeley: University of California Press, 2012); Lizzie Collingham, *Curry: A Tale of Cooks and Conquerors* (Oxford, UK: Oxford University Press, 2007); Susan Zlotnick, "Domesticating Imperialism: Curry and Cookbooks in Victorian England," *Frontiers: A Journal of Women Studies* 16, nos. 2–3 (1996): 51–68; Arjun Appadurai, "How to Make a National Cuisine: Cookbooks in Contemporary India," *Comparative Studies in Society and History* 30, no. 1 (1988): 2–34.

71. Dean Nelson, "American Pastor Says Yoga Is 'Demonic,'" *Telegraph,* October 19, 2010, www.telegraph.co.uk/news/worldnews/northamerica/usa /8071253/American-pastor-says-yoga-is-demonic.html; William Kremer, "Does Doing Yoga Make You a Hindu?," BBC, November 21, 2013, www.bbc .co.uk/news/magazine-25006926. Also see Tamara Lizette Brown and Baruti N. Kopano, eds., *Soul Thieves: The Appropriation and Misrepresentation of African American Popular Culture* (New York: Palgrave MacMillan, 2014); Bruce Ziff and Pratima V. Rao, *Borrowed Power: Essays on Cultural Appropriation* (New Brunswick, NJ: Rutgers University Press, 1997).

72. Raj Kumar Gupta, *The Great Encounter: A Study of Indo-American Literature and Cultural Relations* (New Delhi: Abhinav, 1986), 154; "Opera on Mahatma Gandhi: Satyagraha," *Span* (January 1982): 5; Peter Lavezzoli, *The Dawn of Indian Music in the West* (London and New York: Continuum, 2006).

73. Bradley Shope, *American Popular Music in Britain's Raj* (Rochester, NY: University of Rochester Press, 2016).

74. For a thoughtful analysis of *Amar Akbar Anthony* and its legacy, see William Elison, Christian Lee Novetzke, and Andy Rotman, *Amar Akbar Anthony: Bollywood, Brotherhood, and the Nation* (Cambridge, MA: Harvard University Press, 2016).

75. "Niranjan Jhaveri Talks about Indian Music and Jazz," *Span* (May 1978): 29.

76. Lavezzoli, *The Dawn of Indian Music in the West*, 267–295; J. C. Thomas, *Chasin' the Trane: The Music and Mystique of John Coltrane* (New York: Doubleday, 1975), 199–200.

77. Franya J. Berkman, *Monument Eternal: The Music of Alice Coltrane* (Middletown, CT: Wesleyan University Press, 2010), 2; Hua Hsu, "Alice Coltrane's Devotional Music," *New Yorker*, April 24, 2017, www.newyorker.com/magazine /2017/04/24/alice-coltranes-devotional-music; Andrew Katzenstein, "Alice Coltrane's Songs of Bliss," *New York Review of Books*, August 24, 2017, www .nybooks.com/daily/2017/08/24/alice-coltranes-songs-of-bliss/.

78. As R. N. Mookerjee has discussed, Dreiser's wife, Helen, had a deep interest in Hindu philosophy and seems to have strongly influenced the concluding section of *The Stoic*. Theodore Dreiser, *The Stoic* (New York: Doubleday, 1947); R. N. Mookerjee, "Dreiser's Use of Hindu Thought in *The Stoic*," *American Literature* 43, no. 2 (May 1971): 273–278.

79. John Steinbeck, *Cannery Row* (New York: Viking, 1945).

80. Henry Miller, *The Books in My Life* (New York: New Directions, 1969), 150; Pupul Jayakar, *J. Krishnamurti: A Biography* (New York: Penguin, 2003).

81. Allen Ginsberg, *Indian Journals* (New York: Grove Press, 1970), 128–129.

82. Joshua M. Greene, *Swami in a Strange Land: How Krishna Came to the West* (San Rafael, CA: Mandala, 2016); Edwin Bryant and Maria Ekstrand, eds., *The Hare Krishna Movement: The Postcharismatic Fate of a Religious Transplant* (New York: Columbia University Press, 2004); Allen Ginsberg, "Swami Bhaktivedanta Chanting God's Song in America," *Allen & Prabhupada* (Krishna Weekend 2), March 3, 2013, http://ginsbergblog.blogspot.com/2013/03/allen -prabhupada-krishna-weekend-2.html; "A Conversation between A.C. Bhaktivedanta Swami & Allen Ginsberg," posted on April 2, 2016, https:// theharekrishnamovement.org/2016/04/02/a-conversation-between-a-c -bhaktivedanta-swami-allen-ginsberg/#more-9675.

83. Gita Mehta, *Karma Cola: Marketing the Mystic East* (New York: Simon and Schuster, 1979), 17, 19, 179, 192.

84. On Bhagwan Shree Rajneesh and Rajneeshpuram, see the documentary *Wild, Wild Country*, directed by Maclain Way and Chapman Way, *Netflix*, 2018; Paul Heelas, *The New Age Movement: The Celebration of the Self and the Sacralization of Modernity* (Oxford: Blackwell Publishers, 1996); James S. Gordon, *Golden Guru: The Strange Journey of Bhagwan Shree Rajneesh* (Brattleboro, VT: Stephen Greene Press, 1987); Judith Thompson and Paul Heelas, *The Way of the Heart: The Rajneesh Movement* (Wellingborough: Aquarian Press, 1986).

85. Allen Ginsberg, "Swami Bhaktivedanta Chanting God's Song in America," Allen & Prabhupada (Krishna Weekend 2), March 3, 2013, http://ginsbergblog .blogspot.com/2013/03/allen-prabhupada-krishna-weekend-2.html.

86. Merton to Loña Luisa Coomaraswamy, January 13, 1961 and February 12, 1961, in *Thomas Merton: A Life in Letters,* eds. Shannon and Bochen, 379–380; Chakravarty to Merton, March 29, 1967, and Merton to Chakravarty, April 13, 1967, in *Thomas Merton: A Life in Letters,* eds. Shannon and Bochen, 381–382.

87. Douglas Martin, "Swami Satchidananda, Woodstock's Guru, Dies at 87," *New York Times,* August 21, 2002, www.nytimes.com/2002/08/21/world /swami-satchidananda-woodstock-s-guru-dies-at-87.html; "Woodstock Guru," Woodstock festival opening address by Sri Swami Satchidananda, August 15, 1969, http://swamisatchidananda.org/woodstock-guru.

## Keyword: *Thug*

Epigraph: Mark Twain, *Following the Equator: A Journey around the World* (Hartford, CT: American Publishing Company, 1898), 437.

Epigraph: Tupac Shakur, "Interview Outside of Court, 1994," available at www.youtube.com/watch?v=VmS83RtszV0.

1. William Henry Sleeman, *Rambles and Recollections of an Indian Official,* revised annotated edition by Vincent A. Smith (Oxford, UK: Oxford University Press, 1915); Edward Thornton, *Illustrations of the History and Practice of the Thugs* (London: W. H. Allen, 1837); Philip Meadows Taylor, *Confessions of a Thug* (Oxford, UK: Oxford University Press, 1839); Mary Poovey, "Ambiguity and Historicism: Interpreting *Confessions of a Thug,*" *Narrative* 12, no. 1 (January 2004).

2. Michael Jeffries, *Thug Life: Race, Gender, and the Meaning of Hip-Hop* (Chicago: The University of Chicago Press, 2011); Jeffrey O. G. Ogbar, "Slouching toward Bork: The Culture Wars and Self-Criticism in Hip-Hop Music," *Journal of Black Studies* 30, no. 2 (November 1999): 164–183; Michelle Alexander, *The New Jim Crow: Mass Incarceration in the Age of Colorblindness* (New York: New Press, 2012); Dexter Rogers, "Seattle Seahawks: Is Richard Sherman a Thug?," *Huffington Post,* January 31, 2014, www.huffingtonpost .com/dexter-rogers/richard-sherman-thug_b_4705030.html; Stephen A. Crockett, "Richard Sherman: Thug Is the New N-Word," *Root,* January 23, 2014, https://www.theroot.com/richard-sherman-thug-is-the-new-n-word -1790874236.

3. H. M. Elliot, *The History of India as Told by Its Own Historians, The Muhammadan Period,* vol. III (London: Trubner, 1871), 141.

4. In response to the revisionist debunking of the myth of the thug, a few recent scholars have countered that thuggee should not be seen only as a

colonial invention. While acknowledging that much of the evidence of thuggee came from testimony under various forms of duress, these post-revisionist historians suggest that the evidence indicates wider patterns of criminality and ritual murder than were acknowledged by the revisionists. Radhika Singha, "'Providential' Circumstances: The Thuggee Campaign of the 1830s and Legal Innovation," *Modern Asian Studies* 27, no. 1 (February 1993): 83–146; Parama Roy, *Indian Traffic: Identities in Question in Colonial and Postcolonial India* (Berkeley: University of California Press, 1998), chapter 2; Máire Ní Fhlathúin, "'That Solitary Englishman': W. H. Sleeman and the Biography of British India," *Victorian Review* 27, no. 1 (Winter 2001): 69–85; Martine van Woerkens, *The Strangled Traveler: Colonial Imaginings and the Thugs of India*, trans. Catherine Tihanyi (Chicago: University of Chicago Press, 2002); C. A. Bayly, *Empire and Information: Intelligence Gathering and Social Communication in India, 1780–1870* (Cambridge, UK: Cambridge University Press, 2000), 171–176. Kim A. Wagner, *Stranglers and Bandits: A Historical Anthology of Thuggee* (Delhi: Oxford University Press, 2009); Kim A. Wagner, *Thuggee: Banditry and the British in Early Nineteenth-Century India* (New York: Palgrave Macmillan, 2007); Kim A. Wagner, "The Deconstructed Stranglers: A Reassessment of Thuggee," *Modern Asian Studies* 38, no. 4 (October 2004): 931–963; Mike Dash, *Thug: The True Story of India's Murderous Cult* (London: Grant Books, 2005); Kevin Rushby, *Children of Kali: Through India in Search of Bandits, the Thug Cult, and the British Raj* (New York: Walker, 2003).

5. Jeanne Morefield, *Empires without Imperialism: Anglo-American Decline and the Politics of Deflection* (Oxford, UK: Oxford University Press, 2014), 16.

6. Emerson, "Human Culture: Introductory Lecture Read at the Masonic Temple in Boston," first given December 6, 1837, in *The Selected Lectures of Ralph Waldo Emerson*, eds. Ronald A. Bosco and Joel Myerson (Athens: University of Georgia Press, 2005).

7. Mark Twain, *Following the Equator: A Journey around the World*, vol. 2 (Hartford, CT: American Publishing Company, 1898), 426. Also see Ron Powers, *Mark Twain: A Life* (New York: Free Press, 2005), and Justin Kaplan, *Mr. Clemens and Mark Twain: A Biography* (New York: Simon and Schuster, 1991).

8. Mark Twain, *Mark Twain's Notebook* (New York: Harper, 1935), 276; Twain, *Following the Equator*, 144, 436–438, 446, 469, 514, 626.

9. Swami Vivekananda, "On Duty," in *Eight Lectures on Karma Yoga* (New York: Brentano's, 1896); Swami Virajananda, *The Life of the Swami Vivekananda*, vol. II (Almora: Advaita Asrhama, 1914), 451.

10. Prem Chowdhry, *Colonial India and the Making of Empire Cinema: Image, Ideology and Identity* (Manchester, UK: Manchester University Press, 2000), 153–155; Frederic Cople Jaher and Blair B. Kling, "Hollywood's India: The Meaning of RKO's *Gunga Din*," *Film and History: An Interdisciplinary Journal of Film and Television Studies* 38, no. 2 (Fall 2008): 33–44.

11. Andrew J. Rotter, "Gender Relations, Foreign Relations: The United States and South Asia, 1947–1964," *Journal of American History* 81 (September 1994): 518–542; Katherine Mayo, *Mother India* (London: Jonathan Cape, 1927).

12. "The Thugs of New-York," *New York Times*, August 24, 1852; "The Magnolia Raid," *New York Times*, July 14, 1864; "Pennsylvania's Fugitive Thugs," *New York Times*, August 6, 1881; "Two Sarasota Thugs Convicted," *New York Times*, June 13, 1885; "New Haven Negro Thug Held," *New York Times Magazine* (June 5, 1904); "The Fate of a Thug," *National Police Gazette* (December 27, 1879): 6; Frank H. Sweet, "The Blue Thugs of the Sea," *Forest and Stream: A Journal of Outdoor Life, Travel, Nature Study, Shooting, Fishing, Yachting* (August 1, 1908): 169; Herbert B. Mayer, "Murder and Robbery as a Business," *McClure's* (June 1924): 52.

13. Wendy S. Jacobson, "John Jasper and Thuggee," *Modern Language Review* 72, no. 3 (July 1977): 526–537; Leon F. Fannin, "Thuggee and Professional Criminality," *Michigan Sociological Review* 5 (Fall 1989); Steve Van Dine, John P. Conrad, and Simon Dinitz, "The Incapacitation of the Chronic Thug," *Journal of Criminal Law and Criminology* 70, no. 1 (Spring 1979): 125–135.

14. Butts was not alone in his attack on thugs and "gangsta rap." C. Delores Tucker, a civil rights activist and president of the National Political Congress of Black Women, became an outspoken critic. Tucker argued that "white corporate America has always feared the black male. It wants to suggest black males are inhuman thugs." Daniel Jeffreys, "They're Poisoning Our Kids," *Independent*, July 30, 1995, www.independent.co.uk/news/theyre-poisoning -our-kids-1594030.html; Sewell Chan, "Speakers Debate Rap Lyrics: Performers, Baptist Minister Square Off over Meaning," *Harvard Crimson*, October 12, 1994; "1993 NBC Report on Gangsta Rap," posted on April 25, 2012, www.poetv.com/video.php?vid=107636.

15. Bone Thugs N' Harmony, "Thuggish Ruggish Bone," https://www.youtube .com/watch?v=2tzSjtuMGOQ, accessed April 13, 2018; Tricia Rose, *Black Noise: Rap Music and Black Culture in Contemporary America* (Middletown, CT: Wesleyan, 1994), 145; Nelson George, *Hip Hop America* (New York: Penguin, 2005); Jeffrey O. G. Ogbar, *Hip-Hop Revolution: The Culture and Politics of Rap* (Lawrence: University Press of Kansas, 2007).

16. Tupac Shakur, "When Thugz Cry," lyrics uploaded to RapGenius.com, http:// rapgenius.com/2pac-when-thugz-cry-lyrics, accessed April 13, 2018.

17. Tupac Shakur, "Interview Outside of Court, 1994," available at www.youtube .com/watch?v=VmS83RtszV0; George James, "Rapper Faces Prison Term for Sex Abuse," *New York Times*, February 8, 1995; Helaine Olen, "Rapper Shakur Gets Prison for Assault," *Los Angeles Times*, February 8, 1995.

18. Tupac Shakur, interview with Arsenio Hall, *The Arsenio Hall Show*, March 8, 1994, available at http://www.youtube.com/watch?v=yzQewzGahwg; also see bell hooks, "Gangsta Culture—Sexism and Misogyny: Who Will Take the Rap?" in *Outlaw Culture* (London: Routledge, 1994), 134–144.

19. Peter Holley, Abby Phillip and Abby Ohlheiser, "Alabama police officer arrested after Indian grandfather left partially paralyzed," *Washington Post*, February 12, 2015, www.washingtonpost.com/news/morning-mix/wp/2015/02/11/alabama-cops-leave-a-grandfather-partially-paralyzed-after-frisk-goes-awry/.

## Chapter 5: The Ends of Poverty

Epigraph: Taraknath Das, "The Struggle of Indians to Attain Equal Rights in the United States of America," *Modern Review* (October 1946): 263–266.

1. Harris Wofford, *Of Kennedys and Kings: Making Sense of the Sixties* (New York: Farrar, Straus, Giroux, 1980), 272.

2. David Busch, "The Politics of International Volunteerism in the 1960s: The Peace Corps and Volunteers to America," *Diplomatic History* (August 2017); "Report on the Experiences of the Five Indian Volunteers in America," Volunteer Forum, June 22, 1966, RG 490, Subject Files of the Office of the Director, 1961–1966, National Archives and Records Administration, College Park, MD.

3. I am grateful to Daniel Immerwahr for helping me see the importance of this point. See Daniel Immerwahr, *Thinking Small: The United States and the Lure of Community Development* (Cambridge, MA: Harvard University Press, 2015). Also see Sheyda F. A. Jahanbani, "One Global War on Poverty: The Johnson Administration Fights Poverty at Home and Abroad, 1964–1968," in *Beyond the Cold War: Lyndon Johnson and the New Global Challenges of the 1960s*, eds. Francis J. Gavin and Mark Atwood Lawrence (Oxford, UK: Oxford University Press, 2014), 97–117.

4. Vijay Prashad, *The Karma of Brown Folk* (Minneapolis: University of Minnesota Press, 2000); Ellen D. Wu, *The Color of Success: Asian Americans and the Origins of the Model Minority* (Princeton, NJ: Princeton University Press, 2014).

5. For contrasting approaches to the relationship between growth and poverty, see Jean Drèze and Amartya Sen, *An Uncertain Glory: India and its Contradictions* (Princeton, NJ: Princeton University Press, 2013), and Jagdish Bhagwati and Arvind Panagariya, *Why Growth Matters: How Economic Growth in India Reduced Poverty and the Lessons for Other Developing Countries* (New York: PublicAffairs, 2014).

6. Walter Smoter Frank, "Swastikas on the Colorado," http://smoter.com/flooddam/swastika.htm, accessed April 13, 2018.

7. Ramachandra Guha, *India After Gandhi: The History of the World's Largest Democracy* (New York: HarperCollins Publishers, 2007), 221–223.

8. Max F. Millikan and W. W. Rostow, *A Proposal: Key to an Effective Foreign Policy* (New York: Harper and Brothers, 1957); Edward Shils, *The Culture of the Indian Intellectual* (Chicago: University of Chicago Press, Committee on South Asian Studies, 1959).

9. Albert Mayer, "Americans in India," *Survey Graphic* (March 1947): 202–206; Alice Thorner, "Nehru, Albert Mayer, and Origins of Community Projects," *Economic and Political Weekly* 24 (January 1981): 117–120.

10. My knowledge of community development was shaped by the scholarship of Daniel Immerwahr and Nick Cullather. See Immerwahr, *Thinking Small,* and Nick Cullather, *The Hungry World: America's Cold War Battle against Hunger* (Cambridge, MA: Harvard University Press, 2010). Also see letter from Nehru to Mayer, May 1, 1946, box 8, folder 1, Albert Mayer Papers on India, University of Chicago Library.

11. Nicole Sackley has an excellent article on Etawah: Nicole Sackley, "Village Models: Etawah, India, and the Making and Remaking of Development in the Early Cold War," *Diplomatic History* 37 (2013): 749–778. Also see Chester Bowles, *Ambassador's Report* (New York: Harper and Brothers, 1954), 197–198; Nicole Sackley, "Passage to Modernity: American Social Scientists, India, and the Pursuit of Development, 1945–1961" (PhD diss., Princeton University, 2004); Nick Cullather, *The Hungry World,* 77–94; Dennis Merrill, *Bread and Ballot: The United States and India's Economic Development, 1947–1963* (Chapel Hill: University of North Carolina Press, 1992), 92.

12. Cullather, *The Hungry World,* 87; Perkins, *Geopolitics and the Green Revolution: Wheat, Genes, and the Cold War* (New York: Oxford University Press, 1977), 177.

13. Harry S. Taylor, "Oral History Interview with Douglas Ensminger," June 16 and July 7, 1976, Harry S. Truman Library and Museum, Columbia, MO, www.trumanlibrary.org/oralhist/esmingr.htm. Also see Douglas Ensminger, *A Guide to Community Development* (New Delhi: Ministry of Community Development, 1957).

14. Thakurdas Bang and Suresh Ramabhai, "The Truth about Etawah," *Economic and Political Weekly,* (May 1952), http://www.epw.in/system/files/pdf/1952_4/18/the__truth_about_etawah.pdf; Mayer, "Americans in India"; Albert Mayer and Associates, in collaboration with McKim Marriott and Richard L. Park, *Pilot Project, India: The Story of Rural Development at Etawah, Uttar Pradesh* (Berkeley and Los Angeles: The University of California Press, 1958), 337; S. C. Dube, *India's Changing Villages: Human Factors in Community Development* (Ithica, N.Y.: Cornell University Press, 1958), 82–83; Cullather, *The Hungry World,* 89–90.

15. Immerwahr, *Thinking Small,* 10; Gerald D. Berreman, "Caste and Community Development," *Human Organization* 22 (1963): 93. Also see Daniel and Alice Thorner, *Land and Labour in India* (Bombay: Asia Publishing House, 1962).

16. Timothy Mitchell, *Rule of Experts: Egypt, Techno-Politics* (Berkeley: University of California Press, 2002).

17. Paul Collier, *The Bottom Billion: Why the Poorest Countries Are Failing and What Can Be Done about It* (Oxford, UK: Oxford University Press, 2008); Abhijit Banerjee and Esther Duflo, *Poor Economics: A Radical Rethinking of the Way to*

*Fight Global Poverty* (New York: PublicAffairs, 2011); William Easterly, *The Tyranny of Experts: Economists, Dictators, and the Forgotten Rights of the Poor* (New York: Basic Books, 2015).

18. Srinivas M. Chary, *The Eagle and the Peacock: U.S. Foreign Policy Toward India Since Independence* (Westport, Conn.: Greenwood Press, 1995), 24–27.

19. "Famine, among the world's starving peoples . . . let us remember India," March 28, 1946, *New York Times*, Hoover Institution Library and Archives, https://digitalcollections.hoover.org/objects/36447/famine-among-the -worlds-starving-peoples—let-us-rememb?ctx=f8b5d90c-5c9e-4a47-be95 -3f199c5927eb; "Famine in India," *Chicago Tribune*, September 18, 1946.

20. Buck to Truman, August 4, 1946, quoted in Chary, *The Eagle and the Peacock*, 31–32.

21. Robert Beisner, *Dean Acheson: A Life in the Cold War* (Oxford, UK: Oxford University Press, 2006), 507.

22. *Congressional Record*, 81st Congress, 2nd Session, 1950, XCVI, part 13, p. A51; Merrill, *Bread and the Ballot*, 84–91. On the larger history of development and the Cold War, see Gabrielle Hecht, ed., *Entangled Geographies: Empire and Technopolitics in the Global Cold War* (Cambridge, MA: MIT Press, 2012).

23. Taylor, "Oral History Interview with Douglas Ensminger."

24. Cullather, *The Hungry World*, 144.

25. B. R. Shenoy, *P.L. 480 Aid and India's Food Problem* (New Delhi: Affiliated East-West Press, 1974), 3–8; "If India Falls," *Progressive* (January 1958): 8–11; Also see Walter Lippmann, "India: The Glorious Gamble," *Ladies' Home Journal* (August 1959): 48–49.

26. Letter from President Kennedy to Prime Minister Nehru, January 18, 1962, *Foreign Relations of the United States* (FRUS), vol. XIX, *South Asia* (1961–1963), Document 95.

27. John Kenneth Galbraith, *Ambassador's Journal: A Personal Account of the Kennedy Years House* (Boston: Houghton Mifflin, 1969), 70, 167; Arthur Schlesinger, *A Thousand Days: John F. Kennedy in the White House* (Boston: Houghton Mifflin, 1965), 531.

28. "Foreign Assistance Related Agencies Appropriations for 1967," Sub-Committee on Appropriations, May 6, 1966, Record Group 233.4, United States National Archives.

29. Wofford, *Of Kennedys and Kings*, 272; Elizabeth Cobbs Hoffman, *All You Need Is Love: The Peace Corps and the Spirit of the 1960s* (Cambridge, MA: Harvard University Press, 2000), 192.

30. John Updike, *Rabbit, Run* (New York: Knopf, 1960), 146; Paul Ehrlich, *The Population Bomb* (New York: Ballantine Books, 1968), 1–2.

31. "A Time to Seize the Opportunity," *India Forum* 4 (April 1977): 2; Emily R. Merchant, *Prediction and Control: Global Population, Population Science, and Population Politics in the Twentieth Century* (PhD diss., University of Michigan, 2015); Michelle Murphy, *The Economization of Life* (Durham, NC: Duke University Press, 2017).

32. Prabhu L Pingali, "Green Revolution: Impacts, Limits, and the Path Ahead," *Proceedings of the National Academy of Sciences of the United States of America* 109, no. 31 (2012): 12302–12308; Noel Vietmeyer, *Our Daily Bread: The Essential Norman Borlaug* (Lorton, VA: Bracing Books, 2011); "Father of India's Green Revolution Given Padma Vibhushan," August 24, 2006, Rediff.com, http://www.rediff.com/news/report/borlaug/20060824.htm; "PM Pays Tribute to Father of Green Revolution Borlaug," September 14, 2009, Rediff .com, http://news.rediff.com/report/2009/sep/14/pm-pays-tribute-to-father -of-green-revolution-borlaug.htm.

33. R. E. Evenson and D. Gollin, "Assessing the Impact of the Green Revolution, 1960 to 2000," *Science* 300, (2003): 758–762; Nick Cullather, "Miracles of Modernization: The Green Revolution and the Apotheosis of Technology," *Diplomatic History* 28, no. 2 (April 2004): 227–254; Dietmar Rothermund, *An Economic History of India,* 2d ed. (New York: Routledge, 1993), 139–143.

34. Cullather, *The Hungry World,* 201; Amartya Sen, *Poverty and Famines: An Essay on Entitlement and Deprivation* (Oxford, UK: Clarendon Press, 1981).

35. Telegram from the Embassy in Italy to the Department of State, November 26, 1965, [Johnson Library, National Security File, NSC History, Indian Famine, August 1966–February 1967,] FRUS, vol. XXV, *South Asia* (1964–1968).

36. Chester Bowles, *Promises to Keep: My Years in Public Life, 1941–1969* (New York: Harper & Row, 1971), 534; McMahon, *The Cold War on the Periphery: The United States, India and Pakistan* (New York: Columbia University Press, 1996), 326; Nick Cullather, "LBJ's Third War: The War on Hunger," in *Beyond the Cold War: Lyndon Johnson and the New Global Challenges of the 1960s,* eds. Francis J. Gavin and Mark Atwood Lawrence (New York: Oxford University Press, 2014), 118–140; James Warner Bjorkman, "Public Law 480 and the Policies of Self-Help and Short-Tether: Indo American Relations, 1965–68," in *Making U.S. Foreign Policy toward South Asia: Regional Imperatives and the Imperial Presidency,* eds. Lloyd I. Rudolph and Susanne H. Rudolph (Bloomington: Indiana University Press, 2008), 359–424.

37. Gary J. Bass, *The Blood Telegram: Nixon, Kissinger, and a Forgotten Genocide* (New York: Vintage, 2014).

38. Transcript of telephone conversation between President Nixon and his Assistant for National Security Affairs (Kissinger), March 29, 1971, FRUS, vol. XI, *South Asia Crisis, 1971* (1969–1976): 35–36.

39. Richard Nixon, remarks at Phoenix, Arizona, October 31, 1970, posted online by Gerhard Peters and John T. Woolley, American Presidency Project, www.presidency.ucsb.edu/ws/?pid=2797.

40. U.S. Consulate (Dacca) Cable, dissent from U.S. policy toward East Pakistan, April 6, 1971, FRUS, vol. XI, *South Asia Crisis, 1971* (1969–1976); Bass, *The Blood Telegram.*

41. Letter from Indian Prime Minister Gandhi to President Nixon, December 5, 1971, FRUS, vol. XI, *South Asia Crisis, 1971* (1969–1976): 629–631; Bass, *The Blood Telegram,* 251.

42. Transcript of telephone conversation between President Nixon and his Assistant for National Security Affairs (Kissinger), December 4, 1971, FRUS, vol. XI, *South Asia Crisis, 1971* (1969–1976): 628.

43. Lucian W. Pye, "Foreign Aid and America's Involvement in the Developing World," in *The Vietnam Legacy,* ed. Anthony Lake (New York: New York University Press, 1976), 379.

44. Taylor, "Oral History Interview with Douglas Ensminger."

45. Thomas Friedman, *The World Is Flat: A Brief History of the Twenty-First Century* (New York: Farrar, Straus and Giroux, 2005); Jagdish Bhagwati, *In Defense of Globalization* (New York: Oxford University Press, 2004).

46. Indo-American Chamber of Commerce, "Indo-American Commercial Relations," *Modern Review* (November 1938): 585; Earl Robert Schmidt, "American Relations with South Asia 1900–1940" (PhD diss., University of Pennsylvania, 1955), 387–393.

47. Schmidt, "American Relations with South Asia 1900–1940," 18–19.

48. D.A. Kearns-Preston, "Commercial Relations Between India and the United States," *Foreign Commerce Weekly,* October 10, 1949, 3 and 42; Chary, *The Eagle and the Peacock,* 45;"India: New Economic Frontier?" *Amerasia* (September 8, 1944): 243–253; John P. Lewis, *Quiet Crisis in India: Economic Development and American Policy* (Washington, DC: Brookings Institution, 1962).

49. Bernard Bell, *Report to the President of the International Bank for Reconstruction and Development and the International Development Association on India's Economic Development Effort: Main Report* (Washington, DC: World Bank, 1965); D. B. H. Denoon, *Devaluation under Pressure: India, Indonesia and Ghana* (Cambridge, UK: Cambridge University Press, 1986), 25–53; Mitu Sengupta, "Making the State Change Its Mind: The IMF, the World Bank, and the Politics of India's Market Reforms," *New Political Economy* 14, no. 2 (June 2009): 181–210; John P. Lewis, *India's Political Economy: Governance and Reform* (Oxford, UK: Oxford University Press, 1995), 53–166.

50. Rothermund, *An Economic History of India,* 163–172.

51. Jay Solomon and Kathryn Kranhold, "In India's Outsourcing Boom, GE Played a Starring Role," *Wall Street Journal,* March 23, 2005; Kiran Karnik, *The Coalition of Competitors: The Story of Nasscom and the IT Industry* (New York: Harper Collins, 2012).

52. William Greene, "Growth in Services Outsourcing to India: Propellant or Drain on the U.S. Economy?" U.S. International Trade Commission, Office of Economics Working Paper, no. 2005–12-A, 2006, p. 2; Jagdish Bhagwati, Arvind Panagariya, and T. N. Srinivasan, "The Mudddles over Outsourcing," *Journal of Economic Perspectives* 18, no. 4 (Fall 2004): 93–114.

53. Greene, "Growth in Services Outsourcing to India," 11; Shehzad Nadeem, *Dead Ringers: How Outsourcing Is Changing the Way Indians Understand Themselves* (Princeton, NJ: Princeton University Press, 2013), 2; Mathangi Krishnamurthy, *1–800-Worlds: The Making of the Indian Call Centre Economy* (Delhi: Oxford University Press, 2018).

54. Patrick Thibodeau, "Fury Rises at Disney over Use of Foreign Workers," *Computerworld* (April 29, 2015); Jagdish N. Bhagwati and Alan S. Blinder, *Offshoring of American Jobs: What Response from U.S. Economic Policy?*, ed. Benjamin M. Friedman (Cambridge, MA: MIT Press, 2009); William Milberg and Deborah Winkler, *Outsourcing Economics: Global Value Chains in Capitalist Development* (Cambridge, UK: Cambridge University Press, 2013).

55. "A Faceless, Nameless, Fragmented, Unorganized, and Segregated Labor Force," *SAMAR* (Summer 1996): 8; Mir Ali Husain and Maya Yajnik, "Virtual Work, Real Labor," *SAMAR* (Summer 1996): 7; Tom Schoenberg, David McLaughlin and Tom Korosec, "Infosys Settles With U.S. in Visa Fraud Probe," October 31, 2013, Bloomberg Technology, www.bloomberg.com /news/articles/2013–10–30/infosys-settles-with-u-s-in-visa-fraud-probe; Don Tennant, "Former U.S. Infosys Employees Allege Discrimination on Basis of National Origin," October 14, 2014, ITBusinessEdge, www.itbusinessedge .com/blogs/from-under-the-rug/former-u.s.-infosys-employees-allege -discrimination-on-basis-of-national-origin.html.

56. Norman Matloff, "Immigration and the Tech Industry," *Migration Letters* (May 2013); Roli Varma, *Harbingers of Global Change: India's Techno-Immigrants in the United States* (Lanham, MD: Rowman and Littlefield, 2006).

57. Greene, "Growth in Services Outsourcing to India," 11; Miriam Altman, "Industrial Strategy, Offshoring, and Employment Promotion in South Africa," in *The Oxford Handbook of Offshoring and Global Employment*, eds. Ashok Bardhan, Dwight M. Jaffee, and Cynthia A. Kroll (Oxford, UK: Oxford University Press, 2013), 622; Solomon and Kranhold, "In India's Outsourcing Boom, GE Played a Starring Role"; Ignatius Chithelen, "Outsourcing to India: Causes, Reaction and Prospects," *Economic and Political Weekly* 39, no. 10 (March 6, 2004): 1022–1024; Ajay Agrawal, Devesh Kapur, John McHale, Alexander Oettl, "Brain Drain or Brain Bank? The Impact of Skilled Emigration on Poor-Country Innovation," *Journal of Urban Economics* 69 (2011): 43–55; Mihir A. Desai, Devesh Kapur, John McHale, and Keith Rogers, "The Fiscal Impact of High-Skilled Emigration: Flows of Indians to the U.S.," *Journal of Development Economics* 88, no. 1 (January 2009): 32–44.

58. Ward Morehouse and M. Arun Subramaniam, *The Bhopal Tragedy: A Report for the Citizens Commission on Bhopal* (New York: Apex Press, 1986); Dan Kurzman, *A Killing Wind: Inside Union Carbide and the Bhopal Catastrophe* (New York: McGraw-Hill, 1987); Ward Morehouse, "And Not to Yield: The Long Struggle against Union Carbide," *SAMAR* (Summer / Fall 1997): 4.

59. T. C. A. Srinivasa Raghavan, "Manmohan Pledges $10 Billion to Debt-Ridden Eurozone," *Hindu*, June 19, 2012, www.thehindu.com/news/international /manmohan-pledges-10-billion-to-debtridden-eurozone/article3545849 .ece; Sachin Chaturvedi, "Aid from India, Coming to a Country Near You," *Hindu*, September 5, 2012, www.thehindu.com/opinion/op-ed/aid-from -india-coming-to-a-country-near-you/article3859607.ece.

60. Sam Pitroda, "Taking Silicon Valley Culture to India," *Silicon India* (April 2000), quoted in Aswin Punathambekar, *From Bombay to Bollywood: The Making of a Global Media Industry* (New York: New York University Press, 2013), 121; Pallab Datta, "@India.com: The Frontiers of the New Economy," *India West* 25, no. 17 (February 25, 2000).

61. Asha Sharma, "A Century in Hawaii," *The Hindu*, May 10, 2014, , www.thehindu.com/features/magazine/a-century-in-hawaii/article5996018.ece; Francis Assisi, "Watumull Saga Stretches across 50 Years of Philanthropy," *East West Magazine* (February 1, 1991): 45; Laurel Murphy, "Jhamandas Watumull: Hyderabad to Honolulu," *Honolulu Advertiser*, August 22, 1973.

62. Ravi Kuchimanchi, "Story of How AID Started," https://aidindia.org/about-aid/history-of-aid/, accessed April 13, 2018.

63. Jhumpa Lahiri, *Interpreter of Maladies* (New York: Mariner, 1999), 23–42.

64. Taraknath Das, "The Struggle of Indians to Attain Equal Rights in the United States of America," *Modern Review* (October 1946): 263–266.

65. Eric Yo Ping Lai and Dennis Arguelles, eds., *The New Face of Asian Pacific America: Numbers, Diversity, and Change in the 21st Century* (Los Angeles: UCLA Asian American Studies Center Press, 1998), 105–113; Tom Gjelten, *A Nation of Nations: A Great American Immigration Story* (New York: Simon and Schuster, 2015).

66. Khyati Y. Joshi and Jigna Desai, *Asian Americans in Dixie: Race and Migration in the South* (Urbana-Champaign: University of Illinois Press, 2013); Padma Rangaswamy, *Namasté America: Indian Immigrants in an American Metropolis* (State College, PA: Penn State University Press, 2008).

67. Maritsa V. Poros, "Asian Indians and Asian-Indian Americans, 1870–1940," in *Immigrants in American History: Arrival, Adaptation, and Integration*, ed. Elliott Robert Barkan (Santa Barbara: ABC-CLIO, 2013), 209–218; Rozina Visram: *Asians in Britain: 400 Years of History* (London: Pluto Press, 2002).

68. Pawan Dhingra, *Life behind the Lobby: Indian American Motel Owners and the American Dream* (Stanford, CA: Stanford University Press, 2012); Joshi and Desai, *Asian Americans in Dixie*; Rangaswamy, *Namasté America*; "From the Editorial Collective," *SAMAR* no. 4, *Class Encounters of the South Asian Kind* (Winter 1994): 2; Sujani Reddy, "The Hidden Hand: Remapping Indian Nurse Immigration to the United States," in *The Sun Never Sets: South Asian Migrants in an Age of U.S. Power*, eds. Vivek Bald, Miabi Chatterji, Sujani Reddy, and Manu Vimalassery (New York: NYU Press, 2013), 103–126.

69. Prema Kurien, *A Place at the Multicultural Table: The Development of an American Hinduism* (New Brunswick, NJ: Rutgers University Press, 2007); Khyati Y. Joshi, *New Roots in America's Sacred Ground: Religion, Race, and Ethnicity in Indian America* (New Brunswick, NJ: Rutgers University Press, 2006); Diana Eck, *A New Religious America: How a "Christian Country" Has Become the World's Most Religiously Diverse Nation* (New York: HarperCollins, 2002).

70. Sangay K. Mishra, *Desis Divided: The Political Lives of South Asian Americans* (Minneapolis: University of Minnesota Press, 2016); Arvind Rajagopal, "Hindu Nationalism in the US: Changing Configurations of Political Practice," *Ethnic and Racial Studies* 23, no. 3 (2000): 467–496; Biju Mathew and Vijay Prashad, "The Protean Forms of Yankee Hindutva," *Ethnic and Racial Studies* 23, no. 3 (2000): 516–534.

71. *SAMAR* (Winter 1992), available at South Asian American Digital Archive (SAADA), www.saada.org; Pawan Dhingra, *Managing Multicultural Lives: Asian American Professionals and the Challenge of Multiple Identities* (Stanford, CA: Stanford University Press, 2007); Gita Rajan and Shailja Sharma, eds., *New Cosmopolitanisms: South Asians in the US* (Stanford: Stanford University Press, 2006).

72. Eric Yo Ping Lai and Dennis Arguelles, eds., *The New Face of Asian Pacific America: Numbers, Diversity, and Change in the 21st Century* (Los Angeles: UCLA Asian American Studies Center Press, 1998), 105–113; K. V. Rao, "Indian Americans," *Asian-Nation: The Landscape of Asian America*, 2003, www.asian-nation.org/indian.shtml; Sunaina Marr Maira, *Desis in The House: Indian American Youth Culture in NYC* (Philadelphia: Temple University Press, 2002).

73. Manan Desai, "The Crooner from Kashmir," *Tides: Magazine of the South Asian American Digital Archive,* November 12, 2014, www.saada.org/tides/article/crooner-from-kashmir; "Now We Got Cool Dip," *Life,* December 10, 1956, 107.

74. Marita V. Poros, "Asian Indians and Asian-Indian Americans, 1940–Present."

75. Ariela Schachter, "Finding Common Ground? Indian Immigrants and Asian American Panethnicity," *Social Forces* 92, no. 4 (June 2014): 1487–1512; Vibha Bhalla, "The New Indians: Reconstructing Indian Identity in the United States," *American Behavioral Scientist* 50, no. 118 (2006): 118–136; Y. L. Espiritu, *Asian American Panethnicity: Bridging Institutions and Identities* (Philadelphia: Temple University Press, 1992), 124–125.

76. Joy Cherian, *Our Relay Race: A Compilation of Selected Articles and Speeches* (Lanham, MD: University Press of America, 1997), 6.

77. Cherian, *Our Relay Race,* 10. For a more prominent South Asian American critic of affirmative action, see Dinesh D'Souza, *Illiberal Education: The Politics of Race and Sex on Campus* (New York: Free Press, 1991).

78. See Al Kamen, "After Immigration, an Unexpected Fear: New Jersey's Indian Community is Terrorized by Racial Violence," *Washington Post,* November 16, 1992; Rekha Borsellino, "Tougher Law Asked in Attacks on Indians," *New York Times,* July 10, 1988. Also see Arthur Helwig and Usha Helwig, *An Immigrant Success Story: East Indians in America* (Philadelphia: University of Pennsylvania Press, 1990), 188.

79. On the impact of Apu Nahasapeemapetilon on the racialization of South Asian Americans, see Hari Kondabalu's documentary film, *The Problem with Apu* (2017). Also see Deepa Iyer, *We Too Sing America: South Asian, Arab, Muslim, and Sikh Immigrants Shape Our Multiracial Future* (New York: New Press, 2015);

Aminah Mohammed-Arif, *Salaam America: South Asian Muslims in New York* (London: Anthem Press, 2002), 271; Ahmed Afzal, *Lone Star Muslims: Transnational Lives and the South Asian Experience in Texas* (New York: NYU Press, 2014); Junaid Rana, *Terrifying Muslims: Race and Labor in the South Asian Diaspora* (Durham, NC: Duke University Press, 2011); "Sodhi Murder Trial Begins," September 4, 2003, www.rediff.com/us/2003/sep/03sodhi.htm.

80. Sunil Bhatia, *American Karma: Race, Culture, and Identity in the Indian Diaspora* (New York: NYU Press, 2007); "Vanita: Sworn to Justice," and "Vanita Spelt [*sic*] Hope for Defendants," *Rediff India Abroad*, December 08, 2004; Arvind Rajagopal, "Better than Blacks? Or, Hum Kaale Hain To Kya Hua," *SAMAR* no. 5 (Summer 1995): 4; Ann Morning, "The Racial Self-Identification of South Asians in the United States," *Journal of Ethnic and Migration Studies* 27, no. 1 (January 2001): 61–79.

81. Sunaina Maira, "Identity Dub: The Paradoxes of the Indian American Youth Subculture (New York Mix)," *Cultural Anthropology* 14, no. 1 (1999): 29–60; Ajay Nair and Murali Balaji, *Desi Rap: Hip-Hop and South Asian America* (Lanham, MD: Lexington Books, 2008).

82. Following are the websites for these organizations: http://saalt.org/; www.solidaritysummer.org/; http://eastcoastsolidaritysummer.weebly.com/; www.sakhi.org/; http://maitri.org/. Also see Monisha Das Gupta, *Unruly Immigrants: Rights, Activism, and Transnational South Asian Politics in the United States* (Durham, NC: Duke University Press, 2006); Inderpal Grewal, *Transnational America: Feminisms, Diasporas, Neoliberalisms* (Durham, NC: Duke University Press, 2005); Sangeeta R. Gupta, ed., *Emerging Voices: South Asian American Women Redefine Self, Family and Community* (Thousand Oaks, CA: Sage Publications, 1999); Arpana Sircar, *Work Roles, Gender Roles, and Asian Indian Immigrant Women in the United States* (Lewiston, NY: Edwin Mellen Press, 2000); Margaret Abraham, *Speaking the Unspeakable: Marital Violence among South Asian Immigrants in the United States* (New Brunswick, NJ: Rutgers University Press, 2000); Linta Varghese, "Looking Home: Gender, Work, and the Domestic in Theorizations of the South Asian Diaspora," in *The Sun Never Sets: South Asian Migrants in an Age of U.S. Power*, eds. Vivek Bald, Miabi Chatterji, Sujani Reddy, and Manu Vimalassery (New York: NYU Press, 2013), 156–175.

83. Priyamvada Sinha, "They Have a Right to Love!" SALGA Newsletter, October 1994, available at Digital Public Library of America, http://collections.si.edu/search/results.htm?q=record_ID%3Asiris_arc_305389&repo=DPLA; "SALGA Marches in the NYC Pride '95 Parade," SAADA; Also see Gayatri Gopinath, "Who's Your Daddy? Queer Diasporic Framings of the Region," in *The Sun Never Sets*, eds. Bald, Chatterji, Reddy, and Vimalassery, 274–300.

84. Annie Gowen and Tyler Bridges, "From Piyush to Bobby: How Does Jindal Feel about His Family's Past?," *Washington Post*, June 23, 2015, www

.washingtonpost.com/politics/from-piyush-to-bobby-how-does-jindal-feel
-about-his-familys-past/2015/06/22/7d45a3da-18ec-11e5-ab92
-c75ae6ab94b5_story.html?tid=sm_tw&utm_term=.0d5dfdf9101e; Akhilesh
Pillalamarri, "'Not Indian Enough': Bobby Jindal, Heritage, and Politics,"
*Diplomat,* July 1, 2015, http://thediplomat.com/2015/07/not-indian-enough
-bobby-jindal-heritage-and-politics/; Sarah Pulliam Bailey, "S.C. Gov. Race
Heats Up over Haley's Religion," *Christianity Today,* June 16, 2010, www
.christianitytoday.com/gleanings/2010/june/sc-gov-race-heats-up-over
-haleys-religion.html; Shaila Dewan and Robbie Brown, "All Her Life, Nikki
Haley Was the Different One," *New York Times,* June 13, 2010; www.free
-times.com/index.php?cat=1992912064017974&ShowArticle_ID
=11010308112984607.

85. Daniel Beekman, Lynn Thompson, and Claudia Rowe, "Pramila Jayapal De-
feats Brady Walkinshaw in Washington's 7th Congressional District," *Seattle
Times,* November 8, 2016; Sheenu Sharma, "Raja Krishnamoorthi Becomes
First Indian-American to enter US Congress," *India Today,* November 9, 2016;
"Khanna Defeats Eight-Term Incumbent Honda for Congress," Associated Press, www.nbcbayarea.com/news/local/Khanna-Defeats-Eight-Term
-Incumbent-Honda-For-Congress—400510431.html; Phil Willon, "Kamala
Harris Is Elected California's New U.S. Senator," *Los Angeles Times,* No-
vember 8, 2016; "New California Senator Kamala Harris Leads a Desi Wave
in US Elections," www.ndtv.com/indians-abroad/record-5-indian-americans
-set-to-be-elected-to-us-congress-1623230.

86. Dave Kaup and Aditya Kalra, "Kansas Man Charged with Killing Indian in
Possible Hate Crime," *Reuters,* February 24, 2017; Srinivasa Rao Apparasu,
"US Isn't a Safe Place, Don't Send Your Children There: Father of Indian En-
gineer Injured in Kansas Shooting," *Hindustan Times,* February 28, 2017;
"Olathe, Kansas, Shooting Suspect 'aid he killed Iranians,'" February 28,
2017, BBC, www.bbc.com/news/world-us-canada-39108060.

87. Sebastian Rotella, "The American Behind India's 9/11—and How U.S.
Botched Chances to Stop Him," *ProPublica,* www.propublica.org/article/david
-headley-homegrown-terrorist.

88. Daniel S. Markey, *No Exit from Pakistan: America's Tortured Relationship with
Islamabad* (Cambridge, UK: Cambridge University Press, 2013); Husain
Haqqani, *Magnificent Delusions: Pakistan, the United States, and an Epic History
of Misunderstanding* (New York: PublicAffairs, 2013).

## Chapter 6: Bollywood / Hollywood

1. Chidanand Rajghatta and Bharati Dubey, "My Name Is Khan? Too Bad,"
*Times of India,* August 15, 2009, http://timesofindia.indiatimes.com/india/My
-name-is-Khan-Too-bad-SRK-feels-the-heat-of-American-paranoia
/articleshow/4897426.cms?; "'Ra.One': Shah Rukh Khan as Bollywood

Superhero," *Los Angeles Times,* November 4, 2011, http://latimesblogs
.latimes.com/movies/2011/11/shah-rukh-khan-ra-one-bollywood.html.

2. Saeed Naqvi, *Being the Other: The Muslim in India* (New Delhi: Aleph, 2016);
Laurent Gayer and Christophe Jaffrelot, eds., *Muslims in Indian Cities: Trajectories of Marginalisation* (London: Hurst, 2011); Justice Rajindar Sachar, "Social, Economic and Educational Status of the Muslim Community of India:
A Report," Prime Minister's High Level Committee, Cabinet Secretariat, Government of India, New Delhi, November 2006, www.minorityaffairs.gov.in
/reports/sachar-committee-report.

3. Chidananda Das Gupta, "Cinema: America-India," in *The Traffic of Ideas between India and America,* ed. Robert M. Crunden (Delhi: Chanakya Publications, 1985), 189–195; Earl Robert Schmidt, "American Relations with South
Asia 1900–1940" (PhD diss., University of Pennsylvania, 1955), 387–393;
Chidandanda Das Gupta, "Ray Retrospective Draws Crowds in New York,"
*Span* (October 1981): 43; Rosie Thomas, *Bombay before Bollywood: Film City Fantasies* (Albany: State University of New York Press, 2013).

4. M. Madhava Prasad, "Surviving Bollywood," in *Global Bollywood,* eds.
Anandam P. Kavoori and Aswin Punathambekar (New York: New York University Press, 2008), 41; Madhava Prasad, "This Thing Called Bollywood,"
*Seminar,* www.india-seminar.com/2003/525/525%20madhava%20prasad
.htm, accessed April 10, 2018; Priya Joshi, *Bollywood's India: A Public Fantasy*
(New York: Columbia University Press, 2015), 9.

5. Nitin Govil, *Orienting Hollywood: A Century of Film Culture between Los Angeles
and Bombay* (New York: New York University Press, 2015), 184.

6. On pluralism, see John D. Inazu, *Confident Pluralism: Surviving and Thriving
through Deep Difference* (Chicago: University of Chicago Press, 2016); Martha C.
Nussbaum, *The Clash Within: Democracy, Religious Violence, and India's Future*
(Cambridge, MA: Belknap Press of Harvard University Press, 2007). On polyculturalism versus multiculturalism, see Vijay Prashad, *Everybody Was Kung
Fu Fighting: Afro-Asian Connections and the Myth of Cultural Plurality* (Boston:
Beacon Press, 2001).

7. Joshi, *Bollywood's India,* 14.

8. "'We Are Scared': Africans in India Face Rampant Racism," *Indian Express,*
June 10, 2016, http://indianexpress.com/article/india/india-news-india
/scared-africans-india-constant-racism-2844626/; R. Parameswaran and K.
Cardoza, "Melanin on the Margins: Advertising and the Cultural Politics of
Fair/Light/White Beauty in India," *Journalism and Communication Monographs*
11, no. 3 (2009): 213–274; Neha Mishra, "India and Colorism: The Finer Nuances," *Washington University Global Studies Law Review* 14, no. 4 (2015): 725–
750, http://openscholarship.wustl.edu/law_globalstudies/vol14/iss4/14.

9. Rachel Dwyer, *Bollywood's India: Hindi Cinema as a Guide to Contemporary India*
(London: Reaktion Books, 2014); V. Kishore, A. Sarwal, and P. Patra, eds.,
*Bollywood and Its Other(s): Toward New Configurations* (New York: Palgrave Macmillan, 2014); Ranjani Mazumdar, *Bombay Cinema: An Archive of the City* (Min-

neapolis: University of Minnesota Press, 2007); Jyotika Virdi, *The Cinematic ImagiNation: Indian Popular Films as Social History* (New Brunswick, NJ: Rutgers University Press, 2003); Ashis Nandy, ed., *The Secret Politics of our Desires: Innocence, Culpability and Indian Popular Cinema* (London: Zed Books, 1999); Sumita Chakravarty, *National Identity in Indian Popular Cinema, 1947–1987* (Austin: University of Texas Press, 1993).

10. Louis Bromfield, *The Rains Came* (New York: Harper and Brothers, 1937).

11. The profusion of skulls and other forms of death is emblematic of the long link between phrenology, the thug, and colonial knowledge. See Kim A. Wagner, "Confessions of a Skull: Phrenology and Colonial Knowledge in Early Nineteenth-Century India," *History Workshop Journal* 69 (Spring 2010): 27–51.

12. Mordaunt Hall, "The Screen," *New York Times,* May 23, 1929; James Chapman and Nicholas J. Cull, *Projecting Empire: Imperialism and Popular Cinema* (London: I. B. Tauris, 2009); Prem Chowdhry, *Colonial India and the Making of Empire Cinema: Image, Ideology and Identity* (Manchester, UK: Manchester University Press, 2000); Gina Marchetti, *Romance and the 'Yellow Peril': Race, Sex, and Discursive Strategies in Hollywood Fiction* (Berkeley and Los Angeles: University of California Press, 1994); Jeffrey Richards, "Korda's Empire: Politics and Film in Sanders of the River, The Drum and The Four Feathers," *Australian Journal of Screen Theory* 5, no. 6 (1978): 122–137.

13. Jeffrey Richards, *Visions of Yesterday* (London: Routledge, 1973), 120–123; Ivone Kirkpatrick, *The Inner Circle* (London: Macmillan, 1959), 97.

14. Peter Lev, *Twentieth Century-Fox: The Zanuck-Skouras Years, 1935–1965* (Austin: University of Texas Press, 2013), 39–42.

15. There are obvious resonances here with the way in which African Americans were portrayed in Hollywood—or not portrayed. "So far as Negroes are concerned," Langston Hughes said of Hollywood, it "might just as well be controlled by Hitler." See Arnold Rampersad, *The Life of Langston Hughes: Volume 1, 1902–1941, I, Too, Sing America* (New York: Oxford University Press, 1986), 371. Also see Ellen C. Scott, *Cinema Civil Rights: Regulation, Repression, and Race in the Classical Hollywood Era* (New Brunswick, NJ: Rutgers University Press, 2015).

16. Chowdhry, *Colonial India and the Making of Empire Cinema,* 153–155.

17. Jigna Desai, *Beyond Bollywood: The Cultural Politics of South Asian Diasporic Film* (New York: Routledge, 2003), 67–95.

18. Kal Penn's choice is reminiscent of the "thug" rappers accused of perpetuating stereotypes of blackness. See Michael Jeffries, *Thug Life: Race, Gender, and the Meaning of Hip-Hop* (Chicago: University of Chicago Press, 2011); 16–17. Also see Jada Yuan, "'Harold and Kumar' and '24' Actor Kal Penn on His New Movie 'The Namesake'," *New York Magazine,* http://nymag.com/movies/profiles/28866/, accessed April 10, 2018.

19. Hollywood films are often wrongly held up as the measure of quality. See Meheli Sen, *Haunting Bollywood: Gender, Genre, and the Supernatural in Hindi Commercial Cinema* (Austin: University of Texas Press, 2017), 25.

20. I am grateful to Priya Joshi for directing me to the links between *Bobby,* Archie Comics, and *The Wizard of Oz.* See Joshi, *Bollywood's India,* 96–97.

21. Sangita Gopal and Sujata Moorti, "Bollywood in Drag: *Moulin Rouge!* and the Aesthetics of Global Cinema," *Camera Obscura* 25 (2011): 29–67.

22. Khan quoted in Govil, *Orienting Hollywood,* 1–2; Stephen Alter, *Fantasies of a Bollywood Love Thief* (New York: Harcourt, 2007), 9; Prasad, "Surviving Bollywood," 49. Also see Tejaswini Ganti, "No Longer a Frivolous Singing and Dancing Nation of Movie-Makers: The Hindi Film Industry and Its Quest for Global Distinction," *Visual Anthropology* 25, no. 4 (2012): 340–365; Jigna Desai, "The Scale of Diasporic Cinema: Negotiating National and Transnational Cultural Citizenship," in *Routledge Handbook on Indian Cinema,* eds. K. Moti Gokulsing and Wimal Dissanayake (New York: Routledge, 2013), 206–217.

23. Michael Cieply and Brooks Barnesjan, "A Studio's Real-Life Drama," *New York Times,* January 29, 2012; "Anil Ambani, Spielberg Join Hands to Form Amblin Partners," *The Hindu,* December 17, 2015, http://www.thehindu.com /business/anil-ambani-steven-spielberg-join-hands-to-form-amblin-partners /article8000003.ece; on financial ties between Hollywood and Bollywood, see Govil, *Orienting Hollywood,* 77–114; Tejaswini Ganti, *Producing Bollywood: Inside the Contemporary Hindi Film Industry* (Durham, NC: Duke University Press, 2012).

24. Lavina Melwani, "Made In America: Bollywood Comes to the US," Lassi with Lavina, January 24, 2013, www.lassiwithlavina.com/thebuzz/made-in -america-bollywood-comes-to-the-us/html.

25. Parama Roy, "Discovering India, Imagining Thuggee," *Yale Journal of Criticism* 9, no. 1 (Spring 1996): 121–145.

26. On gender within Indian cinema, see Sangita Gopal, *Conjugations: Marriage and Form in New Bollywood Cinema* (Chicago: University of Chicago Press, 2011); Shoma A. Chatterji, "The Evolution of Representing Female Sexuality in Hindi Cinema, 1991–2010," in *Routledge Handbook on Indian Cinema,* eds. Gokulsing and Dissanayake, 179–192; Asha Kasbekar, "Hidden Pleasures: Negotiating the Myth of the Female Ideal in Popular Hindi Cinema," in *Pleasure and the Nation: The History, Politics and Consumption of Public Culture in India,* eds. Rachel Dwyer and Christopher Pinney (New Delhi: Oxford University Press, 2002), 287–307.

27. Kai Friese, "The Porn Star Sunny Leone's Bollywood Makeover," *New York Times,* May 8, 2015.

28. Jenny Sharpe, "Gender, Nation, and Globalization in Monsoon Wedding and Dilwale Dulhania Le Jayenge," *Meridians: Feminism, Race, Transnationalism* 6, no. 1 (2005): 58–81.

29. Sangita Gopal and Sujata Moorti, eds., *Global Bollywood: Travels of Hindi Song and Dance* (Minneapolis: University of Minnesota Press, 2008); Kat Stoeffel, "Selena Gomez Not Backing Down on Bindi Front," *New York Magazine,* April 25, 2013.

30. John Felstiner, *Translating Neruda: The Way to Machu Picchu* (Palo Alto, CA: Stanford University Press, 1980); George Steiner, *After Babel: Aspects of Language and Translation* (New York: Oxford University Press, 1975).

31. Aswin Punathambekar, *From Bombay to Bollywood: The Making of a Global Media Industry* (New York: New York University Press, 2013), 156–165; Shakuntala Banaji, "Hindi Film Audiences outside South Asia," in *Routledge Handbook on Indian Cinema*, eds. Gokulsing and Dissanayake, 391–401.

32. Purnima Mankekar, *Unsettling India: Affect, Temporality, Transnationality* (Durham, NC: Duke University Press, 2015), 3 and 50; Bakirathi Mani, "Beyond Bollywood: Exhibiting South Asian America," *Journal of Asian American Studies* 18, no. 2 (June 2015): 193–217; Meheli Sen, "Beyond Bollywood?" *Cinema Journal* 52, no. 4 (Summer 2013): 155–160.

33. Aakash Singh Rathore, *Indian Political Theory: Laying the Groundwork for Svaraj* (New York: Routledge, 2017), 149; Sudipta Kaviraj, *The Invention of Private Life: Literature and Ideas* (New York: Columbia University Press, 2015), 11.

## Conclusion

Epigraph: "Statement to the Press," September 17, 1934, *Collected Works of Mahatma Gandhi* (CWMG) Electronic Book (New Delhi: Government of India, 1999).

1. "Right or Wrong," *Harijan*, September 14, 1947, CWMG; "Statement to the Press," September 17, 1934, CWMG; "Statement to the Press," September 17, 1934, CWMG; "Question Box," *Harijan*, May 18, 1940, CWMG. Also see Eva Pföstl, *Between Ethics and Politics: New Essays on Gandhi* (New Delhi: Routledge, 2014); Ramachandra Guha, *Gandhi before India* (New York: Knopf, 2014); Ajay Skaria, *Unconditional Equality: Gandhi's Religion of Resistance* (Minneapolis: University of Minnesota Press, 2016).

2. For critical accounts that question whether India deserves to be called a democracy, see Ayesha Jalal, *Democracy and Authoritarianism in South Asia: A Comparative and Historical Perspective* (Cambridge, UK: Cambridge University Press, 1995), and Arthur Bonner, Kancha Ilaiah, Suranjit Kumar Saha, Ashgar Ali Engineer, and Gerard Hueze, *Democracy in India: A Hollow Shell* (Washington, DC: American University Press, 1994). I agree with Ashutosh Varshney that democracy is best understood as a "continuous variable." See Ashutosh Varshney, *Battles Half Won: India's Improbable Democracy* (New York: Penguin, 2013), 84. Also see Malcolm X, "Democracy Is Hypocrisy," *Great Speeches* vol. 16 (Educational Video Group), DVD; Malcolm X, "The Ballot or the Bullet," April 3, 1964, Cleveland, Ohio, available at www.edchange .org/multicultural/speeches/malcolm_x_ballot.html; Sunil Khilnani, *The Idea of India* (New York: Farrar, Straus, and Giroux, 1997), 35.

3. Ramachandra Guha, "A Fifty-Fifty Democracy," *Telegraph*, January 24, 2015; Lala Lajpat Rai, "The New Internationalism," *Young India* 1 (April 1918), 9;

John Dunn, *Democracy: A History* (New York: Atlantic Monthly Press, 2005); Alexander Keyssar, *Right to Vote: The Contested History of Democracy in the United States* (New York: Basic Books, 2000); Pradeep Chhibber, *Democracy without Associations: Transformation of the Party System and Social Cleavages in India* (Ann Arbor: University of Michigan Press, 2001); Patrick Heller, "Degrees of Democracy: Some Comparative Lessons from India," *World Politics* 52, no. 4 (2000): 484–519; Achin Vanaik, *The Painful Transition: The Bourgeois Democracy of India* (London: Verso Books, 1990).

4. Sanjay Seth, "Rewriting Histories of Nationalism: The Politics of 'Moderate Nationalism' in India, 1870–1905," *American Historical Review* 104, no. 1 (February 1999): 95–116; Naazneen Karmali, "A Record 90 Indians on Forbes Billionaires List 2015," *Forbes,* March 3, 2015, www.forbes.com/sites /naazneenkarmali/2015/03/03/a-record-90-indians-on-forbes-billionaires -list-2015/#5a7691c73524; Pam Fessler, "How Many Americans Live In Poverty?" NPR, November 6, 2013, https://www.npr.org/sections/money/2013 /11/06/243498168/how-many-americans-live-in-poverty.

5. Douglas S. Massey and Nancy A. Denton, *American Apartheid: Segregation and the Making of the Underclass* (Cambridge, MA: Harvard University Press, 1993); Michelle Alexander, *The New Jim Crow: Mass Incarceration in the Age of Color-blindness* (New York: The Free Press, 2010); Joseph Stiglitz, *The Price of Inequality: How Today's Divided Society Endangers Our Future* (New York: Norton, 2012); Katherine Boo, *Behind the Beautiful Forevers: Life, Death, and Hope in a Mumbai Undercity* (New York: Random House, 2012); Christophe Jaffrelot, *Religion, Caste, and Politics in India* (Oxford, UK: Oxford University Press, 2011).

6. James T. Kloppenberg, *Toward Democracy: The Struggle for Self-Rule in European and American Thought* (New York: Oxford University Press, 2016), 22.

7. Timothy Mitchell, *Carbon Democracy: Political Power in the Age of Oil* (London and New York: Verso, 2011), 240.

8. Khilnani, *The Idea of India,* 4; Ramachandra Guha, *India After Gandhi: The History of the World's Largest Democracy* (New York: HarperCollins Publishers, 2007), 329.

9. John Keane, *The Life and Death of Democracy* (New York: Simon & Schuster, 2009), 618; "Indian Students' Meeting to Protest Indira Gandhi's Subversion of Democracy in India," flyer, June 26, 1975, available at South Asian American Digital Archive (SAADA), www.saada.org; Indians for Political Freedom, "India under Indira's Iron Rule," broadsheet, 1975, SAADA; *India Forum,* no. 3, November 1976, SAADA; "Urgent Message from the India Foundation," 1975, SAADA.

10. Charu Kartikeya, "Anand Kumar: An Anti-Emergency Activist Abroad," *Catch News,* June 25, 2015, www.catchnews.com/politics-news/anand-kumar -an-anti-emergency-activist-abroad-1435180264.html; "Urgent Message from the India Foundation"; *Congressional Record,* 93rd Congress, 2nd session, 1974, vol. 120, part 17, p. 22681.

11. "India under Indira's Iron Rule," SAADA; "Surveillance and Intimidation Abroad by the Government of India," *India Forum* 4 (April 1977): 12–13, 22–23, 26, 29.

12. Michel Crozier, Samuel P. Huntington, and Joji Watanuki, *The Crisis of Democracy: On the Governability of Democracies* (New York: NYU Press, 1975), 113–114.

13. Rajni Kothari, *Rethinking Democracy* (New Delhi: Orient Longman, 2005), 155 and 158; Pratap Bhanu Mehta, *The Burden of Democracy* (New Delhi: Penguin India, 2003); Aishwary Kumar, *Radical Equality: Ambedkar, Gandhi, and the Risk of Democracy* (Stanford: Stanford University Press, 2015), 3.

14. W. E. B. Du Bois, *Darkwater: Voices from within the Veil* (New York: Harcourt, Brace, and Howe, 1920), 207.

15. Orlando Patterson, *Slavery and Social Death* (Cambridge, MA: Harvard University Press, 1982), 341–342; Orlando Patterson, *Freedom in the Making of Western Culture* (New York: Basic Books, 1991); Saidiya V. Hartman, *Scenes of Subjection: Terror, Slavery, and Self-Making in Nineteenth-Century America* (New York: Oxford University Press, 1997), 115.

16. Ambedkar, "Evidence before the Southborough Commission," quoted in Anupama Rao, *The Caste Question: Dalits and the Politics of Modern India* (Berkeley: University of California Press, 2009), 133. Also see Kwame Anthony Appiah, *Cosmopolitanism: Ethics in a World of Strangers* (New York: Norton, 2006); David Hollinger, *Cosmopolitanism and Solidarity: Studies in Ethnoracial, Religious, and Professional Affiliation in the United States* (Madison: University of Wisconsin Press, 2006).

17. "Notes Taken by P.M on Non-Violence," March 1940, "Petersburg Bus Incident," file 86, box 4, Pauli Murray Papers, Schlesinger Library, Radcliffe Institute, Cambridge, MA; Richard G. Fox, "Passage from India," in *Between Resistance and Revolution: Cultural Politics and Social Protest*, eds. Richard G. Fox and Orin Starn (New Brunswick, NJ: Rutgers University Press, 1997), 68.

18. Nico Slate, "'I Am a Colored Woman': Kamaladevi Chattopadhyay in the United States, 1939–41," *Contemporary South Asia* 17, no. 1 (March 2009): 7–19; Kamaladevi Chattopadhyay, *Inner Recesses, Outer Spaces: Memoirs* (New Delhi: Navrang, 1986), 253.

19. Pauli Murray, "An American Negro Views the Indian Question," *Call* (September 4, 1942): 4.

20. Charles Tilly, *Democracy* (Cambridge, UK: Cambridge University Press, 2007); Jan Teorell, *Determinants of Democratization: Explaining Regime Change in the World, 1972–2006* (Cambridge, UK: Cambridge University Press, 2010).

21. Walt Whitman, *Poetry and Prose*, ed. Justin Kaplan (New York: Library of America, 1996): 984.

# ACKNOWLEDGMENTS

A Hindu girl told me a story. She is a high school pupil and
the course of history prescribed for her class includes Indian
history. One day she asked her teacher why the latter ignored
that part of the subject. The teacher's reply was, because the
Indians had done nothing to have a history; they were a
backward people having nothing to their credit.

—Lala Lajpat Rai, *The United States of America:*
*A Hindu's Impressions and a Study* (Calcutta:
Brahmo Mission Press, 1916), 419–420

Many of the figures in this book defied distinctions between scholarship and
the struggle for justice. Many recognized, as did Lala Lajpat Rai, that freedom
requires fighting not just for land and power but also for the right to tell our
own histories. I am grateful to all those who have labored to uncover the many
histories that connect the United States and India. Historians, journalists, archivists, and everyone who guarded old letters left by parents and grandparents—
this book depends on your wisdom and your work. Thank you.

My notes demonstrate my indebtedness to the many scholars who have
tackled different facets of this history. I am especially grateful to Carol Anderson,
Vivek Bald, Ramachandra Guha, Vijay Prashad, Maia Ramnath, Andrew Rotter,
and Nayan Shah. In addition to offering the inspiration of their scholarship, Jonathan Eacott, Jeff Hinkelman, Daniel Immerwahr, Priya Joshi, Jonathan Nassim,
Shebani Rao, and Seema Sohi all read particular chapters and offered incisive
and invaluable suggestions.

I am also deeply grateful to the many archivists and librarians who offered
guidance and support, especially Randall Burkett at Emory University; Kathy
Flynn, Head of Reference Service at the Phillips Library of the Peabody Essex
Museum; and Dr. Balakrishnan at the Nehru Memorial Museum and Library.

Special thanks go to Samip Mallick, the Cofounder and Executive Director of the South Asian American Digital Archive (saada.org), an invaluable resource that was of tremendous value to this book.

I am grateful to my colleagues at Carnegie Mellon University for their friendship and inspiration. Ricky Law read the manuscript and offered invaluable suggestions. Joe Trotter provided caring mentorship and unflagging support. My graduate students—David Busch, Levi Pettler, and Clayton Vaughn-Roberson—helped me grow as a historian and a teacher. I am also grateful to my undergraduate students, many of whom offered ideas and suggestions that made their way into this book. My interest in connections between India and the United States began in graduate school. My dissertation adviser, James T. Kloppenberg, continues to shape how I understand democracy. I would also like to thank Lizabeth Cohen, Sugata Bose, and Evelyn Higginbotham.

My friends at the Kamalnayan Jamnalal Bajaj Foundation are a constant inspiration. I would like to thank, in particular, Haribhai Mori, Mahendra Phate, and Apoorv Nayan Bajaj. I would also like to thank my colleagues and friends at SocialChange101.org, especially Michael Pisano and Sarah Ceurvorst.

Connie Mohn sent me a copy of *Karma Cola* just when I needed to read it, and inspired me with her devotion to Hindu spiritual traditions. Aarushi Shah conducted vital research for this book, and amazed me with her curiosity and determination. I would also like to thank Golda Philip, Tenny Thomas, Ali Asani, Diana Eck, and Narayan Shrestha.

I am grateful to my editor, Sharmila Sen, who has been a joy to work with and an inspiration. I would also like to thank all the staff at Harvard University Press, especially Heather Hughes; the two anonymous readers who commented on an earlier version of this book; and Kelley Blewster and Angela Piliouras for their help with copyediting the manuscript.

Finally, I would like to thank my family. My mother, Karena Slate, came with me to India twice and read this manuscript with care and insight. My brother, Peter Slate, inspired my love for democracy and taught me to believe in my dreams without taking myself too seriously. My children, Kai and Lucia, teach me how to find joy in the smallest of things and remind me to be silly. I cannot thank them enough. And what can I say to Emily Mohn-Slate, who read this manuscript multiple times and improved nearly every line, who believes in my better self while somehow still loving the man I am, and whose fierce commitment to writing inspires me every day: *what you do still betters what is done.*

# INDEX

www.ingramcontent.com/pod-product-compliance
Lightning Source LLC
Chambersburg PA
CBHW021830090426
42811CB00032B/2101/J